THE **BCOM** SOLUTION

W9-BXT-882

Print + Online

BCOM⁹ delivers all the key terms and core concepts for the **Business Communication** course.

BCOM Online provides the complete narrative from the printed text with additional interactive media and the unique functionality of **StudyBits**—all available on nearly any device!

What is a StudyBit™? Created through a deep investigation of students' challenges and workflows, the StudyBit™ functionality of **BCOM Online** enables students of different generations and learning styles to study more effectively by allowing them to learn their way. Here's how they work:

COLLECT WHAT'S IMPORTANT
Create StudyBits as you highlight text, images or take notes!

WEAK

FAIR

STRONG

UNASSIGNED

RATE AND ORGANIZE STUDYBITS
Rate your understanding and use the color-coding to quickly organize your study time and personalize your flashcards and quizzes.

StudyBit™

TRACK/MONITOR PROGRESS
Use Concept Tracker to decide how you'll spend study time and study YOUR way!

85%

PERSONALIZE QUIZZES
Filter by your StudyBits to personalize quizzes or just take chapter quizzes off-the-shelf.

CORRECT

INCORRECT

INCORRECT

INCORRECT

CENGAGE
Learning®

BCOM9
Carol Lehman, Debbie DuFrene, Robyn Walker

Senior Vice President,
    General Manager: Balraj Kalsi
Product Manager: Laura Redden
Content/Media Developer: Patricia Hempel
Product Assistant: Eli Lewis
Marketing Manager: Eric Wagner
Marketing Coordinator: Courtney Cozzy
Content Project Manager: Darrell E. Frye
Manufacturing Planner: Ron Montgomery
Sr. Art Director: Bethany Casey
Cover Design: Lisa Kuhn: Curio Press, LLC /
    Trish & Ted Knapke: Ke Design
Internal Design: Lou Ann Thesing / Thesing
    Design
Cover Images: Venus Angel/Shutterstock.com
    Andrey_Popov/Shutterstock.com
    goodluz/Shutterstock.com
Back Cover and Special Page Images:
Computer and tablet illustration:
    iStockphoto.com/furtaev; Smart
    Phone illustration: iStockphoto.com/
    dashadima; Feedback image:
    Rawpixel.com/Shutterstock.com
Intellectual Property Analyst: Diane Garrity
Intellectual Property Project Manager:
    Carly Belcher
Production Service: SPi Global

Library of Congress Control Number: 2016960911

Student Edition ISBN: 978-1-337-11687-9

Student Edition with Online ISBN: 978-1-337-11684-8

Cengage Learning
20 Channel Center Street
Boston, MA 02210
USA

Cengage Learning is a leading provider of customized learning solutions with employees residing in nearly 40 different countries and sales in more than 125 countries around the world. Find your local representative at **www.cengage.com**

Cengage Learning products are represented in Canada by Nelson Education, Ltd.

To learn more about Cengage Learning Solutions, visit **www.cengage.com**

Purchase any of our products at your local college store or at our preferred online store **www.cengagebrain.com**

Printed in the United States of America
Print Number: 03   Print Year: 2018

LEHMAN/DUFRENE
BCOM⁹ BRIEF CONTENTS

© Photo Credit Here

CONTENTS

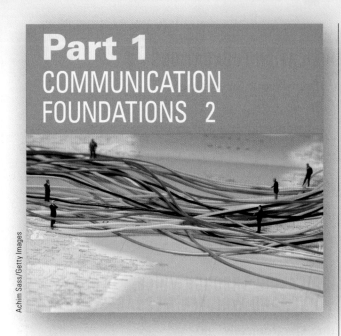
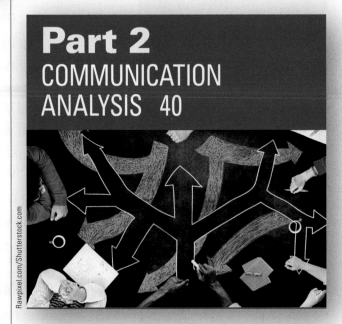

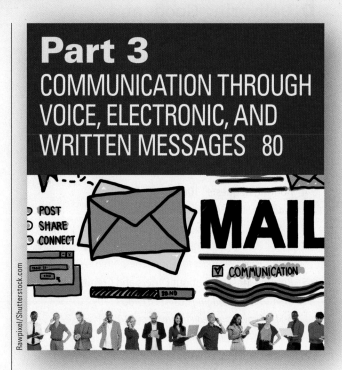

Rawpixel/Shutterstock.com

Part 3
COMMUNICATION THROUGH VOICE, ELECTRONIC, AND WRITTEN MESSAGES 80

Part 4

COMMUNICATION THROUGH REPORTS AND BUSINESS PRESENTATIONS 156

Andrey_Popov/Shutterstock.com

10 Managing Data and Using Graphics   176

11 Organizing and Preparing Reports and Proposals   190

12 Designing and Delivering Business Presentations   212

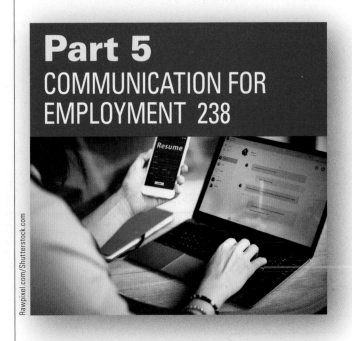

Part 5
COMMUNICATION FOR EMPLOYMENT   238

Rawpixel.com/Shutterstock.com

13 Preparing Résumés and Application Messages   238

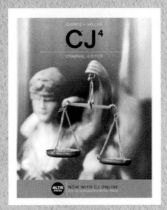

1 | Establishing a Framework for Business Communication

Achim Sass/Getty Images

LEARNING OBJECTIVES

After studying this chapter, you will be able to...

1-1 Define communication and describe the value of communication in business.

1-2 Explain the communication process model and the ultimate objective of the communication process.

1-3 Discuss how information flows in an organization.

1-4 Explain how legal and ethical constraints, diversity challenges, changing technology, and team environment act as contextual forces that influence the process of business communication.

After finishing this chapter, go to **PAGE 21** for **STUDY TOOLS.**

1-1 VALUE OF COMMUNICATION

We communicate to satisfy needs in both our work and private lives. Each of us wants to be heard, appreciated, and wanted. We also want to accomplish tasks and achieve goals. Generally people communicate for three basic purposes: to inform, to persuade, and to entertain. However, in the professional workplace some of these purposes have greater importance. Informing and persuading are common purposes of communication in the workplace; entertainment is less so. In addition, establishing and maintaining our credibility and positive relationships with others are also important purposes in an organizational setting.

What is communication? Communication is the process of exchanging and interpreting information and meaning between or among individuals through a system of symbols, signs, and behavior. In ideal situations, the goal is to reach mutual understanding. Studies indicate that managers typically spend 60% to 80% of their time involved in communication. In your career activities, you will communicate in a wide variety of ways, including

- listening and contributing to decision making and problem solving while attending meetings;
- writing various types of messages to inform and persuade others about your ideas and the services and products your organization provides;
- presenting information and persuasive messages to large and small groups in face-to-face and virtual environments;
- explaining and clarifying management procedures and work assignments;
- coordinating the work of various employees, departments, and other work groups;

> Abilities in writing and speaking are major determinants of career success.

- evaluating and counseling employees and;
- promoting the company's products, services, and image using a variety of channels in various contexts.

1-2 THE COMMUNICATION PROCESS

Effective business communication is essential to success in today's work environments. Recent surveys of executives demonstrate that abilities in writing and speaking are major determinants of career success in many fields.[1] Although essential to personal and professional success, effective business communication does not occur automatically. Your own experiences likely have taught you that a message is not interpreted correctly just because you transmitted it. An effective communicator anticipates possible breakdowns in the communication process—the unlimited ways the message can be misunderstood. This mind set provides the concentration to plan and design the initial message effectively and to be prepared to intervene at the appropriate time to ensure that the message received is on target.

Consider the transactional process model of communication presented in Figure 1.1. These seemingly simple steps actually represent a very complex process.

A number of communication process models exist. The transactional model is useful, though, because it illustrates the complexity of the communication process and reveals some of the challenges to effective communication that might emerge in a communication encounter.

According to the transactional process model, two parties involved in a communication encounter are potentially both communicating at the same time, particularly if the encounter is face-to-face. That's because in face-to-face communication situations, parties to the encounter are continuously interpreting each other's nonverbal signals. Some scholars say more than 90% of the information in a face-to-face encounter may be sent nonverbally. But even in a cellphone conversation, silences and tone of voice may be interpreted in various ways. Even a written message may provide information about the writer that he or she did not intend to convey.

FIGURE 1.1 THE TRANSACTIONAL PROCESS MODEL OF COMMUNICATION

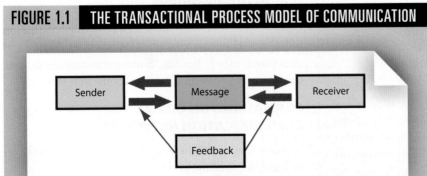

Interruptions or distractions can create barriers to understanding.

nonverbally, it can be very challenging to ensure that the information is received as intended. For this reason, it is particularly important to check for understanding rather than assume that it has taken place, particularly when communicating important messages to audiences that are less familiar to us.

You can surely compile a list of other barriers that affect your ability to communicate with friends, instructors, coworkers, supervisors, and others. By being aware of them, you can concentrate on removing these interferences.

In an ideal communication situation, one party would be able to encode his or her message in such a way that the receiving party would understand it exactly as intended. However, this goal can be challenging for a variety of reasons, or what are called **interferences** or *barriers* to effective communication. For example,

- differences in educational level, experience, culture, and other characteristics of the sender and the receiver increase the complexity of encoding and decoding a message;

- physical interferences in the channel, including a noisy environment, interruptions, and uncomfortable surroundings, can occur and;

- mental distractions, such as being preoccupied with other matters and developing a response, rather than listening, create barriers to understanding.

Because of these barriers, and because both parties engaged in a communication encounter may be simultaneously sending information both orally and

interferences also called *barriers*; numerous factors that hinder the communication process

organizational communication the movement of information within the company structure

formal communication network a network of communication flow typified by the formal organizational chart; dictated by the technical, political, and economic environment of the organization

COMMUNICATING WITHIN ORGANIZATIONS

In order to be successful, organizations must create an environment that energizes and encourages employees to accomplish tasks by promoting genuine openness and effective communication.

Organizational communication is communication that occurs with an organizational context. Regardless of your career or level within an organization, your ability to communicate will affect not only the success of the organization but also your personal success and advancement within that organization.

1-3a Communication Flow in Organizations

Communication occurs in a variety of ways within an organization. Some communication flows are planned and structured, others are not. Some communication flows can be formally depicted, whereas some defy description.

FORMAL AND INFORMAL COMMUNICATION NETWORKS

Communication within an organization involves both formal and informal networks.

- **Formal communication network**. This channel is typified by the formal organizational chart, which is created by management to define individual and group relationships and to specify lines of responsibility. Essentially, the formal system is dictated by the managerial, technical, cultural, and structural environment of the organization. Within this system, people are required to behave and to communicate in certain ways simply to get work done.

- **Informal communication network**. This network, which is commonly called "the grapevine," continuously develops as people interact within the formal system to accommodate their social and psychological needs. Because the informal network undergoes continual changes and does not parallel the organizational chart, it cannot be depicted accurately by any graphic means.

The office grapevine carries informal messages.

The Formal Communication Network When employees rely almost entirely on the formal communication system as a guide to behavior, the system might be identified as a *bureaucracy*. Procedure manuals, job descriptions, organizational charts, and other written materials dictate the required behavior. Communication channels are followed strictly, and red tape is abundant. Procedures are generally followed exactly; terms such as *rules* and *policies* serve as sufficient reasons for actions. Even the most formal organizations, however, cannot function long before an informal communication system emerges. As people operate within the organized system, they interact on a person-to-person basis and create an environment conducive to meeting their personal emotions, prejudices, likes, and dislikes.

In a workplace, employees are generally expected to satisfy a formal system of arriving at work on time, fulfilling their job duties, working well with others, and addressing their supervisor's requests. However, some employees may not openly accept these expectations and may arrive at work late and spend an undue amount of time "around the water cooler." If these informal practices become more widely spread, the purposes of the group may move from a focus on completing tasks to that of socializing with others or speculating about organizational events or activities. Obviously, the informal system benefits people because it meets their needs, but it also may affect the overall communication of the group in important ways.

The Informal Communication Network As people talk casually during breaks, text one another, or chat online, the focus usually shifts from topic to topic. One of the usual topics is work—the company, supervisor, or fellow employees. Even though the formal system includes definite communication channels, the grapevine tends to develop and operate within all organizations. Consider these points related to the accuracy and value of grapevine communication:

- As a communication network, the grapevine has a reputation for being speedy but inaccurate. In the absence of alarms, the grapevine might be the most effective way to let occupants know that the building is on fire. It certainly beats sending an email.

- Although the grapevine often is thought of as a channel for inaccurate communication, in reality it is no more or less accurate than other channels. Even formal communication can become inaccurate and filtered as it passes from level to level in the organizational hierarchy.

- The inaccuracy of the grapevine has more to do with the message input than with the output. For example, the grapevine is noted as a carrier of rumors, primarily because it carries informal messages. If the input is a rumor, and nothing more, the output obviously will be inaccurate. But the output might be an accurate description of the original rumor.

- In a business office, news about promotions, personnel changes, company policy changes, and annual salary adjustments often is communicated through the grapevine long before being

informal communication network a network of communication flow that continuously develops as people interact within the formal system to accommodate their social and psychological needs conveyed through formal channels. The process works similarly in colleges, where information about instructors typically is not officially published but is known by students, often through word-of-mouth. How best to prepare for examinations, instructor attitudes on attendance and homework, and even faculty personnel changes are messages that travel over the grapevine.

- A misconception about the grapevine is that the message passes from person to person until it finally reaches a person who can't pass it on: the end of the line. Actually, the grapevine works as a network channel. Typically, one person tells two or three others, who each tell two or three others, who each tell two or three others, and so on. Thus, the message might spread to a huge number of people in a short time, especially now that the grapevine includes digital forms of communication, such as social networking sites.

- The grapevine has no single, consistent source. Messages might originate anywhere and follow various routes.

Due at least in part to widespread downsizing and corporate scandals during the last few years, employees in many organizations are demanding that they be better informed. Some companies have implemented new formal ways, such as newsletters and intranets, as well as informal ways, including blogs, wikis, Twitter, and other social networking platforms, for sharing information with their internal constituents. Company openness with employees about management decisions, process changes, and financial issues means conveying more information through the formal system rather than risking its miscommunication through informal channels. Online eyewear retailer Warby Parker, for example, grew from a small start-up to a 300-employee company in just three years. In order to keep the lines of communication open, the company has an "Ask Anything" segment of its weekly meetings, in which employees can ask anything. The Warby Parker Wiki enables employees to add notes from meetings, key lessons from the past or present, or team updates. The transparent company culture extends to each of its employees submitting weekly "happiness ratings" (on a 0 to 10 scale) and participating in quarterly, one-on-one, "360 reviews" in which brutal honesty is encouraged.[2]

downward communication a type of communication that flows from supervisor to employee, from policy makers to operating personnel, or from top to bottom on the organizational chart

upward communication a type of communication that is generally a response to requests from supervisors

An informal communication network will emerge from even the most carefully designed formal system. Managers who ignore this fact are attempting to manage blindfolded. Instead of denying or condemning the grapevine, the effective manager will learn to use the informal communication network. The grapevine, for instance, can be useful in counteracting rumors and false information.

DIRECTIONS OF COMMUNICATION FLOW

The direction in which communication flows in an organization can be downward, upward, or horizontal, as shown in Figure 1-2. Because these three terms are used frequently in communication discussions, they deserve clarification. Although the concept of flow seems simple, direction has meaning for those participating in the organizational communication process.

Downward Communication The communication that flows from supervisor to employee, from policy makers to operating personnel, or from top to bottom on the organizational chart is called **downward communication**. A simple policy statement from the top of the organization might grow into a formal plan for operation at lower levels. Teaching people how to perform their specific tasks is an element of downward communication. Another element is orientation to a company's rules, practices, procedures, history, and goals. Employees learn about the quality of their job performance through downward communication.

Downward communication normally involves both written and spoken methods and makes use of the following assumptions:

DOWNWARD COMMUNICATION

- People at high levels in the organization usually have greater knowledge of the organization's mission and goals than do people at lower levels.

- Both spoken and written messages tend to become larger as they move downward through organizational levels. This expansion results from attempts to prevent distortion and is more noticeable in written messages.

- Spoken messages are subject to greater changes in meaning than are written messages.

When a supervisor sends a message to a subordinate employee who then asks a question or nods in agreement, the employee has given signs of feedback. Feedback can flow both downward and upward in organizational communication through traditional as well as informal channels.

FIGURE 1.2 | FLOW OF INFORMATION WITHIN AN ORGANIZATION

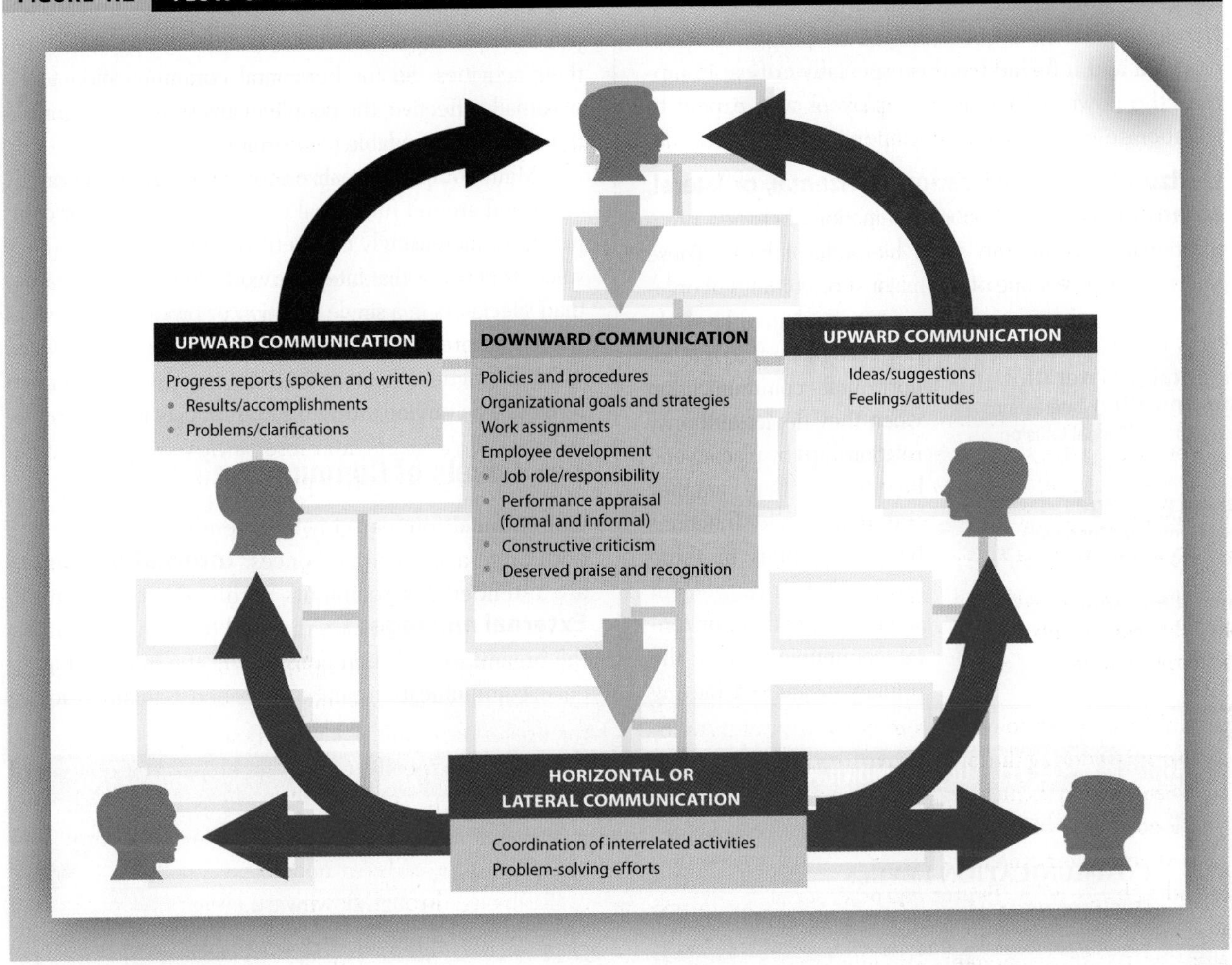

UPWARD COMMUNICATION

Progress reports (spoken and written)
- Results/accomplishments
- Problems/clarifications

DOWNWARD COMMUNICATION

Policies and procedures
Organizational goals and strategies
Work assignments
Employee development
- Job role/responsibility
- Performance appraisal (formal and informal)
- Constructive criticism
- Deserved praise and recognition

UPWARD COMMUNICATION

Ideas/suggestions
Feelings/attitudes

HORIZONTAL OR LATERAL COMMUNICATION

Coordination of interrelated activities
Problem-solving efforts

Upward Communication The information that flows from the front lines of an organization to the top is **upward communication**. When management requests information from lower organizational levels, the resulting information becomes feedback to that request. Employees talk to supervisors about themselves, their fellow employees, their work and methods of doing it, customer needs and perceptions, and their own perceptions of the organization. These comments are commonly feedback in response to the downward flow transmitted in both spoken and written forms by group meetings, emails, procedures or operations manuals, company news releases, the company intranet, and the grapevine.

Although necessary and valuable, upward communication involves risks. The box that follows lists important upward communication factors to consider.

When effectively used, upward communication keeps management informed about the feelings of lower-level employees, taps the expertise of employees, helps management identify both difficult and

UPWARD COMMUNICATION

▶ Upward communication is primarily feedback to the requests and actions of supervisors.

▶ Upward communication can be misleading because lower-level employees often tell their superiors what they think their superiors want to hear. Therefore, their messages might contradict their true observations and perceptions.

▶ Upward communication frequently involves risk to an employee and is dependent on his or her trust in the supervisor.

▶ Employees will reject superficial attempts by management to obtain feedback.

potentially promotable employees, and paves the way for even more effective downward communication. Upward communication is key to keeping employees engaged and informed and is especially critical in tapping the power of younger employees who expect to collaborate rather than to be supervised.[3]

Horizontal Communication Horizontal, or lateral, **communication** describes interactions between organizational units on the same hierarchical level. These interactions reveal one of the major shortcomings of organizational charts: They do not recognize the role of horizontal communication when they depict authority relationships by placing one box higher than another and define role functions by placing titles in those boxes. Yet management should realize that horizontal communication is the primary means of achieving coordination in a functional organizational structure. Units coordinate their activities to accomplish task goals just as adjacent workers in a production line coordinate their activities. So for horizontal communication to be maximally effective, the people in any system or organization should be available to one another.

Many companies realize that the traditional hierarchy organized around functional units is inadequate for competing in increasingly competitive global markets. They value work teams that integrate work-flow processes rather than specialists in a single function or product. Such work teams can break down communication barriers between isolated functional departments, and communication patterns take on varying forms to accommodate team activities.

1-3b Levels of Communication

Communication can involve sending messages to both large and small audiences. **Internal messages** are intended for recipients within the organization. **External messages** are directed to recipients outside the organization. When considering the intended audience, communication can be described as taking place on

FIGURE 1.3	LEVELS OF COMMUNICATION

COMMUNICATION LEVELS	EXAMPLES
INTRAPERSONAL • Communication within oneself • Not considered by some to be true communication as it does not involve a separate sender and receiver	*Individual considers how others respond to his or her verbal and/or nonverbal communication*
INTERPERSONAL • Communication between two people • Task goal is to accomplish work confronting them • Maintenance goal is to feel better about themselves and each other because of their interaction	*Supervisor and subordinate, two coworkers*
GROUP • Communication among more than two people • Goal of achieving greater output than individual efforts could produce	*Work group, project team, department meeting*
ORGANIZATIONAL • Groups combined in such a way that large tasks may be accomplished • Goal of providing adequate structure for groups to achieve their purposes	*Company, organization*
PUBLIC • The organization reaching out to its public to achieve its goals • Goal of reaching many with the same message	*Media advertisement, website communication, annual report*

five levels: intrapersonal, interpersonal, group, organizational, and public. Figure 1.3 depicts the five audience levels. An effective communicator has a clearly defined purpose for each message, and has selected strategies for targeting his or her intended audience.

1-4 CONTEXTUAL FORCES INFLUENCING BUSINESS COMMUNICATION

All communication occurs within a **context**, which is the situation or setting. Context can influence the content, the quality, and the effectiveness of a communication event. The effective communicator will recognize the importance of context, identify the contextual elements that will influence communication, and adjust his or her messages in response. Four important contextual forces influence the communication process today and help determine and define the nature of the communication that should occur, as shown in Figure 1.4. These forces are legal and ethical constraints, diversity challenges, changing technology, and team environment.

1-4a Legal and Ethical Constraints

Legal and ethical constraints act as contextual or environmental forces on communication because they set boundaries in which communication rightfully occurs. International, federal, state, and local laws affect the way that various business activities are conducted. For instance, laws specify that certain information must be stated in messages that reply to credit applications and those dealing with the collection of outstanding debts.

Furthermore, one's own ethical standards will often influence what a person is willing to say in a message. For example, a system of ethics built on honesty might require that the message provide full disclosure rather than a shrouding of the truth. Legal responsibilities, then, are the starting point for appropriate business communication. One's ethical belief system, or personal sense of right and wrong behavior, provides further boundaries for professional activity.

The press is full of examples of unethical conduct in business and political communities, but unethical behavior is not relegated to the papers—it has far-reaching consequences. Those affected by decisions, the **stakeholders**, can include people inside and outside the organization. Employees and stockholders are obvious losers when a company fails.

context a situation or setting in which communication occurs

stakeholders people inside and outside the organization who are affected by decisions

---

FIGURE 1.4 — FACTORS INFLUENCING BUSINESS COMMUNICATION

LEGAL AND ETHICAL CONSTRAINTS	CHANGING TECHNOLOGY	DIVERSITY CHALLENGES	TEAM ENVIRONMENT
• International Laws	• Accuracy and Security Issues	• Cultural Differences	• Trust
• Domestic Laws	• Telecommunications	• Language Barriers	• Team Roles
• Codes of Ethics	• Software Applications	• Gender Issues	• Shared Goals and Expectations
• Stakeholder Interests	• "High-Touch" Issues	• Education Levels	• Synergy
• Ethical Frameworks	• Telecommuting	• Age Factors	• Group Reward
• Personal Values	• Databases	• Nonverbal Differences	• Distributed Leadership

Fotoluminate LLC/Shutterstock.com

Competitors in the same industry also suffer because their strategies are based on what they perceive about their competition. Beyond this, financial markets as a whole suffer due to the erosion of public confidence.

Business leaders, government officials, and citizens frequently express concern about the apparent erosion of ethical values in society. Even for those who want to do the right thing, matters of ethics are seldom clear-cut decisions of right versus wrong, and they often contain ambiguous elements. In addition, the pressure appears to be felt most strongly by lower-level managers, who are often recent business school graduates who are the least experienced at doing their jobs.

THE FOUNDATION FOR LEGAL AND ETHICAL BEHAVIOR

Although ethics is a common point of discussion, many find defining ethics challenging. Most people immediately associate ethics with standards and rules of conduct, morals, right and wrong, values, and honesty. Dr. Albert Schweitzer defined *ethics* as "the name we give to our concern for good behavior. We feel an obligation to consider not only our own personal well-being, but also that of others and of human society as a whole."[4] In other words, **ethics** refers to the principles of right and wrong that guide you in making decisions that consider the impact of your actions on others as well as yourself.

Although the recorded accounts of legal and ethical misconduct would seem to indicate that businesses are dishonest and unscrupulous, keep in mind that millions of business transactions are made daily on the basis of honesty and concern for others. Why should a business make ethical decisions? What difference will it make? Johan Karlstrom, global chief executive officer of construction giant Skanska, gave a powerful reply to these questions:

> When you understand that profits and a strong values base go together then you have a company that employees are so proud of. We want our team to feel that they're doing something that has a higher meaning, that they feel like "I'm part of something bigger, part of a bigger puzzle driving society in a positive direction."[5]

ethics the principles of right and wrong that guide one in making decisions that consider the impact of one's actions on others as well as on the decision maker

> Learning to analyze a dilemma from both legal and ethical perspectives will help you find a solution that conforms to your own personal values.

CAUSES OF ILLEGAL AND UNETHICAL BEHAVIOR

Understanding the major causes of illegal and unethical behavior in the workplace will help you become sensitive to signals of escalating pressure to compromise your values. Unethical corporate behavior can have a number of causes:

- **Excessive emphasis on profits.** Business managers are often judged and paid on their ability to increase business profits. This emphasis on profits might send a message that the end justifies the means.

- **Misplaced corporate loyalty.** A misplaced sense of corporate loyalty might cause an employee to do what seems to be in the best interest of the company, even if the act is illegal or unethical.

- **Obsession with personal advancement.** Employees who wish to outperform their peers or are working for the next promotion might feel that they cannot afford to fail. They might do whatever it takes to achieve the objectives assigned to them.

- **Expectation of not getting caught.** Thinking that the end justifies the means, employees often believe illegal or unethical activity will never be discovered. Unfortunately, a great deal of improper behavior escapes detection in the business world. Believing no one will ever find out, employees are tempted to lie, steal, and perform other illegal acts.

- **Unethical tone set by top management.** If top managers are not perceived as highly ethical, lower-level managers might be less ethical as a result. Employees have little incentive to act legally and ethically if their superiors do not set an example and encourage and reward such behavior. The saying "The speed of the leader is the speed of the pack" illustrates the importance of leading by example.

- **Uncertainty about whether an action is wrong.** Many times, company personnel are placed in situations in which the line between right and wrong is not clearly defined. When caught in this gray area, the perplexed employee asks, "How far is too far?"

- **Unwillingness to take a stand for what is right.** Often employees know what is right or wrong but are not willing to take the risk of challenging a wrong action.

They might lack the confidence or skill needed to confront others with sensitive legal or ethical issues. They might remain silent and then justify their unwillingness to act.

FRAMEWORK FOR ANALYZING ETHICAL DILEMMAS

Determining whether an action is ethical can be difficult. Learning to analyze a dilemma from both legal and ethical perspectives will help you find a solution that conforms to your own personal values. Figure 1.5 shows the four conclusions you might reach when considering the advisability of a particular behavior.

Dimension 1: Behavior that is illegal and unethical When considering some actions, you will reach the conclusion that they are both illegal and unethical. The law specifically outlines the "black" area—those alternatives that are clearly wrong—and your employer will expect you to become an expert in the laws that affect your particular area. When you encounter an unfamiliar area, you must investigate any possible legal implications. Obviously, obeying the law is in the best interest of all

FIGURE 1.5	FOUR DIMENSIONS OF BUSINESS BEHAVIOR

DIMENSION 1 Behavior that is illegal and unethical	**DIMENSION 2** Behavior that is illegal yet ethical
DIMENSION 3 Behavior that is legal yet unethical	**DIMENSION 4** Behavior that is both legal and ethical

concerned: you as an individual, your company, and society. Contractual agreements between two parties also offer guidance for legal decision making. Frequently, your own individual sense of right and wrong will also confirm that the illegal action is wrong for you personally. In such situations, decisions about appropriate behavior are obvious.

Dimension 2: Behavior that is illegal yet ethical Occasionally, a businessperson will decide that even though a specific action is illegal, there is a justifiable reason to break the law. A case in point is a law passed in Vermont

ETHICAL DILEMMAS ...

Identifying ethical issues in typical workplace situations can be difficult, and coworkers and superiors might apply pressure for seemingly logical reasons. To illustrate, examine each of the following workplace situations for a possible ethical dilemma:

Stokkete/Shutterstock.com

▶ In order to achieve profit expectations, a stockbroker hides the financial risk of an investment product from potential clients.

▶ To prevent an adverse effect on stock prices, corporate officers deliberately withhold information concerning a possible corporate takeover.

▶ To protect the organization, management decides not to publicize a design flaw in an automobile that could lead to possible injury and even death to consumers, because the announcement might result in legal action.

▶ A supervisor takes advantage of his position and threatens an employee with dismissal if she does not acquiesce to his inappropriate requests and language use.

▶ Angry because of an unfavorable performance appraisal of a colleague, an employee leaks confidential information to the colleague that creates distrust among others in the department and results in a lawsuit.

Your fundamental morals and values provide the foundation for making ethical decisions. However, as the previous examples imply, even seemingly minor concessions in day-to-day decisions can gradually weaken an individual's ethical foundation.

FIGURE 2.1 | **THE JOHARI WINDOW**

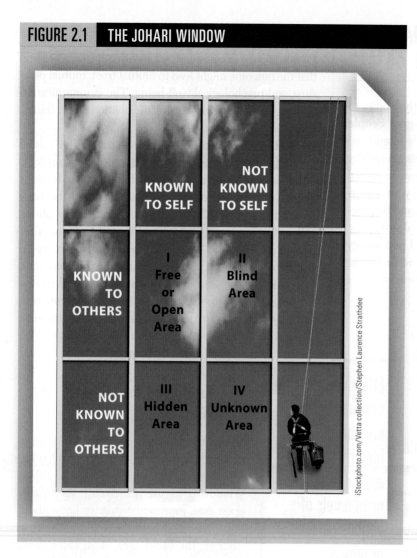

	KNOWN TO SELF	NOT KNOWN TO SELF
KNOWN TO OTHERS	**I** Free or Open Area	**II** Blind Area
NOT KNOWN TO OTHERS	**III** Hidden Area	**IV** Unknown Area

iStockphoto.com/Vetta collection/Stephen Laurence Strathdee

development (OD) are concerned with developing successful organizations by building effective small groups. They believe small-group effectiveness evolves mostly from a high level of mutual trust among group members. The aim of OD is to open emotional as well as task-oriented communication. To accomplish this aim, groups often become involved in encounter sessions designed to enlarge the open areas of the Johari Window.[2]

2-1d Contrasting Management Styles

Douglas McGregor, a management theorist, attempted to distinguish between the older, traditional view that workers are concerned only about satisfying lower-level needs, and the more contemporary view that productivity can be enhanced by assisting workers in satisfying higher-level needs. Under the older view, management exercised strong control, emphasized the job to the exclusion of concern for the individual, and sought to motivate solely through external incentives—a job and a paycheck. McGregor labeled this management style Theory X. Under the contemporary style, Theory Y, management strives to balance control and individual freedom. By treating the individual as a mature person, management lessens the need for external motivation; treated as adults, people will act as adults.

The situational leadership model developed by Paul Hersey and Kenneth Blanchard does not prescribe a single leadership style, but advocates that what is appropriate in each case depends on the follower (subordinate) and the task to be performed. **Directive behavior** is characterized by the leader's giving detailed rules and instructions and monitoring closely that they are followed. The leader decides what is to be done and how. In contrast, **supportive behavior** is characterized by the leader's listening, communicating, recognizing, and encouraging. Different degrees of directive and supportive behavior can be desirable, given the situation.[3] Combining the ideas of Maslow and McGregor with those of Hersey and Blanchard leads to the conclusion that "the right job for the person" is a better philosophy than "the right person for the job."

be trusted, trust is reinforced and leads to an expansion of the open area on the Johari Window. Usually we are willing to tell people about various things that aren't truly personal. But we share personal thoughts, ambitions, and inner feelings only with selected others—those whom we have learned to trust. The relationships existing between supervisor and employee, doctor and patient, and lawyer and client are those of trust, but only in specific areas.

In more intimate relationships with significant others, siblings, and parents, deeper, personal feelings are entrusted to each other.

The idea that trust and openness leads to better communication between two people also applies to groups. Managers engaged in *organizational*

directive behavior
characterized by leaders who give detailed rules and instructions and monitor closely that they are followed

supportive behavior
characterized by leaders who listen, communicate, recognize, and encourage their followers

The **total quality management** move-ment focuses on creating a more responsible role for the worker in an organization. In a total quality management environment, deci-sion-making power is distributed to the people closest to the problem, who usually have the best information sources and solutions. Each employee, from the president to the custodian, is expected to solve problems, participate in team-building efforts, and expand the scope of his or her role in the organization. The goal of employee empowerment is to build a work environment in which all employees take pride in their work accomplishments and begin motivating themselves from within, rather than through traditional extrinsic incentives.[4] Managers of many companies understand that empowering employees to initiate continu-ous improvements is critical for survival. Only companies producing quality products and services will survive in today's world market.

Leadership studies have taken a new turn in recent years with the emergence of the social constructionist view of leadership. A social constructionist view sees leadership differently than the psychological approach to management discipline. A social constructionist view sees leadership as a co-constructed reality that emerges from the interaction of social actors. What this means is that certain leadership behaviors are acceptable to group members while others are not. Because of this, a person may position him- or herself as a leader, but others may not perceive these communication behaviors as corre-sponding with their perception of a leader.

From this perspective, the leader of a group may not be the formally appointed manager or, in certain situations, as discussed in Chapter 1, leadership may be distributed among team members. The value of this approach to leadership is its focus on the importance of communication practices in creating leadership.

 2-2 ## NONVERBAL COMMUNICATION

Managers use verbal and nonverbal messages to communi-cate ideas to employees. *Verbal* means "through the use of words," either written or spoken. *Nonverbal* means "with-out the use of words." Although major attention in commu-nication studies is given to verbal messages, studies show that nonverbal elements can account for more than 90% of the total meaning of a message.[5] Nonverbal communi-cation includes *metacommunication* and *kinesic messages*.

A frown is one form of visual kenesic messaging.

2-2a **Metacommunication**

A **metacommunication** is a message that, although *not* expressed in words, accompanies a message that *is* expressed in words. For example, "Don't be late for work" communicates caution; yet the sentence might imply (but not express in words) such additional ideas as "You are frequently late, and I'm warning you," or "I doubt your dependability." "Your solution is perfect" might also con-vey a metacommunication such as "You are efficient," or "I certainly like your work." Whether you are speaking or writing, you can be confident that those who receive your messages will be sensitive to the messages expressed in words, and to the accompanying messages that are present but not expressed in words.

2-2b **Kinesic Messages**

People constantly send meanings through kinesic communication, which is an idea expressed through nonverbal behavior. In other words, receivers gain additional meaning from what they see and hear—the visual and the vocal:

- **Visual kinesic communication**—gestures, winks, smiles, frowns, sighs, attire, grooming, and all kinds of body movements.

total quality management focuses on creating a more responsible role for the worker in an organization by distributing decision-making power to the people closest to the problem, empowering employees to initiate continuous improvements

metacommunication a nonverbal message that, although not expressed in words, accompanies a message that is expressed in words

visual kinesic communication gestures, winks, smiles, frowns, sighs, attire, grooming, and all kinds of body movements

- **Vocal kinesic communication**—intonation, projection, and resonance of the voice.

Following are some examples of kinesic messages and the meanings they can convey.

Action	Possible Kinesic Message
A wink or light chuckle follows a statement.	"Don't believe what I just said."
A manager is habitually late for staff meetings and with email replies.	"My time is more important than yours. You can wait for me." Alternately, the action might be ordinary for a manager not born in the United States.
A group leader sits at a position other than at the head of the table.	"I want to demonstrate my equality with other members."
An employee wears clothing that reveals tattoos, which violates the company's dress code.	"Rules are for other people; I can do what I want." Alternately, "I do not understand the expectations."
A job applicant submits a résumé containing errors.	"My language skills are deficient." Alternately, "I didn't care to do my best."

2-2c Understanding Nonverbal Messages

Metacommunications and kinesic messages have characteristics that all communicators should take into account.

- **Nonverbal messages cannot be avoided.** Both written and spoken words convey ideas in addition to the ideas contained in the words used. All actions—and even the lack of action—have meaning to those who observe them.

- **Nonverbal messages can have different meanings for different people.** If a team member smiles after making a statement, one member might conclude that the speaker was trying to be funny; another might conclude that the speaker was pleased about having made such a great contribution; and another might see the smile as indicating friendliness.

- **Nonverbal messages vary between and within cultures.** Not only do nonverbal messages have different meanings from culture to culture, but men and women from the same culture typically exhibit different body language. As a rule, US men make less body contact with other men, than do women with other women. Acceptable male body language might include a handshake or a pat on the back, whereas women are afforded more flexibility in making body contact with each other.

- **Nonverbal messages can be intentional or unintentional.** "You are right about that" can be intended to mean "I agree with you" or "You are right on *this* issue, but you have been wrong on all others discussed."

- **Nonverbal messages can contradict the accompanying verbal message and affect whether your message is understood or believed.** The adage "actions speak louder than words" reveals much about how people perceive messages. Picture a person who says, "I'm happy to be here," but looks at the floor, talks in a weak and halting voice, and clasps his or her hands timidly in front of his or her body. Because his or her verbal and nonverbal messages are contradictory, his or her audience might not trust his or her words. Similarly, consider the negative effect of a sloppy personal appearance by a job candidate.

- **Nonverbal messages can receive more attention than verbal messages.** If a supervisor repeatedly glances at his smartphone for text messages, or rhythmically taps a pen while making a statement, the words might not register in the employee's mind. An error in basic grammar might receive more attention than the idea that is being transmitted.

- **Nonverbal messages provide clues about the sender's background, attitudes, and motives.** For example, excessive use of big words might suggest that a person reads widely or has an above-average education. It might also suggest a need for social recognition or insecurity about his or her social background.

- **Nonverbal messages are influenced by the circumstances surrounding the communication.** Assume that two men, Ganesh and Jacob, are friends at work. When they are together on the job, Ganesh sometimes puts his hand on Jacob's shoulder. To Jacob, the act could mean nothing more than "We are close friends." But suppose Ganesh is a member of a committee that subsequently denies a promotion for Jacob. Afterward, the same act could mean "We are still friends," but it could also cause resentment. Because of the circumstances, the same act could now mean something such as "Watch the hand that pats; it can also stab."

- **Nonverbal messages can be beneficial or harmful.** Words or actions can be accompanied by nonverbal messages that help or hurt the sender's purpose.

vocal kinesic communication intonation, projection, and resonance of the voice

Metacommunications and kinesic communications can convey such messages as "I am competent and considerate of others," or they can convey the opposite. They cannot be eliminated, but you can make them work for you instead of against you by recognizing their value and becoming more aware of them.

racorn/Shutterstock.com

2-3 LISTENING AS A COMMUNICATION SKILL

Despite the fact that many professionals believe, incorrectly, that business communication is about presentation and not interaction, most employees spend a major part of their day listening to others. In fact, listening is our most used communication skill. In the corporate world, managers may devote more than 60% of their workday to listening to others.[6] Chief executives may spend as much as 75% of their communicating time listening.[7] Listening to supervisors, employees, customers, and colleagues commonly consumes more of employees' time than reading, writing, and speaking combined.

With smartphones, tablets, and 24/7 access to information, it is harder than ever to pay attention to something without a screen, let alone be an effective listener. But although people may be glued to their device of choice, listening is even more crucial to effective communication, and real knowledge. Learning not only happens by reading, researching, or through today's favorite shiny object—Big Data. True learning comes from *sharing* ideas through conversation, which involves being fully engaged in listening, business, and life. Only then can ideas evolve, leaders lead, and teams flourish. Strategist Peter Senge emphasizes the value of developing "learning organizations" to deal with the rapid changes of a globalized world, and listening to others is a critical component of such an organization.[8]

Listening depends on your abilities to receive and decode both verbal and nonverbal messages. The best-devised messages and sophisticated communication systems will not work unless people on the receiving end of spoken messages actually listen.

2-3a Listening for a Specific Purpose

Individuals satisfy a variety of purposes through listening: (1) interacting socially, (2) receiving information, (3) solving problems, (4) sharing feelings with

EFFECTIVE LISTENING HABITS PAY OFF IN SEVERAL WAYS

- ▶ Good listeners are liked by others because they satisfy the basic human needs of being heard and being wanted.

- ▶ People who listen well are able to separate fact from fiction, cope effectively with false persuasion, and avoid having others use them for personal gain.

- ▶ Effective listening leads to sensitivity and tolerance toward key individuals who are critical to the organization's success, such as employees, customers, and suppliers.

- ▶ Effective listeners are engaged and constantly learning—gaining knowledge and skills that lead to increased creativity, job performance, advancement, and satisfaction.

- ▶ Job satisfaction increases when people know what is going on, when they are heard, and when they participate in the mutual trust that develops from good communication.

others, and (5) showing interest and resolving conflict. Listening is a more complex behavior than is typically acknowledged, with some suggesting more than two dozen different types. Each activity may call for a different style of listening or for a combination of styles.

- **Casual listening.** Listening for pleasure, recreation, amusement, and relaxation is casual listening. Some people listen to music all day long for relaxation and to mask unwanted sounds during daily

Casual listening listening for pleasure, recreation, amusement, and relaxation

routines, work periods, and daily commutes. Aspects of casual listening are as follows:

- ° It provides relaxing breaks from more serious tasks and supports our emotional health.

- ° It illustrates that people are selective listeners. You listen to what you want to hear. In a crowded room in which everyone seems to be talking, you can block out all the noise and engage in the conversation that you are having with someone.

- ° It doesn't require much emotional or physical effort.

- **Listening for information.** Listening for information involves the search for data or material. In a lecture class, for example, the instructor usually has a strategy for guiding the class to desired goals. The instructor will probably stress several major points and use supporting evidence to prove or to reinforce them. When engaged in this type of listening, you could become so focused on recording every detail that you take copious notes with no organization. When listening for information:

  - ° Use an outlining process to help you capture main ideas and supporting sub-points in a logical way.

  - ° Watch the speaker as you listen to him or her, because most speakers exhibit a set of mannerisms composed of gestures and vocal inflections to indicate the degree of importance or seriousness that they attach to portions of their presentations.

- **Intensive listening.** When you listen to obtain information, solve problems, or persuade or dissuade (as in arguments), you are engaged in intensive listening. Intensive listening involves greater use of your analytical ability to proceed through problem-solving steps. When listening intensively:

  - ° Become a good summarizer.

  - ° Trace the development of the discussion, and then move from there to your own analysis.

- **Active listening.** Active listening requires that the listener fully concentrates, understands, responds, and then remembers what is being said. It is useful when receiving important instructions, resolving conflict, and providing or receiving critical feedback. When listening actively:

  - ° Observe the speaker's behavior and body language. Having the ability to interpret a person's body language lets the listener develop a more accurate understanding of the speaker's message.

  - ° Paraphrase the speaker's words. In doing so, the listener is not necessarily agreeing with the speaker—simply stating what was said to ensure understanding.

  - ° Ask questions as needed to ensure accurate understanding.

- **Empathetic listening.** *Empathy* occurs when a person attempts to share another's feelings or emotions. Counselors attempt to use empathetic listening in dealing with their clients, and good friends listen empathetically to each other. Empathy is a valuable trait developed by people skilled in interpersonal relations. When you take the time to listen to another, the courtesy is usually returned. When listening empathetically:

  - ° Avoid preoccupation with your own problems. Talking too much and giving strong nonverbal signals of disinterest destroy others' desire to talk.

  - ° Remember that total empathy can never be achieved simply because no two people are exactly alike. The more similar our experiences, however, the better the opportunity to put ourselves in the other person's shoes. Listening with empathy involves some genuine tact along with other good listening habits.

You might have to combine listening intensively, actively, and empathetically in some situations. Performance appraisal interviews, disciplinary conferences, and other sensitive discussions between supervisors and employees require listening intensively and actively in order to gain an accurate understanding of the message and background, as well as to understand feelings and preconceived points of view.

2-3b Bad Listening Habits

Most of us have developed bad listening habits in one or more of the following areas:

- **Faking attention.** Have you ever been introduced to someone only to realize 30 seconds later that you missed the name? We can look directly at a person, nod, smile, and *pretend* to be listening.

- **Allowing disruptions.** We welcome disruptions of almost any sort when we are engaged in somewhat difficult listening. The next time someone enters

listening for information
listening that involves the search for data or material

intensive listening
listening to obtain information, solve problems, or persuade or dissuade

active listening requires that the listener fully concentrates, understands, responds, and then remembers what is being said

empathetic listening
listening to others in an attempt to share their feelings or emotions

your classroom or meeting room, notice how almost everyone in the room turns away from the speaker, and the topic, to observe the latecomer.

- **Over listening.** When we attempt to record many details in writing or in memory, we can *over listen* and miss the speaker's major points.

- **Stereotyping.** We make spontaneous judgments about others based on such issues as appearances, mannerisms, dress, and speech delivery. If a speaker doesn't meet our standards in these areas, we simply turn off our listening and assume the speaker can't have much to say.

- **Dismissing subjects as uninteresting.** People tend to use disinterest as a rationale for not listening. Unfortunately, the decision is usually made before the topic is ever introduced. A good way to lose an instructor's respect when you have to miss class is to ask, "Are we going to do anything important in class today?"

- **Failing to observe nonverbal aids.** To listen effectively, you must observe the speaker. Facial expressions and body motions always accompany speech and contribute a lot to messages.

Many bad listening habits develop simply because the speed of spoken messages is far slower than our ability to receive and process them. Normal speaking speeds are between 100 and 150 words a minute. The human ear can actually distinguish words in speech in excess of 500 words a minute, and many people read at speeds well beyond 500 words a minute. Finally, our minds process thoughts at thousands of words per minute.

A second reason for poor listening habits is that it takes effort to listen, as opposed to simply hearing. We need to take steps to concentrate on what we are hearing to eliminate distractions, and to take notes, and engage in active listening techniques as described in the box found on page 28.

Although much of your spoken communication in business will occur in one-to-one relationships, another frequent spoken-communication activity will likely occur when you participate in groups, committees, and teams.

2-4a Increasing Focus on Groups

In recent years, developments among US businesses have shifted attention away from the employment of traditional organizational subunits as the only mechanisms for achieving organizational goals, and toward the increased use of groups.

- **Flat organizational structures.** Many businesses today have downsized and eliminated layers of management. Companies implementing Total Quality Management programs are reorganizing to distribute the decision-making power throughout the organization. The trend is to eliminate functional or departmental boundaries. Instead, work is reorganized in cross-disciplinary teams that perform broad core processes (e.g., product development and sales generation) and not narrow tasks (e.g., forecasting market demand for a particular product).

In a flat organizational structure, communicating across the organization chart (among cross-disciplinary teams) becomes more important than communicating up and down in a top-heavy hierarchy. An individual can take on

Although much research has been conducted in the area of group size, no optimal number of members has been identified. Groups of five to seven members are thought to be best for decision-making and problem-solving tasks. An odd number of members is often preferred because decisions are possible without tie votes.

SUGGESTIONS FOR EFFECTIVE LISTENING

You can enhance the effectiveness of your face-to-face listening by following these suggestions:

▶ **Minimize environmental and mental distractions.** Take time to listen. Move to a quiet area where you are not distracted by noise or other conversation. Avoid becoming so preoccupied with what you will say next that you fail to listen.

▶ **Get in touch with the speaker.** Maintain an open mind while attempting to understand the speaker's background, prejudices, and points of view. Listen for emotionally charged words and watch for body language, gestures, facial expressions, and eye movements as clues to the speaker's underlying feelings.

▶ **Use your knowledge of speakers to your advantage.** Some people seem to run on and on with details before making the point. With this kind of speaker, you must anticipate the major point, but not pay much attention to details. Other speakers give conclusions first and perhaps omit support for them. In this case, you must ask questions to obtain further information.

▶ **Let the speaker know you are actively involved.** Show genuine interest by remaining physically and mentally involved. Provide nonverbal feedback by maintaining eye contact and smiling or nodding at statements with which you agree. Signal that you understand with such verbal messages as "I see," "go on," and "I agree."

▶ **Do not interrupt the speaker.** Try to understand the speaker's full meaning, and wait patiently for an indication of when you should enter the conversation.

▶ **Ask reflective questions that assess understanding.** Simply restate in your own words what you think the other person has said. This paraphrasing will reinforce what you have heard and allow the speaker to correct any misunderstanding or add clarification.

▶ **Use probing prompts to direct the speaker.** Use probing statements or questions to help the speaker define the issue more concretely and specifically.

▶ **Use lag time wisely.** Listening carefully should be your primary focus; however, you can think ahead at times as well. Making written or mental notes allows you to provide useful feedback when the opportunity arises. If you cannot take notes during the conversation, record important points as soon as possible so you can summarize the speaker's key points.

---

an expanded **role** as important tasks are assumed. This role can involve power and authority that surpass the individual's **status**, or formal position in the organizational chart. Much of the communication involves face-to-face meetings with team members rather than numerous, time-consuming "handoffs" as the product moves methodically from one department to another. Companies such as IKEA, the Swedish furniture manufacturer and retailer, are using flat organizational structures within stores to build an employee attitude of job involvement and ownership.

- **Heightened focus on cooperation.** Competition has been a characteristic way of life in US companies. Organizations and individuals compete for a greater share of scarce resources, for a limited number of positions at the top of organizations, and for esteem in their professions. Such competition is a healthy sign of the human desire to succeed, and in terms of economic behavior, competition is fundamental to the private enterprise system. At the same time, when excessive competition replaces the cooperation necessary for success, communication can be diminished, if not eliminated.

Just as you want to look good in the eyes of your coworkers and supervisors, units within organizations want to look good to one another. This attitude can cause behavior to take a competitive form, or a "win/lose" philosophy. When excessive competition has a negative influence on the performance of the organization, everyone loses.

Although competition is appropriate and desirable in many situations, many companies have taken steps through open communication and information, and reward systems to reduce competition and to increase cooperation. Cooperation is more likely when the competitors (individuals or groups within an organization) have an understanding of, and appreciation for, others' importance and functions. This cooperative spirit is characterized as a "win/win" philosophy. One person's success is not achieved at the expense or exclusion of another. Groups identify a solution that everyone finds satisfactory and is committed to achieving. Reaching this mutual understanding requires a high degree of trust and effective

role tasks employees assume that can involve power and authority that surpass their formal position in the organizational chart

status one's formal position in the organizational chart

interpersonal skills, particularly empathetic and intensive listening skills, and the willingness to communicate long enough to agree on an action plan acceptable to everyone (see Figure 2.2 for a discussion of interpersonal styles).

2-4b Characteristics of Effective Groups

Groups form for synergistic effects. Through pooling their efforts, members can achieve more collectively than they could individually. At the same time, the social nature of groups contributes to the individual as well. Although communication in small groups leads to decisions that are generally superior to individual decisions, the group process can motivate members, improve thinking, and assist attitude changes.

As you consider the following factors of group communication, try to visualize your relationship to the groups to which you have belonged, such as in school, religious organizations, athletics, and social activities.

- **Common goals.** In effective groups, participants share a common goal, interest, or benefit. This focus on goals allows members to overcome individual differences of opinion and to negotiate acceptable solutions.

- **Role perception.** People who are invited to join groups have perceptions of how the group should operate and what it should achieve. In addition, each member has a self-concept that dictates how he or she will behave. Those known to be aggressive will attempt to be confrontational and forceful; those who like to be known as moderates will behave in moderate ways by settling arguments rather than initiating them. In successful groups, members play a variety of necessary roles and seek to eliminate nonproductive ones.

- **Longevity.** Groups formed for short-term tasks, such as arranging a dinner and program, will spend more time on the task than on maintenance. However, groups formed for long-term assignments, such as an accounting team auditing a major corporation, may devote much effort to maintenance goals. Maintenance includes division of duties, scheduling, recordkeeping, reporting, and assessing progress.

- **Size.** The smaller the group, the more its members have the opportunity to communicate with each other. Large groups often inhibit communication because the opportunity to speak and interact is limited. However, when broad input is desired, large

FIGURE 2.2 — FOUR INTERPERSONAL COMMUNICATION STYLES

Aggressive	Verbally attacking someone else, being controlling, provoking, and maybe even physically intimidating or violent. *Example: "What is wrong with you? All you ever think about is yourself!"*
Passive-Aggressive	Retaliating in an indirect manner rather than expressing negative feelings, such as anger, directly. This type of behavior may cause confusion because the person on the receiving end may feel "stung" but can't be sure how or why. *Example: An employee who is angry about his low salary may make negative comments on Twitter about the company rather than discuss the issue with his supervisor.*
Passive	Withdrawing in an attempt to avoid confrontation. Passive people let others think for them, make decisions for them, and tell them what to do. *Example: An employee feels a colleague is treating her poorly. She feels resentful but doesn't express it because she believes her colleague will not listen to her concerns anyway. She is likely to feel down, perhaps even depressed, and avoids interacting with her colleague.*
Assertive	Knowing what you feel and what you want. This behavior involves expressing feelings and needs directly and honestly without violating the rights of others. Assertive people accept responsibility for their feelings and actions. *Example: "I was angry when you didn't show up for our meeting. I know that your time is as valuable to you as my time is to me. I would appreciate it if in the future you would call me if you know you can't make an appointment or if you are going to be late."*

Dean Drobot/shutterstock.com

have an important part to play. The ability of a group leader to work toward task goals, while contributing to the development of group and individual goals, is often critical to group success. Leadership activities may be shared among several participants, and leadership may also be rotated, formally or informally. As part of the group, the leader can affect the establishment of norms by determining who can speak and when, encouraging contribution, and providing motivation for effective group activity.[9]

2-4c Group Roles

Groups are made up of members who play a variety of roles, both positive and negative. Negative roles detract from the group's purposes and include those in the following list.

groups can be good, if steps are taken to ensure that there is effective communication. Interestingly, large groups generally divide into smaller groups for maintenance purposes, even when the large group is task oriented.

- **Status.** Some group members will appear to have higher ranking than others. Consider a group in which the chief executive of an organization is a member. When the chief executive speaks, members agree. When members speak, they tend to direct their remarks to the one with high status—the chief executive. People are inclined to communicate with peers as their equals, but they tend to speak upward to their supervisor and downward to lower-level employees. In general, groups require balance in status and expertise.

- **Group norms.** A **norm** is a standard or average behavior. All groups possess norms. An instructor's behavior helps establish classroom norms. If some students are allowed to arrive late for class, others will begin to arrive late. If some are allowed to talk during lectures, the norm will be for students to talk. People conform to norms because conformity is easy, and nonconformity is difficult and uncomfortable. Conformity leads to acceptance by other group members and creates communication opportunities.

- **Leadership.** The performance of groups depends on several factors, but none is more important than leadership. Some hold the mistaken view that leaders are not necessary when an organization moves to a group concept. The role of leaders changes substantially, but they still

norm a standard or average behavior

NEGATIVE GROUP ROLES

▶ **Isolator**—one who is physically present but fails to participate

▶ **Dominator**—one who speaks too often and too long

▶ **Free rider**—one who does not do his or her fair share of the work

▶ **Detractor**—one who constantly criticizes and complains

▶ **Digresser**—one who deviates from the group's purpose

▶ **Airhead**—one who is never prepared

▶ **Socializer**—one who pursues only the social aspect of the group

A list of positive group roles can be found as follows:

POSITIVE GROUP ROLES

▶ **Facilitator** (also known as *gatekeeper*)—one who makes sure everyone gets to talk and be heard

▶ **Harmonizer**—one who keeps tensions low

▶ **Record keeper**—one who maintains records of events and activities and informs members

▶ **Reporter**—one who assumes responsibility for preparing materials for submission

▶ **Leader**—one who assumes a directive role

In healthy groups, members may fulfill multiple roles, which rotate as the need arises. Negative roles are extinguished as the group communicates openly about its goals, strategies, and expectations. The opinions and viewpoints of all members are encouraged and expected.

2-4d From Groups to Teams

Some use the terms *group* and *team* interchangeably; others distinguish between them. The major distinction between a group and a team is in members' attitudes and level of commitment. A team is typified by a clear identity and a high level of commitment on the part of members. A variety of strategies has been used for organizing workers into teams:

- A **task force** is generally given a single goal and a limited time to achieve it.

- A **quality assurance team**, or *quality circle*, focuses on product or service quality, and projects can be either short or long term.

- A **cross-functional team** brings together employees from various departments to solve a variety of problems, such as productivity

task force a team of workers that is generally given a single goal and a limited time to achieve it

quality assurance team a team that focuses on product or service quality; projects can be either short or long term

cross-functional team a team that brings together employees from various departments to solve a variety of problems issues, contract estimations and planning, and multi-department difficulties.

- A **product development team** concentrates on innovation and the development cycle of new products, and is usually cross-functional in nature.

Whereas chain of command is still at work in formal organizational relationships and responsibilities, team structures unite people from varying portions of the organization. Work teams are typically given the authority to act on their conclusions, although the level of authority varies, depending on the organization and the purpose of the team. Typically, the group supervisor retains some responsibilities, some decisions are made completely by the team, and the rest are made jointly.

Merely placing workers into a group does not make them a functional team. A group must go through a developmental process to begin to function as a team. The four stages of team development include the following:

1. **Forming**—becoming acquainted with each other and the assigned task

2. **Storming**—dealing with conflicting personalities, goals, and ideas

3. **Norming**—developing strategies and activities that promote goal achievement

4. **Performing**—reaching the optimal performance level

For a variety of reasons, teams are often unable to advance through all four stages of development. Even long-term teams might never reach the optimal performing stage, settling instead for the acceptable performance of the norming stage. Studies indicate that virtual teams require additional attention to the planning and use of technology, as well as to members' attitudes and knowledge of such technology. See Figure 2.3 for a discussion of the stages of virtual team formation.

Research into what makes workplace teams effective indicates that training is beneficial for participants in such areas as problem solving, goal setting, conflict resolution, risk-taking, active listening, and recognizing the interests and achievements of others. Participants need to be able to satisfy one another's basic needs for belonging, personal recognition, and support. Team members at the performing stage of team development exhibit the following behaviors[10]:

- **Commitment.** They are focused on the mission, values, goals, and expectations of the team and the organization.

- **Cooperation.** They have a shared sense of purpose, mutual gain, and teamwork.

- **Communication.** They know that information must flow smoothly between top management and workers. Team members are willing to face confrontation and unpleasantness when necessary.

- **Contribution.** All members share their different backgrounds, skills, and abilities with the team.

Teams have existed for hundreds of years throughout many countries and cultures. Teams are more flexible than larger organizational groupings because they can be assembled, deployed, refocused, and disbanded more quickly, usually in ways that enhance rather than disrupt more permanent structures and processes. Organizational changes are often necessary, however, because support must be in place for performance evaluation, recognition, communication, and training systems. Strategies for bringing about needed change might include arranging site visits to similar organizations that already have teams, bringing in a successful team to speak to the organization, and bringing in consultants to discuss the team development process.

 2-5 ## MEETING MANAGEMENT

Meetings are essential for communication in organizations. They present opportunities to acquire and disseminate valuable information, develop skills, and make favorable impressions on colleagues, supervisors, and subordinates. US businesses spend more money on conducting meetings than any other country in the world, and they also spend more time in meetings than people of other countries.[11] International meetings are imperative for solid business reasons but are facing greater planning scrutiny because of tightening travel budgets and a recovering global economy.

Workers frequently have negative attitudes toward meetings because they are perceived as a waste of time. Studies support this opinion, revealing that as much as one-third of the time spent in meetings is unproductive.

---

product development team usually cross-functional in nature; a group of employees who concentrate on innovation and the development cycle of new products

forming stage one of team development, in which team members become acquainted with each other and the assigned task

storming stage two of team development, in which team members deal with conflicting personalities, goals, and ideas

norming stage three of team development, in which team members develop strategies and activities that promote goal achievement

performing stage four of team development, in which team members reach the optimal performance level

FIGURE 2.3   STAGES OF VIRTUAL TEAM FORMATION

Forming	Members begin to develop codes of virtual conduct, to review software and hardware requirements, and to raise and answer questions about how they will use technology to accomplish the group's goals. Some groups arrange a face-to-face meeting before going online, especially when members do not know each other and the project or work is complex and requires a high degree of interaction.
Storming	Members must deal with the added complication imposed by the virtual environment. In addition to expressing opinions and debating substantive issues, the group may encounter technical problems and different levels in member expertise. For example, what should the group do if technical systems are not compatible or if some members are technically unskilled or apprehensive about using advanced technology? Virtual groups must solve technical problems if they hope to address task-related issues and move beyond this stage.
Norming	Virtual groups define members' roles, resolve conflicts, solve most technical problems, and accept the group's norms for interaction. They will be ready to focus on the task. They will also resolve issues related to differences in time, distance, technology, member cultures, and organizational environments.
Performing	Members engage in ongoing virtual interaction and encourage equal participation by all members. They have overcome or adjusted to technical roadblocks and have become comfortable with the virtual media used by the group.
Adjourning	A group may rely on virtual communication to blunt the separation anxiety that comes with the adjourning stage. If a group has matured and performed well, its members will be reluctant to give up relationships with colleagues. Even if a virtual group no longer operates in an official capacity, members may continue to use technological media to consult and interact with one another.

Source: I. N. Engleberg and D. R. Wynn. (2012). *Working in Groups: Communication Principles and Strategies*, 6th ed. Pearson.

Negative attitudes toward meetings can be changed when meetings are conducted properly, giving attention to correct procedures and behavior. Successful meetings don't just happen; rather, they occur by design. Careful planning and attention to specific guidelines can help ensure the success of your meetings, whether they are conducted in a face-to-face format or electronically.

2-5a Face-to-Face Meetings

Face-to-face meetings continue to be the most used meeting format in most organizations. They offer distinct advantages and are appropriate in the following situations[12]:

- When you need the richest nonverbal cues, including body, voice, proximity, and touch

Face-to-face meetings continue to be a frequently used format in most organizations.

Konstantin Chagin/Shutterstock.com

- When the issues are especially sensitive
- When the participants don't know one another
- When establishing group rapport and relationships is crucial
- When the participants can be in the same place at the same time

Face-to-face meetings can be enhanced with the use of various media tools such as flip charts, handouts, and electronic slide decks. Although face-to-face meetings provide a rich nonverbal context and direct human contact, they also have certain limitations. In addition to the obvious logistical issues of schedules and distance, face-to-face meetings may be dominated by overly vocal, quick-to-speak, and high-status members.

2-5b Electronic Meetings

Electronic meetings allow companies to reduce travel budgets, save professional time, and minimize the environmental impact caused by travel. Electronic meetings are common for those working in virtual teams. A variety of technologies is available to facilitate electronic meetings. Participants may communicate with one another through telephones, computers, or video broadcast equipment using groupware or meeting management software applications. Electronic meetings offer certain advantages. They facilitate geographically dispersed groups because they provide the choice of meeting at different places/same time, different places/different times, same place/same time, or same place/different times. Electronic meetings also speed up meeting follow-up activities because decisions and action items can be recorded electronically. Electronic meetings also have certain limitations[13]:

- They cannot replace face-to-face contact, especially when group efforts are just beginning and when groups are trying to build group values, trust, and emotional ties.

- They can make it harder to reach consensus, because more ideas are generated, and it might be harder to interpret the strength of other members' commitment to their proposals.

- The success of same-time meetings is dependent on all participants having excellent keyboarding skills to engage in rapid-fire, in-depth discussion. This limitation might be overcome as the use of voice input systems becomes more prevalent.

2-5c Suggestions for Effective Meetings

Whether you engage in face-to-face or electronic meetings, observing the following guidelines can help ensure that your meetings are productive:

- **Identify the purpose of the meeting.** Meetings typically have various purposes: to inform, to gather information, and to make decisions. Consider whether sending an email would be a better option as a channel choice.

- **Limit meeting length and frequency.** Any meeting held for longer than an hour, or more frequently than once a month should be scrutinized. Ask yourself whether the meeting is necessary. Perhaps the purpose can be achieved in another way, such as email, instant messaging, or telephone.

- **Make satisfactory arrangements.** Select a date and time convenient for the majority of expected participants. For face-to-face meetings, plan the meeting site with consideration for appropriate seating for attendees, media equipment, temperature and lighting, and necessary supplies. For electronic meetings, check hardware and software and connectivity components.

- **Distribute the agenda well in advance.** The **agenda** is a meeting outline that includes important information: date, beginning and ending times, place, topics to be discussed, and responsibilities of those involved. Having the agenda prior to the meeting allows participants to know what is expected of them. A sample agenda template is provided in Figure 2.4.

- **Encourage participation.** Although it is certainly easier for one person to make decisions, the quality of decision making is often improved by involving the team. Rational decision making may begin with **brainstorming**, that is, the generation of many ideas by team members. Brainstormed ideas can then be discussed and ranked, followed by some form of voting.

- **Maintain order.** An organized democratic process ensures that the will of the majority prevails; the minority is heard; and group goals are achieved as expeditiously as possible. Proper parliamentary procedure may be followed in formal meetings, as outlined in sources such as *Robert's Rules of Order* and *Jones' Parliamentary Procedure at a Glance*. For less

agenda a meeting outline that includes important information (e.g., date, beginning and ending times, place, topics to be discussed, and responsibilities of those involved)

brainstorming the generation of many ideas by team members

FIGURE 2.4   FORMAL GENERIC AGENDA FOR MEETINGS

Agenda for [name of group] **Meeting**
Prepared on [date agenda created]
By [*name of author of agenda*]

Attendees: [those invited to attend, often in alphabetical order]
Date and time of meeting:
Location of meeting:
Subject: [major issues to be discussed or purpose of meeting]
Agenda items:

1. Call to order
2. Routine business [procedural or administrative matters]   (10–15 minutes)
    a.   Approval of agenda for this meeting
    b.   Reading and approval of minutes of last meeting
    c.   Committee reports
3. Old business [unfinished matters from previous meeting]   (15–20 minutes)
    (a)   Discussion of issue(s) carried over from previous meeting
    (b)   Issue(s) arising from decision(s) made at previous meeting
4. New business   (20–25 minutes)
    (a)   Most important issue
    (b)   Next most important issue
    (c)   Other issues in decreasing order of importance
    (d)   Business from the floor not included on the agenda
         [only as time permits; otherwise, these issues should be
         addressed in the next meeting]
5. Adjournment

formal meetings, the use of parliamentary procedure may not be necessary to ensure effective contribution by attendees.

- **Manage conflict.** In an autocratic organization, conflict might be avoided because employees are conditioned to be submissive. Such an environment, however, leads to smoldering resentment. On the other hand, conflict is a normal part of any team effort and can lead to creative discussion and superior outcomes. Maintaining focus on issues and not personalities helps ensure that conflict is productive rather than destructive.

- **Seek consensus.** Although unanimous agreement on decisions is an optimal outcome, total agreement cannot always be achieved. **Consensus** represents the collective opinion of the group, or the informal rule that all team members can live with at least 70% of what is agreed upon.

- **Prepare thorough minutes.** Minutes provide a concise record of meeting actions, ensure the tracking and

follow-up of issues from previous meetings, and assist in the implementation of previously reached decisions.

In addition to these general rules for meetings, preparing for and holding virtual meetings include some extra considerations. First, it is important that participants are knowledgeable about the use of the meeting technology, therefore, training may be required. At the beginning of the meeting, individuals should introduce themselves, particularly if a meeting tool is being used that does not provide visual access to attendees. For clarity, questions and comments should be directed to specific individuals. It is also important that noise is reduced to ensure clear reception, so smartphones and pagers should be turned off, and side conversations should be avoided. For video-conferences, participants need to be aware of their

consensus represents the collective opinion of the group, or the informal rule that all team members can live with at least 70% of what is agreed upon

nonverbal behaviors to avoid distracting or disconcerting practices, such as tapping a pen or reviewing text messages. Because you are on camera, it is important to maintain eye contact by looking at the camera.

Meetings are an important management tool and are useful for idea exchange. They also provide opportunities for you, as a meeting participant, to enhance your credibility and communicate impressions of power, competence, and status. Knowing how to present yourself, and your ideas, and exhibiting knowledge about correct meeting management will assist you in your career advancement.

STUDY TOOLS 2

LOCATED AT THE BACK OF THE TEXTBOOK
☐ Tear-Out Chapter Review Card

LOCATED AT WWW.CENGAGEBRAIN.COM
☐ Review Key Term flashcards and create your own cards

☐ Track your knowledge and understanding of key concepts in business communication

☐ Complete practice and graded quizzes to prepare for tests

☐ Complete interactive content within BCOM9 Online

☐ View the chapter highlight boxes for BCOM9 Online

BCOM
ONLINE

ACCESS TEXTBOOK CONTENT ONLINE—
INCLUDING ON SMARTPHONES!

Includes Videos & Other
Interactive Resources!

MANAGE MY COURSE ∨   STUDENT

BCOM

CHAPTER
1

Establishing a Framework for
Business Communication

CHAPTER
2

3 | Planning and Decision Making

Rawpixel.com/Shutterstock.com

LEARNING OBJECTIVES

After studying this chapter, you will be able to …

3-1 Consider the contextual forces that may affect whether, how, to whom, and when a message is sent.

3-2 Identify the purpose of the message and the appropriate channel and medium.

3-3 Develop clear perceptions of the audience to enhance the impact and persuasiveness of the message, improve goodwill, and establish and maintain the credibility of the communicator.

3-4 Apply tactics for adapting messages to the audience, including those for communicating ethically and responsibly.

3-5 Recognize the importance of organization when planning the first draft.

After finishing this chapter, go to **PAGE 55** for **STUDY TOOLS.**

In a report titled "Writing: A Ticket to Work . . . or a Ticket Out," the National Commission on Writing reported that two-thirds of salaried employees in large companies have some writing responsibilities, and getting hired and promoted in many industries requires strong writing abilities. Although writing is important in most managerial-level jobs, the Commission also concluded that one-third of employees in corporate America write poorly. Knowing that effective communication is tied to the corporate bottom line, and that many employees can't write well, businesses are investing $3.1 billion annually to train employees to write.[1] Remedies are needed to prevent confusion, waste, errors, lost productivity, and a damaged corporate image, which are all caused by employees, customers, and clients muddling their way through unreadable messages.

As a capable communicator, you can immediately add value to your organization and positively set yourself apart from your peers, who are struggling to articulate ideas in writing and in presentations. Communication that commands attention and can be understood easily is essential for survival during the information explosion that we are experiencing today. On the job, you will be expected to process volumes of available information and shape useful messages that respond to the needs of customers or clients, coworkers and supervisors, and other key business partners. Additionally, increased use of electronic communication (email, texts, instant messages, blogs, wikis, videoconferences, etc.) will require

Increased use of technological communication will require you to be technologically savvy . . .

you to be technologically savvy and capable of adapting the rules of good communication to the demands of emerging technology.

How can you learn to plan and prepare powerful business messages? The process of systematic analysis, outlined in Figure 3.1, will help you develop messages that save you and your organization valuable time and resources, and portray you as a capable, energetic professional. A thorough analysis of the audience and your specific communication assignment will empower you to create a first draft efficiently, and to revise and proofread your message for accuracy, conciseness, and appropriate tone.

3-1 STEP 1: CONSIDER THE APPLICABLE CONTEXTUAL FORCES

Chapter 1 discussed four contextual forces that may affect whether, how, to whom, and when a message is sent. These were legal and ethical constraints, diversity challenges, changing technology, and team environment. In addition to these four forces, communication patterns within an organization are a contextual force that should also be considered when planning a message. The organizational culture as well as the four dimensions of context may influence how, whether, to whom, and when a message is sent. These two issues are discussed in the sections that follow.

FIGURE 3.1 | **PROCESS FOR PLANNING AND PREPARING SPOKEN AND WRITTEN MESSAGES**

STEP 1	STEP 2	STEP 3	STEP 4	STEP 5	STEP° 6
Consider the applicable contextual forces	Determine the purpose and select an appropriate channel and medium	Envision the audience	Adapt the message to the audience's needs and concerns	Organize the message	Prepare the first draft

° You will focus on the planning process (Steps 1–5) in this chapter; you will learn to prepare the message in Chapter 4 (Step 6).

3-1a Organizational Culture

Organizational culture can be variously defined depending on the theoretical assumptions of the definer. One perspective of culture is that it is "a pattern of shared basic assumptions that the group learned as it solved its problems of external adaptation and internal integration and which has worked well enough to be taught to new members as the correct way to perceive, think, and feel in relation to these problems."[2] This view assumes that culture exists outside of the participants and their communication patterns.

Another perspective of organizational culture is that it is created and reproduced through the communication practices of its participants, with an expansive view of what constitutes communication: symbols; artifacts, such as company logos and accepted employee dress; and structural elements, such as office layout and design. Regardless of the perspective applied to defining the phenomenon, an organization's culture determines what it can and cannot do, and to the extent of individual members' socialization into that culture, it determines what they can and cannot do as well. This is true of actions, behaviors, communicative practices, and the use and inclusion of accepted artifacts.

Keith Bell/Shutterstock.com

In other words, organizational culture affects the type, amount, and quality of communication that is generally accepted within an organization (and vice versa in the latter definition of corporate culture). The culture of a business provides part of the *context* for interpreting the meaning of everyday organizational life, as well as determining what are considered appropriate messages, the proper or expected ways to convey them, and to whom.

For example, Mindvalley, a progressive personal development company based in Malaysia, has declared "Love Week" to honor the values of Valentine's Day. During this annual one-week event in February, each employee is assigned a Secret Angel who anonymously performs acts of caring and kindness for him or her. Studies show that employees are more engaged and productive when they are happy and when their interactions with colleagues are positive. The event has been so powerful that Mindvalley is globally encouraging and inspiring other companies to try it as well.[3]

Compare these values with the type of culture that you might find in an investment banking firm in which competition, individualism, and the drive for profits and bonuses would likely be key elements, and it should be easy to see how culture might affect how communication occurs and what is expected and accepted within an organization in terms of behaviors.

Theorists have constructed a variety of models to try to capture the essence of corporate culture, a discussion of which goes beyond the scope of this text. But one simple model, based on the Competing Values Framework, distinguishes four culture types, which are summarized here to illustrate the differences that might emerge in corporate cultures:

- **Clan culture (internal focus and flexible)**— A friendly workplace where leaders act like father figures.

- **Adhocracy culture (external focus and flexible)**— A dynamic workplace with leaders who stimulate innovation.

- **Market culture (external focus and controlled)**— A competitive workplace where leaders are hard drivers.

- **Hierarchy culture (internal focus and controlled)**— A structured and formalized workplace where leaders act like coordinators or administrators.

Generally speaking, the culture of business can be characterized as typically having a bias toward action, a demand for confidence, and a results orientation. The culture of business can be seen in everyday office interactions. Being knowledgeable about an organization's culture can help you gauge the type and quality

organizational culture
a pattern of shared basic assumptions that the group has learned as it solved its problems with external adaptation and internal integration, and which has worked well enough to be taught to new members as the correct way to perceive, think, and feel in relation to these problems

of communication that takes place, as well as whether you are a good match with the organization. For example, does the organization have an open door policy, or are you expected to obey the hierarchical order of management when communicating concerns? Does the office have an open floor plan, or do employees have private offices? Do people wear T-shirts and shorts or suits to work every day? The first situation in each of these cases probably signals that the culture is less formal in terms of its expectations and communication patterns, whereas the second situation may indicate a culture that is more formal in terms of its expectations regarding punctuality and communication choices and behaviors.

3-1b Dimensions of Context

In addition to the other elements of context discussed in previous chapters and sections, there are several dimensions to context, including the physical, social, chronological, and cultural. The *physical* context or setting can influence the content and quality of interaction. For example, if you were to ask your boss for a raise, the effect of the setting might dramatically affect your chances for success. How might the following settings affect the success of such an interaction, how it might take place, or whether it should take place: In the boss's office? At a company picnic? Over lunch at a restaurant? In your work area with others observing?

The *social context* refers to the nature of the relationship between the communicators, as well as who is present. In the same situation mentioned above, imagine how the relationship between your manager and yourself might affect your request for a raise, depending on the various scenarios that follow:

- You and the manager have been friends for several years, as opposed to a situation in which you and your manager have no personal relationship.

- You are the same age as your manager, or she or he is 15 years older (or younger) than you.

- You and the manager have gotten along well in the past, compared to a situation in which you and the manager have been involved in an ongoing personal conflict.

The *chronological context* refers to the ways time influences interactions. For example, how might the time of day affect the quality of an interaction? How might the communicator's personal preferences regarding time affect communication and its success? Is it a busy time of year for employees and managers? Has there just been

Contextual forces may affect how a message is sent.

iStockphoto.com/Sirgunhik

a major layoff, downsizing, or profit loss? In this last case, you might want to put off your request for a raise until conditions improve.

The *cultural context* includes both the organizational culture as well as the cultural backgrounds of the people with whom you may be communicating. A person's cultural influences also can affect the kind and quality of communication that takes place, and they can help determine approaches that will be more effective. For example, young people have different expectations than seniors; Hispanics have different expectations than Asians; Californians have different expectations than people from the Midwest or East Coast; and men may communicate differently than women.

Environmental factors may also affect what should be communicated and how. For example, if the economy is doing poorly, then some messages may be inappropriate or may have little chance for success. If you work in a highly litigious environment or one that is strongly regulated, then constraints may exist for what you can communicate and how. Larger social, political, or historical events may affect whether certain messages are appropriate or have a chance of success. As mentioned earlier, in an economic downturn, it may be difficult, depending on the industry, to be successful at negotiating a pay raise, because the employer may feel that employees should feel lucky to simply have a job during difficult times.

As this discussion shows, context is a complex, multi-dimensional force that should be considered when planning a message, and determines whether it should be sent, when it should be sent, to whom, and how.

3-2

STEP 2: DETERMINE THE PURPOSE, AND SELECT AN APPROPRIATE CHANNEL AND MEDIUM

To speak or write effectively, you must think through what you are trying to say and understand it thoroughly before you begin. Ask yourself why you are preparing the message and what you hope to accomplish. Is the purpose to get information, to answer a question, to accept an offer, to deny a request, or to seek support for a product or idea? Condense the answers into a brief sentence that outlines the purpose for writing or the central idea of your message. You will use the central idea to organize your message to achieve the results you desire.

The major purpose of many business messages is to have the receiver understand logical information. Informative messages are used to convey the vast amounts of information needed to complete the day-to-day operations of the business: explain instructions to employees, announce meetings and procedures, acknowledge orders, accept contracts for services, and so forth. Some messages are intended to persuade: to influence or change the attitudes or actions of the receiver. These messages include promoting a product or service, and seeking support for ideas and worthy causes presented to supervisors, employees, stockholders, customers or clients, and others. Additional purposes include establishing a good relationship with your audience, which is discussed later in this chapter, and establishing and maintaining your own credibility as a professional, both of which can help increase your persuasiveness. You will learn to prepare messages that are for each of these purposes later in this text. In addition to identifying the purposes of the message, it is also important to decide which channel and medium would be most effective and appropriate.

3-2a Selecting the Channel and Medium

Broadly speaking, four channels of communication exist: visual, written, oral, and nonverbal. However, these broad categories can be broken down further. For example, written

> Face-to-face communication provides participants with a rich source of information, including vocal cues, facial expressions, bodily movement and appearance, the use of space and time, touching, and clothing and other artifacts.

communication can be disseminated using a variety of media or forms, including memos, letters, emails, instant or text messaging, faxes, press releases, company websites, blogs, blog applications, wikis, and reports. Oral communication can also use various media or forms such as face-to-face or interpersonal, telephone, voice messages, teleconferences and videoconferences, speeches, meetings, and podcasts. Typically, nonverbal communication supplements oral forms, but it shouldn't be underestimated because most communication in face-to-face situations is often nonverbal. Similarly, visual communication supplements both written and oral forms of communication in the form of slide presentations, diagrams, photographs, charts, tables, video, and artwork.

Channel choice might be influenced or informed by earlier steps in the planning process. For instance, the contextual forces may affect how a message is sent. If the organization typically conveys most routine messages using email, for instance, this may be the most obvious choice. The purpose of communication might affect channel choice as well. In a situation in which the purpose is primarily to establish a relationship or convey goodwill, a face-to-face meeting might be the best choice to achieve this goal. Audience analysis might yield information that indicates it prefers a particular medium of communication such as email or phone discussions.

Common channel choice considerations include the following:

- **Richness versus leanness.** Some channels of communication provide more information than others. Generally, the richest channels of communication provide nonverbal information in addition to that provided in written or oral form. For this reason, the richest channel of communication is face-to-face, or interpersonal. Face-to-face communication provides participants a rich source of information, including vocal cues, facial expressions, bodily movement, bodily appearance, the use of space, the use of time, touching, and clothing and other artifacts. In addition, face-to-face communication provides opportunities to facilitate feedback and establish a personal focus. These aspects also contribute to the richness of interpersonal communication as a channel of communication.

- **Need for interpretation.** Some channels of communication are more ambiguous, or leave more room for interpretation of the message being sent, than others. Nonverbal communication may be the most ambiguous channel of communication because it requires the audience to interpret almost the entirety of the message. Nonverbal communication is difficult to interpret for a variety of reasons, mainly because it is not generally considered a coded language. Because of this, one nonverbal code may communicate a variety of meanings. Similarly, nonverbal communication can be difficult to interpret because a variety of codes may communicate the same meaning. A third issue that may affect a person's ability to interpret nonverbal codes accurately is intentionality. Some nonverbal codes are sent intentionally, and others unintentionally.

- **Speed of establishing contact.** Another important consideration, particularly in the business world, is the time it will take for a message to be delivered. For this reason, electronic forms of communication have become popular. Using the telephone, writing an email or text message, using blogs and blog applications (such as Twitter) or other social media such as Facebook or LinkedIn, posting to wikis, Skyping, using virtual team applications, or sending a fax are nearly instantaneous channels of communication. In contrast, sending a written message or package by mail may take days.

- **Time required for feedback.** Just as we may need to contact someone immediately, we may also need a response from that person just as rapidly. The most rapid forms of communication, as explained previously, are generally electronic. However, depending on the person with whom you are communicating, his or her personality, and your relationship, communicating with a person via an electronic channel does not guarantee prompt feedback. In other words, corporate cultures and individual people may have preferences for specific communication channels or mediums and differing communication practices.

- **Cost.** Many channels of communication are relatively inexpensive for business users. Mail, email, text messages, telephones, faxes, wikis, blogs and blog applications, social media, videoconferencing and teleconferencing tools, and Skype are generally considered inexpensive forms of communication. These tools have made it much less expensive for stakeholders, both inside and outside organizations, to communicate with each other, regardless of their location. Still, there are times when it may be appropriate to choose the greater expense of arranging a face-to-face meeting, such as when introducing

members of a virtual team who will be working on an important project for some time or interviewing job applicants for key positions.

- **Amount of information conveyed.** The best channel for conveying large amounts of information is generally a written one. One reason is that most of us are generally poor listeners. Studies indicate that we retain only 10% or so of what we hear. Therefore, if you want people to have the opportunity to process and remember the information you have to deliver, particularly if the message is long or complex, then it is generally best delivered using a written channel rather than an oral one.

- **Need for a permanent record.** Businesspeople are often involved in situations where they must keep records of what occurred during various work activities throughout the day or week. These situations include the need to record what occurred at a department meeting, an employee's work history, the findings of an audit of a client's financial records, and an employee's travel expenses. Most legal documents, including contracts, use the written channel of communication for this reason: the need to maintain a record. Email messages and other electronic forums such as websites, social networking sites, and blogs, if stored and backed up properly, can also serve as a record.

- **Control over the message.** Written channels of communication also are often the best choice when you wish to maintain greater control of the message that you send. why? If information is presented orally and interpersonally, you have a greater chance of persons who disagree with you speaking out and potentially derailing or confusing the message. That is why many negative messages, such as informing a job applicant that he or she was not selected, are sent using a written channel of communication.

Figure 3.2 provides a summary of the proper use of differing media within an organizational context.

 ## 3-3 STEP 3: ENVISION THE AUDIENCE

Perception is the part of the communication process that involves how we look at others and the world around us. Perception is a three-phase process of selecting, organizing, and interpreting information, objects, people, events, or situations. It's a natural tendency to perceive situations from our own limited viewpoint. We use the context of the situation and our five senses to absorb and interpret the information bombarding us in unique ways.

FIGURE 3.2   USE OF COMMUNICATION MEDIA

MEDIUM	BEST USES	MEDIUM	BEST USES
Memo	• Simple, routine messages • Confirming policies • Distributing to a large, internal audience • Providing information when a response isn't required	Telephone	• Providing quick feedback or response • Sending confidential information • Discussing bad news • Confirming • Great for creating a personal connection • Easy to measure impact
Letter	• Communicating with an external audience • Conveying formality • Providing a written record • Writing a complaint • Communicating condolences or thanks	Voice mail	• Informing when feedback isn't needed • Confirming • Sending a simple message
		Video conferencing	• Making a personal connection with a large audience • Economical and efficient • Training
Email	• Sending brief, impersonal, or routine messages • Can reach mass audiences fast • Cost effective and simple to use • A consistent and controlled message • Reaches the recipient directly • Providing a hard copy	Twitter	• Great for short bursts of information • Good for directing attention to other forms of communication, such as a website • Real-time tweets can make people, who are off-site, feel involved in site-based events • Good for generating a following • Quick, easy, and cheap • Attracts younger audiences
Fax	• Sending a visual display of information • Communicating general information about a company and its products or services	Facebook and other social networks	• Easy and cheap to do. • Good way of directing readers' attentions to other forms of communication, such as a website • Good for gathering information about individuals • Good way to build a general profile • Allowing people to interact rather than receiving information passively
Web page	• Sharing information with large audiences in an economical fashion • Inspiring and motivating others • Demonstrating products or training • Allowing people to interact rather than receiving information passively		
Oral presentation	• Introducing a persuasive message or following up on one when goodwill and credibility are especially important • Delivering bad news to a large audience when goodwill and credibility are especially important	LinkedIn and other professional networks	• Easy and cheap to do • Good way of directing the reader's attention to other forms of communication, such as a website • Good for gathering information about individuals • Good for providing additional benefits to prospects through peer-to-peer networking and posting career opportunities
Face-to-face	• Communicating confidential information • Negotiating • Promoting or firing an employee • Communicating personal warmth or care • Reading nonverbal communication cues	Team meetings	• Can make communication personal and relevant to the team involved • Opportunity for discussion, feedback, questioning, and ideas • Can help build understanding and involvement

Individual differences in perception account for the varied and sometimes conflicting reports given by eyewitnesses to the same accident. Our senses can be tricked when there is a difference in what we expect and what really is happening. For example, consider how your *perception* affects your ability to accurately or completely interpret an optical illusion.

Perception of reality is also limited by previous experiences and our attitudes toward the sender of the message. We support ideas that are in line with our own and decide whether to focus on the positive or the negative aspects of a situation. We may simply refuse to hear a message that doesn't fit into our view of the world.

> Overcoming perceptual barriers is difficult but essential if you are to craft messages that meet the needs and concerns of your audience

Much of the confusion in communication is caused by differences in the sender's and receiver's perceptions. For example, a manager's brief email requesting a status report on a task may come across as curt to the employees. Perceptions vary between individuals with similar backgrounds, and even more so when people from different cultures, generations, and genders communicate.

Overcoming perceptual barriers is difficult but essential if you are to craft messages that meet the needs and concerns of your audience. To help you envision the audience, first focus on relevant information you know about the receiver. The more familiar you are with the receiver, the easier this task will be. When communicating with an individual, you immediately recall a clear picture of the receiver: his or her physical appearance, background (education, occupation, religion, and culture), values, opinions, preferences, and so on. Most importantly, your knowledge of the receiver's reaction in similar, previous experiences will aid you in anticipating how this receiver is likely to react in the current situation. Consider the following audience characteristics:

- **Age.** A message answering an elementary-school student's request for information from your company would not be worded the same as a message answering a similar request from an adult.

- **Economic level.** A solicitation for a business donation for a charity project written to a small business owner would likely differ from one written to a representative of a major corporation.

- **Educational/occupational background.** The technical jargon and acronyms used in a financial proposal sent to bank loan officers may be inappropriate in a proposal sent to a group of private investors.

- **Needs and concerns of the audience.** Just as successful sales personnel begin by identifying the needs of the prospective buyer, an effective manager attempts to understand the receiver's frame of reference as a basis for organizing the message and developing the content.

- **Culture.** The vast cultural differences between people (e.g., language, expressions, customs, values, and religion) increase the complexity of the communication process as was discussed in Chapter 1. An email

Alex Staroseltsev/Shutterstock.com

Stimulus → Stimulus → Stimulus → Selection → Organization → Interpretation

▶ Airbnb, a community marketplace for people to list and book accommodations around the world, was founded in 2008 out of San Francisco, California.

▶ Since then, Airbnb has grown to more than 1,500,000 listings in 34,000-plus cities worldwide. A large contributor to the company's explosive global success has been its creative use of social media.

▶ In January 2015, Airbnb launched a social media campaign around the hashtag #OneLessStranger. The company referred to the campaign as a "global, social experiment," in which Airbnb asked the community to perform random acts of hospitality for strangers. Brian Chesky, Airbnb's CEO, gifted 1 million in the form of $10 into the accounts of 100,000 people in the Airbnb community. He urged them to put this donation towards committing one act of hospitality for a stranger, document it, and upload it onto social media with the hashtag #OneLessStranger.

▶ Just three weeks after the launch of the campaign, more than 3 million people worldwide engaged, created content, or were talking about the campaign. "We empowered our community to bring our brand vision to life with this pay-it-forward approach to inspire participation." The result is that visitors to Airbnb's web page have been spending on average more than 6 minutes, well above industry averages, on the landing page, engaging with all of the user-generated acts of #OneLessStranger.

Consider the audience in order to determine whether to use the inductive or deductive sequence. If an audience might be antagonized by the main idea in a deductive message, lead up to the main idea by making the message inductive. If a sender wants to encourage audience involvement (to generate some concern about where the details are leading), use the inductive approach. Inductive organization can be especially effective if the main idea confirms the conclusion that the audience has drawn from the preceding details—a cause is worthy of support, a job applicant should be interviewed, a product/service should be selected, and so on. As you learn in later chapters about writing letters, memos, and email messages, and about planning spoken communications, you will comprehend the benefits of using the appropriate outline for each receiver reaction:

Deductive Order (main idea first)	Inductive Order (details first)
When the message *will* please the audience	When the message will *displease* the audience
When the message is *routine* (will not please nor displease)	When the audience *might* not be *interested* (will need to be persuaded)

For determining the sequence of minor ideas that accompany the major idea, the following bases for idea sequence are common:

- **Time.** When writing a report or email message about a series of events or a process, paragraphs proceed from the first step through the last step.

- **Space.** If a report is about geographic areas, ideas can proceed from one area to the next until all areas have been discussed.

- **Familiarity.** If a topic is complicated, the presentation can begin with a known or easy-to-understand point and proceed to progressively more difficult points.

- **Importance.** In analytical reports in which major decision-making factors are presented, the factors can be presented in order of most important to least important, or vice versa.

- **Value.** If a presentation involves major factors with monetary values, paragraphs can proceed from those with greatest values to those with least values, or vice versa.

The same organizational patterns are recommended for written and spoken communication.

These patterns are applicable in email messages, blogs, letters, memos, and reports.

STUDY TOOLS 3

LOCATED AT THE BACK OF THE TEXTBOOK
☐ Tear-Out Chapter Review Card

LOCATED AT WWW.CENGAGEBRAIN.COM
☐ Review Key Term flashcards and create your own cards

☐ Track your knowledge and understanding of key concepts in business communication

☐ Complete practice and graded quizzes to prepare for tests

☐ Complete interactive content within BCOM9 Online

☐ View the chapter highlight boxes for BCOM9 Online

4 | Preparing Written Messages

Shahril KHMD/Shutterstock.com

LEARNING OBJECTIVES

After studying this chapter, you will be able to . . .

4-1 Apply techniques for developing effective introductions, sentences, and unified and coherent paragraphs.

4-2 Prepare visually appealing documents that grab the reader's attention and increase comprehension.

4-3 Identify factors affecting readability, and revise messages to improve readability.

4-4 Revise and proofread a message for content, organization, style, and tone, as well as mechanics, format, and layout.

After finishing this chapter, go to **PAGE 78** for **STUDY TOOLS**.

In Chapter 3, you learned about the importance of following a systematic process to develop business messages. The applications in Chapter 3 guided you in developing a clear, logical plan for your message that focused on the needs of the receiver (Steps 1–5). Effectively capturing your ideas for various business communication situations involves skillful use of language and careful attention to accuracy and readability issues—the remaining two steps in this important process are shown in Figure 4.1.

> Business communicators normally use active voice more than passive voice.

for new inspiration, and rereading preceding sentences.

Concentrating on getting your ideas down as quickly as you can is an efficient approach to writing. During this process, remember that you are preparing a draft and not the final copy. If you are composing at the computer, you can quickly and easily revise your draft throughout the writing process. This seamless approach to writing allows you to continue to improve your working draft until the moment you are ready to submit the final copy. Numerous electronic writing tools are available, and technology will continue to unfold to enhance the writing process.

4-1 EFFECTIVE INTRODUCTIONS, COHERENT PARAGRAPHS, AND POWERFUL SENTENCES

STEP 6: PREPARE THE FIRST DRAFT

Once you have determined whether the message should be presented deductively (main idea first) or inductively (explanation and details first) and have planned the logical sequence of minor points, you are ready to begin composing the message.

Normally, writing rapidly (with intent to rewrite certain portions, if necessary) is better than slow, deliberate writing (with intent to avoid any need for rewriting portions). The latter approach can be frustrating and can reduce the quality of the finished work. Time is wasted in thinking of one way to express an idea, discarding it either before or after it is written, waiting

4-1a Select the Type of Introduction

Deductively organized messages will likely differ in the type of introduction used compared to an inductively organized message. Deductively organized messages typically start with a direct and straightforward introduction that immediately announces the purpose of the message from the audience's perspective and provides a brief overview of its contents or organization to aid in quickly grasping the overall scope of the message and its ordering.

For example, a message intended to respond to a reader's query for more information about a company's product offerings might begin as follows:

In response to your request, you will find an overview of TechPro's line of commercial networking products. The information provided is categorized by both the number of users served and the functionality provided.

FIGURE 4.1	PROCESS FOR PLANNING AND PREPARING SPOKEN AND WRITTEN MESSAGES

STEP 1	STEP 2	STEP 3	STEP 4	STEP 5	STEP* 6	STEP* 7
Consider the applicable contextual forces	Determine the purpose, and select an appropriate channel and medium	Envision the audience	Adapt the message to the audience's needs and concerns	Organize the message	Prepare the first draft	Revise and proofread for accuracy and the desired impact

*You will focus on the planning process (Steps 1–5) in Chapter 3; you will learn to prepare the message (Steps 6–7) in this chapter.

This introduction recognizes the reader's request for information and provides additional explanation of what he or she will find in the body of the message. This latter information orients the reader so he or she can quickly skim the document to find the specific information for which he or she is looking. It is important that the writer fulfills his or her promise to the reader to organize the information as announced.

For an inductively organized message, though, a buffer or goodwill opening might be used to soften the approach and the reader's reception.

For example, a message to a job applicant informing him or her that he or she was not selected might begin as follows:

Dietrich Fine Foods greatly appreciates your interest in contributing to our continued success.

This example illustrates the use of a single sentence to convey goodwill to the recipient for his or her interest in the company as well as to act as a buffer for the next paragraph, which delivers the bad news in a tactful way that he or she was not selected for the job opening.

4-1b Develop Coherent Paragraphs

Well-constructed sentences are combined into paragraphs that discuss a portion of the topic being covered. To write effective paragraphs, you must learn to (a) develop deductive or inductive paragraphs consistently, (b) link ideas to achieve coherence, (c) keep paragraphs unified, and (d) vary sentence and paragraph length.

POSITION THE TOPIC SENTENCE APPROPRIATELY

Typically, paragraphs contain one sentence that identifies the portion of the topic being discussed and presents the central idea. That sentence is commonly called a **topic sentence**. For example, consider the operating instructions prepared for company-owned GPS navigation systems. The overall topic is how to get satisfactory performance from the device. One portion of that topic is setup, another portion (paragraph) discusses operation, and so forth. Within each paragraph, one sentence serves a special function. Sentences that list the steps can appear as one paragraph, perhaps with steps numbered as follows:

topic sentence a sentence that identifies the portion of the topic being discussed and presents the central idea of the paragraph

deductive paragraph a paragraph in which the topic sentence precedes the details

inductive paragraph a paragraph in which the topic sentence follows the details

To set up the system, take the following steps:

1. *Connect . . .*
2. *Go to menu settings to . . .*

In this illustration, the paragraphs are **deductive**; that is, the topic sentence *precedes* details. When topic sentences *follow* details, the paragraphs are **inductive**. As discussed previously, the receiver's likely reaction to the main idea (pleased, displeased, interested, or not interested) aids in selecting the appropriate sequence.

When the subject matter is complicated and the details are numerous, paragraphs sometimes begin with a main idea, follow with details, and end with a summarizing sentence. But the main idea might not be in the first sentence; the idea could need a preliminary statement. Receivers appreciate consistency in the placement of topic sentences. Once they catch on to the writer's or speaker's pattern, they know where to look for main ideas. It is important to remember, though, that most messages are deductive in organization because of the subject matter and because of the audience's needs. In other words, inductive organization is typically only used in bad news messages and persuasive messages written to resistant audiences. All other types of messages are typically deductive in organization.

This is because business audiences are typically pressed for time and deductively organized messages are easier to read if well crafted. Well-crafted deductive messages are easy to skim; the audience can quickly ascertain the purpose of the message, its contents, and its location in just a few seconds. This type of writing enables the audience to quickly grasp the message and immediately find the information they are seeking.

What this means is that most business readers do not read an entire document carefully, but may jump to a specific section that contains information that is immediately needed, or is more important for their specific tasks. A good writer anticipates that the reader might skim a message and attempts to make this process easier for the reader.

To pass the "skim test," ensure that a deductively organized message has the following:

1. A clearly stated purpose in the introduction, as well as a brief overview of its contents
2. If it is a longer, more complex document, it uses clear headings to identify important sub-topics
3. Uses topic sentences that clearly identify the sub-topics listed in the introduction

These suggestions seldom apply to the first and last sentences of letters, memos, and email messages. Such sentences frequently appear as single-sentence paragraphs. But for reports and long paragraphs of letters, strive for paragraphs that are consistently deductive or inductive. Regardless of which is selected, topic sentences are clearly linked with details that precede or follow.

LINK IDEAS TO ACHIEVE COHERENCE

Careful writers use coherence techniques to keep receivers from experiencing abrupt changes in thought. Although the word **coherence** is used sometimes to mean "clarity" or "understandability," it is used throughout this text to mean "cohesion." If writing or speaking is coherent, the sentences stick together; each sentence is in some way linked to the preceding sentences. Avoid abrupt changes in thought, and link each sentence to a preceding sentence.

The following techniques for linking sentences are common:

tanewpix/Shutterstock.com

1. **Repeat a word that was used in the preceding sentence.** The second sentence in the following example is an obvious continuation of the idea presented in the preceding sentence.

    . . . to take responsibility for the decision. This responsibility can be shared . . .

2. **Use a pronoun that represents a noun used in the preceding sentence.** Because *"it"* means "responsibility," the second sentence below is linked directly with the first.

    . . . to take this responsibility. It can be shared . . .

3. **Use connecting words.** Examples include *however, therefore, yet, nevertheless, consequently, also,* and *in addition.* "However" implies "We're continuing with the same topic, just moving into a different phase." Remember, though, that good techniques can be overused. Unnecessary connectors are space consuming and distracting. Usually they can be spotted (and crossed out) in proofreading.

    . . . to take this responsibility. However, few are willing to . . .

Just as sentences within a paragraph must be linked together, paragraphs within a document must also be linked together. Unless a writer or speaker is careful, the move from one major topic to the next will seem abrupt. A good transition sentence can bridge the gap between the two topics by summing up the preceding topic and leading a receiver to expect the next topic:

Once the new accounting system is put into place, training employees in its operation is vital.

This sentence could serve as a transition between "Installation" and "Training" division headings. Because a transition sentence comes at the end of one segment and before the next, it emphasizes the central idea of the preceding segment and confirms the relationship of the two segments. Although transition sentences are helpful if properly used, they can be overused. For most reports, transition sentences before major headings are sufficient. Normally, transition sentences before subheadings are unnecessary.

KEEP PARAGRAPHS UNIFIED

Receivers expect the first paragraph of a message to introduce a topic, additional paragraphs to discuss it, and a final paragraph to tie all of the paragraphs together. The middle paragraphs should be arranged in a systematic sequence, and the end must be linked easily to some word or idea presented in the beginning.

coherence cohesion, so that each sentence is linked to the preceding sentences in some way

The effect of a message that is *not* unified is like that of an incomplete circle or a picture with one element obviously missing.

- A unified email message, letter, memo, or report covers its topic adequately but does not include extraneous material. The document should have a beginning sentence that is appropriate for the expected receiver's reaction, paragraphs that present the bulk of the message, and an ending sentence that is an appropriate closing for the message presented.

- A unified report or presentation begins with an introduction that identifies the topic, reveals the thesis, and previews upcoming points. The introduction often includes some background, sources of information, and the method for treating data. Between the beginning and the ending, a unified report should have paragraphs arranged in a systematic sequence. A summary or conclusion brings all major points together.

Laboko/Shutterstock.com

VARY SENTENCE AND PARAGRAPH LENGTH

Sentences of short or average length are easy to read and preferred for clear communication. However, keeping *all* sentences short is undesirable because the message might sound monotonous, unrealistic, or elementary. A 2-word sentence is acceptable; so is a 60-word sentence—if it is clear. Just as sentences should vary in length, they should also vary in structure. Some complex or compound sentences should be included with simple sentences.

Variety is just as desirable in paragraph length as it is in sentence length. A paragraph can be from one line in length to a dozen lines or more. However, just as with sentence length, average paragraph length also should be kept short, as appropriate to the document type:

- Paragraphs in letters, memos, and email messages are typically shorter than paragraphs in business reports.

- First and last paragraphs are normally short (one to four lines), and other paragraphs are normally no longer than *six lines*. A short first paragraph is more inviting to read than a long first paragraph, and a short last paragraph enables a writer to emphasize parting thoughts.

- The space between paragraphs is a welcome resting spot. Long paragraphs are difficult to read and make a message appear uninviting. Paragraph length will vary depending on the complexity of the subject matter. However, as a general rule paragraphs should be no longer than *eight to ten lines*. This length usually allows enough space to include a topic sentence and three or four supporting statements. If the topic cannot be discussed in this space, divide the topic into additional paragraphs.

To observe the effect that large sections of unbroken text can have on the overall appeal of a document, examine the memos in Figure 4.2. Without question, the memo with the short, easy-to-read paragraphs is more inviting than the memo with one bulky paragraph.

Although variety is a desirable quality, it should not be achieved at the expense of consistency. Using *I* in one part of a message and then, without explanation, switching to *we* is inadvisable. Using the past tense in one sentence and the present tense in another sentence creates variety at the expense of consistency—unless the shift is required to indicate actual changes in time. Unnecessary changes from active to passive voice and from third to first person are also discouraged.

4-1c Craft Powerful Sentences

Well-developed sentences help the receiver to understand the message clearly and to react favorably to the writer or speaker. In this section, you will learn how to predominately use the active voice and to emphasize important points, which affect the clarity and goodwill of your message.

RELY ON ACTIVE VOICE

Business communicators normally use the active voice more heavily than the passive voice because the active voice conveys ideas more vividly. In sentences in which the subject is the *doer* of an action, the verbs are called

OLD MESSAGE	NEW MESSAGE
To: All employees	**To:** All employees
From: Gina Park [gina.park@xyzco.com]	**From:** Gina Park [gina.park@xyzco.com]
Subject: Travel card changes	**Subject:** Travel card changes
Everyone,	Everyone,
For those of you who hold or wish to have a company credit card for travel purposes, we will be switching from MasterCard to Visa in 30 days. You can sign up for the new card online. Please just access the Human Resources' web page at www.xyzco.com/human resources and click on the link "Travel Card Application." Fill out the form that appears and submit it. You will receive a confirmation message if your submission was successful. In about two weeks, Human Resources will notify you via email when your card is available for pick up.	For those of you who hold or wish to have a company credit card for travel purposes, we will be switching from MasterCard to Visa in 30 days.
	You can sign up for the new card online. Please just access the Human Resources' web page at www.xyzco.com/human resources and click on the link "Travel Card Application." Fill out the form that appears and submit it. You will receive a confirmation message if your submission was successful. In about two weeks, Human Resources will notify you via email when your card is available for pick up.
If you currently have a MasterCard, you should return it to Human Resources by March 30. If you have questions about this change, please contact me at gina.park@xyzco.com.	If you currently have a MasterCard, you should return it to Human Resources by March 30.
	If you have questions about this change, please contact me at gina.park@xyzco.com.

active. In sentences in which the subject is the *receiver* of an action, the verbs are called *passive*. Review the differences in the impact of the **passive voice** and **active voice**:

Passive Voice	Active Voice
Reports are transferred electronically from remote locations to the corporate office.	Our sales reps transfer reports from remote locations to the corporate office.

The active sentence invites the receiver to see the sales reps as actively engaged in setting expectations, whereas the passive sentence draws attention to the reports. Using active voice makes the subject the actor, which places greater emphasis on his or her concerns.

Even when a passive sentence contains additional words to reveal the doer, the imagery is less distinct than it would be if the sentence were active: *Free refills of soft drinks are expected by our customer base and shouldn't be the focus of cutbacks. Free refills* gets the most attention because it is the subject. The sentence seems to let the audience know the *result* of the action before revealing the doer; therefore, the sentence is less emphatic.

Although active voice conveys ideas more vividly, passive voice is useful for the following purposes:

- Concealing the doer: "Shortages in inventory have been found," rather than employees are the cause of inventory shortages.

passive voice when the subject of a sentence is the receiver of an action

active voice when the subject of a sentence is the doer of an action

- Placing more emphasis on *what* was done and who or what it was *done* to than on *who* did it: "The reports have been compiled by our sales representatives."
- Subordinating an unpleasant thought or avoiding finger-pointing: "The printer on the second floor is not working properly," rather than "Lucy apparently fouled up the printer on the second floor."

EMPHASIZE IMPORTANT IDEAS

A landscape artist wants some features in a picture to stand out boldly and others to get little attention. A musician sounds some notes loudly and others softly. Likewise, a writer or speaker wants some ideas to be *emphasized* and others to be *de-emphasized*. Normally, pleasant and important ideas should be emphasized; unpleasant and insignificant ideas should be de-emphasized. Emphasis techniques include sentence structure, repetition, words that label, position, and space and format.

SENTENCE STRUCTURE

For emphasis, place an idea in a simple sentence. The simple sentence in the following example has one independent clause. Because no other idea competes with it for attention, this idea is emphasized.

A Simple Sentence Is More Emphatic	A Compound Sentence Is Less Emphatic
Travis accepted a position in marketing.	Travis accepted a position in marketing, but he would have preferred a job in finance.

For emphasis, place an idea in an independent clause; for de-emphasis, place an idea in a dependent clause. In the following compound sentence, the idea of finance work is in an independent clause. Because an independent clause makes sense if the rest of the sentence is omitted, an independent clause is more emphatic than a dependent clause. In the complex sentence, the idea of finance work is in a dependent clause. Compared with the independent clause that follows ("Travis accepted a position . . ."), the idea in the dependent clause is de-emphasized.

Compound Sentence Is More Emphatic	Complex Sentence Is Less Emphatic
Travis accepted a position in marketing, but he would have preferred a job in finance.	Although he would have preferred a job in finance, Travis accepted a position in marketing.

REPETITION

To emphasize a word, let it appear more than once in a sentence. For example, a clever advertisement by OfficeMax used the word *stuff* repeatedly to describe generically several types of office-supply needs ranging from paper clips to color copies, and then ended succinctly with "OfficeMax . . . for your office stuff." Likewise, in the following example, "successful" receives more emphasis when the word is repeated.

Less Emphatic	More Emphatic
The meeting was successful because . . .	The meeting was successful; the success was attributed to . . .

WORDS THAT LABEL

For emphasis or de-emphasis, use words that label ideas as significant or insignificant. Note the labeling words used in the following examples to emphasize or de-emphasize an idea:

> But most important of all . . .
> A less significant aspect was . . .

POSITION

To emphasize a word or an idea, position it first or last in a sentence, clause, paragraph, or presentation. Note that the additional emphasis placed on the words "success" or "failure" (or its equivalent) in the examples in the right column, because these phrases appear early or late in their clauses.

Less Emphatic	More Emphatic
Our efforts ensured the success of the project; without them, failure would have been the result.	Success resulted from our efforts; failure would have resulted without them.
The project was successful because of our efforts; without them, failure would have been the result.	Success resulted; without our efforts, failure would have been the outcome.

In paragraphs, the first and last words are in particularly emphatic positions. An idea that deserves emphasis can be placed in either position, but an idea that does not deserve emphasis can be placed in the middle of a long paragraph. The word *I*, which is frequently overused in messages, is especially noticeable if it appears as the first word. *I* is more noticeable if it appears as the first word in *every* paragraph. Avoid using the word *However* as the first word in a paragraph if the preceding paragraph is neutral or positive. These words imply that the next idea will be negative. Unless the purpose is to place emphasis on negatives, such words as *denied*, *rejected*, and *disappointed* should not appear as the last words in a paragraph.

Likewise, the central idea of a written or spoken report appears in the introduction (the beginning) and the conclusion (the end). Good transition sentences synthesize ideas at the end of each major division.

SPACE AND FORMAT

The various divisions of a report or spoken presentation are not expected to be of equal length, but an extraordinary amount of space devoted to a topic attaches special significance to that topic. Similarly, a topic that receives an especially small amount of space is de-emphasized. The manner in which information is physically arranged affects the emphasis it receives and consequently the overall impact of the message.

4-1d Select the Appropriate Conclusion

Conclusions can serve a variety of purposes. First, they provide a positive sense of closure to the reader. In certain cases, they may emphasize an important topic or takeaway from a message. Finally, they might encourage the reader to take action. These options are respectively called goodwill, summary, and call-to-action conclusions.

A goodwill conclusion is typically used for short routine messages or good news or thank you messages.

An example of a goodwill conclusion for a routine message reminding the recipient of an upcoming meeting might be as simple as "I look forward to seeing you tomorrow."

A summary conclusion is often used for more complex, informative messages. An example summary conclusion for a message outlining a change in travel expense filing might emphasize the following points:

The new method of filing your travel expenses should streamline the process by eliminating paperwork and by making expense processing quicker and more convenient. The result is that you will also receive your travel reimbursement in less time. Please remember the new process goes into effect next month. Any questions you might have should be directed to your human resources adviser.

Not only does this conclusion remind the reader of the key points of the body of the message in a more general way, it is also persuasive in that it reminds the reader of the benefits of the new process.

The third type of conclusion, a call to action, is often used in persuasive or sales messages. The call-to-action conclusion attempts to "seal the deal" by encouraging the reader to take the next step in the process. In today's time-pressured world, it is easy to avoid following up on a persuasive request, so a call-to-action should be easy to comply with in order to better ensure follow through.

An example of a call-to-action conclusion for ensuring the completion of a report by a deadline is as follows:

It is important that we meet deadline on this project so that the company can report completion to shareholders in the meeting two weeks from today. Remember to please share your section of the report with the team by Tuesday at 1 p.m. by posting it in the team Dropbox.

Even for the most routine message, a conclusion should be provided to provide closure and convey goodwill to the reader. But conclusions can also be used to emphasize important points and to better ensure that a specific action is taken. Because of the immediacy principle—the last part of a message is more likely to be remembered—the importance of a good conclusion should not be overlooked, therefore, savvy writers will take advantage of this final opportunity to make an impact on the reader.

4-2 REVISE TO GRAB YOUR AUDIENCE'S ATTENTION

Professional writers often recognize that the real work of writing occurs during the revision process. It is this step, however, that is often overlooked or given short shrift by those who do not write for a living. Revising and proofreading effectively, therefore, require a change in mind-set.

4-2a Cultivate a Frame of Mind for Effective Revising and Proofreading

The following suggestions will guide your efforts in developing business documents that achieve the purpose for which they were intended.

- **Attempt to see things from your audience's perspective rather than from your own.** Being empathetic with your audience isn't as simple as it seems, particularly when dealing with today's diverse workforce. Erase the mind-set, "I know what I need to say and how I want to say it." Instead, ask, "How would my audience react to this message? Is this message worded so that my audience can easily understand it? Does it convey a tone that will build goodwill?"

- **Revise your documents until you cannot see any additional ways to improve them.** Resist the temptation to think of your first draft as your last draft. Instead, look for ways to improve, and be willing to incorporate valid suggestions once you have completed a draft. Experienced writers believe that there is no such thing as good writing, but there is such a thing as good rewriting. Author Dorothy Parker, who wrote for *Vanity Fair* and *Esquire*, once said, "I can't write five words but that I change seven."[1] Skilled speech writers might rewrite a script 15 or 20 times. Writers in public relations firms revise brochures and advertising

> Cluttered text is unappealing and difficult to read. *Chunking*—a desktop publishing term—is an answer to the problem.

copy until perhaps only a comma in the final draft is recognizable from the first draft. Even simple email messages require revision for clarity and mechanical errors, with extra passes needed depending on the number of recipients and the context of the message. Regardless of the message type, your careful revising will aid you in creating accurate, readable documents that produce results.

- **Be willing to allow others to make suggestions for improving your writing.** Because most of us consider our writing personal, we often feel reluctant to share it with others and can be easily offended if they suggest changes. This syndrome, called *writer's pride of ownership*, can prevent us from seeking needed assistance from experienced writers—a proven method of improving communication skills. On the job, especially in today's electronic workplace, your writing will be showcased to your supervisor, clients/ customers, members of a collaborative writing team, and more. You have nothing to lose but much to gain by allowing others to critique your writing. This commitment is especially important considering the mistake hardest to detect is your own. However, you have the ultimate responsibility for your document; don't simply trust that someone else will catch and correct your errors.

The ability you've gained in following a systematic process for developing effective business messages will prove valuable as you direct your energies to developing effective messages as a member of a team. Refer to the "Check Your Communication" checklist on the Chapter 4 Review Card to review the guidelines for preparing and proofreading a rough draft.

The speed and convenience of today's electronic communication have caused many communicators to confuse informality with sloppiness. Sloppy messages

Revising and proofreading are critical steps in business writing.

contain misspellings, grammatical errors, unappealing and incorrect formats, and confusing content—all of which create a negative impression of the writer and the company, and affect the receiver's ability to understand the message. Some experts believe the increased use of email is leading to bosses becoming ruder. To combat against the harsh tone that often sets in when managers must respond to 300 to 500 emails weekly, Unilever is providing writing training and urging staff to think before they press the send button.[2]

As the sender, you are responsible for evaluating the effectiveness of each message you prepare. You must not use informality as an excuse to be sloppy. Instead, take one consultant's advice: "You can still be informal and not be sloppy. You can be informal and correct."[3] Take a good hard look at the messages you prepare. Commit to adjusting your message to the audience, designing appealing documents that are easily read, and following a systematic proofreading process to ensure error-free messages. This effort could save you from being embarrassed or jeopardizing your credibility.

4-2b Apply Visual Enhancements to Improve Readability

The vast amount of information created in today's competitive global market poses a challenge to you as a business writer. You must learn to create visually appealing documents that entice the audience to read rather than discard your message. Additionally, an effective design will enable you to highlight important information for maximum attention and to transition a receiver smoothly through sections of a long, complex document. These design techniques can be applied easily using word processing software. However, add visual enhancements only when they aid in comprehension. Overuse will cause your document to appear cluttered and will defeat your purpose of creating an appealing, easy-to-read document.

ENUMERATIONS

To emphasize units in a series, place a number, letter, or bullet before each element. Words preceded by numbers, bullets, or letters attract the receiver's special attention and are easier to locate when the page is reviewed.

Original	Highlighted
The department problems have been identified as tardiness, absenteeism, and low productivity.	The department problems have been identified as • tardiness, • absenteeism, • low productivity.

ENUMERATED OR BULLETED LISTS

Writers often want to save space; however, cluttered text is unappealing and difficult to read. *Chunking*—a desktop publishing term—is an answer to the problem. Chunking involves breaking down information into easily digestible pieces. It's the communication equivalent of Butterfinger BBs rather than the whole candy bar. The added white space divides the information into blocks, makes the page look more organized, and increases retention by 50%.[4]

Enumerated or bulleted lists can be used to chunk and add even greater visual impact to items in a series. Items appear on separate lines with numerals, letters, or various types of bullets (•, ◊, □, ✓, and so on) at the beginning. Multiple-line items often are separated by a blank line. This design creates more white space, which isolates the items from other text and demands attention. Bullets are typically preferred over numerals unless the sequence of the items in the series is critical (e.g., steps in a procedure that must be completed in the correct order). In the following excerpt from a long analytical report, the four supporting reasons for a conclusion are highlighted in a bulleted list:

Original	Highlighted
Although there are some disadvantages that should not be overlooked, virtual teams provide many benefits, including cost savings from reduced travel, convenient access to team members, time savings and greater productivity, and the potential for greater creativity and better solutions.	Although there are some disadvantages that should not be overlooked, virtual teams provide many benefits, including these: • Cost savings from reduced travel • Convenient access to team members • Time savings and greater productivity • Potential for greater creativity and better solutions

HEADINGS

Headings are signposts that direct the receiver from one section of the document to another. Studies have shown that readers find documents with headings easier to grasp and that they are more motivated to pay attention to the text, even in a short document such as a half-page warranty.[5] You'll find that organizing the content of various types of documents with logical, well-written headings will make the documents more readable and appealing. Follow these general guidelines for writing effective headings:

Sergey Nivens/Shutterstock.com

- Compose brief headings that make a connection with the receiver, giving clear cues as to the usefulness of the information (e.g., "How Do I Apply?"). Consider using questions rather than noun phrases to let readers know they are reading the information they need (i.e., choose "Who Is Eligible to Apply?" rather than "Eligible Loan Participants").[6] Consider talking headings that reveal the conclusions reached in the following discussion, rather than general topic headings. For example, "Costs Are Prohibitive" is more emphatic than "Cost Factors."

- Strive for parallel structure of readings within a section. For example, mixing descriptive phrases with questions requires additional mental effort and distracts readers who expect parallel writing.

- Follow a hierarchy, with major headings receiving more attention than minor headings or paragraph headings. To draw more attention to a major heading, center it and use a heavier, larger typestyle or brighter text color.

TABLES AND GRAPHS

Tables and graphs are used to simplify and clarify information and to add variety to long sections of dense text. The clearly labeled rows and columns in a table organize large amounts of specific numeric data and facilitate analysis. Graphics such as pie, line, and bar charts visually depict relationships within the data. They provide quick estimates rather than specific information.

LINES AND BORDERS

Horizontal and vertical lines can be added to partition text or to focus attention on a specific line or lines. For example, a thin line followed by a thick line effectively separates the identification and qualifications sections of a résumé. Placing a border around a paragraph or section of text sets that information apart and adding shading inside the box adds greater impact. For example, a pull-quote format might spotlight a testimonial from a satisfied customer in a sales letter, important dates to remember in a memorandum, or a section of a document that must be completed and returned.

RELEVANT IMAGES

A variety of interesting shapes can be used to highlight information and add appeal. Examples include creating a rectangular call-out box highlighting a key idea, with an arrow pointing to a specific number in a table; surrounding a title with a shaded oval for added impact; and using built-in designs to illustrate a process, cycle, hierarchy, or other relationships. Clip art or photos can also be added to reinforce an idea and add visual appeal. The following example from the Plain Language website shows how visual communication can convey important safety information more effectively than words can.

Battling to manage an avalanche of information, the recipients of your messages will appreciate your extra effort to create an easy-to-read, appealing document. These fundamental techniques will be invaluable as you enhance printed documents, such as letters, memos, reports, agendas, handouts, and minutes for meetings.

This is a multipurpose passenger vehicle which will handle and maneuver differently from an ordinary passenger car, in driving conditions which may occur on streets and highways and off road. As with other vehicles of this type, if you make sharp turns or abrupt maneuvers, the vehicle may roll over or may go out of control and crash. You should read driving guidelines and instructions in the Owner's Manual, and WEAR YOUR SEAT BELTS AT ALL TIMES.

WARNING: HIGHER ROLLOVER RISK

Avoid Abrupt Maneuvers and Excessive Speed.

Always Buckle Up.

See Owner's Manual For Further Information.

Courtesy of National Highway Traffic Safety Administration

4-3 IMPROVE READABILITY

STEP 7: REVISE FOR STYLE AND TONE

4-3a Improve Readability

Although sentences are arranged in a logical sequence and are written coherently, the receiver might find reading the sentences difficult. Several programs have been developed to measure the reading difficulty of your writing. Electronic tools aid you in making computations and identifying changes that will improve readability.

The grammar and style checker feature of leading word-processing software calculates readability measures to aid you in writing for quick and easy reading and listening. The Fog Index, a popular readability index developed by Robert Gunning, and the Flesch–Kincaid Grade Level calculator available in Microsoft Word consider the length of sentences and the difficulty of words, to produce the approximate grade level at which a person must read in order to understand the material. For example, a grade level of 10 indicates a person needs to be able to read at the tenth-grade level to understand the material. Fortunately, you don't have to calculate readability manually, but understanding the manual calculation of the Fog index will illustrate clearly how sentence length and difficulty of words affect readability calculations and will guide you in adapting messages.

Trying to write at the exact grade level of the receiver is not advised. You may not know the exact grade level, and even those who have earned advanced degrees appreciate writing they can read and understand quickly and easily. Also, writing a passage with a readability index appropriate for the audience does not guarantee the message will be understood. Despite simple language and short sentences, the message can be distorted by imprecise words, biased language, jargon, and translations that ignore cultural interpretations, to name just a few. The value of calculating a readability measure lies in the feedback you gain about the average length of sentences and the difficulty of the words. Revise and recalculate the readability index, and continue revising until you feel that the reading level is appropriate for the intended audience.

The grammar and style feature in word-processing programs also locates grammatical errors, including misspellings and common usage errors, such as the use of fragments, run-on sentences, subject–verb disagreement, passive voice, double words, and split infinitives. Because it can only guess at the structure of a sentence and then apply a rigid set of rules, a grammar and style checker, such as a spell checker, must be used cautiously. It is not a reliable substitute for a human editor who has an effective writing style and is familiar with the rules the software displays. Allow the software to flag misspellings and writing errors as you write; then, accept or reject the suggested changes based on your knowledge of effective writing, and use the readability measures to adjust your writing levels appropriately, as shown in Figure 4.3.

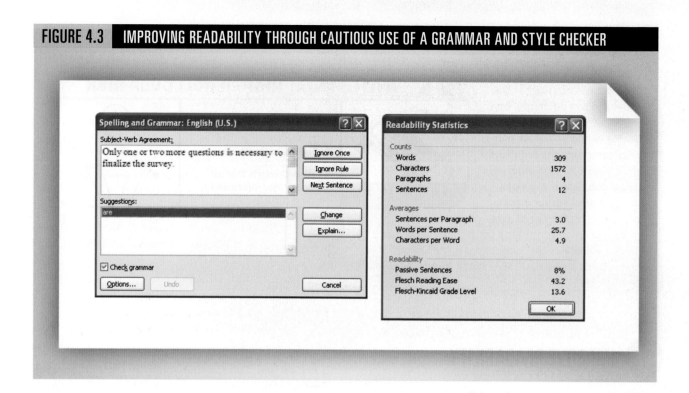

4-3b Eliminate Outdated Expressions

In addition to using software tools to approve readability, several additional steps can be taken to improve the style and tone of a written message. For example, using outdated expressions will give your message a dull, stuffy, unnatural tone. Instead, substitute fresh, original expressions that reflect today's language patterns.

Outdated Expressions	Improvement
As per your request, the report has been submitted to the client.	As you requested, the report has been submitted to the client.
Enclosed please find a copy of my transcript.	The enclosed transcript should answer your questions.
Very truly yours (used as the complimentary close in a letter)	Sincerely

4-3c Curb Clichés

clichés, or overused expressions, are common in our everyday conversations and in business messages. These handy verbal shortcuts are convenient, quick, easy to use, and often include simple metaphors and analogies that effectively communicate the most basic

clichés overused expressions that can cause their users to be perceived as unoriginal, unimaginative, lazy, and perhaps even disrespectful

idea or emotion or the most complex business concept. However, writers and speakers who routinely use stale clichés may be perceived as unoriginal, unimaginative, lazy, and perhaps even disrespectful. Less frequently used words capture the receiver's attention because they are original, fresh, and interesting.

Clichés present another serious problem. Consider the scenario of shoppers standing in line at a discount store with the cashier saying to each, "Thanks for shopping with us today. Please come again." Because the last shopper has heard the words several times already, he or she may not consider the statement genuine. The cashier has used an expression that can be stated without thinking and possibly without meaning. A worn expression can convey messages such as "You are not special," or "For you, I won't bother to think. The phrases I use in talking with others are surely good enough for you." Original expressions convey sincerity and build strong human relations.

Cliché	Improvement
Pushed (or stretched) the envelope	Took a risk or considered a new option
Skin in the game	Committed to the project
Cover all the bases	Get agreement/input from everyone
That sucks!	That's unacceptable/needs improvement

4-3d Eliminate Profanity

Increasing tolerance of profanity is an issue of concern to society as a whole, and also for employers and employees as they communicate at work. You must consider the potential business liabilities and legal implications resulting from the use of profanity that may offend others or create a hostile work environment. Recognize that minimizing or eliminating profanity is another important way in which you must adapt your language for communicating effectively in order to foster human relations in a professional setting.

marekuliasz/Shutterstock.com

4-3e Use Simple, Informal Words

Business writers prefer simple, informal words that are readily understood and less distracting than more difficult, formal words. If a receiver questions the sender's motive for using formal words, the impact of the message may be diminished. Likewise, the impact would be diminished if the receiver questioned a sender's use of simple, informal words. This distraction is unlikely, however, if the message contains good ideas that are well organized and well supported. Under these conditions, simple words enable a receiver to understand the message clearly and quickly.

To illustrate, consider the unnecessary complexity of a notice that appeared on a corporate bulletin board: "Employees impacted by the strike are encouraged to utilize the hotline number to arrange for alternative transportation to work. Should you encounter difficulties in arranging for alternative transportation to work, please contact your immediate supervisor." A simple, easy-to-read revision would be, "If you can't get to work, call the hotline or your supervisor." For further illustration, note the added clarity of the following words:

Formal Words	Informal Words
terminate	end
procure	get

Formal Words	Informal Words
remunerate	pay
corroborate	support

Using words that have more than two or three syllables when they are appropriate is acceptable. However, you should avoid regular use of a long, infrequently used word when a simpler, more common word conveys the same

idea. Professionals in some fields often use specialized terminology, referred to as **jargon**, when communicating with colleagues in the same field. In this case, the audience is likely to understand the words, and using the jargon saves time. However, when communicating with people outside the field, professionals should select simple, common words to convey messages. Using clear, jargon-free language that can be readily understood by non-native recipients and easily translated is especially important in international communication.

You should build your vocabulary so that you can use just the right word for expressing an idea and can understand what others have said. Just remember the purpose of business messages is not to advertise a knowledge of infrequently used words, but to transmit a clear and tactful message. For the informal communication practiced in business, use simple words instead of more complicated words that have the same meaning.

4-3f Communicate Concisely

Concise communication includes all relevant details in the fewest possible words. Abraham Lincoln's two-minute Gettysburg Address is a premier example of concise communication. Mark Twain alluded to the skill needed to write concisely when he said, "I would have written a shorter book if I had had time."

Some executives have reported that they read memos that are two paragraphs long but may only skim or discard longer ones. Yet it's clear that this survival technique can lead to a vital message being discarded or misread. Concise writing is essential for workers struggling to handle an avalanche of information, which is often read on the run on their smartphone. Concise messages save time and money for both the sender and the receiver, as the receiver's attention is directed toward the important details and is not distracted by excessive words and details.

The following techniques will produce concise messages:

- **Eliminate redundancies.** A **redundancy** is a phrase in which one word unnecessarily repeats an idea contained in an accompanying word.

jargon specialized terminology that professionals in some fields use when communicating with colleagues in the same field

redundancy a phrase in which one word unnecessarily repeats an idea contained in an accompanying word (e.g., "exactly identical")

FIGURE 4.4 ROUGH DRAFT OF A LETTER (EXCERPT)

September 8, 2016
FAX Transmission

Conrad Harris, Owner
Xcess
2054 Pioneer Square
Portland, OR ~~Oregon~~ 85301

Dear Mr. Haris:
Congratulations on the recent opening of your innovative chocolate and wine bar! We are excited to learn of your interest in the Trayne commercial oven line and believe you will find a model that meets your exact needs.

Available with radiant, direct-fired convection and hybrid radiant/convection heating, Trayne ovens are highly energy efficient owing to both heating system design and their low surface area to volume ratio. Fully automated, they incorporate a user-friendly touch-screen interface, plus full-length viewing doors for visual inspection of the bake at every level with easy access for cleaning and maintenance.

Trayne ovens provide enormous advantages over conventional oven technologies, including
- Iimproved product quality and consistency.; The ultra-compact design is based on a transport technology where pans are conveyed horizontally through the oven via a vertical 'S' configuration.
- Typically one-tenth the footprint of an equivalent tunnel oven, Trayne ovens offer a crucial advantage in environments where production floor space is at a premium ~~and~~.
- Trayne ovens offer superior flexibility, allowing product changes by simply changing pans~~,~~ and ~~ancillary~~ additional tooling.

Mr. Harris, we're eager to schedule your visit to our nearby showroom to introduce our product line. At your convenience, please review the enclosed brochures and I will call you next week to schedule an appointment.

Annotation callouts (right margin):
- Adds mailing notation.
- Uses two-letter abbreviation.
- Corrects spelling of name.
- Adds smooth transition to next paragraph.
- Bullet list for emphasis and conciseness.
- Eliminates unnecessary comma.
- Replace with simple word for clarity.
- Errors Undetectable by Spell-Check — Check correctness of word substitutions: "to" for "too" and "your" for "you."
- Correct proofreading error.

TO RECAP:

▸ Use the spell checker to locate simple keying errors and repeated words.

▸ Proofread once, concentrating on errors in content, organization, and style.

▸ Proofread a second time, concentrating on mechanical errors.

▸ Edit for format and layout.

▸ Print a draft copy of the document.

▸ Proofread a third time if the document is nonroutine and complex.

▸ For documents to be delivered on paper, print on high-quality paper.

STUDY TOOLS 4

LOCATED AT THE BACK OF THE TEXTBOOK
☐ Tear-Out Chapter Review Card

LOCATED AT WWW.CENGAGEBRAIN.COM
☐ Review Key Term flashcards and create your own cards
☐ Track your knowledge and understanding of key concepts in business communication
☐ Complete practice and graded quizzes to prepare for tests
☐ Complete interactive content within BCOM9 Online
☐ View the chapter highlight boxes for BCOM9 Online

BCOM
ONLINE

STUDY YOUR WAY
WITH STUDYBITS!

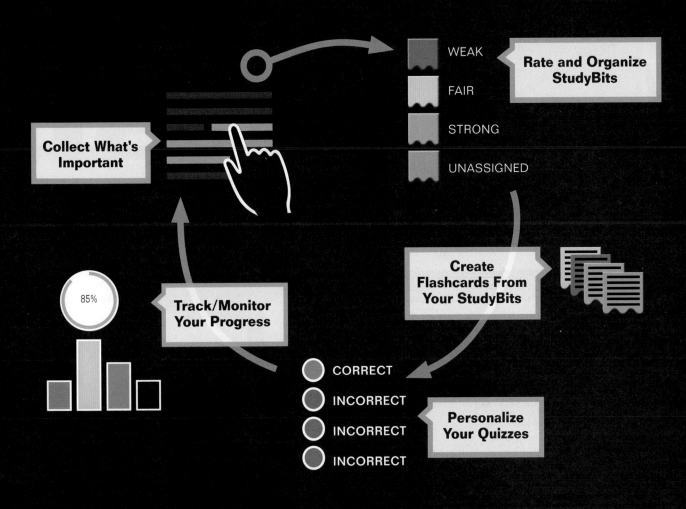

WEAK

FAIR

STRONG

UNASSIGNED

Rate and Organize StudyBits

Collect What's Important

Track/Monitor Your Progress

85%

Create Flashcards From Your StudyBits

CORRECT

INCORRECT

INCORRECT

INCORRECT

Personalize Your Quizzes

4LTR
PRESS

Access BCOM ONLINE at www.cengagebrain.com

PART 3

5 | Communicating Electronically

Rawpixel/Shutterstock.com

LEARNING OBJECTIVES

After studying this chapter, you will be able to . . .

5-1 Discuss the effective use of email, instant messaging, and text messaging in business communication.

5-2 Explain the principles for writing effectively for the Web.

5-3 Discuss the effective use of voice and wireless technologies in business communication.

5-4 Consider the legal and ethical implications associated with the use of communication technology.

After finishing this chapter, go to **PAGE 97** for **STUDY TOOLS**.

5-1 DATA SECURITY

In the past several decades, computer technology has revolutionized the way that communication occurs in most organizations. Communication, using a variety of text-, audio-, and video-enabled tools, can be achieved almost instantaneously with others located around the globe. But with the many advantages of computer-mediated communication, a similar rise in the potential hazards associated with its use has occurred. Concerns about maintaining the privacy of, and information about, employees, partners, and customers, as well as corporate resources, have reached a critical point. In fact, since 2005, more than 75 data breaches by hackers in which 1,000,000 or more records were compromised have been publicly disclosed.[1] A practice that is more difficult to judge in terms of its ethicality is that of data mining, which is used by many organizations on their social networking sites to learn more about customers for the enhancement of marketing techniques.

Organizations may be held liable for providing outside access to private information of their employees, customers, and other external groups. This information includes customers' credit card, bank account, and social security numbers, as well as employee details, such as health records, home addresses, email addresses, and login information. U.S. retailer, Target, agreed to a $39 million settlement with several U.S. banks in 2015 over a data breach two years earlier that affected roughly 40 million customers.[2] The banks lost millions when they were forced to reimburse customers who lost money in the massive 2013 hack of Target's database. In August 2015, Target settled with Visa for $67 million over the data hack. Earlier that year, Target settled a federal class action lawsuit brought by customers for $10 million.

In addition to protecting employee, supplier, distributor, and customer privacy, organizations are also concerned about protecting proprietary information about products, services, and business strategies.

Because of these concerns, many organizations have enacted policies to guide employees in the proper use of technology in order to safeguard information. These policies often address three data security risks: breaches of confidentiality, failing to offer choice in what information is shared, and reputational damage caused by data breaches. Often, everyone in the company is expected to ensure that data is collected, handled, and stored properly.

Such policies generally require that employees are properly trained in data use and storage, and how to keep data secure, making sure that data is not shared informally, that no information is shared with unauthorized individuals, and that no longer needed data is properly deleted or disposed of. It is very important to be well informed about an organization's data use policies, and to follow policies to the letter in order to avoid breaches of data security.

5-2 APPROPRIATE USE OF TECHNOLOGY

Technology offers numerous advantages, but a technological channel is not always the communication method of choice. Before sending a message, be certain the selected channel of communication is appropriate by considering the message's purpose, confidentiality issues, and human relations factors.

5-2a Determine the Purpose of the Message

If a message is straightforward and informative, chances are a technological option might be appropriate. Although the use of instantaneous and efficient communication methods is quite compelling, keep in mind that written communication, printed or online, cannot replace the personal interaction so essential in today's team-based work environments. Employees who are floors apart or in different offices or time zones benefit from email and Web communications, but two people sitting side by side, or on the same floor, shouldn't have to communicate solely by electronic means.

A second question when selecting among communication options is whether a permanent record of the message is needed or if a more temporary form, such as a phone call or instant message, would suffice.

5-2b Determine Whether the Information Is Personal or Confidential

As a general guideline, keep personal correspondence off-line if you don't want it to come back and haunt you. The content of an email message could have embarrassing consequences since such documents often become a part of public records, and wireless communications

> Many organizations have enacted policies to guide employees in the proper use of technology in order to safeguard information.

might be unexpectedly intercepted. Your company technically "owns" your electronic communications and, thus, can monitor them to determine legitimate business use or potential abuse. Undeliverable email messages are delivered to a mail administrator, and many networks routinely store backups of all email messages that pass through them.

Even deleted messages can be "resurrected" with little effort, as several public figures discovered when investigators retrieved archived email as evidence in court cases. For sensitive situations, a face-to-face encounter is often preferred.

5-2c Decide Whether Positive Human Relations Are Sacrificed

Be wary of using an electronic communication tool as an avoidance mechanism. Remember, too, that some people do not regularly check their email or voice mail, and some have unreliable systems that are slow or prone to losing messages. Some news will be received better in person than through an electronic format, which might be interpreted as cold and impersonal.

Additionally, some people, especially those of certain cultures, prefer a personal meeting, even if you perceive that an electronic exchange of information would be a more efficient use of everyone's time. Choose the communication channel carefully to fit both your purpose and the preference of the receiver.

5-3 ELECTRONIC MAIL COMMUNICATION

As you read in Chapter 1, the continuous evolution of technology has expanded communication options. Email, instant messaging, Web communications, and voice and wireless technologies are important tools for accomplishing company goals. In fact, email has overtaken the telephone in terms of the most common workplace communication tool.[3] The ability to use email communications effectively is essential for success in virtually every career.

5-3a Advantages of Email

Electronic mail, or email, offers numerous advantages. Its widespread availability, convenience, and ease of use have resulted in its skyrocketing popularity. The advantages of email are numerous:

- **It facilitates the fast, convenient flow of information among users at various locations and time zones.** Mail service is often too slow for communicating timely

information, and the telephone system is inconvenient and costly when communicating with people located in several locations and time zones. For these reasons, email is especially effective when sending a single message to several recipients, and when needing to communicate 24 hours a day, 365 days a year.

- **It increases efficiency.** Email reduces "telephone tag" and unnecessary telephone interruptions caused when delivering messages that are unlikely to require a verbal response.

- **It reduces costs.** Sending email messages represents substantial savings for companies in long-distance telephone costs and postal mail-outs.

- **It reduces paper waste.** Often an electronic message can be read and immediately discarded without the need for a printed copy.

5-3b Guidelines for Preparing Email Messages

Following these guidelines will enable you to use email efficiently and effectively when communicating with both valued coworkers and outside parties:

- **Send to single or multiple addressees.** The same message can be sent to one or many recipients simultaneously. Routinely sending an email message to multiple recipients involves keying the email address of each recipient into a distribution list and selecting the distribution list as the recipient.

- **Provide a useful subject line.** A descriptive subject line assists the receiver's understanding of the message and is helpful for future reference to it. Additionally, a well-written subject line in an email message will help the receiver sort through an overloaded mailbox and read messages in priority order. When writing a subject line, think of the five Ws—Who, What, When, Where, and Why—to give you some clues for wording. For instance, "Budget Committee Meeting on Thursday" is a more meaningful subject line than "Meeting."

- **Restate the subject in the body of the message.** The body of the message should be a complete thought and should not rely on the subject line for elaboration. A good opening sentence might be a repetition of most of the subject line. Even if the reader skipped the subject line, the message would still be clear, logical, and complete.

- **Focus on a single topic directed toward the receiver's needs.** An email message is generally limited to one idea rather than addressing several issues. If

- **Use graphic highlighting to add emphasis.** Enumerated or bulleted lists, tables, graphs, pictures, or other images can be either integrated into the content of the email or attached as supporting material.

- **Revise your email before sending.** Even the average email requires at least one pass to ensure that the intended message is clear, concise, and error-free. The number of passes increases depending on the number of people receiving the email and the complexity of the message. Revising for brevity and conciseness is a primary goal for messages that are often read on the run and on mobile devices. Keep to one screen, eliminate redundancies, and tighten wording. Avoid off-topic material that detracts from the email's single subject, as well as clever or amusing statements that are funny only to the writer.[4]

Direct, concise messages sometimes sound impersonal and curt if not revised for goodwill. Question whether a phone call would be more appropriate for the message; a businesslike, yet conversational tone might sound less aggressive or demanding. Revise emails to achieve a similar tone.[5] Use the email spell checker and then proofread onscreen for content and grammatical errors.

you address more than one topic in a single email message, chances are the recipient will forget to respond to all points discussed. Discussing one topic allows you to write a descriptive subject line, and the receiver can file the single subject message in a separate mailbox if desired. If you must send a lengthy email, preview the topics to be covered in the introduction, and then divide the message into logical sections for easy comprehension.

- **Sequence your ideas based on the anticipated reader reaction.** As you learned previously, ideas should be organized deductively when a message contains good news or neutral information. Inductive organization is recommended when the message contains bad news or is intended to persuade. Email messages should be organized according to the sequence of ideas, for example, time order, order of importance, or geography. As a general rule, present the information in the order that it is likely to be needed. For example, describe the nature and purpose of an upcoming meeting before giving the specifics (date, place, and time).

- **Make careful use of jargon, technical words, and shortened terms.** The use of jargon and technical terms is more common in email messages than in business letters. Such shortcuts save time with audiences who will understand the intent. In practicing empathy, however, consider whether the receiver will likely understand the terms used.

5-3c Effective Use of Email

The email message in Figure 5.1 illustrates guidelines for using professional email. The sender begins the email message by announcing the topic of enhanced shipping services. The paragraphs that follow include timely instructions to find more detailed pickup and delivery times as well as how to schedule service.

Although email offers various advantages in speed and convenience, problems arise when it is managed inappropriately. Learning fundamental **netiquette**, the buzzword for proper behavior on the Internet, will ensure your online success. The following guidelines will assist you in using email effectively:

- **Check mail promptly.** Generally, a response to email is expected within 24 hours. Ignoring messages from coworkers can erode efforts to create an open, honest, and cooperative work environment. On the other hand, responding every

netiquette the buzzword for proper behavior on the Internet

FIGURE 5.1 **GOOD EXAMPLE OF AN EMAIL MESSAGE** Good

New Message

To: Freda Ruiz [fruiz@happy!.com]

From: Martin Curtin [mcurtin@speedxpress.com]

Subject: Enhanced delivery service

Hi Freda,

SpeedXPress has resumed its regular pickup and delivery schedule for freight packages. You can now take advantage of more frequent pickup and delivery times to ensure faster service to your customers. For schedule details, please go to our company website: www.speedxpress.com.

To schedule a pickup, please use the same website. We are able to provide same-day service for last-minute shipments. You may also call our automated scheduling system at 1-888-422-7533.

We look forward to providing you the fastest delivery services in the New York area.

Regards,
Martin Curtin, Operations

- *Provides subject line that is meaningful to the reader and writer.*

- *Includes a salutation and closing to personalize the message.*

- *Conveys a short, concise message limited to one idea and one screen.*

---

second could indicate that you are paying more attention to your email than your job.

- **Do not contribute to email overload.** To avoid clogging the system with unnecessary messages, follow these simple guidelines:

  ○ Be certain individuals need a copy of the email, and forward an email from another person only with the original writer's permission.

  ○ Never address an email requesting general action to more than one person if you want to receive an individual response. Sharing responsibility will lead to no one taking responsibility.

  ○ Avoid sending formatted documents. Messages with varying fonts, special print features (bold, italics, etc.), and images take longer to download, require more storage space, and could be unreadable on some computers. In addition, enhancing routine email messages does not support the goals of competitive organizations, and employees, clients, or customers might resent such frivolous use of time.

  ○ Edit the original message when you reply to email if the entire body of the original message

is not needed for context. Instead, you can cut and paste pertinent sections that you believe will help the recipient understand your reply. You can also key brief comments in all caps below the original section.

  ○ Follow company policy for personal use of email. Obtain a private email account if you are job hunting or sending many private messages to friends and relatives.

- **Use email selectively.** Send short, direct messages for routine matters that need not be handled immediately (scheduling meetings, giving your supervisor quick updates, or addressing other uncomplicated issues).

- **Do not send messages when you are angry.** Email containing sensitive, highly emotional messages could be easily misinterpreted because of the absence of nonverbal communication (facial expressions, voice tone, and body language). Sending a *flame*, the online term used to describe a heated, sarcastic, sometimes abusive message or posting, might prompt a receiver to send a retaliatory response. Email messages written in anger and filled with emotion and sarcasm could result in embarrassment or even end up as evidence in litigation. Because of the potential damage to relationships and legal liability, read email messages carefully before sending them. Unless a response is urgent, store a heated message for an hour until you have cooled off and thought about the issue clearly and rationally. When you *must* respond immediately, you might acknowledge that your response is emotional and has not been thoroughly considered. Give this warning by using words such as "I need to vent my frustration for a few paragraphs" or "flame on—I'm writing in anger."[6]

GokGak/Shutterstock.com

- **Exercise caution against email viruses and hoaxes.** An ounce of prevention can avert the problems caused by deadly *viruses* that destroy data files or annoying messages that simply waste your time while they are executing. Install an *antivirus software program* that will scan your hard drive each time you start the computer or access external devices, and keep backups of important files. Be suspicious of email messages that contain attachments if they are from people you don't know. Email text is usually safe to open, but the attachment could contain an executable file that can affect your computer's operations. **Social networking sites**, such as Facebook and MySpace are also common sources of viruses and spyware.

- Additionally, be wary of *computer hoaxes*—email messages that incite panic, typically related to risks of computer viruses or deadly threats, and urge you to forward them to as many people as possible. Forwarding a hoax can be embarrassing and causes inefficiency by overloading email boxes and flooding computer security personnel with inquiries from alarmed recipients of your message. Investigate the possible hoax by visiting websites such as the following that post virus alerts and hoax information and provide tips for identifying a potential hoax:

  ○ Urban legends: www.urbanlegends.com

  ○ Snopes: www.snopes.com

  ○ Truth or Fiction: www.truthorfiction.com

If a bogus message is forwarded to you, reply to the person politely that the message is a hoax. This action allows you to help stop the spread of the malicious message and will educate one more person about the evils of hoaxes.

- **Develop an effective system for handling email.** Some simple organization will allow you to make better use of your email capability:

  ○ Set up separate accounts for receiving messages that require your direct attention.

  ○ Keep your email inbox clean by reading an email and taking action immediately. Delete messages you are not using and those not likely to be considered relevant for legal purposes.

  ○ Move saved messages into a limited number of email folders for quick retrieval. The email search feature is also useful for identifying saved messages quickly. If you receive many messages, consider setting up your account to sort and prioritize messages, send form letters as replies to messages received with a particular subject line, automatically forward specified email, and sound an alarm when you receive a message from a particular person.

To Recap—Email Advantages

  ○ Allows communication 24 hours a day, 365 days a year

  ○ Reduces telephone interruptions by delivering messages that are unlikely to require a verbal response

  ○ Saves companies the costs of long-distance telephone bills and postal mail-outs

  ○ Reduces the need to print messages

To Recap—Effective Use of Email

  ○ Check email promptly.

  ○ Do not contribute to email overload.

social networking sites
websites that provide virtual communities in which people with shared interests can communicate

FIGURE 5.2   GOOD EXAMPLE OF AN INSTANT MESSAGE

Good

Output Interaction Box

Ahsan:>>Is this a good time to talk about the Thomson software project?

Marla:>>Sure. What do u have?

Ahsan:>>I've talked to Jana about the delay that came up in our last convo.

Marla:>>Great. Will this cause problems with the client?

Ahsan:>>Hard to say without scheduling a meeting with them to discuss alternatives.

Marla:>>IC. What about making changes on our end instead?

Ahsan:>>It might mean some cost cutting or other cutbacks.

Marla:>>Should we schedule a meeting with the team?

Ahsan:>>Yes. Can you take care of that?

Marla:>>Absolutely. When can u meet?

Ahsan:>>Any time this week after lunch. CU then.

Users Logged On

☐ Entry Chime

Enter your message below

Send URL

Quit

- *Opens message by "knocking" to ask if he is interrupting.*
- *Keeps conversation brief by limiting it to a few short sentences.*
- *Uses a few easily recognized abbreviations and acronyms but avoids informal slang that could be confusing and unprofessional.*
- *Uses instant messaging to arrange for sudden report revisions.*

- Use email selectively.
- Do not send messages when you are angry.
- Exercise caution against email viruses and hoaxes.
- Develop an effective system for handling email.

5-3d   Instant and Text Messaging

Business use of **instant messaging (IM)** has seen phenomenal growth. Analysts estimate that in 90% of companies, some employees use IM, whether to close a sale, collaborate with a colleague, or just trade pleasantries with a colleague.[7] This real-time email technology allows the sender to know when someone is available to respond immediately.

The best-known IM programs are free and require no special hardware and little training. With some programs, users can exchange graphics and audio and video clips. To use instant messaging, you maintain a list of people with whom you want to interact. You can send messages to any or all of the people on your

> **instant messaging (IM)** a real-time email technology that blends email with conversation; sender and receiver who are online at the same time can type messages that both see immediately

list as long as the people are online. Sending a message opens up a window in which you and your contact can key messages that you both can see immediately. Figure 5.2 illustrates a sample IM conversation that occurred to arrange for last-minute project changes.

Many of the guidelines that apply to the use of email for business purposes also apply to instant messaging. With IM, however, spelling and grammar matter less when trading messages at high speed. IM users often use shorthand for common words and phrases. IM and telephone communication also share common challenges: being sure that the sender is who he or she claims to be and that the conversation is free from eavesdropping.

Some managers worry that employees will spend too much work time using IM to chat with buddies inside and outside the company. They also emphasize that IM is not the right tool for every business purpose. Employees should still rely on email when they need a record and use the telephone for a personal touch.

5-3e   Text Messaging

Text messaging has grown in popularity as cellphones and other handheld devices with text capability have proliferated. Messages can be sent from one cellphone to another, a cellphone to a computer, or computer to computer. **Text messaging** on a cellphone or personal digital assistant is a refinement of computer instant messaging. The typical cellphone screen can accommodate no more than 160 characters, and because the keypad is far less versatile, text messaging puts an even greater premium on conciseness. An entire code book of acronyms and abbreviations has emerged, ranging from CWOT (complete waste of time) to DLTBBB (don't let the bed bugs bite). The use of emoticons has also advanced far beyond the traditional smiley face and includes drooling (:-). . .) and secrecy (:X). Inventive and young users frequently insert their own style, substituting "z" for "s," or "d" for "th." Shortened lingo or text gets right to the point. For instance, a sender might send the following message that can be easily deciphered by most: "Pk u up @730." Cellphone programs are also available to assist in efficiency when texting. T9 (text on nine keys) and similar programs use predictive text to finish words after the first few characters are keyed. T9 can be "trained" to recognize new vocabulary.[8]

Texting is a viable alternative to phone calls for those with hearing impairments. Economic and cultural factors have also driven the advancement of text messaging in some parts of the world where voice conversations are more expensive than texting and short conversations are considered impolite. Some of the most avid users of text messaging are clustered in Southeast Asia. The Chinese language is particularly well suited to text messaging because in Mandarin the names of the numbers are also close to the sounds of certain words.[9] Japanese commuters use their cellphones to text silently, as talking on a phone on the train would be impolite. In the United States, teenagers have popularized texting and carry the habit into places of work. Both abroad and at home, text messaging can be used as an avoidance mechanism that preserves the feeling of communication without the burden for actual intimacy or substance. Most text messages are superficial greetings and are often sent when the two parties are within speaking distance of each other. Like a CHAPTER 5: Communicating Electronically 79 wave or nod, they are meant to merely establish connection without getting specific.

Although text messaging is generally considered a social communication tool, it is finding more use for business. Text messages can be sent or retrieved in situations when a ringing phone would be inappropriate, such as during meetings. With research showing that many more text messages are opened than are email messages, advertisers are using text messages to send their marketing messages.[10] Refer to Figure 5.3, which compares the completeness and relative formality of an email message to the informal nature of the instant message and

You are responsible for the content of any electronic message you send, which could have legal ramifications.

the abbreviated style of the text message. Each medium requires its own appropriate writing style to maximize effectiveness and social expectations.

5-3f Electronic Messages and the Law

US courts have established the right of companies to monitor the electronic mail of an employee because they own the facilities and intend them to be used for job-related communication only. On the other hand, employees typically expect that their email messages will be kept private. To protect themselves against liability imposed by the Electronic Communications Privacy Act (ECPA), employers simply provide a legitimate business reason for the monitoring (e.g., preventing computer crime, retrieving lost messages, and regulating employee morale) and obtain written consent to intercept email or at least notify employees. Employees who use the system after the notification may have given implied consent to the monitoring.[11]

The legal status of text messaging has been murkier. A 2008 court ruling made a distinction between electronic communications employers store on their servers and communication that is contracted out to third parties. Employers must have either a warrant or the employee's permission to view messages stored by someone other than the employer. Employers who intend to monitor electronic communications must be specific in their written employee policy statements that they intend to access text messages sent with company-issued devices.[12]

text messaging messages that can be sent from one cellphone to another, a cellphone to a computer, or computer to computer; a refinement of computer instant messaging

FIGURE 5.3   LEVELS OF FORMALITY REQUIRED BY VARIOUS TECHNOLOGIES

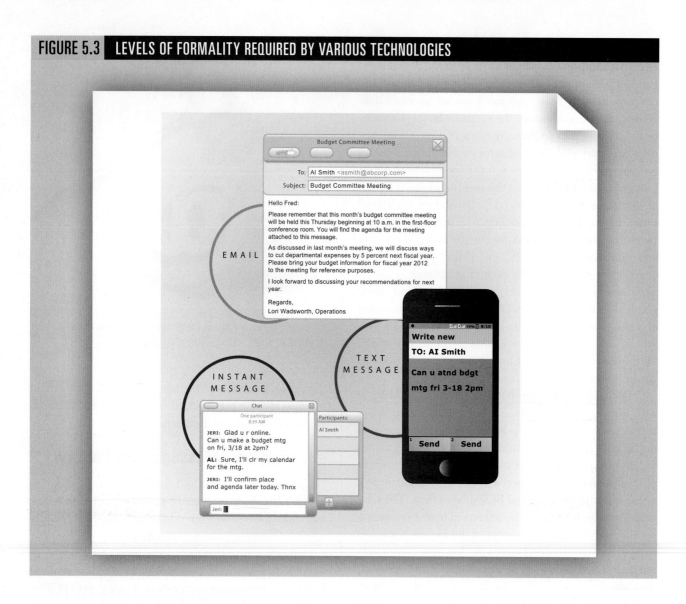

Remember that you are responsible for the content of any electronic message you send. Because electronic messages move so quickly between people and often become very informal and conversational, individuals might not realize (or might forget) their responsibility. If a person denies commitments made via an electronic message, someone involved can produce a copy of the message as verification.

Electronic communicators must abide by copyright laws. Be certain to give credit for quoted material, and seek permission to use copyrighted text or graphics from printed or electronic sources. Unless you inform the reader that editing has occurred, do not alter a message you are forwarding or reposting, and be sure to ask permission before forwarding it.

Federal and state bills related to employee privacy are frequently introduced for legislative consideration. Although litigation related to present privacy issues is underway, the development of law is lagging far behind

technology; nevertheless, employers can expect changes in the laws as technology continues to develop. Electronic messages have often become the prosecutor's star witness, the corporate equivalent of DNA evidence, as it and other forms of electronic communication are subject to subpoena in litigation. Referring to this issue, former New York Attorney General Eliot Spitzer had this to say: "Never write when you can talk. Never talk when you can nod. And never put anything in an email [that you don't want on the front page of the newspaper]."[13] Several perils of "evidence" mail that companies must address are illustrated in these cases:

- Including inappropriate content in an email can humiliate and lead to indictment. Detroit Mayor Kwame Kilpatrick and his chief of staff were charged in a 12-count indictment including perjury and obstruction of justice when text messages exchanged between the two were revealed. The pair's secret love affair played out in the messages was also disclosed to a shocked public.[14] The press dubbed the resulting disastrous professional result as "death by Blackberry."

- Failing to preserve, or destroying, email messages in violation of securities rules is a sure path to destruction. Deleting Enron scandal-related messages led to Arthur Andersen's criminal conviction and eventually to Enron's implosion.

- Inability to locate emails and other relevant documents demanded by the courts is unacceptable and considered negligence by the courts. Penalties have included monetary fines, assessment of court costs or attorney's fees, and dismissal of the case in favor of the opposing side.[15]

On the other hand, evidence mail can protect a company from lawsuits. A company being sued by a female employee because a male executive had allegedly sexually abused her retrieved a trail of emails with lurid attachments sent by the female employee to the male executive named in the case.[16]

To avoid the legal perils of electronic communications, employees must be taught not to write loose, potentially rude, and overly casual messages; to avoid carelessly deleting messages; and to take the time to identify and organize relevant messages for quick retrieval.

5-4 WEB PAGE COMMUNICATION AND SOCIAL MEDIA

Most organizations now have their own websites to accomplish a number of activities, such as updating employees and customers about organizational changes; selling products and services; advertising employment opportunities; and creating a first point of contact for customers through order entry, customer service systems, and online call centers. Although effective web page development is a highly specialized activity, understanding the process will be useful to any business communicator. Organizations can use the Web not only to communicate with customers and clients but also to interact with business associates.

Designing web pages that are accessible by the millions of people with permanent or temporary disabilities, including visual impairments, is good for business.[17] Research by the 2004 Disability Rights Commission has found that the websites that were most accessible for users with disabilities were also easier for people without disabilities to operate, with some online tasks performed 35% faster on the more accessible sites.[18] US businesses have legal requirements for online content to be available

TIP SHEET

The following tips will help you compose appropriate Web content:[19]

▶ **Be brief.** A good rule is to reduce the wording of any print document by 50% when you put it on the Web.

▶ **Keep it simple.** Use short words that allow for fast reading by people of various educational backgrounds. Use mixed case because all caps are slower to read.

▶ **Consider appropriate jargon.** If all of your site users share a common professional language, use it. Otherwise, keep to concise yet effective word choices.

bleakstar/Shutterstock.com

▶ **Use eye-catching headlines.** They catch interest, ask a question, present the unusual, or pose a conflict.

▶ **Break longer documents into smaller chunks.** Provide ways to easily move through the document and return to the beginning.

▶ **Use attention-getting devices judiciously.** Bolding, font changes, color, and graphics do attract attention but can be overdone, causing important ideas to be lost.

▶ **Avoid placing critical information in graphic form only.** Many users are averse to slow-loading graphics and skip over them.

6 | Delivering Good- and Neutral-News Messages

Westend61/Getty Images

LEARNING OBJECTIVES

After studying this chapter, you will be able to …

6-1 Describe the deductive outline for good and neutral news and its adaptations for specific situations and for international audiences.

6-2 Prepare messages that convey good news, including thank-you and appreciation messages.

6-3 Write messages presenting routine claims and requests, and favorable responses to them.

6-4 Write messages acknowledging customer orders, providing credit information, and extending credit.

6-5 Prepare procedural messages that ensure clear and consistent application.

After finishing this chapter, go to **PAGE 115** for **STUDY TOOLS**.

6-1 DEDUCTIVE ORGANIZATIONAL PATTERN

You read in Chapter 4 that you can organize business messages either *deductively* or *inductively* depending on your prediction of the audience's reaction to your main idea. Learning to organize business messages according to the appropriate outline will improve your chances of preparing a document that elicits the response or action you desire.

In this chapter, you will learn to compose messages that convey ideas that your audience will likely find either *pleasing* or *neutral*. Messages that convey pleasant information are referred to as **good-news messages**. Messages that are of interest to your audience, but are not likely to generate an emotional reaction are referred to as **neutral-news messages**. The strategies discussed for structuring good- and neutral-news messages can generally be applied to North American audiences. Because message expectations and social conventions differ from culture to culture, the effective writer will adapt as necessary when writing for various audiences. People in organizations use a number of channels to communicate with internal and external audiences. When sending a message that is positive or neutral, you have numerous choices, as shown in Figure 6.1. Depending on the message, audience, and constraints of time and location, the best channel might be spoken or electronic. In addition to the electronic and verbal tools presented in Chapter 5 (email, instant messaging, Web communications, and phone), companies also use written documents such as memorandums and letters to communicate information.

The principles for preparing memorandums (commonly referred to as *memos*) are similar to those that you've already applied when composing email messages, as both are channels for sharing information of a somewhat informal nature. Memos provide a more formal means of sharing information with people inside an organization. Letters are a more formal method of conveying information to external audiences, such as customers, clients, business partners, or suppliers. Regardless of whether the audience is an internal or external one, communication should be carefully structured to achieve the desired purpose.

Good-news or neutral-news messages follow a **deductive** or **direct sequence**—the message begins with the main idea. To present good news and neutral information deductively, begin with the major idea, followed

> Whether the audience is internal or external, communication should be structured to achieve the desired purpose.

by supporting details, as depicted in Figure 6.1. In both outlines, the third point (closing thought) might be omitted without seriously impairing effectiveness; however, including it unifies the message and avoids abruptness.

The deductive pattern has several advantages:

- The first sentence is easy to write. After it is written, the details follow easily.
- The first sentence gets the attention it deserves in this emphatic position.
- Encountering good news in the first sentence puts your audience in a pleasant frame of mind, so it is more receptive to the details that follow.
- The arrangement might save your audience some time. Once it understands the important idea, it can move rapidly through the supporting details.

As you study sample deductive messages in this chapter, note the *poor example* notations that clearly mark the examples of ineffective writing. Detailed comments highlight important writing strategies that have been applied or violated. While gaining experience in developing effective messages, you will also learn to recognize standard business formats. Fully formatted messages are shown as printed documents (letters on company letterhead or paper memos) or as electronic formats (email messages or online input screens).

6-2 GOOD-NEWS MESSAGES

Messages delivering good news are organized using a direct approach, as illustrated in Figure 6.1. For example, you'll study examples of messages that convey positive news as well as thank-you and appreciation messages that generate goodwill.

6-2a Positive News

The memo sent to all employees in Figure 6.2 begins directly with the main idea: a new work-at-home policy for employees. The discussion that follows includes a brief review of the policy and ends positively by encouraging employees to seek

good-news messages messages that convey pleasant information

neutral-news messages messages that are of interest to the reader but are not likely to generate an emotional reaction

deductive (or direct) sequence when the message begins with the main idea followed by supporting details

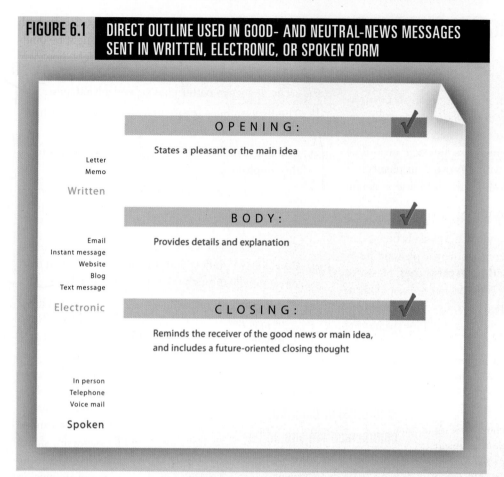

FIGURE 6.1 DIRECT OUTLINE USED IN GOOD- AND NEUTRAL-NEWS MESSAGES SENT IN WRITTEN, ELECTRONIC, OR SPOKEN FORM

OPENING:
States a pleasant or the main idea

Letter
Memo
Written

BODY:
Provides details and explanation

Email
Instant message
Website
Blog
Text message
Electronic

CLOSING:
Reminds the receiver of the good news or main idea, and includes a future-oriented closing thought

In person
Telephone
Voice mail
Spoken

additional information from the company website or contact the supervisor.

6-2b Thank-You and Appreciation Messages

Empathetic managers take advantage of occasions to write goodwill messages that build strong, lasting relationships with employees, clients, customers, and various other groups. People are usually not reluctant to say, "Thank you," "What a great performance," "You have certainly helped me," and so on. Despite good intentions, however, people don't often get around to sending thank-you and appreciation messages. Because of their rarity, written appreciation messages are especially meaningful—even treasured.

THANK-YOU MESSAGES

After receiving a gift, being a guest, attending an interview, or benefiting in various other ways, a thoughtful person will take the time to send a written thank-you message. A simple handwritten note or email is sufficient for some social situations. However, when written from a professional office to respond

to a business situation, the message might be printed on company letterhead. Your message should be written deductively and reflect your sincere feelings of gratitude. The thank-you messages shown on this page (1) identify the circumstances for which the writer is grateful and (2) provide specific reasons the action is appreciated.

APPRECIATION MESSAGES

You will write appreciation messages to recognize, reward, and encourage the receiver; however, you will also gain satisfaction from commending a deserving person. Such positive thinking can be a favorable influence on your own attitude and performance. In appropriate situations, you might wish to address an appreciation message to an individual's supervisor and send a copy of the document to the individual to share the positive comments. In any case, an appreciation message should be sent to commend deserving people and not for possible self-gain.

For full potential value, follow these guidelines for appreciation messages:

patpitchaya/Shutterstock.com

FIGURE 6.2 **GOOD EXAMPLE OF A GOOD-NEWS MESSAGE**   Good

INTEROFFICE MEMORANDUM

To: Data Analysis Department Employees

From: Roberto Rodriquez, Manager, Data Analysis Department

Date: June 10, 2017

Subject: New Work-at-home Policy

A policy allowing employees to work at home has been approved by Montgomery Retail Group effective August 1. This change is being made in response to the results of our recent employee survey.

Starts with the main idea—announcement of award.

Because of our use of cloud storage of customer data, you are now able to access that information anytime, anywhere. This enables you to fulfill your 40-hour-a-week work requirement however you choose in terms of where you complete your duties, and on what days. The data analysis system will automatically track the hours you work and transfer that information to human resources.

Provides a clear explanation to ensure the policy is understood. Format uses a bulleted list for quick, easy reference to specific details.

Since your responsibilities do not require you to interact with external audiences, you can login to the data analysis system wherever you might be, as long as you have an Internet connection.

You are still required to fulfill your 40-hour-a-week work obligation, but you can also apportion your work hours however you like. For example, you might choose to work

- five eight-hour days each week,
- four 10-hour days each week,
- five to six hours every day of the week,
- variable hours depending on your personal obligations.

These examples are just an illustration of how you might decide to apportion your work week; your schedule is completely up to you as long as you work 40 hours weekly.

Please visit the HR website for the complete work-at-home policy. If you have specific questions about how to use the policy, please speak to me directly.

Encourages readers to ask questions or view additional information on company intranet.

Format Pointers
Uses template with standard memo headings for efficient production. Includes writer's initials after printed name and title.

TO EXPRESS THANKS FOR A GIFT

Thank you for the gift certificate to Bath Bubbles Boutique. You know how much I like to relax in a hot, aromatic bath after a stressful day at work! I was happy to fill in for you during the hiring meeting, since our input is so important to our team. I hope your sister's wedding was a success.

TO EXTEND THANKS FOR INFORMATION

Thank you for informing me of the recent job opening in Russell's marketing department. That information led to an interview with Ms. LeVal this morning, and that interaction made me feel confident that I could contribute effectively to her team's efforts. Please accept my invitation to lunch in appreciation for learning about this opportunity.

Written appreciation messages are meaningful.

- **Send in a timely manner.** Sending an appreciation message within a few days of the circumstance will emphasize your genuineness. The receiver might question the sincerity of appreciation messages that are sent long overdue.

- **Avoid exaggerated language that is hardly believable.** You might believe the exaggerated statements to be true, but the recipient might find them unbelievable and insincere. Strong language with unsupported statements raises questions about your motive for the message.

- **Make specific comments about outstanding qualities or performance.** Compared to Figure 6.3, the following message might lack the impact of one that contains more detail and is written with more care. Although the sender cared enough to say thank you, the message could have been given to any speaker, even if the sender had slept through the entire workshop. Similarly, a note merely closed with "sincerely" does not necessarily make the ideas seem sincere. Including specific remarks about understanding and applying the speaker's main points makes the message meaningful and sincere.

Original: Your workshop on using the new database software program was very much appreciated. I'm sure it will help staff tremendously. Thanks.

Improved: Your workshop on the use of our new

claim a request for an adjustment

database software program has enabled staff to apply its broad array of features much more quickly.

One of the most important takeaways from the workshop was the emphasis you placed on creating and communicating clear procedures for work processes. Based upon your suggestions, our team created a draft of these guidelines during our first meeting. Thank you for the suggestions that have put my colleagues and me on the path to becoming a more effective virtual team.

The appreciation message in Figure 6.3 sent from a project administrator to a government employee conveys sincere appreciation for the positive results of a presentation. The net effects of this message are positive: The sender feels good for having passed on a deserved compliment, and the receiver is encouraged by the recipient's recognition of the value of his organization's work.

An apology is written much like an appreciation message. A sincere written apology is needed to preserve relationships when regrettable situations occur. Though difficult to prepare, a well-written apology will usually be received favorably.

6-3 ROUTINE CLAIMS

A **claim** is a request for an adjustment. When business communicators ask for something to which they think they are entitled (such as a refund, replacement, exchange, or payment for damages), the message is called a *claim message*.

FIGURE 6.3 | **GOOD EXAMPLE OF AN APPRECIATION MESSAGE** Good

New Message

To: Howard Chin [hchin@citygovernment.buildingcodes.org]
From: Maury Lewis [mlewis@lewisconstruction.com]
Subject: Appreciation for New Earthquake Code Presentation

Hi, Howard,

Our team is very grateful for the well-structured presentation you provided to explain the city's new earthquake requirements for building construction. We were also very appreciative to learn of the detailed web page the city has made available to help us meet the new requirements.

Extends appreciation for the company providing quality opportunities for leadership development.

Your presentation was particularly helpful in providing the specific building specifications for the types of buildings that we commonly construct in the city. We appreciate the time you took to make the presentation so focused on our specific needs and uses.

Provides a specific example without exaggerating or using overly strong language or insincere statements.

The service orientation of your approach drove home for our company how important it is to maintain a close working relationship with you department. Thanks for emphasizing this additional dimension of our responsibilities to the city and our clients.

Reciprocates goodwill.

Sincerely,

Maury Lewis, Project Administrator
Lewis Construction, Inc.
509-269-4100, Fax: 509-269-4103
mlewis@lewisconstruction.com

Format Pointers
Uses short lines, mixed case; omits special formatting, such as emoticons and email abbreviations, for improved readability.

6-3a Claim Message

Requests for adjustments can be divided into two groups: **routine claims** and **persuasive claims**. Persuasive claims, which are discussed in Chapter 8, assume that a request will be granted only after explanations and persuasive arguments have been presented. Routine claims (possibly because of guarantees, warranties, or other contractual conditions) assume that a request will be granted quickly and willingly, without persuasion. Because you expect routine claims to be granted willingly, a forceful, accusatory tone is inappropriate.

When the claim is routine, the direct approach shown in Figure 6.1 is appropriate. Let's consider the situation referred to in Figures 6.4 and 6.5. Surely, the computer company intended its laptop computers to be fully functioning. Because the damage is obvious, the computer company can be expected to correct the problem without persuasion. Thus the manager can ask for an adjustment before providing an explanation, as shown in Figure 6.5. Beginning with the request for an adjustment gives it the emphasis

routine claims messages that assume that a claim will be granted quickly and willingly, without persuasion

persuasive claims messages that assume that a claim will be granted only after explanations and persuasive arguments have been presented

it deserves. Note, however, that the message in Figure 6.4 is written inappropriately using an indirect approach—the details are presented before the main idea, and it ends abruptly.

6-3b Favorable Response to a Claim Message

Businesses *want* their customers to communicate when merchandise or service is not satisfactory. They want to learn of ways in which goods and services can be improved, and they want their customers to receive value for the money they spend. With considerable confidence, they can assume that writers of claim messages think their claims are valid. By responding fairly to legitimate requests in **adjustment messages**, businesses can gain a reputation for standing behind their goods and services. A loyal customer is likely to become even more loyal after a business has demonstrated its integrity.

adjustment messages messages that are fair responses by businesses to legitimate requests in claim messages by customers

resale a discussion of goods or services already bought

sales promotional material statements made about related merchandise or service

Ordinarily, a response to a written message is also a written message. Sometimes people communicate to confirm ideas they have already discussed on the phone. When the response to a claim is favorable, present ideas in the direct sequence. Although the word *grant* is acceptable when talking about claims, its use in adjustment messages is discouraged. An expression such as "Your claim is being granted" unnecessarily implies that you are in a position of power.

Because the subject of an adjustment is related to the goods or services provided, the message can include a brief sales idea. With only a little extra space, the message can include resale or sales promotional material. **Resale** refers to a discussion of goods or services already bought. It reminds customers and clients that they made a good choice in selecting a company with which to do business, or it reminds them of the good qualities of their purchase. **Sales promotional material** refers to statements made about related merchandise or service. For example, a message about a company's recently purchased office furniture might also mention available office equipment. Mentioning the office equipment is using sales promotional material. Subtle sales messages that are included in adjustments have a good chance of being read, whereas direct sales messages might not be read at all.

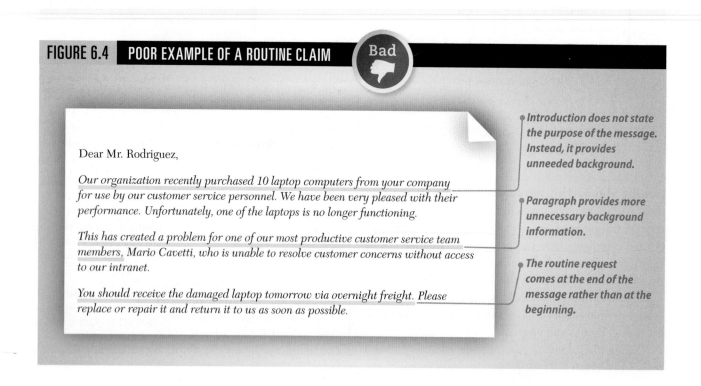

FIGURE 6.4   POOR EXAMPLE OF A ROUTINE CLAIM   Bad

Dear Mr. Rodriguez,

Our organization recently purchased 10 laptop computers from your company for use by our customer service personnel. We have been very pleased with their performance. Unfortunately, one of the laptops is no longer functioning.

This has created a problem for one of our most productive customer service team members, Mario Cavetti, who is unable to resolve customer concerns without access to our intranet.

You should receive the damaged laptop tomorrow via overnight freight. Please replace or repair it and return it to us as soon as possible.

• Introduction does not state the purpose of the message. Instead, it provides unneeded background.

• Paragraph provides more unnecessary background information.

• The routine request comes at the end of the message rather than at the beginning.

FIGURE 6.5 GOOD EXAMPLE OF A ROUTINE CLAIM

New Message

To: Juan Rodriguez [jrodriquez@computernet.com]
From: Laura Sinclair [lsinclair@autoworld.com]
Subject: Laptop Repair or Replacement Needed

Mr. Rodriguez,

Please repair or send us a replacement for the broken laptop computer listed on the attached sales agreement. You should receive the computer tomorrow via overnight freight.

The computer was purchased three months ago under our agreement with your company to provide our customer service team with laptops. The computers are covered by a 12-month warranty for faulty parts replacement. I spoke with your sales manager, Theo Clemens, this morning, and he instructed me to contact you for extradited service.

Our salesperson Mario Cavetti eagerly awaits the return of his laptop. Our customer service team is highly dependent on its computers to access customer product records and to provide them time-sensitive information.

Thanks,
Laura Sinclair
Purchasing Manager

- Limits message to a single idea expressed in a meaningful subject line.
- Emphasizes the main idea (request for adjustment) by placing it in the first sentence.
- Provides an explanation.
- Ends on a positive note, reminding reader of immediate need.

Format Pointers

Composes a short, concise message that fits on one screen.

Includes a salutation and closing to personalize the message.

FIGURE 6.6 POOR EXAMPLE OF A POSITIVE RESPONSE TO A ROUTINE CLAIM

Thank you for your letter on January 21. It has been referred to me for reply.

We have received the laptop of which you wrote and have identified a faulty battery as the cause of the computer malfunction.

We will replace the battery and return it to you soon.

We apologize for any inconvenience.

- This introduction states the obvious and does not address the reader's concerns.
- The paragraph is too descriptive of the writer's experience.
- The ending is too generic to effectively promote.

New Message

To: Laura Sinclair [lsinclair@autoworld.com]
From: Juan Rodriguez [jrodriguez@computernet.com]
Subject: Repaired Laptop Delivered Tomorrow

Ms. Sinclair,

The repaired laptop has been shipped to you via overnight freight. You should receive it tomorrow.

The battery has been replaced, and we have conducted a systems test to ensure that all of the computer components are in working order.

We pride ourselves on our timely service response. Please do not hesitate to contact us with any concerns regarding your laptop orders or their performance.

Sincerely,

Juan Rodriguez
Manager, Customer Service

Begins with good news (main idea) with an assurance of desired action.

Presents explanation and assurance of a process for quality control.

Attempts to regain possible lost goodwill by offering personalized assistance.

Consider the ineffective response in Figure 6.6 to Laura Sinclair's claim letter and the message it sends about the company's commitment. Now notice the deductive outline and the explanation in the revision in Figure 6.7. Because the writer knows that Laura Sinclair will be pleased that the laptop has been repaired and shipped, the good news appears in the first sentence. The details and closing sentence follow naturally and show a desire to correct the problem.

6-4   ROUTINE REQUESTS

routine requests messages that assume that a request will be granted quickly and willingly, without persuasion

persuasive requests messages that assume that a requested action will be taken after persuasive arguments are presented

Like claims, requests are divided into two groups: **routine requests** and **persuasive requests**. Persuasive requests, which are discussed in Chapter 8, assume that action will be taken after persuasive arguments are presented.

Routine requests and favorable responses to them follow the deductive sequence.

6-4a   Requests for Information

Requests for information about people, prices, products, and services are common. Because these requests from customers and clients are door openers for future business, businesses accept them optimistically. At the same time, they arrive at an opinion about the sender based on the quality of the message. Follow the points in the deductive outline for preparing effective requests that you are confident will be fulfilled.

The message in Figure 6.8 does not follow an appropriate deductive outline for a routine request. The request is too vague and the sales manager receiving the message is not provided with enough useful information.

Note that the revision in Figure 6.9 starts with a direct request for specific information. Then as much detail as necessary is presented to enable the receiver to answer specifically. The revision ends

Subject: Need information

Our company is doing a periodic review of computer service providers to ensure that we are contracted with the company who provides the best quality service for the most competitive price. Based on a review of your website, it appears that your organization provides the type of service we need. Obviously, a website is a limited source of information, so I am uncertain as to whether your organization will be able to accommodate our needs.

Our organization has 500 networked desktops and 100 printers that need to be maintained and upgraded as needed. In addition, computer service personnel would be expected to provide technical support to our computer users. Does your company provide resources to support these needs?

I look forward to receiving your reply as quickly as possible.

The subject line could be more informational.

The introduction could more clearly state the purpose of the message.

The writer's needs could be stated more clearly and systematically.

The generic close fails to build goodwill or a sense of urgency.

6-4b Favorable Response to a Routine Request

The message in Figure 6.10 on page 109 responds favorably but with little enthusiasm to an online request for detailed information related to IT services provided by Global Tech. With a little planning and consideration for the needs outlined in the request, the message in Figure 6.11 on page 110 could have been written just as quickly. Note the specific answers to the questions prepared in the convenient Q&A format and the helpful, sincere tone.

6-4c Positive Response to a Favor Request

Occasionally, as a business professional, you will be asked for special favors. You might receive invitations to speak at various civic or education events, spearhead fund-raising and other service projects, or offer your expertise in other ways. If you say "Yes," you might as well say it enthusiastically. Sending an unplanned, stereotyped acceptance suggests that the contribution will be similar.

confidently with appreciation for the action requested. The email message is short, but because it conveys enough information and has a tone of politeness, it is effective.

Rawpixel.com/Shutterstock.com

FIGURE 6.9   GOOD EXAMPLE OF A ROUTINE REQUEST

New Message

To: Donna Peters [dpeters@ElegantCatering.com]
From: Arun Gupta [agupta@gmail.com]
Subject: Request for Catering Estimate

Ms. Peters,

Our association is planning its annual meeting event and is seeking information from local caterers regarding their services. To assist us in this task, please email me the following information:

- Are you available to cater a luncheon for approximately 50 attendees on August 15, 2017 at the War Memorial Hall?
- If so, would you be able to provide a meal for each attendee at a cost of between $20 and $24?
- If so, what are the menu options that fall within this price range?
- Are there any additional fees that you charge and if so, what are these costs specifically?

The information you provide will help us to determine whether you are the catering service that will best meet our needs and budget.

At any time that you would like to contact me directly, please call (307) 213-6770.

Thanks,

Arun Gupta, Event Chair
Children's Hope Fund
307-213-6770, Fax: 307-213-6775
agupta@gmail.com

States request clearly.

Asks specific questions with a necessary explanation; uses a list for emphasis.

Expresses appreciation and alludes to the benefits for quick action.

Opens the door for personal dialogue by providing telephone number.

Format Pointers

Provides a salutation appropriate for the company.

Includes a complete signature block below the writer's name for complete reference.

If you find yourself responding to invitations frequently, you can draft a form message that you'll revise for each invitation you receive.

6-4d Form Messages for Routine Responses

Form messages are a fast and efficient way of transmitting frequently recurring messages to which the anticipated receiver reaction is likely to be favorable or neutral. Inputting the customer's name, address, and other variables (information that differs for each receiver) personalizes each message to meet the needs of its receiver.

Companies might use form paragraphs that have been saved as template documents. When composing a document, select the appropriate paragraph according to your receiver's request. After assembling the selected files on the computer screen, input the particular information for the situation (e.g., name and address), and print a copy of the personalized message on letterhead to send to the receiver.

Form letters have earned a negative connotation because of their tendency to be impersonal. Many people simply refuse to read such letters for that reason. Personalizing a form letter can circumvent this problem.

FIGURE 6.10   POOR EXAMPLE OF A POSITIVE RESPONSE TO A ROUTINE REQUEST

RE: Information Needed

Ms. Taylor,

I read your request, and hopefully my hurried response will provide you the information you need.

As a full-service IT management service provider, we offer ways to save your company time and money with

- flexible and cost-effective technology solutions for your business to stay competitive;
- cost-saving "outsourced" IT support;
- innovative technology solutions specific to your business needs; and
- equipment procurement.

We are happy you're considering Global Tech as your IT service provider. Please contact either me or my staff to make the necessary reservations.

The subject line could be more informational.

The introduction could be more positive and speak more narrowly to the reader's concerns.

This discussion could provide the specific information requested.

The close could be more effective at building goodwill and demonstrating a sincere interest in meeting the organization's needs.

6-5 ROUTINE MESSAGES ABOUT ORDERS AND CREDIT

Routine messages, such as customer order acknowledgments, are written deductively. Normally, credit information is requested and transmitted electronically from the national credit reporting agencies to companies requesting credit references. However, when companies choose to request information directly from other businesses, individual credit requests and responses must be written.

6-5a Acknowledging Customer Orders

When customers place orders for merchandise, they expect to get exactly what they ordered as quickly as possible. Most orders can be acknowledged by shipping the order; no message is necessary. For an initial order, and for an order that cannot be filled quickly and precisely, companies typically send an **acknowledgment message**, a document that indicates that an order has been received and is being processed. Typically,

acknowledgment messages are preprinted letters, or copies of the sales order. An immediate email message acknowledges a new customer and assures quality service, as shown in Figure 6.12 on page 112. Individualized letters are not cost effective and will not reach the customer in a timely manner. Although the form message is impersonal, customers appreciate the order acknowledgment, and information on when the order will arrive.

Nonroutine orders, such as initial orders, custom orders, and delayed orders, require individualized acknowledgment messages. When well-written, these messages not only acknowledge the order but also create customer goodwill and encourage the customer to place additional orders.

6-5b Providing Credit Information

Replies to requests for credit information are usually simple—just fill in the blanks and return the document. If the request does

> **acknowledgment message** a document that indicates that an order has been received and is being processed

FIGURE 6.11   GOOD EXAMPLE OF A POSITIVE RESPONSE TO A ROUTINE REQUEST

New Message

To: Lana Taylor [ltaylor@worldwide.com]
From: Don Pearson [dpearson@globaltech.com]
Subject: Providing your IT management service needs

Global Tech is the ideal provider for your information technology management needs. My staff and I can assist you with maintaining and upgrading your current computer network, providing technical support to your employees, and other support services, all at prices that are competitive.

As a full-service IT management service provider, we offer ways to save your company time and money in the following ways:

- Set up an infrastructure that works for your staff, ultimately allowing it to use the new technologies that will increase its work output, productivity, and company-wide communication.
- Provide a talented staff of experts ready to help, over the phone or online. The resources that we provide will allow your business to get access to specialized expertise at a fraction of the cost of in-house development and maintenance.
- Provide a planned approach to systems maintenance, data backup, disaster recovery, and system security to significantly reduce downtime in the future, while also keeping your business running smoothly and reliably for your employees on a day-to-day basis.
- Purchase equipment at lower costs due to economies of scale and to provide the best solutions for your needs due to our deep knowledge of products, machines, and software.

With technology changing rapidly, it's critical to have a trusted and experienced resource on your side to provide you with the latest in technical capabilities. We keep our staff trained and up-to-date with the changing world of technology so that you don't have to.

Whether it's updating your business with the right equipment in order to get to the next level, or implementing a streamlined technical solution to maximize workflow optimization, or a combination thereof, we employ our knowledge of more than 18 years of information technology experience to get you there.

As your technology provider, we instill our values into every interaction with every client so that you can expect to be treated with professionalism and respect.

In order to provide you with an accurate cost estimate for our services, one of our service managers will need to visit your organization to gather specific information about your current setup and assess your future needs. May I call you next Monday to schedule a site visit?

Regards,
Don Pearson
President
Global Tech, Inc.

Revises subject line after clicking "Reply" to communicate enthusiasm for providing exceptional personalized service.

Highlights specific answers to recipient's questions using an articulate, concise writing style.

Shows a sincere interest in the request and the person.

Addresses the audience's concerns using an articulate, concise writing style.

Provides more useful information that communicates genuine interest in the person, and expertise in the area of information technology.

Format Pointers

Uses a bulleted list format to enhance readability.

not include a form, follow a deductive plan in writing the reply: the major idea first, followed by supporting details.

When providing credit information, you have an ethical and legal obligation to yourself, the credit applicant, and the business from which the credit information is requested. You must be able to document any statement you make to defend yourself against a defamation charge. Thus, good advice is to stick with facts; omit any opinions. "I'm sure he will pay promptly" is an opinion that should be omitted, but include the documentable fact that "His payments have always prompt." Can you safely say a customer is a good credit risk when all you know is that the customer had a good credit record when purchasing from you?

6-5c Extending Credit

A timely response is preferable for any business document, but it is especially important when communicating about credit. The Equal Credit Opportunity Act (ECOA) requires that a credit applicant be notified of the credit decision within 30 days of receipt of the request or application. The party granting the credit must also disclose the terms of the credit agreement, such as the address for sending or making payments, due dates for payments, and the interest rate charged.

When extending credit, follow these guidelines as you write deductively:

1. **Open by extending credit and acknowledging shipment of an order.** Because of its importance, the credit aspect is emphasized more than the acknowledgment of the order. In other cases (in which the order is for cash or the credit terms are already clearly understood), the primary purpose of writing might be to acknowledge an order.

2. **Indicate the basis for the decision to extend credit and explain the credit terms.** Indicating that you are extending credit on the basis of an applicant's prompt paying habits with present creditors might encourage this new customer to continue these habits with you.

3. **Present credit policies.** Explain policies (e.g., credit terms, authorized discounts, and payment dates). Include any legally required disclosure documents.

4. **Communicate a genuine desire to build a strong business relationship.** Include resale, sales promotional material, and comments that remind the customer of the benefits of doing business with you and encourage additional orders.

FIGURE 6.12 GOOD EXAMPLE OF AN ONLINE ORDER CONFIRMATION

Good

New Message

To: Daria Tibbens [dtibbens@gmail.com]

From: Mark Fry [mfry@solefull.com]

Subject: SoleFull.Com welcomes Daria as a member!

Hi Daria,

Welcome to SoleFull.Com's wonderful world of foot delight! I'm excited to see that you have enrolled as a member of our service.

As a new member, you will receive daily text messages announcing our new arrivals, allowing you to be the first to order our unique designs. With just one order of $20 or more a month, you will receive points toward a free pair of designer shoes.

SoleFull.Com prides itself on carrying the latest styles by top designers from around the world. We also guarantee that our shoes will meet your quality expectations. If you are not happy with the quality of manufacturing of any order, please return it to us within 30 days and we will put your payment toward your next order.

We look forward to your next visit at SoleFull.Com and welcome your comments and requests for specific products and product lines.

Thank you for trusting us to provide you stylish, yet affordable footwear.

Best regards,

Mark Fry
Customer Service Manager
SoleFull.Com

P.S. Be sure to watch your mailbox for our Welcome to SoleFull.Com's package, which is sent to all of our new customers. You will receive a discount for your next order as well as other special offers for fashion selections from our online partners.

Provides a warm, personal subject line.

Welcomes the new customer.

Reiterates the benefits of the service to the customer.

Emphasizes the focus on the customer's needs.

The letter in Figure 6.13 was written to a retailer; however, the same principles apply when writing to a consumer. Each message should be addressed in terms of individual interests. Dealers are concerned about markup, marketability, and display; consumers are concerned about price, appearance, and durability. Individual consumers might require a more detailed explanation of credit terms.

Companies receive so many requests for credit that the costs of individualized letters are prohibitive; therefore, most favorable replies to credit requests are form letters. To personalize the letter, however, the writer should merge the customer's name, address, amount of the loan, and terms into the computer file containing the form letter information. Typically, form messages read something like this:

Although such form messages are effective for informing the customer that credit is being extended, they do little to build goodwill and promote future sales. Managers can personalize form messages so that recipients do not perceive them as canned responses.

FIGURE 6.13   GOOD EXAMPLE OF A LETTER EXTENDING CREDIT

Good.

Global Home
123 Pike Avenue
Seattle, WA 89001

January 24, 2017

Frank Benjamin
Purchasing Department
World Interiors, Inc.
123 Colville Avenue
Salt Lake City, UT 84001

Dear Mr. Benjamin:

Welcome to the most unique designs in home furnishings available in the U.S. Our expert buyers tour every region of the world to find the most innovative designs in furnishings for every room in the house.

Because of your favorable current credit rating, we are pleased to provide you with a $15,000 credit line subject to our standard 2/10, n/30 terms. By paying your invoice within ten days, you can save 2 percent on your purchases.

You can use our convenient online ordering system to search our extensive line of home furnishings and to place your orders. If you need additional assistance, please call our 24-hour service line, where you will be assisted with our number one rated customer service personnel.

The most innovative home furnishings are now available to you and your customers, so please take some time to familiarize yourself with our extensive line.

Sincerely,

Candice Clark

Candice Clark
Credit Manager

- Recognizes the dealer for earning credit privilege and gives the reason for the credit extension.

- Includes credit terms, and encourages taking advantage of discount.

- Presents reseller with a reminder of product benefits and encourages future business.

- Includes sales promotion; assumes satisfaction with initial order, and looks confidently for future business.

Legal and Ethical Considerations
Provides answer to request for credit within required time frame (30 days from receipt of request) and mentions terms of credit that will be provided, as required by law.

Uses letter channel rather than email to communicate a contractual message.

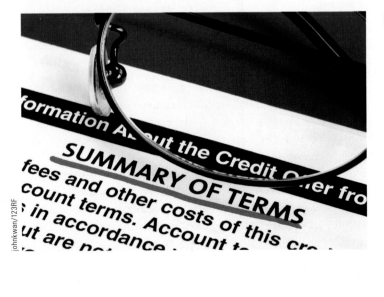

johnkwan/123RF

6-6   PROCEDURAL MESSAGES

Memos or email messages are the most frequently used methods for communicating standard operating procedures and other instructions, as well as changes related to personnel or the organization, and other internal matters for which a written record is needed.

Instructions to employees must be conveyed clearly and accurately in order to facilitate the day-to-day operations of the business, and to prevent negative feelings that occur when mistakes are made and work must be redone.

FIGURE 6.14 **GOOD EXAMPLE OF A PROCEDURAL EMAIL WITH AN ATTACHMENT**

To: All Employees
From: Edward Lawson [elawson@officetemps.com]
Subject: New Procedures for Requesting Technology Services

Attachment: Computer_Service_Request_Procedures.docx 📎

Hi all,

The number of computer service requests has increased proportionately with the growth of our organization. In order to continue to provide you with timely responses to your requests, additional technicians have been hired, and a new service reporting system will be put in to place, beginning September 1.

To report a computer problem, or to request technology services, please follow the procedure provided in the attached file. (This file can also be found on the company intranet under "Technology Resources.") You can complete these procedures at any computer, including your home machine.

Thanks,
Edward Lawson
Information Technology Manager

Procedures for Requesting Technology Services

1. Access http://www.officetemps.com/it and click the Technology Services link.

2. Provide the information requested in the form. Be certain to complete the required items denoted with asterisks.

3. Check your email for the response to your request, which typically will arrive within 48 hours.

4. Complete normal shutdown when leaving your computer station or other device. Service work will be completed after hours; technicians will start your device using their personal login procedures.

5. Check your email for a service completion notification. Please contact us if the work was not completed to your satisfaction. Our email is itservices@officetemps.com. A coordinator will contact you within 24 hours.

Dated 02/22/2017

Includes an attached file of a document requiring involved formatting.

Introduces the main idea.

Explains the new procedures outlined in the attached file.

Provides a descriptive title that clearly identifies the procedures.

Enumerates to direct attention to each step and emphasize the need for sequence.

Begins each item with an action verb to help employees visualize completing procedures.

Includes the date of the last revision to ensure currency.

DEAR [TITLE] [LAST NAME]

▶ Trueman's Electronics is pleased to extend credit privileges to you. Initially, you may purchase up to [CREDIT LIMIT] worth of merchandise. Our credit terms are [TERMS]. We welcome you as a credit customer at Trueman's Electronics and look forward to serving your needs for the latest electronics devices designed and manufactured by the world's top companies.

Managers must take special care in writing standard operating procedures to ensure that all employees complete the procedures accurately and consistently.

Before writing instructions, walk through each step in order to understand it and to locate potential trouble spots. Then attempt to determine how much employees already know about the process, and to anticipate any questions or problems. Then, as you write instructions that require more than a few simple steps, follow these guidelines:

1. **Begin each step with an action statement in order to create a vivid picture of the employee completing the task.** Using an action verb and the understood subject, *you*, is more vivid than a sentence written in the passive voice. For example, a loan officer attempting to learn new procedures for evaluating new venture loans can more easily understand "*identify* assets available to collateralize the loan" than "assets available to collateralize the loan should be identified."

2. **Itemize each step on a separate line to add emphasis and to simplify reading.** Number each step to indicate that the procedures should be completed in a particular order. If the order of steps is not important, use bullets rather than numbers.

3. **Consider preparing a flow chart depicting the procedures.** The cost and effort involved in creating a sophisticated flow chart might be merited for extremely important and complex procedures. For example, take a look at the flow chart in Figure 10.7, which demonstrates the steps in the sales process.

4. **Complete the procedure by following your instructions step-by-step.** Correct any errors that you locate.

5. **Ask a colleague or employee to walk through the procedures.** This walk through will allow you to identify ambiguous statements, omissions of relevant information, and other sources of potential problems.

Consider the seemingly simple task of requesting technology assistance. The IT manager might respond to such a request, "No need for written instructions; just make a request for technology help any way that you wish." Ambiguous verbal instructions (reported in haste) could lead to confusion about technology assistance and bad feelings about the efficiency of the process. The clear, consistent procedure in Figure 6.14 was prepared after the manager anticipated employee issues in requesting technology services. The policy is sent as an email attachment and posted to the company intranet for easy reference.

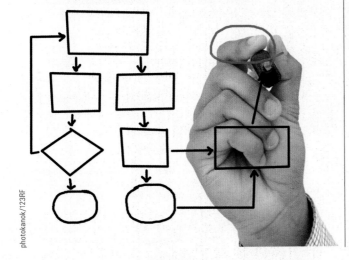

photokanok/123RF

7 | Delivering Bad-News Messages

Nikada/Getty Images

LEARNING OBJECTIVES

After studying this chapter, you will be able to …

7-1 Explain the steps in the inductive outline, and understand its use for specific situations.

7-2 Discuss strategies for developing the five components of a bad-news message.

7-3 Prepare messages refusing requests and claims.

7-4 Prepare messages handling problems with customers' orders and denying credit.

7-5 Prepare messages providing constructive criticism.

7-6 Prepare messages communicating negative organizational news.

7-7 Prepare messages responding to crises.

After finishing this chapter, go
to **PAGE 136** for
STUDY TOOLS.

7-1 CHOOSING AN APPROPRIATE CHANNEL AND ORGANIZATIONAL PATTERN

An organization's ability to handle difficult situations with tact and empathy powerfully influences the perceptions of employees, local citizens, and the public at large. As a skilled communicator, you will attempt to deliver bad news in such a way that the recipient supports the decision and is willing to continue a positive relationship. To accomplish these goals, allow empathy for your audience to direct your choice of an appropriate channel and outline when presenting a logical discussion of the facts or an unpleasant idea. Use tactful and effective language to aid you in developing a clear, yet sensitive, message.

7-1a Channel Choice and Commitment to Tact

Personal delivery has been the preferred medium for delivering bad news because it signals the importance of the news and shows empathy for the recipient. Face-to-face delivery also provides the benefit of nonverbal communication and immediate feedback, which minimizes misinterpretation of these highly sensitive messages. Personal delivery, however, carries a level of discomfort and the potential for the escalation of emotion. A voice on the telephone triggers the same discomfort as a face-to-face meeting, and the increased difficulty of interpreting the intensity of nonverbal cues over the telephone only adds to the natural discomfort associated with delivering negative information.

You must be cautious when you deliver bad news electronically, whether by email or electronic postings. While you might feel more comfortable avoiding the discomfort of facing the recipient, the impersonal nature of the computer might lead to careless writing that is tactless and lacking in empathy, and, perhaps, may even be defamatory. Stay focused and follow the same communication strategies you would apply if you were speaking face-to-face or writing a more formal message. Regardless of the medium, your objective is to help your audience understand and accept your message, and this requires empathy and tact.

"You're fired" became a familiar phrase immortalized by Donald Trump on the hit show *The Apprentice*.

> If the bad news is presented in the first sentence, the reaction is likely to be negative.

Though such bluntness might work on television, it is rarely recommended in actual work situations. Tactlessness can have serious effects when your personal response fails to soothe negative feelings and ensure a harmonious relationship with a customer, client, or employee. You might find it difficult to show tact when you doubt the legitimacy of a request or simply don't have the time to prepare an effective bad-news message. When this conflict exists, you must remember that any message delivered on behalf of the company is a direct reflection on the company's image.

7-1b Use of the Inductive Approach to Build Goodwill

Just as good news is accompanied by details, bad news is accompanied by supporting reasons and explanations. If the bad news is presented in the first sentence, the reaction is likely to be negative: "They never gave me a fair chance," "That's unfair," "This just can't be." Having made a value judgment on reading the first sentence, receivers are naturally reluctant to change their minds before the last sentence—even though the intervening sentences present a valid basis for doing so. Once disappointed by the idea contained in the first sentence, receivers are tempted to concentrate on *refuting* (instead of *understanding*) supporting details.

From the communicator's point of view, details that support a refusal are very important. If the supporting details are understood and believed, the message might be readily accepted and good business relationships preserved. Because the reasons behind the bad news are so important, the communicator needs to organize the message in such a way as to emphasize the reasons.

The chances of getting your audience to understand the reasons are much better *before* the bad news is presented than *after* the bad news is presented. If the bad news precedes the reasons, the message might be discarded before this important portion is even read, or the disappointment experienced when reading the bad news might interfere with your audience's ability to comprehend or accept the supporting explanation.

The five-step outline shown in Figure 7.1 simplifies the process of organizing bad-news messages. These five steps are applied in messages illustrated in this chapter.

Although the outline has five points, a bad-news message may or may not have five paragraphs. More than one paragraph might be necessary for conveying supporting

FIGURE 7.1 INDUCTIVE OUTLINE USED IN BAD-NEWS MESSAGES

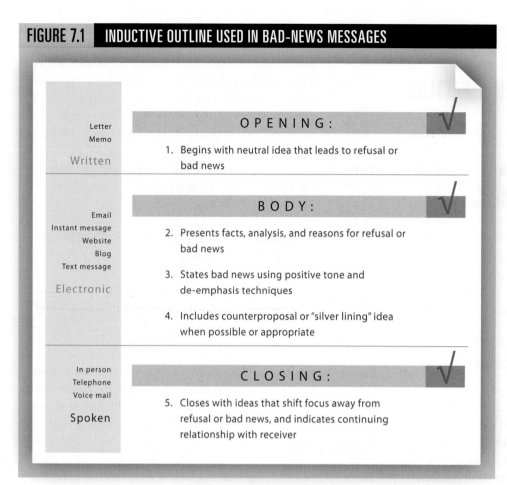

Written — Letter, Memo

OPENING: ✓
1. Begins with neutral idea that leads to refusal or bad news

Electronic — Email, Instant message, Website, Blog, Text message

BODY: ✓
2. Presents facts, analysis, and reasons for refusal or bad news
3. States bad news using positive tone and de-emphasis techniques
4. Includes counterproposal or "silver lining" idea when possible or appropriate

Spoken — In person, Telephone, Voice mail

CLOSING: ✓
5. Closes with ideas that shift focus away from refusal or bad news, and indicates continuing relationship with receiver

reasons. In the illustrations in this chapter, note that the first and final paragraphs are seldom longer than two sentences. In fact, one-sentence paragraphs at the message's beginning look inviting to read.

You might speculate that your audience might become impatient when a message is inductive. Concise, well-written explanations are not likely to make a reader impatient. They relate to the audience's problem, present information not already known, and help your audience understand. However, if a receiver becomes impatient while reading a well-written explanation, that impatience is less damaging to understanding than would be the anger or disgust that often results from encountering bad news in the first sentence.

7-1c Exceptions to the Inductive Approach

Normally, the writer's purpose is to convey a clear message and retain the recipient's goodwill; thus, the inductive outline is appropriate. In the rare circumstances in which a choice must be made between clarity and goodwill, clarity is the better choice. When the deductive approach will serve a communicator's purpose better, it should be used. For example, if you submit a clear and tactful refusal and your audience submits a second request, a deductive presentation might be justified in

---

THE INDUCTIVE SEQUENCE OF IDEAS HAS THE FOLLOWING ADVANTAGES:

▸ Sufficient identification of the subject of the message without first turning off the audience.

▸ Presentation of the reasons *before* the refusal, where they are more likely to be understood and will receive appropriate attention.

▸ Avoidance of a negative reaction. By the time the reasons are read, they seem sensible, and the refusal is foreseen. Because it is expected, the statement of refusal does not come as a shock.

▸ De-emphasis of the refusal by closing on a neutral or pleasant note. By showing a willingness to cooperate in some way, the sender conveys a desire to be helpful.

PLACING A REFUSAL IN THE FIRST SENTENCE CAN BE JUSTIFIED WHEN ONE OR MORE OF THE FOLLOWING CIRCUMSTANCES EXIST:

▸ The message is the second response to a repeated request.

▸ A very small, insignificant matter is involved.

▸ The request is obviously ridiculous, immoral, unethical, illegal, or dangerous.

▸ The sender's intent is to "shake" the receiver.

▸ The sender–recipient relationship is so close and longstanding that satisfactory human relations can be taken for granted.

▸ The sender *wants* to demonstrate authority.

the second refusal. Apparently, the refusal needs the emphasis provided by a deductive outline.

In most situations, the preceding circumstances do not exist. When they do, a sender's goals might be accomplished by stating bad news in the first sentence.

wavebreakmedia/Shutterstock.com

7-2 DEVELOPING A BAD-NEWS MESSAGE

Developing a bad-news message following the inductive outline is challenging. The following suggestions will aid you in writing the (1) introductory paragraph, (2) explanation, (3) bad-news statement, (4) counterproposal or "silver lining" idea, and (5) closing paragraph.

7-2a Writing the Introductory Paragraph

The introductory paragraph in the bad-news message should accomplish the following objectives: (1) provide a buffer to cushion the bad news that will follow, (2) let the audience know what the message is about without stating the obvious, and (3) serve as a transition into the discussion of reasons without revealing the bad news or leading the audience to expect good news. If these objectives can be accomplished in one sentence, then this sentence can be the first paragraph.

Here are several ideas that can be incorporated into an effective beginning paragraph:

- **Compliment**. A message denying a customer's request could begin by recognizing the customer's promptness in making payments.

- **Point of agreement.** A sentence that reveals agreement with a statement made in the message could get the message off to a positive discussion of other points.

- **Good news.** When a message contains a request that must be refused and another that is being answered favorably, beginning with the favorable answer can be effective.

- **Resale**. A claim refusal could begin with some favorable statement about the product.

- **Review.** Refusal of a current request could be introduced by referring to the initial transaction or by reviewing certain circumstances that preceded the transaction.

- **Gratitude**. In spite of the unjustified request, the audience might have done or said something for which you are grateful. An expression of gratitude could be used as a positive beginning.

AVOID THE FOLLOWING WEAKNESSES WHEN WRITING THE INTRODUCTORY PARAGRAPH:

▸ **Empty acknowledgments of the obvious.** *"I am writing in response to your letter requesting . . . "* or *"Your message on the 14th has been given to me for reply"* wastes space and presents points of no value. Beginning with *I* signals the message might be writer-centered.

▸ **Tipping off the bad news too early.** *"Although the refund requested in your letter of May 1 cannot be approved . . ."* might cause an immediate emotional reaction resulting in the message being discarded or it might interfere with understanding the explanations that follow.

The neutral statement *"Your request for an adjustment has been considered. However, . . . "* does not reveal whether the answer is "Yes" or "No," but the use of "however" signals that the answer is "No" before the reasons are presented. Such a beginning has about the same effect as an outright "No."

▸ **Starting too positively so as to build false hopes.** Empathetic statements such as *"I can understand how you felt when you were asked to pay an extra $54"* might lead the audience to expect good news. When a preceding statement has implied that an affirmative decision will follow, a negative decision is all the more disappointing.

7-2b Presenting the Facts, Analysis, and Reasons

The reasons section of the bad-news message is extremely important because people who are refused want to know why. If a message is based on a sound decision, and if it has been well written, recipients will understand and accept the reasons, and the forthcoming refusal statement, as valid.

To accomplish this goal, begin with a well-written first paragraph that transitions the reader smoothly into the reasons section. Then develop the reasons section following these guidelines:

- **Provide a smooth transition from the opening paragraph to the explanation.** The buffer should help set the stage for a logical movement into the discussion of the reasons.

- **Include a concise discussion of one or more reasons that are logical to the reader.** Read the section aloud to identify flaws in logic or the need for additional explanation.

- **Show audience benefit and/or consideration.** Emphasize how your audience will benefit from the decision. Avoid insincere, empty statements such as "To improve our service to you, …"

STUDY THE FOLLOWING EXAMPLES THAT USE TRANSITION STATEMENTS TO ACHIEVE A COHERENT OPENING:

Your employment application package has been reviewed by Human Resources.	Reveals the topic as a reply to a recipient's employment application.
Human Resources personnel …	Uses "Human Resources personnel" to transition from the first to second paragraph.
Following your request for permission to submit a proposal to continue subsidizing employees' access to exercise facilities, we reviewed recent records of attendance.	Reveals the subject of the message as a reply to an employee's request.
In the past two years, attendance …	Uses "recent" and "attendance" to tie the second paragraph to the first.

- **Avoid using "company policy" as the reason.** Disclose the reason behind the policy, which likely will include benefits to the reader. For example, a customer is more likely to understand and accept a 15% restocking fee if the policy is not presented as the "reason" for the refusal.

The principles for developing the reasons section are illustrated in Figure 7.2: a letter written by an attorney refusing a request to represent a client.

7-2c Writing the Bad-News Statement

A paragraph that presents the reasoning behind a refusal at least partially conveys the refusal before it is stated directly or indirectly. Yet one sentence needs to convey (directly or by implication) the conclusion to which the preceding details have been leading. A refusal (bad news) needs to be clear; however, you can subordinate the refusal so that the reasons get the deserved emphasis. The following techniques will help you achieve this goal.

- **Position the bad-news statement strategically.** Using the inductive outline positions the bad-news statement in a less important position—sandwiched between an opening buffer statement and a positive closing. Additionally, the refusal statement should be included in the same paragraph as the reasons, since placing it in a paragraph by itself would give too much emphasis to the bad news. When the preceding explanation is tactful and relevant, resentment over the bad news is minimized. Positioning the bad-news statement in the dependent clause of a complex sentence will also cushion the bad news. This technique places the bad news in a less visible, less emphatic position. In the sentence, *"Although the company's current financial condition prevents us from providing raises this year, we hope to make up for the freeze when conditions improve,"* the emphasis is directed toward a promise of raises at another time.

- **Use passive voice, general terms, and abstract nouns.** Review the *emphasis techniques* that you studied in Chapter 3 as you consider methods for presenting bad news with human relations in mind.

- **Use positive language to accentuate the positive.** Simply focus on the good instead of the bad, the pleasant instead of the unpleasant, or what can be done instead of what cannot be done. Compared with a negative idea presented in negative terms, a

FIGURE 7.2   DEVELOPING THE COMPONENTS OF A BAD-NEWS MESSAGE

Selecting a law firm to represent your organization provides a continuity of services that better protects your officers, board of directors, and investors. It is an important decision that requires careful consideration from a range of perspectives.

Reveals the subject of the message and transitions into reasons.

One important consideration is protection against a conflict of interest. One of our current clients is a key competitor with your firm. For that reason, we believe it is in your best interest to select another law firm to represent your organization and protect you from any potential negative charges.

Supports the refusal with logical reasoning.

States refusal positively and clearly using complex sentences and positive language.

If our current client list changes, we will contact you about our availability in case you are still looking for a law firm to represent you. We appreciate the trust that you hold in our services.

Ends with a forward-looking message to enhance goodwill.

---

negative idea presented in positive terms is more likely to be accepted. When you are tempted to use the following terms, search instead for words or ideas that sound more positive:

Words That Evoke Negative Feelings

complaint   incompetent   misled
regrettable   error   inexcusable   mistake
unfortunate   failure   lied   neglect   wrong

Words That Evoke Positive Feelings

accurate   concise   enthusiasm   productive
approval   durable   generous   recommendation
assist   energetic   gratitude   respect

- **Imply the refusal when the audience can understand the message without a definite statement of the bad news.** By *implying* the "No" answer, the response has the following positive characteristics: (1) it uses positive language, (2) it conveys reasons or at least a positive attitude, and (3) it seems more respectful. For example, during the noon hour one employee says to another, "Will you go with me to see this afternoon's baseball game?" "No, I won't," communicates a negative response, but it seems unnecessarily direct and harsh. The same message (invitation is rejected) can be clearly stated in an *indirect* way (by implication) by saying "I must get my work done," or even, "I'm a football fan." Note the positive tone of the following implied refusals:

Implied Refusal	Underlying Message
I wish I could.	• Other responsibilities prohibit, but recipient would like to accept.
Had you selected our newest calling plan, you could have reduced your monthly rates by 10% or more.	• States a condition under which the answer would have been "Yes" instead of "No." Note the use of the subjunctive words "had" and "could."
By accepting the new terms, Southern Wood Products would have doubled its energy costs.	• States the obviously unacceptable results of complying with a request.

7-2d Offering a Counterproposal or "Silver Lining" Idea

Following negative news with an alternative action, referred to as a **counterproposal**, will assist in preserving a relationship with the reader. Because it states what you *can* do, including a counterproposal might eliminate the need to state the refusal directly. The counterproposal can follow a refusal stated in a tactful, sensitive manner. When global Internet services and media company AOL

counterproposal in a bad-news message, an alternative to the action requested that follows the negative news and can assist in preserving future relationships with the audience

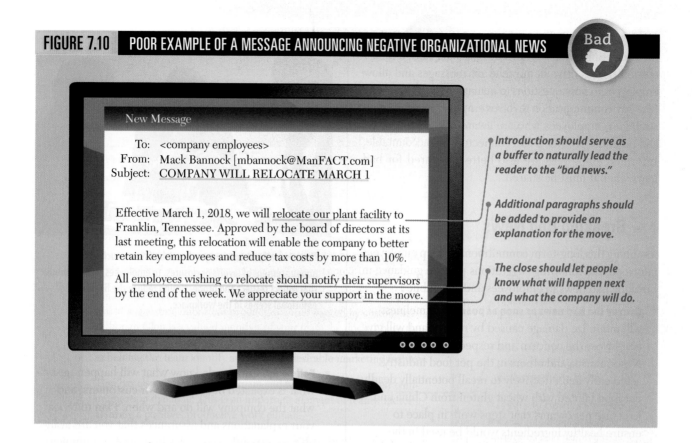

New Message

To: <company employees>
From: Mack Bannock [mbannock@ManFACT.com]
Subject: COMPANY WILL RELOCATE MARCH 1

Effective March 1, 2018, we will relocate our plant facility to Franklin, Tennessee. Approved by the board of directors at its last meeting, this relocation will enable the company to better retain key employees and reduce tax costs by more than 10%.

All employees wishing to relocate should notify their supervisors by the end of the week. We appreciate your support in the move.

Introduction should serve as a buffer to naturally lead the reader to the "bad news."

Additional paragraphs should be added to provide an explanation for the move.

The close should let people know what will happen next and what the company will do.

---

deliberate maliciousness. When crises occur, the communication that is offered can either help ease situations or worsen them. Rather than waiting for a crisis to occur, an organization should examine its state of preparedness and have a carefully considered plan of action that includes the following steps:

- **Anticipate potential crises in terms of areas of vulnerability and what could happen.**

- **Establish emergency procedures, including an alternate command center and chain of command.** Ensure that more than one employee is media trained and able to respond appropriately if needed.

- **Identify who will need to be contacted, and plan for multiple means of disseminating information.** Cellphones and text messaging have proven themselves valuable when other contact means might not work, but keep in mind that telecommunication circuits can be overloaded in mass disaster situations, necessitating multiple means for sharing news.

- **Ensure current contact information is available for employees, media, and other pertinent parties.**

- **Maintain an up-to-date fact sheet about the company, its products/services, locations, and operations.**

RESPONSE IN A CRISIS

In responding to a crisis, the message conveyed is extremely important in reassuring employees and business partners, and in shaping public opinion. These guidelines can help ensure an effective message:

▶ Determine what your message is, and prepare a checklist of what it should contain before writing.

▶ Keep the message simple, and arrange it in logical sections.

▶ Include verbiage that demonstrates your concern, compassion, and control.

▶ Prepare separate messages for internal and external audiences, including the appropriate level of detail.

While crises can seldom be predicted, an organization can position itself to respond to them appropriately when they do occur by preparing for crises before they occur.

Adequate pre-crisis planning is necessary for a rapid, effective crisis response—the second stage of

Good

INTEROFFICE MEMORANDUM

TO:	All Employees
FROM:	Mack Bannock, President
DATE:	January 4, 2017
SUBJECT:	Proposed Plan for Managing Future Growth

Our company has weathered the recent recession by taking advantage of international business opportunities in Southeast Asia. Our location in Southern California has provided us a well-educated and skilled workforce to produce the innovation needed in today's automobile market.

However, the rise in the cost-of-living due to high taxes, comparatively high housing costs, and relatively higher costs for food and utilities has made it more difficult to retain top employees. The cost of living in Southern California is 15% higher than in many other parts of the country. The school system in Los Angeles is one of the poorest in the country in terms of graduation rates from high school. Similarly, L.A. ranks at the top of the list in terms of time spent commuting on overcrowded freeways.

Housing prices, although dramatically lower than they were several years ago, are still well above the national average, particularly in safe neighborhoods with good schools. All of these issues make it much more difficult to retain skilled employees who have the option to move to other parts of the country without these challenges. In fact, three of our top engineers have left in the past year, citing the high cost of living and poor school system as their reasons.

While relocating could provide a long-term economic benefit to the company in terms of tax savings, moving out of Los Angeles could enhance the quality of life for all of us. Consequently, we have been working with state and local governments in other parts of the country to find an area with a lower cost of living, good neighborhoods and schools, and a skilled labor force. This search has led us to identify Franklin, Tennessee, a thriving suburb located approximately 18 miles south of Nashville, as our new plant location.

Your supervisor will explain the logistics of the relocation at your next team meeting. In the meantime, please visit the Franklin link on the company intranet to read more about what Tennessee can offer us and our families. Check back for updates on the FAQ page designed to provide responses to your concerns. Now let us work together for a smooth transition to Franklin.

Uses the subject line to introduce the topic but does not reveal the bad news.

Uses a buffer to introduce the topic familiar to employees through previous communication and leads into reasons.

Provides a rational explanation, including benefits.

Presents the bad news while reminding receiver of the benefits.

Follows up by assuring continued exchange of timely information through discussions and web pages.

Ends with a positive appeal for unity.

Legal and Ethical Consideration
Uses memo channel rather than email for conveying a sensitive message.

© Mike Baldwin / Cornered

"You have a major fiasco at 10:30, followed by a shocking scandal at 2:15."

Mike Baldwin / CartoonStock.com

crisis, the organization is viewed as a victim of the event. This type includes natural disasters, workplace violence, product tampering, and rumors. In an accident crisis, the event is considered unintentional or uncontrollable by the organization, and includes accidents or harm from technical errors or equipment failure. In a preventable crisis, the event is considered purposeful and includes accidents or harm caused by human error as well as organizational misdeeds such as fraud.[8]

After identifying the type of crisis, you can select the appropriate components of an effective crisis message, as depicted in Figures 7.12 and 7.13.

Figure 7.14 provides an example of an effective response to an accident crisis. It includes the appropriate crisis communication components of showing concern, explaining corrective actions, providing instructions, and giving a brief justification.

During a crisis, the organization should monitor the situation carefully and provide quick and accurate communication to all stakeholders through all available communication channels. After the crisis has passed—the post-crisis stage of crisis management—the organization should carefully plan and create a consistent stream of messages to help repair any damage to its reputation sustained by the crisis.

crisis management. A key task during crisis response is to identify the type of crisis in order to better develop communication messages. Three broad types of crises exist: victim, accident, and preventable crises.[7] In a victim

---

FIGURE 7.12   COMPONENTS OF CRISIS COMMUNICATION RESPONSES

Concern	Express concern for all affected by the crisis.
Corrective Actions	Describe specific steps the organization is taking to correct the problem.
Instructions	Tell those affected what to do to stay informed and to protect themselves.
Excuse	Deny intent to harm, or point out inability to control events.
Justification	Minimize the perceived damage of the crisis.
Compensation	Offer money or gifts to victims.
Apology	Take full responsibility for the crisis.

Sources: W. T. Coombs (2007). Protecting organization reputations during a crisis: The development and application of situational crisis communication theory. *Corporate Reputation Review 10* (3), 163–176; W. T. Coombs (2004). Impact of past crisis on current crisis communications: Insights from situational crisis communication theory. *Journal of Business Communication 41* (3), 265–289; W. T. Coombs & S. J. Holladay (2002). Helping crisis managers protect reputational assets: Initial tests of the situational crisis communication theory. *Management Communication Quarterly 16* (2), 165–186.

Type of Crisis	Concern	Corrective Actions	Instructions	Excuse/Justification	Compensation/ Apology
Victim	X	X	X		
Accident	X	X	X	X	
Preventable	X	X	X	X	X

Sources: W. T. Coombs (2007). Protecting organization reputations during a crisis: The development and application of situational crisis communication theory. *Corporate Reputation Review 10* (3), 163–176; W.T. Coombs (2004). Impact of past crisis on current crisis communications: Insights from situational crisis communication theory. *Journal of Business Communication 41* (3), 265–289; W.T. Coombs & S. J. Holladay (2002). Helping crisis managers protect reputational assets: Initial tests of the situational crisis communication theory. *Management Communication Quarterly 16* (2), 165–186.

FIGURE 7.14   EXAMPLE OF CORPORATE WEB SITE POST FOR A VICTIM CRISIS

At 4:30 p.m. this afternoon (March 12), EastAir Flight EA3201 was involved in an incident upon landing at Los Angeles International Airport. All passengers and crew have been deplaned from the aircraft, and 23 passengers and crew who sustained non-life-threatening injuries have been transported to local hospitals for observation and treatment.   *Shows concern.*

EastAir personnel are currently on site providing assistance to passengers, and additional EastAir teams are on their way to provide additional support. This assistance will include:

1. Providing accommodations for passengers and families until transportation to their final destination can be arranged.
2. Arranging for transportation to final destinations of passengers and families.
3. Providing access to counseling services for passengers and families as needed.   *Explains corrective action.*

No further details are available at this time; however, EastAir will provide regular updates on Twitter and on its website at EastAir.com as information becomes known. Family members who seek information about passengers on Flight EA3201 may telephone EastAir at 1-800-912-7099.   *Provides instructions.*

EastAir will be cooperating fully with authorities in their investigation.

"We at EastAir are greatly relieved that no one was critically injured," said Clyde Gotham, Executive Vice President and Chief Operating Officer of EastAir. "Yet we fully appreciate that this has been a very unsettling experience for our customers and their families, as well as our employees, and we are focused on caring for all those affected. We will also fully cooperate with the Transportation Safety Board as it begins an investigation to determine the cause."   *Provides a brief justification.*

Flight EA3201 was carrying 133 passengers and five crew members at the time of the incident.

STUDY TOOLS 7

LOCATED AT THE BACK OF THE TEXTBOOK
☐ Tear-Out Chapter Review Cards

LOCATED AT WWW.CENGAGEBRAIN.COM
☐ Review Key Term flashcards and create your own cards

☐ Track your knowledge and understanding of key concepts in business communication

☐ Complete practice and graded quizzes to prepare for tests

☐ Complete interactive content within BCOM9 Online

☐ View the chapter highlight boxes for BCOM9 Online

BCOM
ONLINE

PREPARE FOR TESTS ON
THE STUDYBOARD!

○ CORRECT
○ INCORRECT
○ INCORRECT
○ INCORRECT

**Personalize Quizzes
from Your StudyBits**

**Take Practice
Quizzes by Chapter**

CHAPTER QUIZZES
▶ Chapter 1
Chapter 2
Chapter 3
Chapter 4

4LTR
PRESS

Access BCOM **ONLINE** at www.cengagebrain.com

8 | Delivering Persuasive Messages

marekuliasz/Shutterstock.com

LEARNING OBJECTIVES

After studying this chapter, you should be able to . . .

8-1 Develop effective outlines and appeals for messages that persuade.

8-2 Write effective sales messages.

8-3 Write effective persuasive requests (making a claim or asking for a favor or information) and persuasion within an organization.

After finishing this chapter, go to **PAGE 155** for **STUDY TOOLS.**

8-1 PERSUASION STRATEGIES

Businesspeople regularly seek to persuade others. **Persuasion** is the ability to influence others to accept your point of view. It is not an attempt to trap someone into taking action favorable to the communicator. Instead, it is an honest, organized presentation of information on which a person can choose to act. Professionals in all fields benefit from well-prepared communications that persuade others to accept their ideas or buy their products, services, or ideas.

How do you learn to persuade others through spoken and written communication? Have you ever made a persuasive request, written employment documents or an essay for college entry or a scholarship, or given a campaign speech? If so, you already have experience with this type of communication. While the persuasive concepts discussed in this chapter are directed primarily at written communication, they can also be applied in many spoken communication situations.

For persuasion to be effective, you must understand your product, service, or idea; know your audience; anticipate the arguments that might come from the audience; and have a rational and logical response to those arguments. Remember, persuasion need not be a hard sell; it can simply be a way of getting a client or your supervisor to say yes. Although much of this chapter concentrates on selling products and services, similar principles apply to selling an idea, your organization, and your own abilities.

> Persuasion can simply be a way of getting a client or supervisor to say yes.

8-1a Plan Before You Write

Success in writing is directly related to success in preliminary thinking. If the right questions have been asked and answered, the composing will be easier and the message will be more persuasive. Specifically, you need information about (1) your product, service, or idea; (2) your audience; and (3) the desired action.

KNOW THE PRODUCT, SERVICE, OR IDEA

You cannot be satisfied with knowing the product, service, or idea in a general way; you need details. Get your information by (1) reading available literature; (2) using the product and watching others use it; (3) comparing the product, service, or idea with others; (4) conducting tests and experiments; and (5) soliciting reports from users.

Before you write, you need concrete answers to such questions as these:

- What will the product, service, or idea do for the reader(s)?
- What are its superior features (e.g., design and workmanship or audience benefit)?
- How is the product or service different from its competition?
- How is the proposed idea superior to other viable alternatives?
- What is the cost to the receiver?

Similar questions must be answered about other viable alternatives or competing products. Of particular importance is the question, "What is the major difference?" People are inclined to choose an item (or alternative) that has some distinct advantage. For example, some people might choose a particular car model because of its style and available options; still others might choose the model because of its safety record.

KNOW THE AUDIENCE

Who are the people to whom the persuasive message is directed? What are their wants and needs? Is a persuasive message to be written and addressed to an individual or to a group? If it is addressed to a group, what characteristics do the members have in common? What are their common goals, their occupational levels, and their educational status? To what extent have their needs and wants been satisfied? How might cultural differences affect your message?

Recall the discussion of Maslow's hierarchy of needs in Chapter 2. Some people might respond favorably to appeals to physiological, security, and safety needs (to save time and money, to be comfortable, to be healthy, or to avoid danger). People with such needs would be impressed with a discussion of the benefits of convenience, durability, efficiency, or serviceability. Others might respond favorably to appeals to their social, ego, and self-actualizing needs (to be loved, entertained, remembered, popular, praised, appreciated, or respected). Consider the varying appeals used in a memo to employees and to supervisors seeking support of teleworking. The memo to employees would appeal to the need for greater flexibility and reduced stress. Appeals directed at supervisors would focus

> **persuasion** the ability of a sender to influence others to accept his or her point of view

on increased productivity and morale, reduced costs for office space, and compliance with the Clean Air Act—a federal law requiring companies to reduce air pollution and traffic congestion.

IDENTIFY THE DESIRED ACTION

What do you want the reader to do? Complete an online order and make a payment? Receive a demonstration version for trial? Return a card requesting a representative to call? Email for more information? Approve a request? Accept a significant change in service, style, and procedures? Whatever the desired action, you need to have a clear definition of it before composing your message.

8-1b Use the Inductive Approach

More than 100 years ago, Sherwin Cody summarized the persuasive process into four basic steps called **AIDA**.[1] The steps have been varied somewhat and have had different labels, but the fundamentals remain relatively unchanged. The persuasive approach illustrated in Figure 8.1 is inductive. The main idea, which is the request for action, appears in the *last* paragraph after presenting the details—convincing reasons for the audience to comply with the request.

Each step is essential, but the steps do not necessarily require equal amounts of space. Good persuasive messages do not require separate sentences and paragraphs for each phase of the outline. The message *could* gain the reader's attention and interest in the same sentence, and creating desire *could* require many paragraphs.

nasirkhan/Shutterstock.com

8-1c Apply Sound Writing Principles

The principles of unity, coherence, and emphasis are just as important in persuasive messages as in other messages. In addition, the following principles seem to be especially helpful in preparing persuasive messages:

- **Keep paragraphs short.** The spaces between paragraphs show the dividing place between ideas, improve appearance, and provide convenient resting places for the eyes. Hold the first and last paragraph to three or fewer lines; a one-line paragraph (even a very short line) is acceptable. You can even use paragraphs less than one sentence long by putting four or five words on the first line and completing the sentence in a new paragraph. Be careful to include key attention-getting words that either introduce the product, service, or idea or lead to its introduction.

- **Use concrete nouns and active verbs.** Concrete nouns and active verbs help readers see the product, service, or idea and its benefits more vividly than abstract nouns and passive verbs.

- **Use specific language.** General words won't mean much unless they are well supported with specifics. Specific language is space consuming (saying that something is "great" requires fewer words than telling what makes it so); therefore, persuasive messages are usually longer than other messages. Still, persuasive messages need to be concise; they should say what needs to be said without wasting words.

- **Let readers have the spotlight.** If readers are made the subject of some of the sentences, if they can visualize themselves with the product in their hands, or if they can get the feel of using it for enjoyment or to solve problems, the chances of creating a desire are increased.

- **Stress a central selling point or appeal.** A thorough analysis ordinarily will reveal some feature that is unique or some benefit that is not provided by other viable alternatives—the **central selling point**. This point of difference can be developed into a theme that is woven throughout the entire message. Or, instead of using a point of difference as a central selling point, a writer could choose to stress a major satisfaction to be gained from using the item or doing as asked. A central selling point (theme) should be introduced early and reinforced throughout the remainder of the message.

AIDA the four basic steps of the persuasive process, including gaining attention, generating interest, creating desire, and motivating action

central selling point the primary appeal on which a persuasive message focuses

Letter
Memo

Written

A ATTENTION:
Get the receiver's attention ✓

Email
Instant message
Website
Blog
Text message

Electronic

I INTEREST:
Introduce the product, service, or idea and arouse interest in it ✓

D DESIRE:
Create desire by presenting convincing evidence of the value of the product, service, or idea ✓

In person
Telephone
Voice mail

Spoken

A ACTION:
Encourage action ✓

8-2 SALES MESSAGES

The four-point persuasive outline is appropriate for an *unsolicited sales message*—a letter, memo, or email message written to someone who has not requested it. A *solicited sales message* has been requested by a potential buyer or supporter; that is, the message is prepared to answer this interested person's questions.

A person requesting sales information has given some attention to the product, service, or idea already; therefore, an attention-getting sentence is hardly essential. However,

such a sentence is needed when the audience is not known to have expressed an interest previously. The very first sentence, then, is deliberately designed to make a reader put aside other thoughts and concentrate on the rest of the message.

8-2a Gain Attention

Various techniques have been successful in convincing readers to consider an unsolicited sales message. Regardless of the technique used, the attention-getter should achieve several important objectives: introduce a relationship, focus on a central selling feature, and use an original approach.

SOME COMMONLY USED ATTENTION-GETTING DEVICES INCLUDE:

▶ **A personal experience:** When a doctor gives you instructions, how often have you thought, "I wish you had time to explain" or "I wish I knew more about medical matters"?

▶ **A solution to a problem (outstanding feature/benefit):** Imagine creating a customized multimedia presentation that . . .

▶ **A startling announcement:** One in four auto accidents is the result of texting while driving.

▶ **A what-if opening:** What if I told you there is a savings plan that will enable you to retire three years earlier?

▶ **A question:** Why should you invest in a company that has lost money for six straight years?

▶ **A story:** Here's a typical day in the life of a manager who uses an iPad.

▶ **A proverb or quote from a famous person:** Vince Lombardi, one of the most successful coaches in the history of football, once said, "If winning isn't everything, why do they keep score?" At Winning Edge, we specialize in making you the winner you were born to be.

▶ **A split sentence:** Sandy beaches, turquoise water, and warm breezes . . . it's all awaiting you on your Mesa cruise.

▶ **An analogy:** Like a good neighbor, State Farm is there.

Other attention-getters include a gift, an offer, a bargain, or a comment on an enclosed product sample.

INTRODUCE A RELATIONSHIP BETWEEN THE AUDIENCE AND THE PRODUCT, SERVICE, OR IDEA

Remaining sentences grow naturally from this beginning sentence. If readers do not see the relationship between the first sentence and the sales appeal, they could react negatively to the whole message—they might think they have been tricked into reading it. For example, consider the following poor attention-getter:

> ✗ **Would you like to be the chief executive officer of one of America's largest companies? As CEO of Graham Enterprises, you can launch new products, invest in developing countries, or arrange billion-dollar buyouts. Graham Enterprises is one of several companies at your command in the new computer software game developed by Creative Diversions Software.**

The beginning sentence of the preceding ineffective example is emphatic because it is a short question. However, it suggests the message will be about obtaining a top management position, which it is not. All three sentences, when combined, suggest high pressure. The computer software game has relevant virtues, and one of them could have been emphasized by placing it in the first sentence.

8-2b Focus on a Central Selling Feature

Almost every product, service, or idea will, in some respects be, superior to its competition. If not, such factors as favorable price, fast delivery, or superior service can be used as the primary appeal. This central selling point must be emphasized, and one of the most effective ways to emphasize a point is by its position in the message. An outstanding feature mentioned in the middle of a message might go unnoticed, but it will stand out if mentioned in the first sentence. Note how the following opening sentence introduces the central selling feature and leads naturally into the sentences that follow:

> ✓ **Like running through a sprinkler on a warm summer day, our latest iced coffee creation combines hot and cold in a way that's totally invigorating. The heat comes from the warm cinnamon notes, which you taste on first sip, followed by a sweet orange finish. Our classic Orange Spice iced coffee is there to refresh you all the while. Jump in!**

jpegwiz/Shutterstock.com

8-2c Use an Original Approach

To get the reader's attention and interest, you must offer something new and fresh. Thus, choose an anecdote likely unfamiliar to your audience or use a unique combination of words to describe how a product, service, or idea can solve the reader's problem:

 The nine-year-old boy rushes to the store's toy department, unaware that his parents are far behind him in housewares. Surrounded by the latest action figures, electronic games, and cartoon DVDs, he hardly knows where to start in his search for the perfect gifts to include on his holiday wish list. For the next hour, his parents indulge his enthusiasm as he tries out every displayed product.

In many ways, Adobe Photoshop Elements is like that toy department. The new Photoshop offers a plethora of powerful, useful features that will hold your attention for hours on end.

8-2d Generate Interest by Introducing the Product, Service, or Idea

A persuasive message is certainly off to a good start if the first sentences cause the reader to think, "Here's a solution to one of my problems," "Here's something I need," or "Here's something I want." You can lead the reader to such a thought by introducing the product, service, or idea in the very first sentence. If you do, you can succeed in both getting attention and creating interest in one sentence. An effective introduction of the product, service, or idea is cohesive and action centered, and continues to stress a central selling point.

BE COHESIVE

If the attention-getter does not introduce the product, service, or idea, it should lead naturally into the introduction. In the following example, note the abrupt change in thought and the lack of connection between the attention-getter in the first sentence and the idea presented in the second sentence:

 Employees appreciate a company that provides a safe work environment.

The Adcock Human Resources Association has been conducting a survey for the last six months. Their primary aim is to improve the safety of office work environments.

The last words of the first sentence, "safe work environment," are related to "safety of office work environments"—the last words of the last sentence. No word or phrase in the first sentence connects the words of the second sentence, which creates an abrupt, confusing change in thought. In the following revision, the second sentence is tied to the first by the word *that's*. *Safety* in the second sentence refers to *protection* in the third. The LogicTech low-radiation monitor is introduced as a means of providing a safe work environment. Additionally, notice that the attention-getter leads smoothly into the discussion of the survey results.

Employees appreciate a company that provides a safe work environment.

That's one thing that the Tucker Human Resources Association learned from its six-month survey on office work environment safety. For added protection from radiation emissions, more companies are purchasing LogicTech's low-radiation computer monitors . . .

BE ACTION ORIENTED

To introduce your offering in an interesting way, you must place the product, service, or idea in your audience's hands and talk about using it, or benefiting from accepting your idea. Your audience will get a clearer picture when reading about something happening than when reading a product description. Also, the picture becomes all the more vivid when the reader is in the spotlight. In a sense, you do not sell products, services, or ideas; instead, you sell the pleasure people derive from their use. Logically, then, you have to focus more on that use than on the offering itself. If you put readers to work using your product, service, or idea to solve problems, they will be the subject of most of your sentences.

Some product description is necessary and natural. In the following example, the writer focuses on the product and creates an uninteresting, still picture:

✗ **The Elise CR is a stripped-back racer that doesn't just deliver on the road. Eibach anti-roll bar and springs plus Bilstein sports dampers mean the Elise CR provides fingertip responsiveness on the racetrack, too.**

In the revision, a person is the subject of the message and is enjoying the benefits of the sports car.

✓ **Channel your inner Kimi Räikkönen in this stripped-back racer worthy of the best Formula One tracks in the world. The Elise CR is an uncompromised sports machine that doesn't just deliver on the road. Eibach anti-roll bar and springs plus Bilstein sports dampers mean the Elise CR provides fingertip responsiveness on the racetrack, too. Handling is assisted further with the latest Lotus Dynamic Performance Management (DPM) system, and selectable Sport setting, giving the driver ultimate power and control.[2]**

STRESS A CENTRAL SELLING POINT

If the attention-getter does not introduce a distinctive feature, it should lead to it. Note how the attention-getter in the following example introduces the distinctive

selling feature, app availability, and how the following sentences keep the audience's eyes focused on that feature:

✓ **With more than 375,000 apps made just for iPad, there's almost no end to what you can do. These aren't merely scaled-up versions of phone apps that lack features designed for a larger screen. They're powerful apps tailor-made to take full advantage of everything iPad has to offer. And because iPad and iPad mini are so thoughtfully designed, virtually every app works on both devices.**

With iPad, all that content is available from one source: Apple. The iTunes Store is the world's largest and most trusted entertainment store. Other mobile platforms have a myriad of fragmented store options, resulting in availability issues, developer frustration, and security risks.[3]

By stressing one main point, you do not limit the message to that point. For example, although app availability is being stressed, other features are also mentioned.

8-2e Create Desire by Providing Convincing Evidence

After you have made an interesting introduction to your product, service, or idea, present enough supporting evidence to satisfy your audience's needs. Keep one or two main features uppermost in the reader's mind, and include evidence that supports these features. For example, using fuel economy as an outstanding selling feature of hybrid cars, while presenting abundant evidence about performance, would be inconsistent.

PRESENT AND INTERPRET FACTUAL EVIDENCE

Few people will believe general statements without having supporting factual evidence. Saying a certain method is efficient is not enough. You must say how it is efficient and present some data to illustrate this. Saying a piece of furniture is durable is not enough. Durability exists in varying degrees. You must present information that

shows what makes it durable and also define how durable. Durability can be established, for example, by presenting information about the manufacturing process, the quality of the raw materials, or the skill of the workers:

✓ **If you're looking for plush comfort, then look no further than Ashley's DuraPella® upholstery collection. DuraPella® is a high-tech fabric that is a breakthrough in comfort and durability. DuraPella® consists of 100% MicroDenier Polyester Suede, which gives you the subtle look and elegant feel of suede, yet is durable and stain-resistant . . . the best of both worlds! Everyday spills like coffee, wine, and even ballpoint pen are cleaned easily and effectively with a mixture of low pH balance liquid soap and water. You can enjoy luxury in everyday living with DuraPella®.**

Presenting research evidence (hard facts and figures) to support your statements is another way to increase your chances of convincing your audience. Presenting results of a research study takes space but makes the message much more convincing than general remarks about superior durability and appearance.

Evidence must not only *be* authentic; it must *sound* authentic, too. Talking about pages treated with special protectants to retard aging and machine-sewn construction suggests the sender is well informed, which increases audience confidence. Facts and figures are even more impressive if they reflect comparative advantage, as illustrated in the following example:

✓ **With thousands of new viruses created every day, relying on traditional security updates isn't enough anymore. Unlike the competition, exclusive McAfee Total Protection™ technology instantly analyzes and blocks new and emerging threats in milliseconds, so there's virtually no gap in your protection. McAfee is 99.9% effective in detecting malware, the best rating among competitors.[4]**

Naturally, your audience will be less familiar with the product, service, or idea and its uses than you will be. Not only do you have an obligation to give information, you should interpret it if necessary and point out how the information will benefit the audience. Notice how the following example clearly interprets *why* an induction cooktop is superior to electric or gas cooktops. The interpretation makes the evidence understandable and thus convincing.

Cold Statement Without Interpretation	**Specific, Interpreted Fact**
Cooking with an induction cooktop is the latest in technology for a restaurant environment or for just the average household.	Induction cooking is an entirely new way of cooking. Forget about red-hot electric coils or open gas flames. An induction cooktop converts your cookware into the heating element by using a magnetic field to energize the atoms in the cookware. Your food cooks faster, using less energy, while providing you with instantaneous temperature control.

The previous example uses a valuable interpretative technique—the comparison. You can often make a point more convincing by comparing something unfamiliar with something familiar. Most people are familiar with electric coils and gas flames, so they can now visualize how the cookware becomes the heating element. A comparison can also be used to interpret prices. Advertisers frequently compare the cost of sponsoring a child in a third-world country to the price of a fast-food lunch. An insurance representative might write this sentence: *The monthly premium for $300,000 of term life insurance is $18, the cost of two movie tickets.*

Do not go overboard and bore or frustrate your audience with an abundance of facts or technical data. Never make your reader feel ignorant by trying to impress him or her with facts and figures he or she might not understand.

BE OBJECTIVE

Use language people will believe. Specific, concrete language makes your message sound authentic. Excessive superlatives, exaggerations, flowery statements, unsupported claims, and incomplete comparisons all make your message sound like high-pressure sales talk. Just one such sentence can destroy confidence in the whole message. Examine the statements in the following paragraphs to see whether they give convincing evidence. Would they make a reader want to buy? Or do they merely remind the audience of someone's desire to sell?

This antibiotic is the best on the market today. It represents the very latest in biochemical research. Identifying the best-selling antibiotic requires gathering information about all antibiotics marketed and then choosing the one with superior characteristics. You know the sender is likely to have a bias in favor of the particular drug being sold. However, you do not know whether the sender actually spent time

FIGURE 8.6 | GOOD EXAMPLE OF A PERSUASIVE CLAIM

Anderson Volk
Simplicity Restaurant
3443 Fruit Arbor Street
Boise, ID 82009
May 2, 2017

Donna Hopkins, Partner
Hopkins and Lowe Architects.
234 27th Avenue
Salt Lake City, UT 83201

Dear Donna:

When Simplicity Restaurant negotiated with your firm to design our new building façade, we were impressed with your previous track record of success. Especially impressive was the building you designed for AppWorks Technologies here in Boise with its simplicity of structure and abundant use of glass to bring in natural lighting and provide access to its park-like surroundings.

In our meeting with your architects, we discussed a façade design that incorporated some of these features but relates harmoniously with the existing building. However, after viewing the initial plan and drawings for the facade, we were disappointed with the planned transition from the more traditional design of the existing building with that to the more modern façade.

With Hopkins and Lowe's reputation for innovative architectural designs, we are confident that the plans can be redrawn to better meet our expectations. We are happy to meet with you again if you would like more specific suggestions regarding changes. Please call me at 330-662-4434 if a meeting would be helpful in this regard.

Sincerely,

Anderson Volk
Anderson Volk, Owner

- Seeks attention by giving a sincere compliment that reveals the subject of the message.

- Continues central appeal—commitment to creative production—while providing needed details.

- Presents reasoning that leads to a request and a subtle reminder of the central appeal.

- *Connects the specific request with the firm's commitment to develop a creative production.*

Legal and Ethical Consideration

- *Uses letter rather than less formal email format to add formality to contractual agreement.*

The most serious weakness is asking for action too quickly and providing no incentive for action. Sometimes the reward for taking action is small and indirect, but the message needs to make these benefits evident.

8-3d Persuading Within an Organization

The majority of memos are of a routine nature and essential for the day-to-day operation of the business, for example, giving instructions for performing work assignments, scheduling meetings, and providing project progress reports. In many organizations, such matters are handled through the use of email rather than paper memos. These routine messages, as well as messages conveying good news, are written deductively. However, some circumstances require that a supervisor write a persuasive message that motivates employees to accept a change in their jobs that might have a negative effect on the employees or generate resistance (e.g., a job transfer, a change in work procedures, or a software upgrade).

For example, imagine that Pub on the Green restaurant was faced with the challenge of communicating

FIGURE 8.7 POOR EXAMPLE OF A PERSUASIVE REQUEST (ASKING A FAVOR)

I am unable to buy my spa maintenance supplies at your store. It would be much more convenient for me to be able to do so. I could avoid a trip across town to the pool supply store.

Would you consider stocking hot tub and spa maintenance supplies in your store for my added convenience?

- Does not use an inductive approach to set a more positive tone. Fails to provide good reasons to comply with the request.

- Close does little to build goodwill or encourage compliance.

FIGURE 8.8 GOOD EXAMPLE OF A PERSUASIVE REQUEST (ASKING A FAVOR)

Viann Pope, Owner and Manager
South Shores Hardware
San Pedro, CA 84330

June 21, 2017

Dear Ms. Pope:

As a regular customer of South Shores Hardware, my family and I appreciate being able to buy our home improvement products from a locally owned business that cares about the community. We also are grateful for the expert advice provided by your friendly and helpful staff.

Your store provides all of the products that most do-it-yourselfers might need for their home improvement projects. This includes maintenance products, such as pool supplies. Adding a line of maintenance products for hot tubs and spas would provide additional convenience for your customers and supplement your current pool supply offerings.

By broadening your product offerings, you will continue to build a reputation as a local business that is attentive to its customers' needs and concerns.

Sincerely,

Lars Tingen
Lars Tingen

- Begins with a sincere compliment that sets the stage for the request that follows.

- Explains the rationale for the request with a discussion of the benefits to the store and its customers.

- *Connects a specific action to the rewards for taking the action.*

to its employees about a significant change in service and style, which included new uniforms. Rather than coercing or demanding that employees accept the change, a letter from the president could emphasize the reasons the changes were being made (benefits to guests, the company, and the employees) and the employee's important role in implementing the changes. Using a lighthearted, entertaining approach, the message could include (a) a visual model of the fresh, crisp, and professional look that the company expected with the uniform

Robin Lund/Shutterstock.com

darsi/Shutterstock.com

change and (b) helpful information on ways to achieve this look. The following excerpt shows how a "you" orientation, and "style flashes" could be interwoven into the letter:

- *Make sure your hair is neatly tied back. Messy hair is a problem for guests—they don't want it getting it into their food. You might even get a better tip.*

- *Don't wear a lot of bling. Guests may think you don't need as large a tip.*

- *Remember to smile. Your smile is the first sign to guests that their Pub on the Green experience will be a memorable one. Your smile tells guests, "I'm glad you came!" But don't just take our word for it. A recent Bay College study found that smiling reflects an awareness of other people and their needs. That's probably why a "winning smile" is so charming!*

The detailed language leaves no doubt in an employee's mind as to what management considers clean, crisp, and professional. However, by continually emphasizing the benefits employees gain from the change, management garners support for the high standards being imposed.

Similarly, employees must often make persuasive requests of their supervisors. For example, they might recommend a change in procedure, acquisition of equipment or software, or attendance at a professional development program. They might justify a promotion or job reclassification or recommendation for policy changes, and so on. Persuasive memos and email messages are longer than most routine messages because of the extra space needed for developing an appeal and providing convincing evidence.

When preparing to write the memo in Figure 8.9, a manager recognizes that implementation costs could affect the president's reaction to his or her proposal to implement a work-at-home policy. Anticipating resistance, the manager writes inductively and builds a logical, compelling argument for his or her proposal.

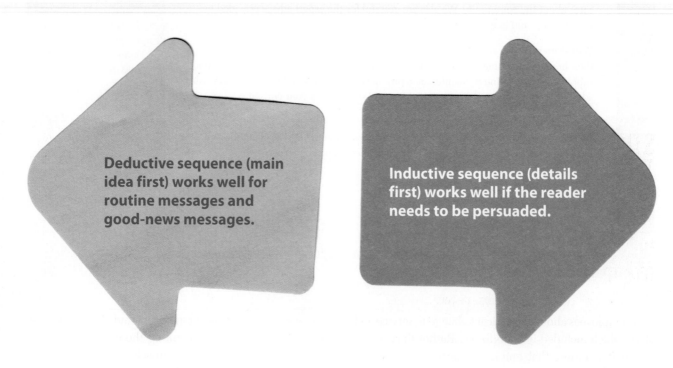

Deductive sequence (main idea first) works well for routine messages and good-news messages.

Inductive sequence (details first) works well if the reader needs to be persuaded.

FIGURE 8.9 GOOD EXAMPLE OF A PERSUASIVE MESSAGE

To: Sara Azhang [sazhang@johnsonassociates.com]
From: Larry Brown [lbrown@johnsonassociates.com]
Subject: Work-at-home policy

During our supervisors' meeting last month, HR Director Cal Waters noted a significant increase in lost productivity because of employee absences. He provided a brief summary of the reasons cited by management, many having to do with personal obligations, such as trips to the doctor, teacher conferences, and other absences related to children's needs. As you may recall, I offered to do some research on how departments like our own have responded to this issue.

My research has found that many departments charged with data-analysis duties have responded by implementing work-at-home policies. There are some important benefits to organizations that implement work-at-home policies, such as dramatically lowering capital expenditures on office and parking spaces, as well as higher satisfaction among employees. Little evidence exists to support such common fears as lower productivity.

In my research, I found that it is important to have a well-planned, specific policy statement regarding work-at-home programs to ensure effectiveness. I have taken the liberty of gathering a sample of work-at-home policies from similar departments that might be used to author a similar document for our department.

With our goals of decreasing employee absences and enhancing productivity, would you allow me to present a summary of my findings to Waters next month? I would be eager to gain your feedback and suggestions on such a presentation. I believe I can put together a draft of such a presentation for your review within a week with your approval of this proposal.

- **Opens with a reference to a meeting discussion and company goal.**
- **Presents a solution to the identified problem.**
- **Builds interest by mentioning the benefits of the program.**
- *Alludes to the benefits and closes with a specific action to be taken.*

STUDY TOOLS 8

LOCATED AT THE BACK OF THE TEXTBOOK

☐ Tear-Out Chapter Review Card

LOCATED AT WWW.CENGAGEBRAIN.COM

☐ Review Key Term flashcards and create your own cards

☐ Track your knowledge and understanding of key concepts in business communication

☐ Complete practice and graded quizzes to prepare for tests

☐ Complete interactive content within BCOM9 Online

☐ View the chapter highlight boxes for BCOM9 Online

PART 4

9 | Understanding the Report Process and Research Methods

Andrey_Popov/Shutterstock.com

LEARNING OBJECTIVES

After studying this chapter, you should be able to …

9-1 Identify the characteristics of a report and the various classifications of business reports.

9-2 Apply the steps in the problem-solving process.

9-3 Use appropriate printed, electronic, and primary source information.

9-4 Demonstrate the appropriate methods of collecting, organizing, and referencing information.

9-5 Explain techniques for the logical analysis and interpretation of data.

After finishing this chapter, go to **PAGE 174** for **STUDY TOOLS.**

CHARACTERISTICS OF REPORTS

9-1a Types of Reports

"Hi, Kate. This is Lewis in sales. Do you know whether the latest sales figures report is ready? My supervisor wants me to review it in preparation for next week's presentation."

"Hi, Lewis. Yes, I just finished a draft of the report yesterday. I will email it to you right now. If there are any changes, I will let you know."

This brief exchange illustrates a simple reporting task. A question has been posed, and the answer given (along with the supporting information) satisfies the reporting requirement. Although Kate may have never have studied report preparation, she did an excellent job; so Lewis can prepare to report the sales figures. Kate's spoken report is a simple illustration of the four main characteristics of reports:

- **Reports typically travel upward in an organization because they usually are requested by a higher authority.** In most cases, people would not generate reports unless requested to do so.

- **Reports are logically organized.** In Kate's case, she answered Lewis's question first and then supported the answer with evidence to justify it. Through your study of message organization, you learned the difference between deductive and inductive organization. Kate's report was deductively organized. If Kate had given the supporting evidence first and followed with the answer that she would meet the deadline, the organization of her reply would have been inductive and would still have been logical.

- **Reports are objective.** Because reports contribute to decision making and problem solving, they should be as objective as possible. When nonobjective (subjective) material is included, the report writer should make that known.

- **Reports are generally prepared for a limited audience.** This characteristic is particularly true of reports traveling within an organization. This means that reports, like letters, memos, and emails, should be prepared with the receivers' needs in mind.

> Because reports contribute to decision making and problem solving, they should be as objective as possible.

Based on the four characteristics, a workable definition of a *report* is an orderly, objective message used to convey information from one organizational area to another or from one organization to another to assist in decision making or problem solving. Reports have been classified by management and by report-preparation authorities in numerous ways. The form, direction, functional use, and content of the report are used as bases for classification. However, a single report might fit several classifications. The following brief review of classification illustrates the scope of reporting, and establishes a basis for studying reports.

- **Formal or informal reports.** The formal/informal classification is particularly helpful because it applies to all reports. A **formal report** is carefully structured; it is logically organized and objective, contains a lot of detail, and is written in a style that tends to eliminate such elements as personal pronouns. An **informal report** is usually a short message written in natural or personal language. An internal memo generally can be described as an informal report. All reports can be placed on a continuum of formality, as shown in Figure 9.1. The distinction between the degrees of formality of various reports is explained more fully in Chapter 11.

- **Short or long reports.** Reports can generally be classified as short or long. A one-page memo is obviously short, and a report of 20 pages is obviously long. What about in-between lengths? One important distinction generally holds true: as it becomes longer, a report takes on more characteristics of formal reports. Thus, the classifications of formal/informal and short/long are closely related.

- **Informational or analytical reports.** An **informational report** carries objective information from one area

formal report a carefully structured report that is logically organized and objective, contains a lot of detail, and is written in a style that tends to eliminate such elements as personal pronouns

informal report usually a short message written in natural or personal language

informational report a report that carries objective information from one area of an organization to another

FIGURE 9.1   REPORT FORMALITY CONTINUUM

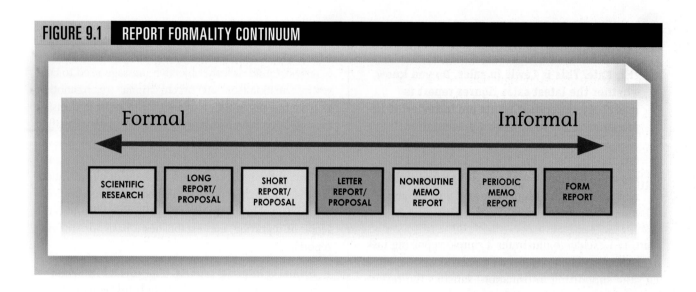

Formal   Informal

| SCIENTIFIC RESEARCH | LONG REPORT/ PROPOSAL | SHORT REPORT/ PROPOSAL | LETTER REPORT/ PROPOSAL | NONROUTINE MEMO REPORT | PERIODIC MEMO REPORT | FORM REPORT |

of an organization to another. An **analytical report** presents suggested solutions to problems. Company annual reports, monthly financial statements, reports of sales volume, and reports of employee or personnel absenteeism and turnover are informational reports. Reports on scientific research, real estate appraisal reports, and feasibility reports by consulting firms are analytical reports.

- **Vertical or lateral reports.** The vertical/lateral classification refers to the directions in which reports travel. Although most reports travel upward in organizations, many travel downward. Both represent vertical reports and are often referred to as *upward-directed* and *downward-directed* reports. The main function of **vertical reports** is to contribute to management *control*, as shown in Figure 9.2. **Lateral reports**, on the other hand, assist in *coordination* in the organization. A report traveling between units on the same organizational level, such as between the

FIGURE 9.2   THE GENERAL UPWARD FLOW OF REPORTS

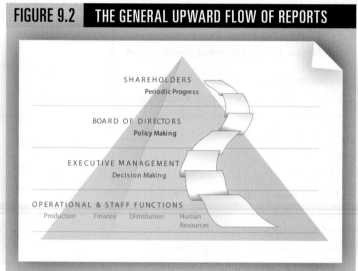

SHAREHOLDERS
Periodic Progress

BOARD OF DIRECTORS
Policy Making

EXECUTIVE MANAGEMENT
Decision Making

OPERATIONAL & STAFF FUNCTIONS
Production   Finance   Distribution   Human Resources

production department and the finance department, is lateral.

- **Internal or external reports.** An **internal report**, such as a production or sales report, travels within an organization. An **external report**, such as a company's annual report to stockholders, is prepared for distribution outside an organization.

- **Periodic reports.** **Periodic reports** are issued on regularly scheduled dates. They are generally directed upward and serve management control purposes. Daily, weekly, monthly, quarterly, semiannual, and annual time periods are typical for periodic reports. Preprinted forms and computer-generated data contribute to the uniformity of periodic reports.

- **Functional reports.** A **functional report** serves a specified purpose within a company. The

analytical report a report that presents suggested solutions to problems

vertical report a report that can be upward- or downward-directed

lateral report a report that travels between units on the same organizational level

internal report a report that travels within an organization, such as a production or sales report

external report a report prepared for distribution outside an organization

periodic report a report that is issued on regularly scheduled dates

functional report a report that serves a specified purpose within a company

functional classification includes accounting reports, marketing reports, financial reports, personnel reports, and a variety of other reports that take their functional designation from their ultimate use. For example, a justification of the need for additional personnel or for new equipment is described as a *justification report* in the functional classification.

9-1b Proposals

A **proposal** is a written description of how one organization can meet the needs of another, for example, by providing products or services or solving problems. Businesses issue *calls for bids* that present the specifications for major purchases of goods and certain services. Most governmental and nonprofit agencies issue *requests for proposals*, or RFPs. Potential suppliers prepare proposal reports telling how they can meet that need. Those preparing the proposal create a convincing document that will lead to obtaining a contract.

Biz Idea Production/Shutterstock.com

In our information-intensive society, proposal preparation is a major activity for many firms. In fact, some companies hire consultants or designate employees to specialize in proposal writing. Chapter 11 presents proposal preparation in considerable detail.

As you review these report classifications, you will very likely decide—correctly—that almost all reports could be included in these categories. A report may be formal or informal, short or long, informational or analytical, vertically or laterally directed, internal or external, or periodic or non-periodic, as well as functionally labeled, a proposal, or some other combination of these classifications. These report categories are in common use and provide necessary terminology for the study and production of reports.

9-2 BASIS FOR REPORTS: THE PROBLEM-SOLVING PROCESS

The upward flow of reports provides management with data that someone might use to make a decision. The purpose is to use the data to solve a problem. Some problems are recurring and call for a steady flow of information;

other problems might be unique and call for information on a one-time basis. A problem is the basis for a report. The following steps are used for finding a solution:

1. Recognize and define the problem.
2. Select a method of solution.
3. Collect and organize the data and document the sources.
4. Arrive at an answer.

Only after all four steps have been completed is a report written for presentation. Reports represent an attempt to communicate how a problem was solved. These problem-solving steps are completed *before* the report is written in final form.

9-2a Recognizing and Defining the Problem

Problem-solving research cannot begin until the researchers define the problem. Frequently, those requesting a report will attempt to provide a suitable definition. Nevertheless, researchers should attempt to state the problem clearly and precisely in order to ensure they are on the right track.

USING PROBLEM STATEMENTS, STATEMENTS OF PURPOSE, AND HYPOTHESES

The **problem statement** is the particular problem that is to be solved by the research. The **statement of purpose** is the goal of the study and includes the aims or objectives that the researcher hopes to accomplish. Research studies often have both a problem statement and a statement of purpose. For example, a real estate appraiser accepts a client's request to appraise a building to determine its market value. The problem is to arrive at a fair market value for the property. The purpose of the appraisal, however, might be to establish a value for a mortgage loan, to determine the feasibility of adding to the structure, or to assess the financial possibility of demolishing the structure and erecting something else. Thus, the purpose might have much to do with determining what elements to consider in arriving at an answer. In other words, unless you know *why* something is wanted, you might have difficulty knowing *what* is wanted. Once you arrive at the answers to the *what* and *why* questions, you will be on your way to solving the problem.

proposal a written description of how one organization can meet the needs of another

problem statement the particular problem that is to be solved by the research

statement of purpose the goal of the study; includes the aims or objectives the researcher hopes to accomplish

Hypotheses are statements that may be proved or disproved through research.

Sergey Nivens/Shutterstock.com

A **hypothesis** is a statement to be proved or disproved through research. For example, a study of work teams might be made to determine the factors that predict success. An observation might lead one to believe that a key factor in determining success was the quality of communication, as defined by equal participation. For this problem, the hypothesis could be formulated in this way:

Hypothesis: Productivity will increase when team members participate equally in discussions, as compared with teams in which one or two members dominate.

Because the hypothesis tends to be stated in a way that favors one possibility or is prejudiced toward a particular answer, many researchers prefer to state hypotheses in the null form. The *null hypothesis* states that no relationship or difference will be found in the factors being studied, which tends to remove the element of prejudice toward a certain answer. The null hypothesis for the previous example could be written as follows:

Null hypothesis: No significant difference will be found in productivity between teams in which members participate in discussions equally, and teams in which one or two members dominate.

Using the problem/purpose approach, the hypothesis approach, or both, is a choice of the researcher. In many ways, the purpose of a study is determined by the intended use of its results.

hypothesis a statement to be proved or disproved through research

LIMITING THE SCOPE OF THE PROBLEM

A major shortcoming that often occurs in research planning is the failure to establish or to recognize desirable limits. The *scope* of the report helps to establish boundaries in which the report will be researched and prepared. Assume, for instance, that you want to study the effectiveness of Internet sales. Imagine the enormity of such a task. Millions of people use the Internet to make product purchases on thousands of different websites. Use the *what, why, when, where,* and *who* questions to reduce such a problem to reasonable proportions.

LIMITS YOU MIGHT SET AS THE SALES MANAGER OF A RETAIL COMPANY:

What:	A study of Internet product sales
Why:	To determine whether to create an Internet sales division
When:	Current
Where:	United States
Who:	Customers who purchase computer products online

Now you can phrase the problem this way:

Statement of purpose: The purpose of this study is to survey online sales of computer products in the United States as compared with storefront sales.

Note that this process of reducing the problem to a workable size has also established some firm limits to the research. You have limited the problem to website functionality, the particular area, and a certain group of users. Note, too, how important the *why* was in helping to establish the limits. Limiting the problem is "zeroing in on the problem."

In some reports, it is desirable to differentiate between the boundaries that were placed on the project outside the control of the researchers and those that were chosen by the researchers. Boundaries imposed outside the control of the researchers are called *limitations*; they might include the assignment of the topic, the allotted budget, and time required in order to complete the report. These boundaries affect what and how the topic can be researched. Boundaries chosen by the researchers to make the project more manageable are called *delimitations*; they might include the sources and methods chosen for research.

DEFINING TERMS CLEARLY

Words often have more than one meaning, and technical or special-use words might occur in the report that are not widely used or understood. Such terms would require a definition in order for the reader to understand the presented information. In the previously used example concerning the Internet product sales a comparison of the Internet product sales with those storefront retail outlets would be meaningful only if the information gathered from the latter is similar to that of the former. A list of products sold by an Internet-based retail outlet, for example, would help ensure that the same products are sold by storefront outlets.

DOCUMENTING PROCEDURES

The procedures or steps a writer takes in preparing a report are often recorded as a part of the written report. This **procedures** section, or **methodology**, adds credibility to the research process and also enables subsequent researchers to repeat, or replicate, the study in another setting or at a later time. Reports that study the same factors in different time frames are called **longitudinal studies**.

The procedures section of a report records the major steps taken in the research, and, possibly, the reasons for their inclusion. It might, for instance, tell the types of printed and electronic sources that were consulted, and the groups of people who were interviewed and how they were selected. Steps in the procedures section are typically listed in chronological order so that the reader has an overall understanding of the timetable that existed for the project.

 9-3 **SELECTING A METHOD OF GATHERING INFORMATION**

After defining the problem, the researcher will plan how to arrive at a solution. The research methods you use to collect necessary information can be secondary, primary, or both.

Kheng Guan Toh/Shutterstock.com

9-3a Secondary Research

Secondary research provides information that has already been created by others. Researchers save time and effort by not duplicating research that has already been undertaken. They can access this information easily through the aid of electronic databases and bibliographic indexes. Suppose that a marketing manager has been asked to investigate the feasibility of implementing a strategic information system. The manager knows other companies are using this technology. By engaging in secondary research, the manager can determine the boundaries of knowledge before proceeding into the unknown.

Certain truths have been established and treated as principles reported in textbooks and other publications. However, because knowledge is constantly expanding, the researcher knows that new information is available. The job, then, is to canvass the literature of the field and attempt to redefine the boundaries of knowledge.

Secondary research can be gathered by means of traditional printed sources or by using electronic tools.

PRINTED SOURCES

Major categories of printed sources are books, periodicals, and government documents. Books are typically cataloged in libraries by call number, with larger libraries using the Library of Congress classification system. Traditional card catalogs in libraries have been replaced by online catalogs, which allow the user to locate desired books by author, title, subject, or keyword. A wide

procedures (or methodology) the steps a writer takes in preparing a report; often recorded as a part of the written report

longitudinal studies reports that study the same factors in different time frames

secondary research provides information that has already been reported by others

10 | Managing Data and Using Graphics

Sergey Nivens/Shutterstock.com

LEARNING OBJECTIVES

After studying this chapter, you will be able to...

10-1 Communicate quantitative information effectively.

10-2 Apply principles of effectiveness and ethical responsibilities in the construction of graphic aids.

10-3 Select and design appropriate and meaningful graphics.

10-4 Integrate graphics within documents.

After finishing
this chapter, go
to **PAGE 188** for
STUDY TOOLS.

10-1 ## COMMUNICATING QUANTITATIVE INFORMATION

Before you can interpret quantitative data, the elements must be classified, summarized, and condensed into a manageable size. This condensed information is meaningful and can be used to answer your research questions. For example, assume that you have been given 400 completed questionnaires from a study of your current clients' future travel destinations. This large accumulation of data is overwhelming until you tabulate the responses for each questionnaire item by manually inputting or compiling responses received through an online survey, or optically scanning the responses into a computer. Then, you can apply appropriate statistical analysis techniques to the tabulated data.

The computer generates a report of the total responses for each possible answer to each item. For example, the tabulation of responses from each client about his or her future travel destinations might appear like this:

Hawaii	329
Caribbean	278
Alaska	218
Europe	185
Mexico	120

The breakdown reduces 400 responses to a manageable set of information. The tabulation shows only five items, each with a specific number of responses from the total of 400 questionnaires. Because people tend to make comparisons during analysis, the totals are helpful. People generally want to know proportions or ratios, and these are best presented as percentage parts of the total.

Future Travel Destinations	Number	Percentage
Hawaii	329	82
Caribbean	278	69.5
Alaska	218	54.5
Europe	185	46.25
Mexico	120	30

Now, analyzing the data becomes relatively easy. Of the survey participants, 82% selected Hawaii, while only 30% selected Mexico. Other observations, depending on how exactly you intend to interpret percentages, could be that more than half selected Alaska. Combining data in two categories allows you to summarize that all respondents intend to take a tropical island vacation in the future.

When tabulating research results of people's opinions, likes, preferences, and other subjective items, rounding off statistics to fractions helps paint a clear picture for readers. In actuality, if the same group of people were asked this question again a day or two later, a few probably would have changed their minds. For example, a participant who had not indicated a desire to travel to Europe may have attended a travel show that increased her or his interest in doing so. The next day, the respondent might indicate a desire to travel to Europe in the future.

> Because people tend to make comparisons during analysis, the totals are helpful.

Fractions, ratios, and percentages are examples of **common language**. In effect, common language reduces difficult figures to the "common denominators" of language and ideas. Although "218 of 400 expect to travel to Alaska in the future" is somewhat easy to understand, "54.4% prefer . . ." is even easier, and "one out of two indicate a preference for traveling to Alaska" is even more understandable.

Common language also involves the use of indicators other than actual count or quantity. The Dow Jones Industrial Average provides a measure of stock market performance and is certainly easier to understand than the complete New York Stock Exchange figures. Similarly, oil is counted in barrels rather than in the quart or gallon sizes purchased by consumers. Because of inflation, dollars are not accurate items to use as comparisons from one year to another in certain areas. For example, automobile manufacturers use "automobile units" to represent production changes in the industry. The important thing for the report writer to remember is that reports are communication media, and everything possible should be done to make sure communication occurs effectively.

10-2 ## USING GRAPHICS

Imagine trying to put in composition style all the information available in a financial statement. Several hundred pages might be necessary to explain

common language
reduces difficult figures to the common denominators of language and ideas

material that could otherwise be contained in three or four pages of balance sheets and income statements. Even then, the reader would no doubt be thoroughly confused! To protect readers from being overwhelmed or simply bored with data, report writers can design visually appealing graphics that are appropriate for the data being presented. Data reported in a table, graph, or picture will make your written analysis clearer to the reader.

Roger Asbury/Shutterstock.com

The term **graphics** is used in this chapter to refer to all types of illustrations used in written and spoken reports. The most commonly used graphics are tables, bar charts, line charts, pie charts, pictograms, maps, flowcharts, diagrams, and photographs.

10-2a **Effective and Ethical Use of Graphics**

graphics all types of illustrations used in written and spoken reports

The use of graphics with a written discussion serves three purposes: to clarify, to simplify, or to reinforce

data. As you read this chapter, ask yourself if the discussion would be effective if the accompanying graphic figures were not included. Use the following questions to help you determine whether using a graphic element is appropriate and effective in a written or spoken report.

- **Is a graphic needed to clarify, reinforce, or emphasize a particular idea?** Or can the material be covered adequately in words rather than in visual ways? To maintain a reasonable balance between words and graphics, save graphics for data that are difficult to communicate in words alone.

- **Does the graphic presentation contribute to the overall understanding of the idea under discussion?** Will the written or spoken text add meaning to the graphic display?

- **Is the graphic easily understood?** Does the graphic emphasize the key idea and spur the reader to think intelligently about this information? Follow these important design principles:

  ° **Avoid *chartjunk*.** This term, coined by design expert Edward Tufte, describes decorative

---

ADAPTING YOUR PRESENTATION FOR YOUTUBE

YouTube is a great potential resource for a business and can be used to distribute your sales message or training material to a wide audience. The easily accessed website can be a great avenue for sharing business presentations; however, some adaptation is necessary for the best effect.

▶ **Keep it short.** The average viewing time for a YouTube clip is 2.5 minutes. If you must stay with a longer presentation format, divide it into several short segments posted as separate videos.

▶ **Make it loud and clear.** Use an external microphone rather than relying on one built into the camera. Your audio quality will be much improved.

▶ **Avoid bulleted PowerPoint slides.** Bullet points will appear blurry on YouTube and be next to impossible to read. Edit your content and change it to full-screen slides before uploading.

Yeamake/Shutterstock.com

Viewers don't have the time or inclination to struggle through a long, poorly prepared video. Make sure your postings on social media sites are "online compatible."[1]

distractions that bury relevant data.[2] Extreme use of color, complicated symbols and art techniques, and unusual combinations of typefaces reduce the impact of the material presented.

○ **Develop a consistent design for graphics.** Arbitrary changes in the design of graphics (e.g., use of colors, typefaces, three-dimensional, or flat designs) within a written or spoken report can be confusing as the receiver expects consistency in elements within a single report.

○ **Write meaningful titles that reinforce the point that you are making.** For example, a receiver can interpret data faster when graphics use a talking title; that is, a title that interprets the data. Consider the usefulness of the following graphic titles for a customer service manager browsing through survey results in preparation for a meeting with top management:

Descriptive Title:	*White-Cell Counts During April*
Talking Title:	*White-Cell Counts have Fallen Throughout April*

• The talking title saves the manager time in understanding the data and also ensures the accuracy of her or his interpretation, recommendations, and the content of her or his presentation. Similarly, poor business decisions can be averted if graphic titles reveal key information. You will learn more about the appropriate use of descriptive and talking headings as you study the preparation of informational and analytical reports in Chapter 11.

• **Is the graphic honest?** Visual data can be distorted easily, leading the reader to form incorrect opinions about the data.

• **Can a graphic used in a presentation be seen by the entire audience?** Electronic presentations, flip charts, whiteboards, and overhead transparencies are the visual means most often used to accompany presentations.

The key to preparing effective graphics is selecting an appropriate graphic for the data and developing a clean, simple design that allows the reader or audience to quickly extract the needed information and meaning.

> We remember more of what we both see and hear than of what we receive through only one sensory channel. When text and graphics are combined, retention goes up an average of 42%.[3]

10-3 TYPES OF GRAPHIC AIDS

Using powerful software programs, managers can perform the data management functions discussed in this chapter, producing highly professional graphics. The information can be reproduced in a variety of ways for integrating into reports and supporting highly effective presentations.

Selecting the graphic type that will depict data in the most effective manner is the first decision you must make. After identifying the idea that you want your receiver to understand, you can choose to use a table, bar chart, line chart, pie chart, flowchart, organizational chart, photographs, models, and so on. Use Figure 10.1 on the next page to help you choose the graphic type that matches the objective you hope to achieve.

Figures 10.2 through 10.7 on the following pages illustrate a variety of graphics commonly used in reports. The figures show

Rawpixel.com/Shutterstock.com

Castleski/Shutterstock.com

chance of errors. The flowchart in Figure 10.7 illustrates the steps in a simple writing process. Presenting this information graphically makes it much easier to understand than a written explanation of the process.

Organizational charts, discussed in Chapter 1, are widely used to provide a picture of the authority structure and relationships within an organization. They provide employees with an idea of what their organization looks like in terms of the flow of authority and responsibility. When businesses change (because of new employees or reorganization of units and responsibilities), organizational charts must be revised. Revisions to organizational charts are simple when prepared using word-processing or graphics software.

10-3g Other Graphics

Other graphics, such as architectural plans, photographs, cartoons, blueprints, and lists of various kinds, may be included in reports. Figure 10.8 shows a blueprint of the Statue of Liberty. The availability of graphics and sophisticated drawing software facilitate inclusion of these more complex visuals in reports and spoken presentations. Photographs are used frequently in annual reports to help the general audience understand complex concepts and to make the documents more appealing to read. Frequently, you must include some graphic material in a report otherwise, the narrative discussion would become unwieldy. In this case, the material might be placed in an appendix and only referred to in the report.

may require slight deviations. For example, if you intend to explode the largest pie slice, placing it in the 12 o'clock position may not be desirable because the slice is likely to intrude into the space occupied by a title positioned above the graphic.

10-3e Maps

A **map** shows geographic relationships. This graphic type is especially useful when a receiver may not be familiar with the geography discussed in a report. The map shown in Figure 10.6 shows the number of persons in the United States with limited English proficiency. The map gives the information visually and thus, eliminates the difficulty of explaining the information in words. In addition to being less confusing, a map is more concise and interesting than a written message.

> Ideally, a graphic should be integrated within the text material immediately after its introduction

10-3f Flowcharts

A **flowchart** is a step-by-step diagram of a procedure, or a graphic depiction of a system or organization. A variety of problems can be resolved by using flowcharts to support written analyses. For example, most companies have procedure manuals to instruct employees in certain work tasks. Including a flowchart with written instructions minimizes the

map a graphic that shows geographic relationships

flowchart a step-by-step diagram of a procedure, or a graphic depiction of a system or organization

 INCLUDING GRAPHICS IN TEXT

Text and graphics are partners in the communication process. If graphics appear before readers have been informed, they will begin to study the graphics and draw their own inferences and conclusions. For this reason, always introduce a graphic in the text immediately before the graphic appears. A graphic that

FIGURE 10.6 | MAP CONVEYING STATISTICAL DATA

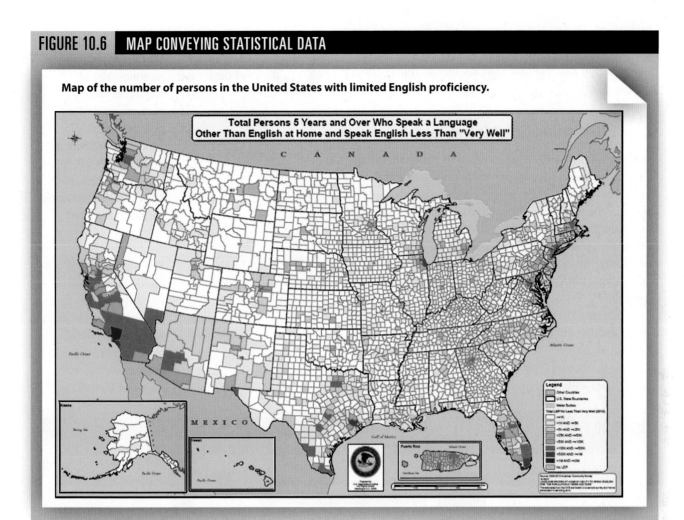

Map of the number of persons in the United States with limited English proficiency.

Source: https://www.lep.gov/maps/

INTRODUCING GRAPHICS IN TEXT

The pattern for incorporating graphics in text is (1) introduce, (2) show, and (3) interpret and analyze. The following range of examples, from poor to best, explain how to introduce graphic and tabular material.

		Example	Rationale
✗	Poor:	Figure 1 shows preferences for shopping locations.	Poor because it tells the reader nothing more than would the title of the figure.
✓	Acceptable:	About two-thirds of the consumers preferred to shop in suburban areas rather than in the city (see Figure 1).	Acceptable because it interprets the data, but it places the figure reference in parentheses rather than integrating it into the sentence.
✓+	Better:	As shown in Figure 1, about two-thirds of the consumers preferred to shop in suburban areas rather than in the city.	Better than the previous examples but puts the reference to the figure at the beginning, thus detracting from the interpretation of the data.
✓++	Best:	About two-thirds of the consumers preferred to shop in suburban areas rather than in the city, as shown in Figure 1.	Best for introducing figures because it talks about the graphic and also includes introductory phrasing, but only after stressing the main point.

follows an introduction and brief explanation will supplement what has been said in the report. Additional interpretation and needed analysis should follow the graphic.

10-4a Positioning Graphics in Text

Ideally, a graphic should be integrated within the text material immediately after its introduction. A graphic that will not fit on the page where it is introduced should appear at the top of the following page. In this chapter, figures are placed as closely as possible to their introductions in accordance with these suggestions. However, in some cases, several figures may be introduced on one page, making perfect placement difficult and sometimes impossible.

When interpreting and analyzing the graphic, avoid a mere restatement of what the graphic obviously shows. Instead, emphasize the main point you are making. Contrast the boring style of the following discussion of graphic data with the improved revision:

Obvious Restatement of Data: When asked to identify the causes of ineffective meetings, 10% of employees blamed poor communication skills, 8% cited egocentric behavior by attendees, 7% attributed nonparticipation, and 6.5% said the discussion became sidetracked.

Emphasis on Main Point: The most cited reason for ineffective meetings is poor communication skills, while issues related to poor interpersonal communication skills were also blamed.

FIGURE 10.7 — FLOWCHART OF SALES PROCESS

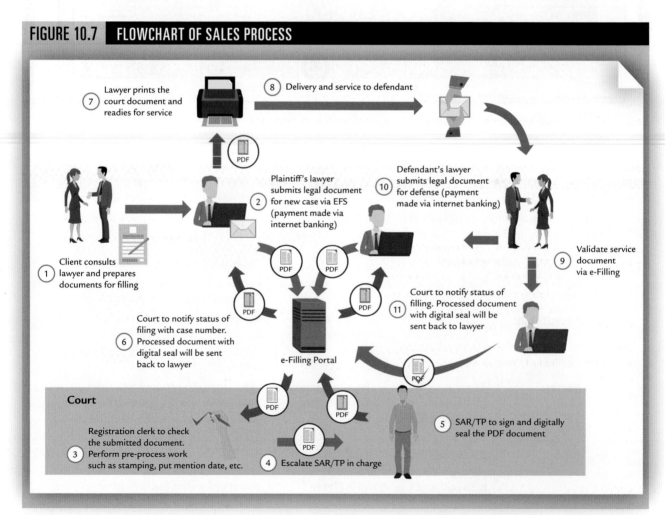

Source: http://www.conceptdraw.com/How-To-Guide/sales-process-flowcharts

FIGURE 10.8   BLUEPRINT

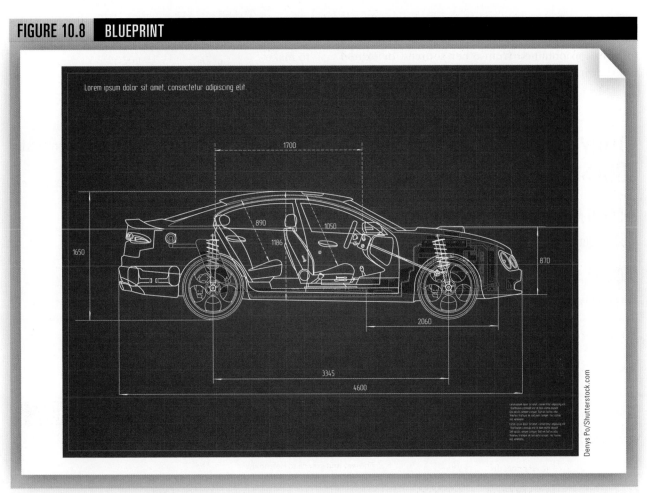

Lorem ipsum dolor sit amet, consectetur adipiscing elit.

Denys Po/Shutterstock.com

Source: https://www.nytimes.com/store/statue-of-liberty-blueprint-libertyblue.html

CONSISTENCY COUNTS

Throughout the discussion of tables and graphs, the term *graphics* has been used to include all illustrations. Although your report may include tables, graphs, maps, and even photographs, you will find organizing easier and writing about the illustrations more effective if you label each item as a "Figure" followed by a number; then number the items consecutively.

Some report writers prefer to label tables consecutively as "Table 1," and so on, and graphs and charts consecutively in another sequence as "Graph 1," and so on. When this dual numbering system is used, readers of the report may become confused if they come upon a sentence that reads, "Evidence presented in Tables 3 and 4 and Graph 2 supports. . . ." Both writers and readers appreciate the single numbering system, which makes the sentence read, "Evidence presented in Figures 3, 4, and 5 supports. . . ."

Khapaev Vladimir/Shutterstock.com

Your analysis may include summary statements about the data, compare information in the figure to information obtained from other sources, or extend the shown data into reasonably supported speculative outcomes. Strive to transition naturally from the discussion of the graphic into the next point you wish to make.

STUDY TOOLS 10

LOCATED AT THE BACK OF THE TEXTBOOK
☐ Tear-Out Chapter Review Card

LOCATED AT WWW.CENGAGEBRAIN.COM
☐ Review Key Term flashcards and create your own cards

☐ Track your knowledge and understanding of key concepts in business communication

☐ Complete practice and graded quizzes to prepare for tests

☐ Complete interactive content within BCOM9 Online

☐ View the chapter highlight boxes for BCOM9 Online

11 | Organizing and Preparing Reports and Proposals

Courtney Keating/Getty Images

LEARNING OBJECTIVES

After studying this chapter, you should be able to …

11-1 Identify the parts of a formal report and the contribution each part makes to the report's overall effectiveness.

11-2 Organize report findings.

11-3 Prepare effective formal reports using an acceptable format and writing style.

11-4 Prepare effective short reports in memorandum, email, and letter formats.

11-5 Prepare effective proposals for a variety of purposes.

After finishing
this chapter, go
to **PAGE 210** for
STUDY TOOLS.

11-1 PARTS OF A FORMAL REPORT

Reports serve a variety of purposes; the type of report you prepare depends on the subject matter, the purpose of the report, and the readers' needs. The differences between a formal report and an informal report lie in the format and, possibly, the writing style. At the short, informal end of the report continuum described in Chapter 9, a report could look exactly like a brief memorandum. At the long, formal extreme of the continuum, the report might include most or all of the parts shown in Figure 11.1 on page 192.

A business report rarely contains all of the parts shown but may include any combination of them. The preliminary parts and addenda are organizational items that support the body of a report. The body contains the report of the research and covers the four steps in the research process. The organization of the body of a report leads to the construction of the contents page.

Because individuals usually write to affect or influence others favorably, they often add report parts as the number of pages increases. When a report exceeds one or two pages, you might add a cover or title page. When the body of a report exceeds four or five pages, you might even add a finishing touch by placing the report in a binder, or binding it in a professional manner. Reports frequently take on the characteristics of the formal end of the continuum simply by reason of length. First, note how the preliminary parts and addenda items shown in Figure 11.2 on page 193 increase in number as the report increases in length. Second, notice the order in which report parts appear in a complete report and the distribution of reports in print and electronic forms.

Memo and letter reports are often one page in length, but they can be expanded into several pages. Long reports may include some special pages that do not appear in short reports. The format you select—long or short, formal or informal—may help determine the supporting preliminary and addenda items to include.

To understand how each part of a formal report contributes to reader comprehension and ease of access to the information in the report, study the following explanations of each part shown in Figure 11.1. The three basic sections—preliminary parts, report text, and addenda—are combined to prepare a complete formal report.

11-1a Preliminary Parts of a Report

Preliminary parts are included to add formality to a report, emphasize report content, and aid the reader in locating information in the report quickly and understanding the report more easily. These parts might include a half-title page, title page, authorization, transmittal, table of contents, table of figures, and executive summary. The most frequently used preliminary parts are described here.

TITLE PAGE

The title page includes the title, author, date, and often the name of the person or organization who requested the report. A title page is often added when opting for a formal report format rather than a memorandum or letter arrangement.

The selected title should be descriptive and comprehensive; its words should reflect the content of the report. Avoid short, vague titles or excessively long titles. Instead, use concise wording to identify the topic adequately. For example, a title such as "Marketing Survey: Internet Providers" leaves the reader confused when the title could have been "Internet Provider Preferences of the Residents of St. Louis."

To give some clues on writing a descriptive title, think of the "five W's": *Who*, *What*, *When*, *Where*, and *Why*. Avoid such phrases as "A Study of …," "A Critical Analysis of …," or "A Review of…."

Follow company procedures, or consult a style manual to place the title attractively on the page. Arrange the title consistently on the half-title page, title page, and the first page of a report.

> Avoid short, vague titles or excessively long titles.

McCarony/Shutterstock.com

TABLE OF CONTENTS

The table of contents provides the reader with an analytical overview of the report and the order in

preliminary parts report sections included to add formality to a report, emphasize report content, and aid the reader in locating information in the report quickly and understanding the report more easily

PRELIMINARY PARTS

Half-title page (Title Fly)	Title page	Authorization	Transmittal	Table of contents	Table of figures	Executive summary
Contains the report title; adds formality.	Includes the title, author, and date; adds formality.	Provides written authorization to complete the report.	Presents the report to the reader and summarizes the main points or analysis.	Provides an overview of the report and order in which information will be presented; contains headings and page numbers.	Includes the number, title, and page number of tables and graphics.	Summarizes the essential elements in the report.

REPORT TEXT

Introduction	Body	Analysis
Orients the reader to the topic and previews the major divisions.	Presents the information collected.	Reviews the main points presented in the body and may include conclusions and recommendations.

ADDENDA

References	Appendix	Index
Includes an alphabetical list of sources used in preparing the report.	Contains supplementary information that supports report, but placing this information in the report would make the report bulky and unmanageable.	Includes an alphabetical guide to subjects in the report.

which information is presented. Thus, this preliminary part aids the reader in understanding the report and in locating a specific section of it. The list includes the name and location (beginning page number) of every report part except those that precede the contents page. Include the list of figures and the transmittal, executive summary, report headings, references, appendixes, and index. Placing spaced periods (leaders) between the report part and the page numbers helps lead the reader's eyes to the appropriate page number.

Word-processing software simplifies the time-consuming, tedious task of preparing many of the preliminary and addenda report parts, including the table of contents. Because the software can generate these parts automatically, report writers can make last-minute changes to a report with updated preliminary and addenda parts.

TABLE OF FIGURES

To aid the reader in locating a specific graphic in a report with many graphics, the writer might include a list of figures separate from the contents. The list should include a reference to each figure that appears in the report, identified by both figure number and name, along with the page number on which the figure occurs. The contents and the figures can be combined on one page if both lists are brief. Word-processing software can be used to automatically generate the list of figures.

EXECUTIVE SUMMARY

The **executive summary** (also called the *abstract, overview,* or *précis*) summarizes the essential elements in an entire report. This overview simplifies the reader's understanding of a long report and is positioned before the first page of the report.

Typically, an executive summary is included to assist the reader in understanding a long, complex report. Because of the increased volume of information that managers must review, some managers require an executive summary regardless of the length and complexity of a report. The executive summary presents the report in miniature: the introduction, body, and summary as well as any conclusions and recommendations. Thus, an executive summary should (1) briefly introduce the report and preview the major divisions, (2) summarize the major sections of the report, and (3) summarize the report summary and any conclusions and recommendations. Pay special attention to topic sentences and to concluding sentences in paragraphs

executive summary
short summary of the essential elements in an entire report; also called an *abstract, overview,* or *précis*

(a) Memo report

(b) Email report

(c) Expanded letter report

(d) Title page

(e) Title page
Transmittal

(f) Title page
Transmittal
Table of contents

(g) Title page
Transmittal
Table of contents
Executive summary

(h) Half-title page
Title page
Transmittal
Table of contents
Executive summary
Addenda

or within sections of reports. This technique helps you write concise executive summaries based on major ideas and reduces the use of supporting details and background information.

To assist them in staying up-to-date professionally, busy executives frequently request assistants to prepare executive summaries of articles they do not have time to read, and conferences and meetings they cannot attend. Many practitioner journals include an executive summary (abstract) of each article. The executive summary provides the gist of the article and alerts the executive to articles that should be read in detail. The executive

12 | Designing and Delivering Business Presentations

michaeljung/Shutterstock.com

LEARNING OBJECTIVES

After studying this chapter, you should be able to …

12-1 Plan a business presentation that accomplishes the speaker's goals and meets the audience's needs.

12-2 Organize and develop the three parts of an effective presentation.

12-3 Select, design, and use presentation visuals effectively.

12-4 Deliver speeches with increasing confidence.

12-5 Discuss strategies for presenting in alternate delivery situations such as culturally diverse audiences, teams, and distance presentations.

After finishing this chapter, go to **PAGE 237** for **STUDY TOOLS.**

12-1 PLANNING AN EFFECTIVE BUSINESS PRESENTATION

The simplicity of writing email and talking on the phone has deterred many workers from learning to communicate in front of people with authority and authenticity.[1] Being a skilled business communicator requires skill in both writing and speaking. A business presentation is an important means of exchanging information for decision making and policy development; relating the benefits of the services offered; and sharing our goals, values, and vision. Because multiple people receive the message at the same time and are able to provide immediate feedback for clarification, presentations can significantly reduce message distortion and misunderstanding.

Many of the presentations you give will be formal, with sufficient time allowed for planning and developing elaborate visual support. You might present information and recommendations to external audiences such as customers and clients whom you've never met or to an internal audience made up of coworkers and managers you know well. You can also expect to present some less formal presentations, often referred to as **oral briefings**. An oral briefing might entail a short update on a current project requested during a meeting without advance notice or a brief explanation in the hallway when your supervisor walks past. Sales representatives give oral briefings daily as they present short, informal pitches for new products and services.

Regardless of the formality of the presentation, the time given to prepare, the nature of the audience (friends or strangers), or the media used (live, distant, Web, or DVD delivery on demand), your success depends on your ability to think on your feet and speak confidently as you address the audience's needs. Understanding the purpose you hope to achieve through your presentation and conceptualizing your audience will enable you to organize the content in a way the audience can understand *and* accept.

As with written messages, presentations should be well planned. The steps in the process for planning, preparing, and rehearsing presentations are shown in Figure 12.1.

> A business presentation is an important means of exchanging information for decision making and policy development.

12-1a Identify Your Purpose and Consider the Channel

Determining what you want to accomplish during a presentation is a fundamental principle of planning an effective presentation. Some speech coaches recommend completing the following vital sentence to lay the foundation for a successful presentation: "At the end of my presentation, the audience will _____." In his book *Do's and Taboos of Public Speaking,* Roger E. Axtell provides two excellent mechanisms for condensing your presentation into a brief, achievable purpose that will direct you in identifying and supporting the major points[2]:

- Ask yourself, "What is my message?" Then, develop a phrase, a single thought, or a conclusion you want the audience to take with them from the presentation. This elementary statement will likely be the final

oral briefings informal presentations prepared and presented with little time for planning and developing

---

FIGURE 12.1 PROCESS FOR PLANNING, PREPARING, AND REHEARSING PRESENTATIONS

STEP 1	STEP 2	STEP 3	STEP 4	STEP 5	STEP 6	STEP 7
Consider the applicable contextual forces.	Determine the purpose and consider channel constraints and benefits.	Envision the audience.	Adapt the message to the audience's needs and concerns.	Organize the message.	Prepare visual aids.	Rehearse delivery.

sentence in your presentation—the basic message you want the audience to remember.

- Imagine a member of your audience has been asked to summarize your message. Ideally, you want to hear him or her describe your central purpose.

If your purpose for presenting is primarily informative and you plan to provide a good deal of information and details, you might wish to select a two-channel approach to message delivery. In other words, you might find it more appropriate to deliver the bulk of the information via email or informal report, and then follow up with a presentation to answer questions or emphasize key points to ensure the accuracy of the message's reception. Although a presentation is a useful medium for establishing rapport and receiving and providing feedback, it is also one of the most misused communication channels. This is because presentations are often used to deliver large amounts of detailed information, which may only succeed in boring the audience. The challenge of keeping an audience's attention for an extended period of time becomes obvious when we consider that the average attention span in 2013 was eight seconds,[3] and most educators and psychologists agree that attention spans have been decreasing over the past decade with the increase in external stimulation. Because of this single challenge, the decision to communicate with a presentation deserves due consideration and, if selected, generally requires substantial planning so as to be effective and enhance, rather than detract, from the presenter's credibility.

For this reason, it is important to emphasize when to choose an oral presentation as the method of message delivery. Presentations are good for the following situations:

- **Inspiring and motivating others.** If the presenter is able to bring enthusiasm and energy and an inspirational message to the situation, then oral message delivery is highly appropriate.

- **Demonstrations of products or for training purposes.** Oral presentations work well when audience members are able to view how a product works and better understand its functions. They are also useful for training purposes, particularly, if the audience

is able to apply the presented material through practice or use as part of the presentation.

- **To introduce a complex persuasive written message (generally a report or a proposal).** This helps increase audience interest by emphasizing the key benefits of the proposal in an engaging manner and allows the presenter to answer audience questions.

- **As a follow-up to a complex persuasive written message (generally a report or a proposal).** The personal presence of an advocate can help establish goodwill and credibility and move the persuasive process forward. In these cases, the oral message should generally emphasize the benefits of the proposal and answer audience questions.

- **To deliver bad news to a large audience.** In some circumstances, the personal presence of an organizational representative helps to establish or maintain goodwill and credibility and, by extension, the image and reputation of the firm.

Once the decision has been made that a presentation is the best medium for message delivery, then the preparer needs to do additional planning by analyzing her audience and considering the context of the presentation.

12-1b Know Your Audience and Consider the Context

A common mistake that many presenters make is to presume they know the audience without attempting to find out about it. If you expect to get results, you must commit the time to know your audience and focus your presentation on it—from planning your speech to practicing its delivery.

As a general rule, audiences *do* want to be in tune with a speaker. Yet people listen to speeches about things of interest to them. "What's in it for me?" is the question most listeners ask. A speech about climate change to a farm group should address the farmers' problems, for example, and not focus on theories of global

Rawpixel.com/Shutterstock.com

warming. Additionally, different strategies are needed for audiences who think and make decisions differently. Audiences from different cultures have different expectations regarding public-speaking norms as explained in the sidebar "Cultural Contexts in Public Speaking." For instance, different strategies are needed for making a successful presentation to sell software to a group of lawyers than to a group of doctors. Lawyers typically think quickly and are argumentative and decisive, whereas doctors are often cautious, skeptical, and don't make quick purchasing decisions.[4]

To deliver a presentation that focuses on the wants and expectations of an audience, you must determine who it is, what motivates it, how members think, and how members make decisions. Helpful information you can obtain about most audiences includes ages, genders, occupations, educational levels, attitudes, values, broad and specific interests, and needs. In addition, you should also consider certain things about the occasion and location. Patriotic speeches to a group of military veterans will differ from speeches to a group of new recruits, just as Fourth of July speeches will differ from Veterans Day speeches. Seek answers to the following questions when you discuss your speaking engagement with someone representing the group or audience:

1. **Who is the audience and who requested the presentation?** General characteristics of the audience should be considered, as well as the extent of their knowledge and experience with the topic, attitude toward the topic and you as a credible speaker, the anticipated response to the use of electronic media, and required or volunteer attendance.

2. **Why is this topic important to the audience?** What will the audience do with the information presented?

How will the information benefit audience members?

3. **What environmental factors affect the presentation?**

   ° How many will be in the audience?

   ° Will I be the only speaker? If not, where does my presentation fit in the program? What time of day?

   ° How much time will I be permitted? Minimum? Maximum?

   ° What are the seating arrangements? How far will the audience be from the speaker? Will a microphone or other equipment be available?

   ° What are my technical requirements and will they be met at the presentation location?

   ° Will I have time to test my media before the presentation? If not, how can I ensure that my presentation will go off without any problems or snags?

Answers to these questions reveal whether the speaking environment will be intimate or remote, whether the audience is likely to be receptive and alert or nonreceptive and tired, and whether you will need to use additional motivational or persuasive techniques.

12-2 ORGANIZING THE CONTENT

With an understanding of the purpose of your business presentation—why you are giving it and what you hope to achieve—the constraints and benefits of the oral medium, and a conception of the size, interest, and background of the audience, you are prepared to outline your presentation and identify appropriate content.

The biggest mistake that presenters often make is not clearly understanding that oral presentations, as a medium of communication, are quite different from written messages in terms of the kinds of information they are useful for conveying. In other words, the biggest mistake that presenters make is treating a presentation as if it were a written document or formal report. The written channel and the oral channel are generally good for communicating different kinds of information and for achieving quite different goals. Even if a presentation is based on written material, the presenter should start planning as if he or she was developing an entirely new message because of this fact. If this isn't understood from the beginning, an oral presentation is likely to fall flat—and the presenter with it. What this means is that rather than writing a script or working from a report, a presenter should begin with an outline of the presentation contents.

First introduced by famous speech trainer Dale Carnegie, and still recommended by speech experts today, the simple but effective basic presentation structure includes an introduction, the body, and a closing.

12-2a Introduction

What you say at the beginning sets the stage for your entire presentation and initiates your rapport with the audience. However, inexperienced speakers often settle for unoriginal and overused introductions that reduce the audience's desire to listen, such as "My name is …, and my topic is …" or "It is a pleasure …"; or negative statements, such as apologies for lack of preparation, boring delivery, or late arrival. An effective introduction accomplishes the following goals:

- **Captures the attention of, and involves, the audience.** Choose an attention-getter that is relevant to the subject and appropriate for the situation.

To involve the audience directly, ask for a show of hands in response to a direct question; allow the audience time to think about the answer to a rhetorical question; or explain why the information is important and how it will benefit the listeners. Consider the following examples.

An alcohol awareness speech to young people might begin with a true story:

"My son was a straight 'A' student who had just been accepted by Harvard. But his dream of becoming a psychologist ended the night he drove his car into a tree, after a party with friends, and suffered serious brain trauma."

A report presenting a plan for restructuring could introduce the subject and set the stage for the findings (inductive sequence) or the recommendation (deductive sequence).

ATTENTION-GETTING TECHNIQUES MIGHT INCLUDE:

- ▶ A shocking statement or startling statistic
- ▶ A quotation by an expert or well-known person
- ▶ A rhetorical or open-ended question that generates discussion from the audience
- ▶ An appropriate joke or humor
- ▶ A demonstration or dramatic presentation aid
- ▶ An anecdote or timely story from a business periodical
- ▶ A personal reference, a compliment to the audience, or a reference to the occasion of the presentation

Inductive: "When the company experienced a dramatic downturn in stock values, a management team immediately began to put together a plan to cut costs and improve productivity."

Deductive: "By reducing levels of management and cutting red tape, we can decrease costs and improve productivity, ensuring future growth of our company."

- **Establishes rapport.** Initiate rapport with the listeners; convince them that you are concerned that they benefit from the presentation and that you are qualified to speak on the topic. You might share a personal story that relates to the topic but reveals something about yourself, or discuss your background or a specific experience with the topic being discussed.

- **Presents the purpose statement and previews the points that will be developed.** To maintain the interest you have captured, present your purpose statement directly so that the audience is certain to hear it. Use original statements and avoid clichés such as "My topic today is …" or "I'd like to talk with you about …"

"The acquisition and construction cost of all three sites were comparable. The decision to locate the new

Seregam/Shutterstock.com

distribution facility in Cincinnati, Ohio, is based on the quality of living, transportation accessibility, and an adequate work force."

Next, preview the major points you will discuss in the order you will discuss them. For example, you might say, "First, I'll discuss …, then …, and finally. …" Revealing the presentation plan will help the audience understand how the parts of the body are tied together to support the purpose statement, thus increasing their understanding. For a long, complex presentation, you might display a presentation visual that lists the points in the order they will be covered. As you begin each major point, display a slide that contains that point and perhaps a related image. These section slides partition your presentation just as headings do in a written report, and thus move the listener more easily from one major point to the next.

12-2b Body

In a typical presentation of 15–20 minutes, limit your presentation to only a few major subpoints (typically three to five) that support or flesh out your primary theme or topic in order to avoid overwhelming and boring your audience. Making every statement in a presentation into a major point— something to be remembered—is impossible, unless the presentation lasts only 2 or 3 minutes.

Once you have selected your major subpoints, locate your supporting material. You can use several techniques to ensure the audience understands your point and to reinforce it:

- **Provide support in a form that is easy to understand.** Three techniques will assist you in accomplishing this goal:

  1. **Use simple vocabulary and short sentences that the listener can understand easily and that sound conversational and interesting.** Spoken communication is more difficult to process than written communication; therefore, complex, varied vocabulary and long sentences often included in written documents are not effective in a presentation.

  2. **Avoid jargon or technical terms that the listeners might not understand.** Instead, use plain English that the audience can easily comprehend. Make your speech more interesting and memorable by using word pictures to make your points. Matt Hughes, a speech consultant, provides this example: "If your message is a warning of difficulties ahead, you might say: 'We're

climbing a hill that's getting steeper, and there are rocks and potholes in the road.'"[5]

  3. **Use a familiar frame of reference.** Drawing analogies between new ideas and familiar ones is another technique for generating understanding. For example, noting that the US blog-reading audience is already one-half the size of the newspaper-reading population helps clarify an abstract or complex concept. Saying that "info dumping" is the verbal equivalent of email spam is a good explanation of the expected consequences of overloading an audience with too many details.[6]

- **Provide relevant statistics.** Provide statistics or other quantitative measures to lend authority and credibility to your points. A word of warning: Do not overwhelm your audience with excessive statistics. Instead, round off numbers and use broad terms or word pictures that the listener can remember. Instead of "68.2%" say "more than two-thirds"; instead of "112% rise in production" say "our output more than doubled."

- **Use quotes from prominent people.** Comments made by other authorities are helpful in establishing credibility.

- **Use interesting anecdotes.** Audiences like and remember anecdotes or interesting stories that tie into the presentation and make strong emotional connections. In her book *Whoever Tells the Best Story Wins*, Annette Simmons stresses that when telling stories, the storyteller allows the audience to feel his or her presence and reveals a trace of humanity, which is vital for developing understanding, influence, and strong relationships with the audience. She encourages leaders to craft personal stories into specific, intentional messages that communicate values,

Rawpixel.com/Shutterstock.com

vision, and important lessons.[7] By communicating their values, leaders communicate the values they expect from their employees. As with jokes, be sure you can get straight to the point of a story.

- **Use jokes and humor appropriately.** Jokes or humor can create a special bond between you and the audience, ease your approach to sensitive subjects, disarm a nonreceptive audience, or make your message easier to understand and remember. Plan your joke carefully so that you can (1) get the point across as quickly as possible, (2) deliver it in a conversational manner with interesting inflections and effective body movements, and (3) deliver the punch line effectively. If you cannot tell a joke well, use humor instead—amusing things that happened to you or someone you know, one-liners, or humorous quotations that relate to your presentation. Refrain from any humor that reflects negatively on race, color, religion, gender, age, culture, or other personal areas of sensitivity.

- **Use presentation visuals.** Presentation visuals, such as handouts, presentation software, and demonstrations, enhance the effectiveness of the presentation. Develop presentation visuals that will enable your audience to see, hear, and even experience your presentation.

- **Encourage audience involvement.** Skilled presenters involve their audiences through techniques such as asking reflective questioning, role-playing, directing audience-centered activities, and incorporating current events or periodicals that tie directly to the message. One communications coach's advice for getting an audience "to sit up and listen" is to make the presentation contemporary by working Twitter, texting, video, and other technologies into the speech.[8]

12-2c Closing

The closing provides unity to your presentation by "telling the audience what you have already told them." The conclusion should be "your best line, your most dramatic point, your most profound thought, your most memorable bit of information, or your best anecdote."[9] Because listeners tend to remember what they hear last, use these final words strategically. Develop a closing that supports and refocuses the audience's attention on your purpose statement.

- **Commit the time and energy needed to develop a creative, memorable conclusion.** An audience is not impressed with endings such as "That's all I have" or "That's it." Useful concluding techniques include summarizing the main points that have been made

in the presentation and using anecdotes, humor, and illustrations. When closing an analytical presentation, state your conclusion and support it with the highlights from your supporting evidence: "In summary, you should select our communication training program because it offers. …" In a persuasive presentation, the closing is often an urgent plea for the members of the audience to take some action or to look on the subject from a new point of view.

- **Tie the closing to the introduction to strengthen the unity of the presentation.** For example, you might answer the rhetorical question you asked in the opening, refer to and build on an anecdote included in the introduction, and so on. A unifying close to a speech to motivate women business owners might be, "Life is too short to spend it doing other people's work and paying the price with unhappiness. With appropriate planning, you can spend your days as I do, making a life you love."

- **Use transition words that clearly indicate you are moving from the body to the closing.** Attempt to develop original wordings rather than rely on standard statements such as "In closing" or "In conclusion."

- **Practice your closing until you can deliver it without stumbling.** Use your voice and gestures to communicate this important idea clearly, emphatically, and sincerely rather than fade out at the end as inexperienced speakers often do.

- **Smile and stand back to accept the audience's applause.** A solid closing does not require a "thank you"; instead, wait confidently for the audience's spontaneous applause to thank you for a worthwhile presentation. Appear eager to begin a question-and-answer period or walk with assurance to your seat.

12-3 DESIGNING COMPELLING PRESENTATION VISUALS

Speakers who use presentation visuals are considered better prepared and more interesting, and achieve their goals more often than speakers who do not use visuals. Presentation visuals support and clarify a speaker's ideas and help the audience visualize the message. A speaker using presentation visuals reaches the receiver with double impact—through the eyes and the ears—and achieves the results quoted in an ancient Chinese proverb: "Tell me, I'll forget. Show me, I'll remember. But involve me and I'll understand." Research studies confirm that using visuals enhances a presentation.

The effective use of presentation visuals provides several advantages[10]:

- Clarifies and emphasizes important points

- Increases retention from 14% to 38%

- Reduces the time required to present a concept

- Results in a speaker achieving goals 34% more often than when presentation visuals are not used

- Increases the occurrence of group consensus by 21% when presentation visuals are used in a meeting

12-3a Design of Presentation Visuals

PowerPoint still remains the standard presentation software used in most organizational settings, even though its use has given rise to such sayings as "Death by Power-Point" and "PowerPoint poisoning." The problem is that too many presenters approach a presentation as if they were reading a document to their audience rather than delivering an interesting and inspiring message. The result is "docu-points," or presentations composed of too many text slides that are overly complex, difficult to understand, and boring. One example is an "electability" PowerPoint slideshow sent by the 2008 Hillary Clinton Campaign to all House Democrats that contained nine slides, 275 words, one table, three bar charts, and two pie charts. Such "docu-points" are usually less effective than a concise, well-designed handout or summary report.[11]

Even though PowerPoint remains a standard in many professional environments, other presentation software packages are available. Flash is one of the best presentation software tools on the market because of its animation effects and ability to import video. Unfortunately, it also takes a high degree of proficiency to use. Prezi is another popular software tool that is available online and provides a very different experience than PowerPoint in that it is nonlinear and more interactive and dynamic. Apple users can use Apple Keynote. Other presentation tools include Google Docs and SlideRocket.

Regardless of the software package you choose, your goal is to create an appealing, easy-to-read visual aid that supports and enhances your main points without overwhelming the audience. Presentation visuals should possess the same degree of professionalism as your delivery and personal appearance. You can create dynamic and useful presentation visuals, including slides, handouts, and notes pages, by following these simple guidelines:

- **Limit the number of visual aids used in a single presentation.** Although audiences value being able to "see" your points, they also welcome the variety provided by listening and the break from concentrating on visuals. Design compelling visuals that direct the audience's attention to major points and clarify or illustrate complex information. Use precise, vivid language that will involve the audience and enrich your message and delivery style.

- **Limit slide content to key ideas presented in as few words as possible or, better yet, visually.** Well-organized, crisp slide content enhances the audience's ability to grasp the speaker's meaning and find immediate value in the information. Good content also leads to an extemporaneous delivery rather than a speaker's monotonous reading of scripted slides. Short text lines are also easier for the eye to follow and open up the slide with appealing white space. Whenever possible, present complex information using graphic aids, such as tables, charts, or diagrams.

- **Develop only one major idea using targeted keywords the audience can scan quickly, understand, and remember.** Full sentences can be used for a direct quotation; otherwise, less is more. William Earnest, author of *Save Our Slides*, offers a cure for verbalitis: "PowerPoint is not a word processor"—it is a visual medium in which fewer words are always more.[12]

- Keep type sizes large enough to read when projected and to discourage crowding slides with text. Strive for these font sizes: slide titles, 44 point; main bullets, 32 point; sub-bullets, 24 point. Do not use text smaller than 18 point, as it is unreadable when projected.

ra2studio/Shutterstock.com

- Limit slide titles and headings to four words and follow the 7 × 7 rule, which limits text to 7 lines per slide and 7 words per line. Eliminate articles (*a, an, and the*), understood pronouns/possessives (*we, you, and your*), simple verbs and infinitive beginnings (*are, and to*), and repetitive phrasing.

- If you must use text, develop powerful bulleted lists that are easy to follow and remember. For easy recall, limit the list to three to five main bullets, but absolutely no more than seven. To eliminate confusion and rereading, use bulleted lists that are grammatically parallel. One item appearing out of place weakens the emphasis given to each item and can distract audience attention from the message. Be certain each major point relates to the key concept presented in the slide title and each subpoint relates to its major point. Unless sequence is important, use bullets as they add less clutter and are easier to follow than numbers.

- **Choose an effective template and powerful images to reinforce ideas, illustrate complex ideas, and enliven boring content.** Images and shapes are more visually appealing and memorable than words, and they enable audiences to grasp information more easily. Today's audiences expect media-rich, dynamic visuals, not a speaker's dense crutch notes displayed on screen. Although photographs and clip art available in your presentation software gallery are acceptable, avoid images that are overused, outdated, grainy, and convey an unprofessional tone. Instead search for or create high-quality, professional images that convey the desired message and can project onscreen without distortion.

- **Choose an effective color scheme.** The colors you choose and the way you combine them determine the overall effectiveness of your presentation and add a personal touch to your work. Follow these simple rules to plan a nondistracting, complementary color scheme that has unity with the template graphics:

- **Limit colors to no more than three on a slide, to avoid an overwhelming feel.**

- **Begin by selecting a background color that conveys the appropriate formality and tone.** Choose cool colors (blue and green) in muted shades for formal presentations; choose warm colors (red, orange, and yellow) or brighter shades of cool colors for a less formal and perhaps trendy look. Think carefully about whether your color selection has a natural association with your topic or organization. For example, a presentation on environmentally friendly policies might incorporate colors naturally associated with nature and cleanliness (earth tones, white and blue); a presentation to Pepsi-Cola would likely be designed around the company colors of red, white, and blue.

- **Choose complementary foreground (text) colors that have high contrast to the background to ensure readability.** To ensure high contrast, choose either dark text on a light background or light text on a dark background. For example, the often-used color scheme with a yellow slide title text and white bulleted list with a blue background is a good choice because the colors are complementary and have high contrast. Choose a slightly brighter color for the slide title that distinguishes it from the color chosen for the bullet list.

Black text against a white background has the greatest contrast. A blue background with yellow text contrasts well, but a light blue background with white text would be difficult to read because of low contrast. Evaluate the readability of the following contrast variations:

High-contrast options:	Dark text on a light background	Light text on a dark background

Poor contrast options:	White text on a light blue background	Bright text on a bright background

Because the lower resolution of projectors can wash out colors and make them less vibrant than what is seen on a printed page or computer screen, choose options with very high—not minimally high—contrast. Project your presentation ahead of time in the room where you are to present so you can assess the color scheme. You can also double-check for readability and typographical errors at the same time.

- **Choose accent colors that complement the color scheme.** Accent colors are used in small doses to draw attention to key elements: bullet markers; bars/slices in graphs, backgrounds (fills) of shapes and lines, and selected text; or drawings that are color coded for emphasis. Avoid red and green when differentiating important points as almost 10% of the population is color impaired and cannot distinguish between red and green. The red and green bars in a graph would be seen as one large area.

- **Choose an appealing font that can be read on-screen easily.** Avoid delicate, decorative, or condensed choices that are difficult to read when projected. The clean, simple lines of a sans serif font, such as Calibri, Tahoma, or Verdana, are ideal for projecting on a large screen, newspaper headline, sign, or billboard. A *sans serif* font has no short cross-strokes, known as *serifs*, which provide extra detail that helps to guide the eye on print media. Examples of serif fonts are Cambria, Times New Roman, and Garamond.

- **Follow these keyboarding rules for easy reading.** Use capital letters sparingly as they are difficult to read from a distance. Capitalize the first letter of important words in slide titles (initial caps) and the first letter of the first word and proper nouns in a bulleted list (sentence case). Omit hard-to-see punctuation at the end of bulleted lists and elsewhere, and avoid abbreviations and hyphenations that might cause confusion.

- **Reflect legal and ethical responsibility in the design of presentation visuals.** Like the graphics you developed in Chapter 10, presentation visuals should be uncluttered, easily understood, and should depict information honestly.

- **Proofread the visual carefully following the same systematic procedures used for printed letters and reports and electronic communication.** Misspellings in visuals are embarrassing and diminish your credibility. Double-check to be certain that names of people, companies, and products are spelled correctly.

Figure 12.2 offers a review of slide design guidelines. The poor example (left) relies on text to convey the message, whereas the good example (right) illustrates the point.

12-3b Adding Multimedia to PowerPoint Presentations

Multimedia uses a combination of different forms such as text, audio, images, animation, video, and interactive content. Multimedia contrasts with other media that only use rudimentary computer displays, such as text-only, diagrams, or pictures, and other traditional forms of printed or hand-produced material.

FIGURE 12.2   DESIGNING COMPELLING SLIDES

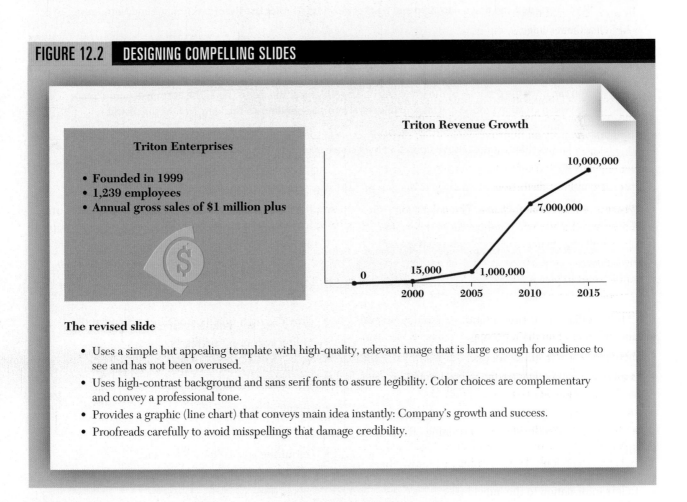

Triton Enterprises

- **Founded in 1999**
- **1,239 employees**
- **Annual gross sales of $1 million plus**

Triton Revenue Growth

10,000,000

7,000,000

0   15,000   1,000,000

2000   2005   2010   2015

The revised slide

- Uses a simple but appealing template with high-quality, relevant image that is large enough for audience to see and has not been overused.
- Uses high-contrast background and sans serif fonts to assure legibility. Color choices are complementary and convey a professional tone.
- Provides a graphic (line chart) that conveys main idea instantly: Company's growth and success.
- Proofreads carefully to avoid misspellings that damage credibility.

SAVE YOUR POWERPOINT PRESENTATION AS A VIDEO

When you want to give a copy of your presentation to colleagues or customers, you can save it as a video that can be burned to a CD or DVD, or published to a video-sharing site, such as YouTube, for easy sharing and distribution.

To save your presentation as a video, follow the instructions below: (Instructions apply to PowerPoint 2013 and 2016 only.)

1. Create your presentation.

2. (Optional) Record and add narration and timings to a slide show and turn your mouse into a laser pointer.

3. Save the presentation.

4. Click File > Export > Create a Video.

5. Under Create a Video, click Computer & HD Displays, and then do one of the following:

    - To create a video with very high quality, yet a large file size, click Computer & HD Displays.

    - To create a video with a moderate file size and medium quality, click Internet & DVD.

    - To create a video with the smallest file size, yet low quality, click Portable Devices.

TIP: You'll want to test these out to see which option meets your needs.

6. Depending on if you did or did not use timed narration and pointer movements, do one of the following:

    - If you did not record and time voice narration and laser pointer movements, click Don't Use Recorded Timings and Narration.

TIP: The default time spent on each slide is set to 5 seconds. To change this, to the right of Seconds to spend on each slide, click the up arrow to increase, or the down arrow to decrease the seconds.

    - If you recorded and timed narration and pointer movements, click Use Recorded Timings and Narrations.

7. Click Create Video.

8. In the File name box, enter a file name for the video, and then browse to locate the file.

9. In the Save As type box, choose a supported video file format, and then click Save.

    - You can track the progress of the video creation by looking at the status bar at the bottom of your screen. The video creation process can take up to several hours depending on the length of the video and the complexity of the presentation.

    - For longer videos, you can set it up so that they create overnight. That way, they'll be ready for you the following morning.

10. To play your newly created video, go to the designated folder location, and then double-click the file.

For more information on turning PowerPoint presentations into videos, visit https://support.office.com/en-us/article/Save-your-presentation-as-a-video-fafb9713-14cd-4013-bcc7-0879e6b7e6ce

Source: Microsoft Office Support. https://support.office.com/en-us/article/Save-your-presentation-as-a-video-fafb9713-14cd-4013-bcc7-0879e6b7e6ce

Multimedia use in presentations provides several advantages, including the following:

- Increases learning effectiveness
- Is more appealing than traditional presentation methods
- Offers significant potential for improving personal communications, education, and training efforts
- Reduces training costs
- Is easy to use
- Tailors information to the individual
- Provides high-quality video images and audio
- Offers system portability[13]

Multimedia use in presentations also presents some potential disadvantages, such as

- being more expensive,
- being more difficult to configure,
- requiring special hardware, and
- introducing potential problems of compatibility with other software or hardware.[14]

Multimedia can be incorporated into PowerPoint simply by copying images from the Web or from personal cameras, and merging them with text and graphic design elements to create engaging presentations that can be used in-house, with clients, or as presentations that are downloadable from the Internet. Links to audio and video files can also be embedded in PowerPoint and played during presentations. Possibilities include playing sounds and movies continuously throughout the slide show, across several sequential slides, or only when clicking on a sound or movie image.

Adobe Flash is another software program that allows you to create presentations with powerful animation. A big advantage of Flash is that it allows you to put presentations directly onto your website because it offers very good video compression technology. The biggest problem with Flash is that it can be a difficult system to use and is somewhat expensive to buy as an add-on to existing software.

dennizn/Shutterstock.com

12-3c Design Tips for Audience Handouts and Notes Pages

Audience handouts should add value for individual audience members; otherwise, the information can better be conveyed in a projected format for group benefit. An effective handout can help audience members remember your message, serve as a reference for later consideration or action, and encourage involvement when space is provided for note taking or response. You can prepare useful presenter notes on small index cards or on pages generated by electronic presentation software.

12-4 REFINING YOUR DELIVERY

After you have organized your message, you must identify the appropriate delivery method, refine your vocal qualities, and practice your delivery.

12-4a Delivery Method

Four presentation methods can be used: memorized, scripted, impromptu, and extemporaneous. Impromptu and extemporaneous styles are generally more useful for business presentations.

Memorized presentations are written out ahead of time, memorized, and recited verbatim. Memorization has the greatest limitations among the speech styles. Speakers are almost totally unable to react to feedback,

and the speaker who forgets a point and develops a mental block might lose the entire speech. Memorized speeches tend to sound monotonous, restrict natural body gestures and motions, and lack conviction. For short religious or fraternal rites, however, the memorized presentation is often impressive.

Manuscript, or *scripted*, **presentations** involve writing the speech word for word and reading it to the audience. For complex material and technical conference presentations, manuscript presentations ensure content coverage. Additionally, this style protects speakers against being misquoted (when accuracy is absolutely critical) and fits into exact time constraints, as in television or radio presentations. Speeches are sometimes read when time does not permit adequate preparation or when several different presentations are given in one day (e.g., the speaking demands of the president of the United States and other top-level executives). Manuscript presentations limit speaker–audience rapport, particularly when speakers keep their eyes and heads buried in their manuscripts. Teleprompters that project the manuscript out of view of the audience allow the speaker to appear to be speaking extemporaneously.

Impromptu presentations are frightening to many people because the speaker is called on without prior notice. Experienced speakers can easily analyze the request, organize supporting points from memory, and present a simple, logical response. In many cases, businesspeople can anticipate a

memorized presentation
a presentation in which a speaker writes out a speech, commits it to memory, and recites it verbatim

manuscript presentation
a presentation in which a speaker writes out the entire speech and reads it to the audience; also called a *scripted presentation*

impromptu presentation
a presentation in which a speaker is called on without prior notice

tmcphotos/Shutterstock.com

phonation are pitch, volume, and rate. These factors permit us to recognize other people's voices over the phone.

- **Pitch.** The highness or lowness of the voice is called pitch. Pleasant voices have medium or low pitch; however, a varied pitch pattern is desirable. The pitch of the voice rises and falls to reflect emotions; for example, fear and anger are reflected in a higher pitch; sadness, in a lower pitch. Lower pitches for both men and women are perceived as sounding more authoritative; higher pitches indicate less confidence and suggest pleading or whining. Techniques discussed later in this section can help you lower the pitch of your voice.

request and be prepared to discuss a particular idea when requested (e.g., a status report on an area of control at a team meeting). Because professionals are expected to present ideas and data spontaneously on demand, businesspeople must develop the ability to deliver impromptu presentations.

Extemporaneous presentations are planned, prepared, and rehearsed, but not written in detail. Brief notes prompt the speaker on the next point, but the words are chosen spontaneously as the speaker interacts with the audience and identifies its specific needs. Extemporaneous presentations include natural body gestures, sound conversational, and can be delivered with conviction because the speaker is speaking "with" the listeners and not "to" them. The audience appreciates a warm, genuine communicator and will forgive an occasional stumble or groping for a word that occurs with an extemporaneous presentation.

12-4b Vocal Qualities

The sound of your voice is a powerful instrument used to deliver your message and to project your professional image. To maximize your vocal strengths, focus on three important qualities of speech: phonation, articulation, and pronunciation.

Phonation involves both the production and the variation of the speaker's vocal tone. You project your voice and convey feelings—even thoughts—by varying your vocal tones. Important factors of

- **Volume.** The loudness of tones is referred to as volume. Generally, good voices are easily heard by everyone in the audience but are not too loud. Use variety to hold the audience's attention, emphasize words or ideas, and create a desired atmosphere (energetic, excited tone versus a dull, and boring one).

- **Rate.** The speed at which words are spoken is called rate. Never speak so quickly that the audience cannot understand your message or so slowly that they are distracted or irritated. Vary the rate with the demands of the situation. For example, speak at a slower rate when presenting a complex concept or emphasizing an important idea. Pause to add emphasis to a key point or to transition to another major section of the presentation. Speak at a faster rate when presenting less important information or when reviewing.

An inherent problem related to speaking rate is verbal fillers—also called non-words. Verbal fillers, such as *uhhh, ahhh, ummm,* and *errr,* are irritating to the audience and destroy your effectiveness. Many speakers fill space with their own verbal fillers; these include *you know, I mean, basically, like I said, okay,* and *as a matter of fact.* Because of the conversational style of impromptu and extemporaneous presentations, a speaker will naturally struggle for a word or idea from time to time. Become aware of verbal fillers you frequently use by critiquing a recording of yourself and then focus on replacing fillers with a three- to five-second pause. This brief gap between thoughts gives you an opportunity to think about what you want to say next and time for your audience to absorb your idea. Presenting an idea (sound bite) and then pausing

extemporaneous presentation a presentation in which a speaker plans, prepares, and rehearses but does not write everything down; brief notes prompt the speaker, but the exact words are chosen spontaneously as the speaker interacts with the audience and identifies its specific needs

phonation the production and variation of a speaker's vocal tone

briefly is an effective way to influence your audience positively. The listener will not notice the slight delay, and the absence of meaningless words will make you appear more confident and polished. Also avoid annoying speech habits, such as clearing your throat or coughing, that shift the audience's attention from the speech to the speaker.

The following activities will help you achieve good vocal qualities:

- **Breathe properly and relax.** Nervousness affects normal breathing patterns and is reflected in vocal tone and pitch. The better prepared you are, the better your phonation will be. Although relaxing might seem difficult to practice before a speech, a few deep breaths, just as swimmers take before diving, can help.

- **Listen to yourself.** A recording of your voice reveals much about pitch, intensity, and duration. Most people are amazed to find their voices are not quite what they had expected. "I never dreamed I sounded that bad" is a common reaction. Nasal twangs usually result from a failure to speak from the diaphragm, which involves taking in and letting out air through the larynx, where the vocal cords operate. High pitch can occur from the same cause, or it can be a product of speaking too fast or experiencing stage fright.

- **Develop flexibility.** A good speaking voice is somewhat musical, with words and sounds similar to notes in a musical scale. Read each of the following sentences aloud, and emphasize the *italicized* word in each. Even though the sentences are identical, emphasizing different words changes the meaning.

I am happy you are here.	*Maybe I'm the only happy one.*
I *am* happy you are here.	*I really am.*
I am *happy* you are here.	*Happy best describes my feeling.*
I am happy *you* are here.	*Yes, you especially.*
I am happy you *are* here.	*You may not be happy, but I am.*
I am happy you are *here.*	*Here and not somewhere else.*

Articulation involves smooth, fluent, and pleasant speech. It results from the way in which a speaker produces and joins sounds. Faulty articulation is often caused by not carefully forming individual sounds. Common examples include:

- Dropping word endings—saying *workin'* for working

- Running words together—saying *kinda* for *kind of* and *gonna* for *going to*

- Imprecise enunciation—saying *dis* for *this*, *wid* for *with*, *dem* for *them*, *pin* for *pen*, or *pitcher* for *picture*

These examples should not be confused with *dialect*, which people informally call an *accent*. A dialect is a variation in pronunciation, usually of vowels, from one part of the country to another. Actually, everyone speaks a dialect; speech experts can often identify, even pinpoint, the section of the country from where a speaker comes. In the United States, common dialects are New England, New York, Southern, Texan, Midwestern, and so forth. Within each of these, minor dialects often arise regionally or from immigrant influence. The simple fact is that when people interact, they influence one another even down to their speech sounds. Many prominent speakers have developed a rather universal dialect, known as Standard American Speech or American Broadcast English that seems to be effective no matter who the audience is. This model for professional language is widely used by newscasters and announcers and is easily understood by those who speak English as a second language because they likely listened to this speech pattern on television as they learned the language.

You can improve the clarity of your voice, reduce strain and voice distortion, and increase your expressiveness by following these guidelines:

- **Stand up straight with your shoulders back, and breathe from your diaphragm rather than your chest.** If you are breathing correctly, you can then use your mouth and teeth to form sounds precisely. For example, vowels are always sounded with the mouth open and the tongue clear of the palate. Consonants are responsible primarily for the distinctness of speech and are formed by an interference with or stoppage of outgoing breath.

- **Focus on completing the endings of all words, not running words together, and enunciating words correctly.** To identify recurring enunciation errors, listen to a recording and seek feedback from others.

- **Obtain formal training to improve your speech.** Pursue a self-study program by purchasing recordings that help you reduce your dialect and move more closely to a universal dialect. You can also enroll in

articulation smooth, fluent, and pleasant speech

a diction course to improve your speech patterns or arrange for private lessons from a voice coach.

Pronunciation involves using the principles of phonetics to create accurate sounds, rhythm, stress, and intonation. People might articulate perfectly but still mispronounce words. A dictionary provides the best source to review pronunciation. Two pronunciations are often given for a word, the first one being the desired pronunciation and the second an acceptable variation. An American adopting a pronunciation commonly used in England, such as *shedule* for *schedule* or *a-gane* for *again*, could be seen negatively. In some cases, leeway exists in pronunciation. The first choice for pronouncing *data* is to pronounce the first *a* long, as in *date*; but common usage is fast making pronunciation of the short *a* sound, as in *cat*, acceptable. Likewise, the preferred pronunciation of *often* is with a silent *t*. Good speakers use proper pronunciation and refer to the dictionary frequently in both pronunciation and vocabulary development.

When your voice qualities combine to make your messages pleasingly receptive, your primary concerns revolve around developing an effective delivery style.

12-4c Delivery Style

Speaking effectively is both an art and a skill. Careful planning and practice are essential for increasing speaking effectiveness.

BEFORE THE PRESENTATION

Follow these guidelines when preparing for your presentation:

- **Prepare thoroughly.** You can expect a degree of nervousness as you anticipate speaking before a group. This natural tension is constructive because it increases your concentration and your energy and enhances your performance. However, even those seasoned to the spotlight can experience a debilitating case of the jitters. In spring 2013, New Kids on the Block singer Jonathan Knight walked offstage in the middle of a concert in New York, prompting him to tweet apologies about his anxiety. Being well prepared is the surest way to control speech anxiety. Develop an outline for your presentation that supports your purpose and addresses the needs of your audience, and take advantage of every opportunity to gain speaking experience.

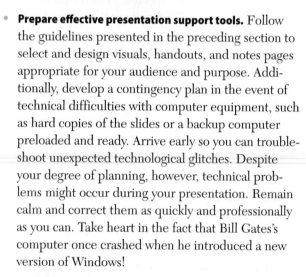

Yuriy Rudyy/Shutterstock.com

- **Prepare effective presentation support tools.** Follow the guidelines presented in the preceding section to select and design visuals, handouts, and notes pages appropriate for your audience and purpose. Additionally, develop a contingency plan in the event of technical difficulties with computer equipment, such as hard copies of the slides or a backup computer preloaded and ready. Arrive early so you can troubleshoot unexpected technological glitches. Despite your degree of planning, however, technical problems might occur during your presentation. Remain calm and correct them as quickly and professionally as you can. Take heart in the fact that Bill Gates's computer once crashed when he introduced a new version of Windows!

- **Practice, but do not rehearse.** Your goal is to become familiar with the key phrases on your note cards so that you can deliver the presentation naturally as if you are talking with the audience—not reciting the presentation or acting out a role. Avoid over practicing, which can make your presentation sound mechanical and limit your ability to respond to the audience.

- **Practice the entire presentation.** This practice will allow you to identify (1) flaws in organization or unity; (2) long, complex sentences or ineffective expressions; and (3) "verbal potholes." Verbal potholes include word combinations that could cause you to stumble, words you have trouble pronouncing ("irrelevant" or "statistics"), and words that accentuate your

pronunciation using principles of phonetics to create accurate sounds, rhythm, stress, and intonation

dialect ("get" can sound like "git" regardless of the intention of a Southern speaker).

- **Spend additional time practicing the introduction and conclusion.** You will want to deliver these important parts with finesse while making a confident connection with the audience. A good closing leaves the audience in a good mood and can help overcome some possible weaknesses during the speech. Depending on the techniques used, consider memorizing significant brief statements to ensure their accuracy and impact (e.g., a direct quotation or an exact statistic).

- **Practice displaying presentation visuals so that your delivery appears effortless and seamless.** Your goal is to make the technology virtually transparent—positioned in the background to support you as the primary focus of the presentation. First, be sure you know the basic commands for advancing through your presentation without displaying distracting menus. Develop the skill to return to a specific slide in the event of a computer glitch or an audience question.

- **Seek feedback on your performance to help you to polish your delivery and improve organization.** Critique your own performance by practicing in front of a mirror and evaluating a recording of your presentation. If possible, present your presentation to a small audience ahead of time for feedback and to minimize anxiety when presenting to the real audience.

- **Request a lectern to hold your notes and to steady a shaky hand, at least until you gain some confidence and experience.** Keep in mind, though, that weaning yourself from the lectern will eliminate a physical barrier between you and the audience. Without the lectern, you will speak more naturally. If you are using a microphone, ask for a portable microphone so that you can move freely.

- **Request a proper introduction if the audience knows little about you.** An effective introduction will establish your credibility as a speaker on the subject and will make the audience eager to hear you. You can prepare your own introduction as professional speakers do, or you can provide concise, targeted information that answers the following three questions: (1) Why is the subject relevant? (2) Who is the speaker? and (3) What credentials qualify the speaker to talk about the subject? Talk with the person introducing you to verify any information, especially the pronunciation of your name, and to review the format of the presentation (time limit, question-and-answer period, and so on). Be certain to thank the person who made the introduction as you begin your presentation. "Thank you for your kind introduction, Ms. Garcia" is adequate. Then follow with your own introduction to your presentation topic.

- **Dress appropriately to create a strong professional image and to bolster your self-confidence.** An audience's initial impression of your personal appearance, your clothing and grooming, affects their ability to accept you as a credible speaker. Because first impressions are difficult to overcome, take time to groom yourself immaculately and to select clothing that is appropriate for the speaking occasion and consistent with the audience's expectations.

- **Arrive early to become familiar with the setup of the room and to check the equipment.** Check the location of your chair, the lectern, the projection screen, light switches, and electrical outlets. Check the microphone and Internet connection and ensure that all equipment is in the appropriate place and working properly. Project your electronic presentation so you can adjust the color scheme to ensure maximum readability. Finally, identify the technician who will be responsible for resolving any technical problems that might occur during the presentation.

DURING THE PRESENTATION

The following are things you can do during your presentation to increase your effectiveness as a speaker:

- **Communicate confidence, warmth, and enthusiasm for the presentation and the time spent with the audience.** "Your listeners won't care how much you know until they know how much you care" is pertinent advice.[14]

  ○ **Exhibit a confident appearance with an alert posture.** Stand tall with your shoulders back and your stomach tucked in. Stand in the "ready position"—no slouching, hunching over the lectern, or rocking. Keep weight forward with knees slightly flexed so that you are ready to move easily, rather than being rooted rigidly in one spot, hiding behind the lectern.

  ○ **Smile genuinely throughout the presentation.** Pause as you take your place behind the lectern, and smile before you speak the first word. Smile as you finish your presentation and wait for the applause.

  ○ **Maintain steady eye contact with the audience in random places throughout the room.** Stay with one person approximately three to five seconds—long enough to finish a complete thought or sentence to convince the listener you are communicating individually with him or her. If the audience is large, select a few friendly faces and concentrate on speaking to them rather than to a sea of nondescript faces.

° **Refine gestures to portray a relaxed, approachable appearance.** Vary hand motions to emphasize important points; otherwise, let hands fall naturally to your side. Practice using only one hand to make points unless you specifically need two hands, such as when drawing a figure or showing dimensions or location. Eliminate any nervous gestures that can distract the audience (e.g., clenching your hands in front of or behind your body, steepling your hands, placing your hands in your pockets, jingling keys or change, or playing with a ring or pen).

° **Move from behind the lectern and toward the audience to reduce the barrier created between you and the audience.** You can stand to one side and casually present a relaxed pose beside the lectern. However, avoid methodically walking without a purpose.

• **Exercise strong vocal qualities.** Review the guidelines provided for using your voice to project confidence and credibility.

• **Watch your audience.** They will tell you how you are doing and whether you should shorten your speech. Be attentive to negative feedback in the form of talking, coughing, moving chairs, and other signs of discomfort.

• **Use your visuals effectively.** Many speakers will go to a great deal of effort to prepare good presentation visuals—and then not use them effectively. Inexperienced speakers often ignore the visual altogether or fall into the habit of simply nodding their heads toward the visual. Neither of these techniques is adequate for involving the audience with the visual. In fact, if the material is complex, the speaker is likely to lose the audience completely.

° **Step to one side of the visual so the audience can see it.** Use a pointer if necessary. Direct your remarks to the audience, so that you can maintain eye contact and resist the temptation to look over your shoulder or turn your back to read the information from the screen behind you.

° **Paraphrase the visual rather than reading it line for line.** To increase the quality of your delivery, develop a workable method of recording what you plan to say about each graphic.

• **Handle questions from the audience during the presentation.** Questions often disrupt carefully laid plans. At the same time, questions provide feedback, clarify points, and ensure understanding. When people ask questions that will be answered later in the presentation, say, "I believe the next slide will clarify that point; if not, we will come back to it." If the question can be answered quickly, you should do so while indicating that it will also be covered more later. Anticipate and prepare for questions that might be raised. You can generate presentation visuals pertaining to certain anticipated questions and display them only if the question is posed.

An audience will appreciate your thorough and complete explanation and your ability to adjust your presentation to their needs—this strategy is much more professional than stumbling through an explanation or delaying the answer until the information is available. Speakers giving electronic presentations have ready access to enormous amounts of information that can be displayed instantly for audience discussion. Hyperlinks created within a presentation file will move a speaker instantaneously to a specific slide, another file, or an embedded music or video file.

• **Keep within the time limit.** Be prepared to complete the presentation within the allotted time. In many organizations, speakers have one or more rehearsals before delivering reports to a group, such as a board of directors. These rehearsals, or dry runs, are made before other executives, and are critiqued, timed, revised, and rehearsed again. Presentation software makes rehearsing your timing as simple as clicking a button and advancing through the slides as you practice. By evaluating the total presentation time and the time spent on each slide, you can modify the presentation and rehearse it again until the presentation fits the time slot.

AFTER THE PRESENTATION

How you handle the time following a presentation is as important as preparing for the presentation itself:

- **Be prepared for a question-and-answer period.** Encourage the audience to ask questions, recognizing an opportunity to ensure that your presentation meets audience needs. Paraphrasing the question allows you time to reflect on what was asked, ensures that everyone heard the question, and assures the questioner that he or she was understood. You can ask the questioner if your answer was adequate. Be courteous even to hostile questioners so you will maintain the respect of your audience. Stay in control of the time by announcing that you have time for one or two more questions, and then invite individual questions when the presentation is over.

- **Distribute handouts.** Distribute the handout when it is needed rather than at the beginning of the presentation. Otherwise, the audience might read the handout while you are explaining background information needed to understand the written ideas. If you expect the audience to take notes directly on the handout, or if the audience will need to refer to the handout immediately, distribute the handout at the beginning of the presentation or before it begins. To keep control of the audience's attention, be sure listeners know when they should be looking at the handout or listening to you. If the handout is intended as resource material only, post the handout to a web page or place it on a table at the back of the room and at the front for those who come by to talk with you after the presentation.

12-5 ADAPTING TO ALTERNATE DELIVERY SITUATIONS

As you've learned, presenting a dynamic presentation that focuses on the audience's needs and expectations is the fundamental principle in presenting effectively. Along with the solid foundation you've set for spoken communication, you'll also need to adapt your presentation style to the ever-changing business environment and the special needs of culturally diverse audiences. Delivering team presentations, and presenting in distance formats are other common situations you'll need to master.

12-5a Culturally Diverse Audiences

When speaking to a culturally diverse audience, you will want to be as natural as possible while adjusting your message for important cultural variations. Using empathy, you can effectively focus on the listener as an individual rather than a stereotype of a specific culture. Be open and willing to learn, and you will reap the benefits by communicating effectively with people who possess a variety of strengths and creative abilities. Additionally, follow these suggestions for presenting to people from outside your own culture:

- **Speak simply.** Use simple English and short sentences. Avoid acronyms and expressions that can be confusing to non-native English speakers—namely slang, jargon, figurative expressions, and sports analogies.

- **Avoid words that trigger negative emotional responses such as anger, fear, or suspicion.** Such "red flag" words vary among cultures; thus, try to anticipate audience reaction and choose your words carefully.

- **Enunciate each word precisely and speak somewhat slowly.** Clear, articulate speech is especially important when the audience is not familiar with various dialects and vocabulary. Avoid the temptation to speak in a loud voice, a habit considered rude in any culture, and especially annoying to the Japanese, who perceive the normal tone of North Americans as too loud.

- **Be extremely cautious in the use of humor and jokes.** Cultures that prefer more formality might think you are not serious about your purpose or find your humor and jokes inappropriate. Many cultures from Asian countries, for instance, do not appreciate jokes about family members and the elderly.

- **Learn the culture's preferences for a direct or indirect presentation.** Although North Americans tend to prefer directness, with the main idea presented first, people from many cultures, such as Japanese, Latin American, and Arabic, consider a straightforward approach tactless and rude.

- **Adapt to subtle differences in nonverbal communication.** The direct eye contact expected by most North Americans is not typical of many cultures from Asian countries listeners, who often keep their eyes lowered and avoid eye contact to show respect. Arab audiences might stare into your eyes in an attempt to "see into the window of the soul." Cultures also vary on personal space and degree of physical contact (slap on the back or arm around the other as signs of friendship).

Even though the western approach to business presentations has spread as a type of ideal throughout much of the globe, it is important to recognize that public speaking is not a universal, but rather, a culturally variable communication practice, one that is often patterned, context-bound, and locally meaningful.[15] Many non-western speakers appear to be guided by norms of eloquence, tradition, authority, and community, rather than beliefs that everyone in the community is on equal footing and, thus, has the opportunity to speak and should do so by delivering fact-filled information in a conversational way.[15]

Although little research has been done on public speaking in other countries, some information exists. For example, Kenyan and Ugandan students found doing research during the preparation process odd and somewhat pedantic. Speaker credibility in Kenya is often determined by factors such as wealth, social status, age, education, ethnicity, and marital status. African speeches are often circular. They resemble a bicycle wheel with spokes wandering out repeatedly to the rim to make a point or tell a story, and then returning back to the center, the thesis. They are one-point speeches with a great deal of supporting material. Americans listening to such a speech might feel bewildered and even bored because they are unable to follow the logic that ties all the points together, whereas Kenyan listeners would be absorbed in the stories and delighted with their subtle convergence back into the central theme.[16]

Even those from cultures within the western world may have other public-speaking ideals. In the United States, the Blackfeet hold that the typical public speaker is the elder male whose experience and wisdom give him the right to speak in public. The most valuable form of communication, according to the Blackfeet, is attentive listening to others (especially the elders) and to one's natural surroundings. Because public speakers hold a high position in society, they deserve community members' respect. Young, inexperienced Blackfeet should feel too embarrassed to speak in public, and elders who are expected to speak should appreciate that the community depends on their guidance. Finally, the Blackfeet hold that the world around them should be listened to rather than talked about.[17]

While the western ideal highlights the role of two types of participants, speakers and audiences, who are on relatively equal footing in terms of social status, and public-speaking practices, non-western speech communities may involve a more stratified set of participants with differently defined social roles and privileges. Western Desert Aboriginal communities in central Australia offer a context in which multiple participants work to build speech sequences.[18] Here, collective decision making is achieved through public discourse in which multiple speakers offer continual, repeating, and overlapping summary accounts, this rapid and "vociferous vocal participation of all present parties" signifies the value of the communal voice over the voice of the individual.[19]

While institutional and personal successes are desired outcomes within the western cultural ideal, these ends are not prominent in many non-western speech communities. Though some non-western speakers valued being perceived as competent or skilled, the public speaking aims of "upward mobility" and "self-improvement" seem uncommon in non-western public-speaking contexts.[20] This may be linked to the fact that many of these contexts exist in stratified social hierarchies in which upward mobility is less attainable or is culturally less desirable.[21] This difference may also be connected to the focus on public speaking as a collective, rather than individual, endeavor in many non-western contexts.

Speaking appropriately in many non-western contexts establishes social authority for the speaker and often works to maintain social hierarchies within speech communities. While western contexts place a large emphasis on the role of the speaker as an individual, many non-western ways of public speaking emphasize community over individuality by placing value on speakers' abilities to speak on behalf of the group as a whole, or to represent subgroups within the larger community.[22]

Pavel L Photo and Video/Shutterstock.com

- **Adapt your dress and presentation style to fit the formality of the culture.** Some cultures prefer a higher degree of formality than the casual style of North Americans. To accommodate, dress conservatively; strive to connect with the audience in a formal, reserved manner; and use highly professional visuals rather than jotting ideas on a flip chart.

- **Seek feedback to determine whether the audience is understanding your message.** Observe listeners carefully for signs of misunderstanding, restating ideas as necessary. Consider allowing time for questions after short segments of your presentation. Avoid asking "Is that clear?" or "Do you understand?" as these statements might elicit a "Yes" answer if the person perceives saying "No" to be a sign of incompetence.

Potential frustrations can also occur when presentations or meetings bring together North Americans, who see "time as money," with people of cultures who are not time conscious and believe that personal relationships are the basis of business dealings (e.g., Asian and Latin American cultures). When communicating with cultures that are not time driven, be patient with what you might consider time-consuming formalities and courtesies, and lengthy decision-making styles when you would rather get right down to business or move to the next point. Recognize that the presentation might not begin on time or stay on a precise schedule. Allow additional time at the beginning of the presentation to establish rapport and credibility with the audience, and perhaps provide brief discussion periods devoted to building relationships during the presentation.

Be patient and attentive during long periods of silence; in many cultures people are inclined to stay silent unless they have something significant to say or if they are considering (not necessarily rejecting) an idea. In fact, some Japanese people have asked how North Americans can think and talk at the same time. Understanding patterns of silence can help you feel more comfortable during these seemingly endless moments, and less compelled to fill the gaps with unnecessary words or to make concessions before the other side has a chance to reply.

Other significant points of difference between cultures are the varying rules of business etiquette. Should you use the traditional American handshake or some other symbol of greeting? Is using the person's given name acceptable? What formal titles should be used with a surname? Can you introduce yourself, or must you have someone else who knows the other person introduce you? Are business cards critical, and what rules should you follow when presenting a business card? Should you have business cards that are printed in two languages?

Gift giving can be another confusing issue. When you believe a gift should be presented to your event host, investigate the appropriateness of gift giving, the types of gifts considered appropriate or absolutely inappropriate, and the colors of wrapping to be avoided in the speaker's culture. Liquor, for example, is an inappropriate gift in Arab countries.

Gaining competence in matters of etiquette will enable you to make a positive initial impression and concentrate on the presentation rather than agonizing over an awkward, embarrassing slip in protocol. Your audience will appreciate your willingness to learn and value their customs. Being sensitive to cultural issues and persistent in learning specific differences in customs and practices can minimize confusion and unnecessary embarrassment.

12-5b Team Presentations

Because much of the work in business today is done in teams, many presentations are planned and delivered by teams of presenters. Well-conducted team presentations give an organization an opportunity to showcase its brightest talent while capitalizing on each person's unique presentation skills. Email, collaborative software, and other technologies make it easy to develop, edit, review, and deliver impressive team presentations.

The potential payoff of many team presentations is quite high—perhaps a $200,000 contract or a million-dollar account. Yet, according to experts, team presentations fail primarily because presenters don't devote enough time and resources to develop and rehearse them.[23] Resist the sure-to-fail strategy of "winging" a team presentation rather than taking the time to do it correctly. Instead, adapt the skills you already possess in planning and delivering an individual presentation to ensure a successful team presentation. Follow these guidelines as you plan and prepare your team presentation:

- **Select a winning team.** Begin by choosing a leader who is well liked and respected by the team, is knowledgeable of the project, is well organized, and will follow through. Likewise, the leader should be committed to leading the team in the development of a cohesive strategy for the presentation as well as the delegation of specific responsibilities to individual members. Frank Carillo, president of Executive Communications Group, warns team presenters that a frequent problem with "divvying up" work into pieces is that the "pieces don't fit together well when they come back."[24] The core team members, along with management, should choose a balanced mix of individuals who each have something important to contribute to

PART 5

13 | Preparing Résumés and Application Messages

Rawpixel.com/Shutterstock.com

LEARNING OBJECTIVES

After studying this chapter, you will be able to …

13-1 Prepare for employment by considering relevant information about yourself as it relates to job requirements.

13-2 Identify career opportunities using traditional and electronic methods.

13-3 Prepare an organized, persuasive résumé that is adapted for print and electronic postings.

13-4 Use employment tools other than the résumé that can enhance employability.

13-5 Write an application message that effectively introduces an accompanying print (designed) or electronic résumé.

After finishing this chapter, go to **PAGE 269** for **STUDY TOOLS.**

13-1 PREPARING FOR THE JOB SEARCH

Managing your career begins with recognizing that securing a new job is less important than assessing the impact of that job on your life. Work isn't something that happens from 8 a.m. to 5 p.m., with life happening after 5 p.m. Life and work are interconnected, and true satisfaction comes from being able to fully express yourself in what you do. This means merging who you are—your values, emotions, capabilities, and desires—with the activities you perform on the job.[1]

An ideal job provides satisfaction at all of Maslow's need levels, from basic economic to self-actualizing needs. The right job for you will not be drudgery; the work itself will be satisfying and give you a sense of well-being. Synchronizing your work with your core beliefs and talents leads to enthusiasm and fulfillment. You will probably work 10,000 days of your life, not including the time spent commuting and on other related activities. Why spend all this time doing something unfulfilling when you could just as easily spend it doing what you enjoy?

Your **résumé** is a vital communication tool that provides a basis for judgment about your capabilities on the job. In preparing this document, your major tasks will be gathering essential information about yourself and the job, using traditional and electronic resources, planning and organizing the résumé to showcase your key qualifications, and adapting the résumé for various types of delivery. You will need to supplement your résumé with examples of your accomplishments and abilities. Finally, you'll prepare persuasive application messages appropriate for the delivery of your résumé.

> You will probably work 10,000 days of your life, not including time spent commuting and on other related activities.

13-1a Gathering Essential Information

The job search begins with research—collecting, compiling, and analyzing information—in order to assess your marketability. The research phase of the job search involves the steps shown in Figure 13.1 on the next page and are summarized as follows:

1. **Gather relevant information for decision making.** Complete a self-assessment to identify your own job-related qualifications, and an analysis of the career field that interests you as well as a specific job in that field. Follow-up in an interview with a career person in your field to acquire additional information.

2. **Prepare a company/job profile.** Compile the information you gathered into a format that allows you to compare your qualifications with the company and job requirements. This organized information will help you determine a possible match between you and the potential job.

3. **Identify unique selling points and specific support.** Determine several key qualifications and accomplishments that enhance your marketability. These are the key selling points you'll target in your résumé and later in a job interview.

13-1b Identifying Potential Career Opportunities

Plan to begin your job search for prospective employers months in advance. Waiting too long to begin and then hurrying through the job search process could affect your ability to land a satisfying job.

Before you begin, take the time to develop an organized strategy for your search efforts. You might download a template such as Microsoft's job search log (**http://office.microsoft.com/en-us/templates/results.aspx?qu=job%20search%20log**) or invest in software such as Winway Résumé and Résumé Maker Deluxe to simplify the task of tracking your contacts. You'll need a record of the name, address, email address, and telephone number of each potential employer. Later, record the date of each job contact you make and receive (along with what you learned from the contact), the name of the contact person, the date you sent a résumé, and so on. Your search for potential career opportunities likely will involve traditional and electronic job search sources.

USING TRADITIONAL SOURCES

Traditional means of locating a job include printed sources, networks, career services centers, employers' offices, employment agencies and contractors, and professional organizations.

PRINTED SOURCES

Numerous printed sources are useful in identifying firms in need of employees. Responses to advertised positions in the employment sections of newspapers

> **résumé** a vital communication tool that provides a basis for judgment about a person's capabilities on the job

FIGURE 13.1 **PROCESS OF APPLYING FOR A JOB**

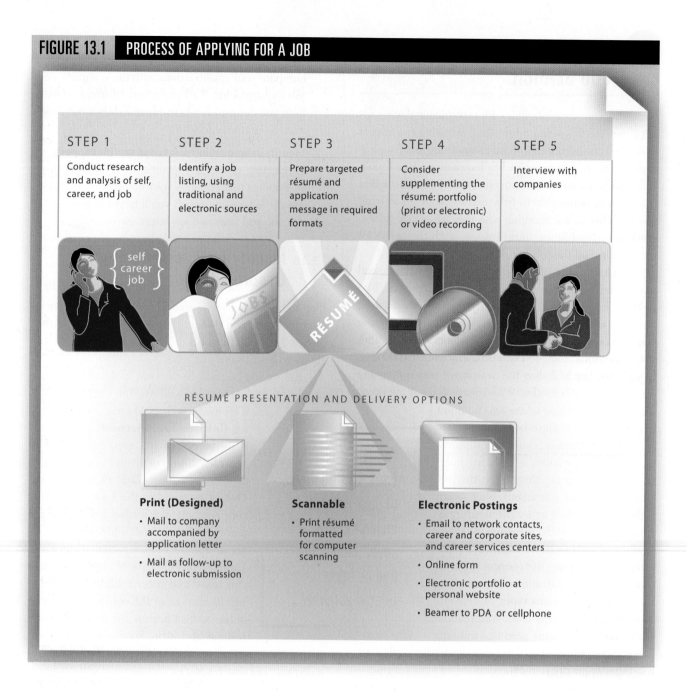

STEP 1

Conduct research and analysis of self, career, and job

STEP 2

Identify a job listing, using traditional and electronic sources

STEP 3

Prepare targeted résumé and application message in required formats

STEP 4

Consider supplementing the résumé: portfolio (print or electronic) or video recording

STEP 5

Interview with companies

RÉSUMÉ PRESENTATION AND DELIVERY OPTIONS

Print (Designed)
- Mail to company accompanied by application letter
- Mail as follow-up to electronic submission

Scannable
- Print résumé formatted for computer scanning

Electronic Postings
- Email to network contacts, career and corporate sites, and career services centers
- Online form
- Electronic portfolio at personal website
- Beamer to PDA or cellphone

should be made as quickly as possible after the ad is circulated. If your résumé is received early and is impressive, you could get a favorable response before other applications are received. If an ad requests that responses be sent to a box number without giving a name, be cautious. The employer could be legitimate but does not want present employees to know about the ad or does not want applicants to phone or drop by. However, you have a right to be suspicious of someone who wants to remain obscure while learning everything you reveal in your résumé. Print job listings can also be found in company newsletters, industry directories, and trade and professional publications, which are often available on the Internet.

NETWORKS

The majority of job openings are never advertised. Therefore, developing a network of contacts is often the most valuable source of information about jobs. A number of professional networking sites exist online. Today, LinkedIn is the most popular networking website for business professionals. Facebook plays the dual role of enabling personal as well as professional networking. Many entrepreneurs actively exploit social media, such as Facebook and Twitter, to promote their businesses and services. These are just a few of the social networking opportunities available.

Gil C/Shutterstock.com

Your network could include current and past employers, guest speakers in your classes or at student organization meetings, business contacts you met while interning or participating in shadowing or over-the-shoulder experiences, professors, and so on. Let these individuals know the type of job you are seeking, and ask their advice for finding employment in today's competitive market.

CAREER SERVICES CENTERS

You will want to register with your college's career services center at least three semesters before you graduate. Typically, the center has a website and a browsing room loaded with career information and job announcement bulletins. Career counseling is available at most career services centers, including workshops on résumé writing, interviewing, etiquette, mock interviews, "mocktail" parties for learning to mingle at pre-interview social events, and more. Through the center, you can learn about job fairs at which you can meet prospective employers and schedule on-campus, phone, and video interviews with company recruiters.

Most career services centers use electronic tracking systems. Rather than submitting printed résumés, students input their résumés into a computer file, following the specific requirements of the tracking system used by the college or university. A search of the résumé database generates an interview roster of the top applicants for a campus recruiter's needs. Some centers assist students in preparing electronic portfolios to supplement their résumés.

> For local businesses, it might be useful to schedule an informational interview to learn more about the employer and the type of skills that it looks for in new employees.

EMPLOYERS' WEBSITES AND OFFICE LOCATIONS

Most organizations post job openings on their website. For local businesses, it might be useful to schedule an informational interview to learn more about the employer and the type of skills that it looks for in new employees. Although you should not ask for a job during an informational interview, the contact you have made may pay off in the future as part of your professional network.

EMPLOYMENT AGENCIES AND CONTRACTORS

City, county, state, and federal employment agencies provide free or inexpensive services. Some agencies offer online listings or phone recordings so that applicants can get information about job opportunities and procedures for using their services. The fee charged by private agencies is paid by either the employee or the employer, and is usually based on the first month's salary and is due within a few months. Some agencies specialize in finding high-level executives or specialists for major firms. Employment contractors specialize in providing temporary employees and might be able to place you in a position on a temporary basis until you find a full-time job.

PROFESSIONAL ORGANIZATIONS

Officers of professional organizations, through their contacts with members, can be good sources of information about job opportunities. A lot of job information is exchanged at meetings of professional associations. In addition to job listings in journals or on organization's websites, interviews are sometimes conducted at conference locations.

In addition to the professional growth that comes from membership in professional organizations, active participation is a good way to learn about jobs. Guest speakers share valuable information about the industry and its career and job opportunities. Employers are often favorably impressed when membership and experiences gained are included on the résumé and discussed during an interview. They are even more impressed if the applicant has been an officer in the organization, as it indicates leadership, community commitment, and willingness to serve without tangible reward, social acceptance, or high level of aspiration. By joining and actively participating in professional, social,

FIGURE 13.2 **TEN MOST POPULAR JOB WEBSITES***

indeed one search. all jobs. 36,000,000—Estimated Unique Monthly Visitors

monster 23,000,000—Estimated Unique Monthly Visitors

careerbuilder 22,400,000—Estimated Unique Monthly Visitors

glassdoor.com 15,000,000—Estimated Unique Monthly Visitors

SimplyHired 11,000,000—Estimated Unique Monthly Visitors

JOBDIAGNOSIS 10,000,000—Estimated Unique Monthly Visitors

Aol Jobs. 8,000,000—Estimated Unique Monthly Visitors

BEYOND.com. 4,750,000—Estimated Unique Monthly Visitors

snagajob.com 4,500,000—Estimated Unique Monthly Visitors

ZipRecruiter 3,500,000—Estimated Unique Monthly Visitors

*The 10 Most Popular Job Sites were derived from the *eBizMBA Rank*, which is a constantly updated average of each website's *Alexa* Global Traffic Rank and U.S. Traffic Rank from both *Compete* and *Quantcast*.

Source: Top 15 Most Popular Job Websites (2014, May). Retrieved October 2016, from http://www.ebizmba.com/articles/job-websites.

both job applicants and employers. Figure 13.2 provides a list of the top 10 job websites as calculated by eBizMBA.[2]

The job sites include jobs of all levels, occupations, and locations. Others specialize in certain kinds of jobs. Most job sites provide the following features and information:

- **Search and apply for job openings.** There are thousands of online job banks. Most work in the same basic way: employers pay to post job openings; job seekers search the openings and apply for those that interest them. Most sites allow you to search by occupation, location, industry, and other characteristics.

- **Post your résumé.** Sometimes you can post your résumé without applying for a specific job. On some job sites, employers can then review your résumé for positions they haven't even posted.

- **Get a feel for job requirements and pay.** Job websites can be a good research tool. They can help you learn what kinds of workers employers want, the skills they expect, and the pay and benefits they offer.

When using job sites, as with other online resources, be aware of possible fraudulent activities. For example, you should not have to pay to post your résumé or search job openings. However, you may have to register to use all of the features of a job website. Likewise, some job postings are scams. Be wary of any that ask you for an "up-front" investment of money for products or instructions. Also, be wary of those that offer commissions or pay thousands of dollars for job duties, such as processing checks on behalf of foreign nationals or reshipping goods from your home.

and honorary organizations, you increase your opportunities to develop rapport with peers and professors and gain an edge over less-involved applicants.

USING ELECTRONIC EMPLOYMENT RESOURCES

An increasing number of companies and job hunters are using the Internet to assist in various stages of the job search process. As part of this trend, a number of job sites have been established that provide a variety of services to

Finally, never give out personal information. A legitimate company won't ask you for your social security number, credit card numbers, bank account information, or any other personal details.

LOCATING CAREER GUIDANCE INFORMATION

According to one career consultant, "Most people in the old days could go into an organization [during a job interview] and not really know about it and hope for the best. Now, people can understand the organization before they even apply."[3] The Internet places at your fingertips a wealth of information that will prepare you for the job interview if you use it as a research tool. Suggestions for effectively using career guidance information on the Internet follow:

- **Visit career sites for information related to various phases of the job search.** You'll find a wide range of timely discussions on career sites: planning a job search, finding a job you love, researching employers, working a career fair, crafting winning résumés and cover letters, negotiating a salary, and so on.

- **Visit corporate websites to learn about companies.** You can locate information online for targeting your résumé appropriately and to prepare for the job interview. Read mission statements or descriptions of services to see how the organization describes itself, and review the annual report and strategic plan to learn about their financial condition and predicted growth rates. Search for "What's New" or "News" sections promoting new developments, as well as career opportunities and job postings. Evaluating the development and professional nature of the website will give you an impression of the organization. Supplement this information with independent sources to confirm the company's stability and status, as negative news likely will not be posted on the website.

- **Identify the specific skills that companies are seeking.** Study the job descriptions provided on corporate home pages and job sites to identify the skills required for the job and the latest industry buzzwords. Use this information to target your résumé to a specific job listing and to generate keywords for an electronic résumé.

- **Network with prospective employers.** It's easy to network online by attending electronic job fairs, chatting with career counselors, participating in news groups and LISTSERVs applicable to your field, and corresponding by email with contacts in companies. The value of these electronic networking experiences is to learn about an industry and career, seek valued opinions, and uncover potential job opportunities. By applying effective communication strategies for an online community, you can make a good impression, create rapport with employment contacts online, and polish your interviewing skills.

USING THE INTERNET TO IDENTIFY JOB LISTINGS

When using the Internet or online databases to search for specific job openings, follow these general suggestions to get started:

- Input words and phrases that describe your skills rather than job titles because job titles vary by company.

- Use specific phrases such as "entry-level job" or "job in advertising" rather than "job search."

- Start with a wider job description term, such as "pharmaceutical sales jobs"; then narrow down to the specific subject, geographic region, state, and so forth.

- Don't limit yourself to one search engine or online job site; try several, and bookmark interesting sites.

- Stay focused on your goal, and don't get distracted as you go.

13-2 PLANNING A TARGETED RÉSUMÉ

In order to match your interests and qualifications with available jobs, you'll need an effective résumé. To win a job interview in today's tight market where job seekers outnumber positions, you need more than a general résumé that documents your education and work history. The powerful wording of a **targeted résumé** reflects the requirements of a specific job listing that you have identified through traditional and electronic job search methods.

An employer typically scans résumés quickly, looking for reasons to reject the applicant, schedule an interview, or place it in a stack for rereading. This initial scan and a second brief look for those who make the cut give little time to explain why you are the best person for the job. To grab an employer's attention, you must selectively choose *what to say, how to say it,* and *how to arrange it* on the page so that it can be read quickly but thoroughly. A concise, informative, easy-to-read summary of your relevant qualifications will demonstrate that you possess the straightforward communication skills demanded in today's information-intensive society.

The goal of the résumé is to get an interview, so your résumé must show that you are, at least on the surface,

> **targeted résumé** a résumé that reflects the requirements of a specific job listing

qualified for the job for which you are applying. The best way to do this is to match your skills to those the employer is seeking. Hopefully, you have already done your homework and familiarized yourself with the type of skills, experience, and qualifications that employers in your field are looking for by finding and analyzing job advertisements for the position you desire. If you have performed this task well, you should have a solid understanding of the skills and qualifications you will need. You should have also spent some time reviewing your own life history in order to identify situations in which you have demonstrated those skills and abilities.

If you have done both of these tasks effectively, you should be well prepared to write a résumé that matches your skills with those an employer is seeking. These are the skills and qualifications that should be easily gleaned from a quick scan of your completed résumé. Other skills and experiences should be omitted so that your résumé is well targeted to the specific position that you are seeking. This fact should be almost immediately obvious to the employer reviewing your materials.

It is also important to remember that your résumé is not being reviewed in a vacuum. It is likely that the employer also is reviewing dozens of other résumés at the same time he or she is reading yours. For this reason, you should also have a solid knowledge of what your competitors bring to the table and how well you compare. A strategic job seeker will have a clear idea of his or her strongest selling points as compared with others and will have considered how to best showcase these favorably.

> An employer typically scans résumés quickly, looking for reasons to reject the applicant, schedule an interview, or place it in a stack for rereading.

Another name for résumé is "*curriculum vitae*" or "CV," which is Latin for "course of one's life."

13-2a Standard Parts of a Résumé

A winning résumé contains standard parts that are adapted to highlight key qualifications for a specific job. The sample résumés and in-depth explanation of each standard part provided in Figures 13.3 to 13.6 (see pages 253–259) will prepare you for creating a résumé that describes your qualifications best.

IDENTIFICATION

Your objective is to provide information that will allow the interviewer to reach you. Include your name, current address, phone number, and email address. Provide a clear, benign email address that reflects a positive impression (e.g., no "mustangsally"). You should also include your website address or professional networking page to provide access to more detailed information.

To ensure that the interviewer can quickly locate the identification information, center it on the page or use graphic design elements to call attention to your name. You should include a permanent address (parent's or other relative's address) if you are interviewing when classes are not in session. In addition, leave a clear, straightforward greeting on your phone that portrays you as a person serious about securing a job. Eliminate music, clever sayings, or background noise.

JOB AND/OR CAREER OBJECTIVE

Following the "Identification" section, state your job/career objective—the job you want. Interviewers can see quickly whether the job you seek matches the one they have to offer. A good job/career objective must be specific enough to be meaningful yet general enough to apply to a variety of jobs. The following example illustrates a general objective that has been revised to describe a specific job:

General Objective	Specific Objective
A challenging position that enables me to contribute to an organization's success.	Position where my creative Web design skills and ability to work under pressure will enable me to contribute to organizational success.
A position with a stable organization that provides an opportunity for development and career advancement.	Position where my accounting knowledge, attention to detail, and strong work ethic will enable me to contribute to a firm's financial success.

In addition to addressing your skills, values, and goals, a useful objective statement is positioned so as to show how these abilities will contribute to an organization. Some employment specialists have criticized objective statements as being generally too self-centered and, thus, not particularly useful. Other experts argue that a statement of your job or career objective can limit your job opportunities; your objective should be obvious from your qualifications. A strategic job applicant will consider the usefulness of including an objective statement when taken into consideration with other aspects of his or her résumé and how well he or she can best compete for a position.

CAREER SUMMARY

To survive the interviewer's 40-second scan, you must provide a compelling reason for a more thorough review of your résumé. To accomplish this goal, another strategy is to craft a persuasive introductory statement that quickly synthesizes your most transferable skills, accomplishments, and attributes, and place it in a section labeled "Summary" or "Professional Profile." As stated earlier, be aware that you are competing with others, so you want to position yourself favorably in comparison by highlighting your personal strengths as they relate to the desired skills or abilities.

In other words, the synopsis of your key qualifications should communicate why you should be hired. Your answer should evolve naturally from the career objective and focus on your ability to meet the needs of the company you have identified from your extensive research.

A high-impact career summary should be developed for your profile on job websites or professional networking sites. A version of this summary can be provided on your résumé as well. Compose a career summary that will interest any interviewer so that he or she will instantly see you as an applicant with exactly the skills needed for the job, as in the following example:

> **Hardworking banking professional with two years of experience processing residential and commercial real-estate loans. Very active in professional organizations locally, resulting in a large network of potential clients. Named "Most Promising Young Banker" by the Iowa Banking Association in 2014.**

This example combines the applicant's career objective—loan officer at a bank—with her unique selling points: her involvement in the local business community and acknowledgment of her promise by a recognized and relevant professional organization.

SEPARATE OBJECTIVE AND CAREER SUMMARY

Objective: Position where my proven customer service skills and strong work habits will enable me to contribute to a growing company.

Career Summary: Six years of experience in a telephone service center; promoted to team leader after two years and supervisor after four.

COMBINED OBJECTIVE WITH CAREER SUMMARY

Professional Profile: Entry-level position in investment banking or finance. Internship experience with two investment banking firms, where I prepared and delivered multiple sales presentations to potential high-volume clients.

LINKED OBJECTIVE AND CAREER SUMMARY

Profile: Position as sales representative in which demonstrated commission selling and hard work bring rewards.

Accomplishments:

▶ Three years' straight commission sales.

▶ Average of $35,000–$55,000 a year in commissioned earnings.

▶ Consistent success in development and growth of territories.

QUALIFICATIONS

The "Qualifications" section varies depending on the information identified in the analysis of self, career, and job. This information is used to divide your qualifications into appropriate parts, label them appropriately, and arrange them in the best sequence. Usually, qualifications stem from your education and work experience (words that appear as headings in the résumé). Order these categories according to which you perceive as more impressive to the employer, with the more impressive category appearing first. For example, education is usually the chief qualification of a recent college graduate. However, a sales representative with related work experience might list experience first, particularly if the educational background is inadequate for the job sought.

EDUCATION

Beginning with the most recent, list the degree, major, school, and graduation date. Include a blank line between schools for easy reading. The interviewer will probably want to know first whether you have the appropriate degree, then the institution, and then other details. Recent

Your résumé should include educational experiences that are beyond requirements, such as study abroad.

WORK EXPERIENCE

The "Work Experience" section provides information about your employment history. For each job held, list the job title, company name, dates of employment, primary responsibilities, and key accomplishments. The jobs can be listed in reverse chronological order (beginning with the most recent) or in order of job relatedness. Begin with the job that most obviously relates to the job being sought if you have gaps in your work history, if the job you are seeking is very different from the job you currently hold, or if you are just entering the job market and have little, if any, related work experience.

Arrange the order and format of information about each job (dates, job title, company, description, and accomplishments) so that the most important information is emphasized—but format all job information consistently. If you have held numerous jobs in a short time, embed dates of employment within the text rather than surround them with white space. Give related job experience added emphasis by listing it first or surrounding it with white space.

Employers are interested in how you can contribute to their bottom line, so a winning strategy involves concentrating on accomplishments and achievements. Begin with the job title and company name that provides basic information about your duties, and then craft powerful descriptions of the quality and scope of your performance. These bullet points will provide deeper insight into your capability, ambition, and personality and set you apart from other applicants who take the easy route of providing only a work history.

Return to the in-depth analysis you completed at the beginning of the job search process to recall insights as to how you can add immediate value to this company. Consider the following questions to spur your recognition of marketable skills from your education, work, and community experiences.[4]

or near college graduates should omit high school activities because that information is "old news." However, include high school activities if they provide a pertinent dimension to your qualifications. For example, having attended high school abroad is a definite advantage to an applicant seeking employment in an international firm. In addition, high school accomplishments could be relevant for freshmen or sophomores seeking cooperative education assignments, scholarships, or part-time jobs. Of course, this information will be replaced with college activities when the résumé is revised for subsequent jobs or other uses.

Include overall and major grade point averages if they are B or better—but be prepared to discuss any omissions during an interview. Some recruiters recommend that every candidate include his or her grade point average because an omission might lead the reader to assume the worst. Honors and achievements that relate directly to education can be incorporated in this section or included in a separate section. Listing scholarships, appearances on academic lists, and initiations into honor societies is common; but consider also including business-relevant skills you've developed, including client projects, team building, and field experiences. If honors and achievements are included in the "Education" section, be sure to include plenty of white space or use bullets to highlight these points (see Figure 13.3 on page 253 and Figure 13.5 on pages 255–256).

The "Education" section could also include a list of special skills and abilities such as foreign language and computer competency. A list of courses typically required in your field is unnecessary and occupies valuable space. However, you should include any courses, workshops, or educational experiences that are not usual requirements, such as internships, cooperative education semesters, "shadowing," and study abroad.

MY MARKETABLE SKILLS

▶ How does my potential employer define success in the job for which I'm applying? How do I measure up?

▶ What is my potential employer's bottom line (money, attendance, sales, etc.)? When have I shown that I know how to address that bottom line?

▶ What project am I proud of that demonstrates I have the skill for my job objective?

▶ What technical or management skills do I have that indicate the level at which I perform?

▶ What problem did I solve, how did I solve it, and what were the results?

SKILLS

right column of the previous example: action words used as first words provide emphasis. One of the best places to find action words is in the advertisements for the jobs for which you are applying. Using key phrases from the job advertisement can help the applicant in two ways: (1) you look like a good fit with the company because you use the same language, and (2) your résumé will more likely be identified by the search software used to select the best qualified applicants for interviews. The following list provides examples of action verbs that are useful in résumés:

Because interviewers spend such a short time reading résumés, the style must be direct and simple. Therefore, a résumé should use crisp phrases to help employers see the value of the applicant's education and experiences. To save space and to emphasize what you have accomplished, use these stylistic techniques:

1. Omit pronouns referring to yourself (*I, me, and my*).

2. Use subject-understood sentences.

3. Begin sentences with action verbs as shown in the following examples:

achieved	drafted	participated
analyzed	increased	planned
assigned	initiated	recruited
assisted	interpreted	researched
boosted	managed	streamlined
compiled	monitored	supervised
developed	organized	wrote

A quick Web search will result in additional action verbs from which to select.

To avoid a tone of egotism, do not use too many adjectives or adverbs that seem overly strong. Plan to do some careful editing after writing your first draft.

Instead of	Use
I had responsibility for developing sales materials.	Developed sales materials, including brochures and website promotions.
My duties included meeting with potential clients to review financial products.	Met with potential clients and used interpersonal communication skills to sell a wide range of financial products.
I was the treasurer of my fraternity and managed a charitable fund-raising event.	Managed a $200,000-plus budget and organized a charitable fund-raising event that garnered $15,000, a 25% increase over previous year.
I worked in retail sales, selling fashions and accessories.	Named salesperson of the year for sales of more than $50,000.
I was the president of the Student Marketing Association and a member of a winning case-competition team.	Demonstrated excellent leadership skills as president of Student Marketing Association and collaborative teamwork skills as member of winning case-competition group.

Action verbs are especially appropriate for résumés because employers are looking for people who will work. Note the subject-understood sentences in the

HONORS AND ACTIVITIES

Make a trial list of any other information that qualifies you for the job. Divide the list into appropriate divisions and then select an appropriate label. Your heading might be "Honors and Activities." You might include a section for "Activities," "Leadership Activities," or "Memberships," depending on the items listed. You might also include a separate section on "Military Service," "Civic Activities," "Volunteer Work," or "Interests." If you have only a few items under each category, use a more general term and combine the lists. If your list is lengthy, divide it into more than one category as interviewers prefer "bite-size" pieces that are easy to read and remember.

Resist the urge to include everything you have ever done; keep in mind that every item you add distracts from other information. Consider summarizing information that is relevant but does not merit several separate lines—for example, "Involved in art, drama, and choral groups." To decide whether to include certain information, ask these questions: How closely related is it to the job being sought? Does it provide job-related information that has not been presented elsewhere?

PERSONAL INFORMATION

Because a résumé should primarily contain information that is relevant to an applicant's experience and qualifications, you must be selective when including personal information that is not related to the job you are seeking. The space could be used more effectively to include more about your qualifications or to add more white space. Personal information is commonly placed at the end of the résumé just above the "References" section because it is less important than qualifications (education, experience, and activities).

Under the 1964 Civil Rights Act (and subsequent amendments) and the Americans with Disabilities Act (ADA), employers cannot make hiring decisions based on gender, age, marital status, religion, national origin, or disability. Employers prefer not to receive information about these protected areas because questions could be raised about whether the information was used in the hiring decision.

Follow these guidelines related to personal information:

- **Do not include personal information that could lead to discriminatory hiring.** Exclude height, weight, color of hair and eyes, and a personal photograph on the résumé.

- **Reveal ethnic background (and other personal information) only if it is job related.** For example, certain businesses might be actively seeking employees in certain ethnic groups because the ethnic background is a legitimate part of the job description. For such a business, ethnic information is useful and appreciated.

- **Include personal information (other than information covered by employment legislation) that will strengthen your résumé.** Select information that is related to the job you are seeking or that portrays you as a well-rounded, happy individual off the job. Include interests, hobbies, favorite sports, and willingness to relocate. You can also include the following topics if you have not covered them elsewhere in the résumé: spoken and written communication skills, computer competency, foreign language or computer skills, military service, community service, scholastic honors, job-related hobbies, and professional association memberships.

- **Consider whether personal information might be controversial.** For example, listing a sport that an interviewer might perceive to be overly time consuming or dangerous would be questionable. An applicant seeking a position with a religious or political organization could benefit from revealing a related affiliation.

REFERENCES

Providing potential employers a list of references (people who have agreed to supply information about you when requested) complements your employment credentials. Listing names, addresses, phone numbers, and email addresses of people who can provide information about you adds credibility to the résumé. Employers, former employers, and college instructors are good possibilities. Friends, relatives, and neighbors are not (because of their perceived bias in your favor). Some career experts recommend including a peer to document your ability to work as a member of a team, an important job skill in today's team-oriented environment.[5] According to Bob

---

LIVING ONLINE?

Your Facebook or Myspace profile, photos, and "innermost" thoughts create a "shadow" résumé that may hurt your employment opportunities far into the future.

A recent employer survey indicated that 44% of employers use social networking sites to examine the profiles of job candidates, and 39% have looked up the profile of a current employee.[6]

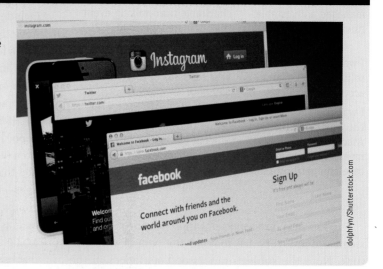

Daugherty, who heads U.S. recruiting for Pricewater-houseCoopers, the best references are people who work for the organization you are looking to join.[7] You'll gain these employee referrals by developing strong relationships through proactive and professional networking via traditional and electronic means. Update your reference list often to be certain that your choices remain relevant and credible (e.g., none are deceased or dismissed for embezzlement).

References can be handled on the résumé in several ways. As the closing section of your résumé, you can provide a list of references; include a brief statement that references are available on request or from a career services center; or omit any statement regarding references, assuming that references are not needed until after an interview. You can list references directly on the résumé if you have limited qualifications to include, if you know that a company interviews applicants *after* references are contacted, or when you believe the names of your references will be recognizable in your career field. You could include a statement such as "For references …," or "For additional information …," and give the address of the career services center of your college or university, the job bank posting your credentials, or the URL of your electronic portfolio.

Withholding the names of references until they are requested prevents unnecessary or untimely requests going to your present employer. This action also conveys genuine courtesy to the references. Even the most enthusiastic references could become apathetic if required to provide recommendations to endless interviewers. For this same reason, be sure to communicate with your references regularly if your job search continues longer than expected. Suggestions for communicating with references are discussed in Chapter 14.

When preparing a separate list of references to be given after a successful interview, place the word *References* and your name in a visible position as shown in Figure 13.4 on page 254. Balance the list (name, address, phone number, and relationship of reference to applicant) attractively on the page, and use the same paper used for printing the résumé. Whether it is handed to the interviewer personally or mailed, the references page professionally complements your résumé. Confident that you have a good message, you are now ready to put it in writing—to construct a résumé that will impress an employer favorably.

13-2b Types of Résumés

The general organization of all résumés is fairly standard: identification (name, address, phone number, and email address), job objective, qualifications, personal information, and references. The primary organizational challenge is in dividing the qualifications section into parts, choosing labels for them, and arranging them in the best sequence. When you review your self-, career, and job analyses data and your career/job profile, you will recognize that your qualifications stem mainly from your education and your experience. Your task is to decide how to present these two categories of qualifications. Résumés usually are organized in one of three ways: reverse chronological order (most recent activity listed first), functional order (most important activity listed first), or a chrono-functional order, which combines the chronological and functional orders, as the name implies. To determine which organizational plan to use, draft your résumé in each.

CHRONOLOGICAL RÉSUMÉ

The **chronological résumé** is the traditional organizational format for résumés. Two headings normally appear in the portion that presents qualifications: "Education" and "Experience." Which one should appear first? Decide which one you think is more impressive to the employer, and put that one first. Within each section, the most recent information is presented first. Reverse chronological order is easier to use and is more common than functional order; however, it is not always more effective.

The chronological résumé is an especially effective format for applicants who have progressed up a clearly defined career ladder and want to move up another rung. Because the format emphasizes dates and job titles, the chronological résumé is less effective for applicants who have gaps in their work histories, are seeking jobs different from the job currently held, or are just entering the job market with little or no experience.[8]

> **chronological résumé** the traditional organizational format for résumés, with headings that spotlight an applicant's education and experience

Sinseeho/Shutterstock.com

If you choose the chronological format, look at the two headings from the employer's point of view, and reverse their positions if doing so is to your advantage. In the "Experience" section, jobs are listed in reverse-chronological order. Assuming you have progressed typically, your latest job is likely to be more closely related to the job being sought than the first job held. Placing the latest or current job first will give it the emphasis it deserves. Include beginning and ending dates for each job.

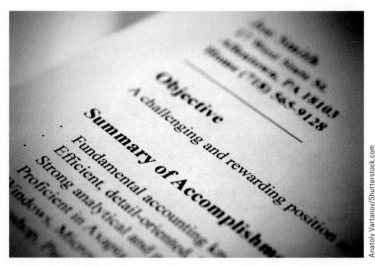

Anatoly Vartanov/Shutterstock.com

FUNCTIONAL RÉSUMÉ

In a **functional résumé**, points of primary interest to employers—transferable skills—appear in major headings. These headings highlight what an applicant can *do* for the employer—functions that the applicant can perform well. Under each heading, an applicant could draw from educational and/or work-related experience to provide supporting evidence.

A functional résumé requires a complete analysis of self, career, and the job sought. Suppose, for example, that a person seeking a job as an assistant hospital administrator wants to emphasize qualifications by placing them in major headings. From the hospital's advertisement of the job and from accumulated job appraisal information, an applicant sees this job as both an administrative and a public-relations job. The job requires skill in communicating and knowledge of accounting and finance. Thus, headings in the "Qualifications" section of the résumé could be "Administration," "Public Relations," "Communication," and "Budgeting." Under "Public Relations," for example, an applicant could reveal that a public relations course was taken at a state university, from which a degree is to be conferred in May, and that a sales job at ABC Store provided abundant opportunity to apply the principles learned. With other headings receiving similar treatment, the qualifications portion reveals the significant aspects of education and experience.

Order of importance is the best sequence for functional headings. If you have prepared an accurate self- and job analysis, the selected headings will highlight points of special interest to the employer. Glancing at headings only, an employer can see that you understand the job's requirements and have the qualities needed for success.

Having done the thinking required for preparing a functional résumé, you are well prepared for a question that is commonly asked in interviews: "What can you do for us?" The answer is revealed in your major headings. They emphasize the functions you can perform and the special qualifications you have to offer.

If you consider yourself well qualified, a functional résumé is worth considering. If your education or experience is scant, a functional résumé could be best for you. Using "Education" and "Experience" as headings (as in a chronological résumé) works against your purpose if you have little to report under the headings; the format would emphasize the absence of education or experience.

> If you have prepared an accurate self and job analysis, the selected headings will highlight points of special interest to the employer.

CHRONO-FUNCTIONAL RÉSUMÉ

The **chrono-functional résumé** combines features of chronological and functional résumés. This format can give quick assurance that educational and experience requirements are met and still use other headings that emphasize qualifications.

functional résumé the organizational format for résumés that highlights an applicant's transferable skills

chrono-functional résumé a résumé that combines features of chronological and functional résumés

13-3 PREPARING RÉSUMÉS FOR PRINT AND ELECTRONIC DELIVERY

Most employers prefer to receive résumés in standard format through electronic media. Whether presented on paper or electronically, the arrangement of a résumé is just as important as the content. If the arrangement is unattractive, unappealing, or in poor taste, the message might never be read. Errors in keyboarding, spelling, and punctuation could be taken as evidence of a poor academic background, lack of respect for the employer, or carelessness. Recognize that résumés serve as your introduction to employers and indicate the quality of work you'll produce.

As in preparing other difficult documents, prepare a rough draft as quickly as you can and then revise as many times as needed to prepare an effective résumé that sells you. After you are confident with the résumé, ask at least two other people to check it for you. Carefully select people who are knowledgeable about résumé preparation and the job you are seeking, and who can suggest ways to present your qualifications more effectively. After you have incorporated those changes, ask a skillful proofreader to review the document.

To accommodate employers' preferences for the presentation and delivery of résumés, you should be aware of three versions of résumés, as shown in Figures 13.3, 13.5, and 13.6: a designed résumé printed on paper, a scannable résumé to be read by a computer, and a designed résumé accessible through email and websites.

13-3a Preparing a Print (Designed) Résumé

Your print (designed) résumé is considered your primary marketing document, and appearance is critical. To win out among hundreds of competing résumés, it must look

professional and reflect current formatting and production standards while maintaining a distinctive conservative tone. Follow these guidelines for designing and producing a highly professional résumé:

- **Develop an appealing résumé format that highlights your key qualifications and distinguishes your résumé.** Use the power of your word-processing software for style enhancements rather than settle for overused, inflexible templates. Study the example résumés in this chapter and models from other sources for ideas for enhancing the style, readability, and overall impact of the document. Then, create a custom design that best highlights your key qualifications.

- **Format information for quick, easy reading.** To format your résumé so that it can be read at a glance, follow these guidelines:

  - Use attention-getting headings to partition major divisions, and add graphic lines and borders to separate sections of text.

  - Use an outline format when possible to list activities and events on separate lines, and include bullets to emphasize multiple points.

  - Use 10-point fonts or larger to avoid reader eye strain.

  - Use type styles and print attributes to emphasize key points. For example, to draw attention to the identification and headings, select a bold sans serif font (e.g., Calibri or Arial) slightly larger than the serif font (e.g., Cambria or Times New Roman) used for the remaining text. Capitalization, indention, and print enhancements (underline, italics, and bold) are useful for adding emphasis. Limit the number of type styles and enhancements, however, so the page is clean and simple to read.

  - Include identification on each page of a multiple-page résumé. Place your name and a page number at the top of the second and successive pages, with "Continued" at the bottom of the first page. The interviewer is re-exposed to your name, and pages can be reassembled if separated.

- **Create an appealing output to produce top professional quality.**

  - Check for consistency throughout the résumé. Consistency in spacing, end punctuation, capitalization, appearance of headings, and sequencing of details within sections will communicate your eye for detail and commitment to high standards.

iStockphoto.com/Tashatuvango

- ° Balance the résumé attractively on the page, with approximately equal margins. Allow generous white space so that the résumé looks uncluttered and easy to read.

- **Consider adding a statement of your creativity and originality.** Be certain that your creativity will not be construed as gimmickry and distract from the content of the résumé. Demonstrating creativity is particularly useful for fields such as advertising, public relations, graphic design, and those requiring computer proficiency.

  - ° Select paper of a standard size (8-1/2" by 11"), neutral color (white, buff, or gray), and high quality (preferably 24-pound, 100% cotton fiber). Consider using a mailing envelope large enough to accommodate the résumé without folding. The unfolded documents on the reader's desk will get favorable attention and will scan correctly if posted to an electronic database.

  - ° Print with a laser printer that produces high-quality output. Position paper so the watermark is read across the sheet in the same direction as the printing.

Some employers insist that the "best" length for a résumé is one page, stating that long résumés are often ignored. However, general rules about length are more flexible. Most students and recent graduates can present all relevant résumé information on one page. However, as you gain experience, you might need two or more pages to format an informative, easy-to-read résumé. A résumé forced on one page will likely have narrow margins and large blocks of run-on text (multiple lines with no space to break them). This dense format is unappealing and complicates the interviewer's task of skimming quickly for key information.

The rule about length is simple: Be certain your résumé contains only relevant information presented as concisely as possible. A one-page résumé that includes irrelevant information is too long. A two-page résumé that omits relevant information is too short.

> Many job banks, corporate sites, and career services centers require you to respond to specific openings by completing an online form or pasting your résumé into a designated section of the form.

beamer a quick version of a résumé designed in a format suitable for broadcasting on smartphones; also called a *beamable résumé*

The résumés illustrated in Figures 13.3 and 13.5 (see pages 253 and 255) demonstrate the organizational principles for chronological and functional résumés. A references page is illustrated in Figure 13.4 on page 254. Study the various layouts to decide on one that will highlight your key qualifications most effectively.

13-3b Preparing Electronic Résumé Submissions

To this point you have focused on the preparation of a print résumé. However, in the digital age of instant information, you'll use various online methods to apply for a job and present your qualifications to prospective employers.

The easiest and most common method of putting your résumé online is through emailing a résumé to a job bank for posting or to a networking contact who asked you to send a résumé. Many job banks, corporate sites, and career services centers require you to respond to specific openings by completing an online form or pasting your résumé into a designated section of the form. Frequently, you can input information directly on the website or download the form to be submitted by email, fax, or mail. You might also choose to post your résumé on your personal website as part of an electronic portfolio that showcases evidence of your qualifications. You could also develop a **beamer**, or *beamable résumé*, a quick version of your résumé designed in a format suitable for broadcasting on smartphones. Recruiting professionals predict that millions of these electronic résumés will be exchanged

Rawpixel.com/Shutterstock.com

FIGURE 13.3   CHRONOLOGICAL RÉSUMÉ

NED AVERS

45 Chester Street

Watertown, IA 62205

(530) 443-1565

na@gmail.com

MORTGAGE LOAN PROCESSOR

- Mortgage industry professional with loan-processing experience and a comprehensive knowledge of conventional and government loan programs.

- Thorough in gathering borrower information, verifying loan documents, and reviewing file documentation to guide each loan from preapproval to closing.

- Computer savvy in MS Office Suite and proprietary mortgage-processing software.

Loan Processing Expertise

Conforming & Nonconforming Loans, FRMs, ARMs, GPMs, Jumbo Loans, Fannie Mae & Freddie Mac Guidelines, FHA, VA, USDA Rural Development Loans

Professional Experience

WATERTOWN FIRST FEDERAL BANK—Watertown, IA

Loan Processor, 2013 to Present

- Regarded as one of the bank's most productive loan processors, handling an average of 22 files monthly.

- Outperformed company average in achieving loan-processing turn-around time of 12 days or less (compared to typical 15 to 20 days).

- Provided expedient service cited as key to consistently high customer satisfaction and a 10% increase in referrals in 2013.

- Ensured all files were complete prior to underwriting hand-off and coordinated effectively with title companies to ensure smooth closings.

- Successfully processed some of the most challenging loan applications (e.g., first-time borrowers, self-employed applicants, and borrowers with problematic credit histories).

BANK OF IOWA—Watertown, IA

Teller, 2011 to 2013

Provided friendly service to individual and commercial bank customers within regional financial institution.

Education

WATERTOWN COMMUNITY COLLEGE—Watertown, IA

Associate of Science in Business, 2013

Overall GPA: 3.95

Includes email address that reflects professional image.

Reveals position sought and powerful summary of qualifications.

Positions education as top qualification for recent graduate. Includes high GPA.

Edges out competition by expanding on related experience and work achievements.

Lists academic recognitions and highlights relevant skills.

Format Pointers

Places name at top center for easy viewing (top right is also acceptable).

Uses bold font to distinguish identification section and headings from remaining text.

Creates visual appeal through custom format rather than commonly used template, short readable sections focusing on targeted qualifications, and streamlined bulleted lists.

Diversity Considerations

Follows standard format and rules for résumés for application with a U.S. company. Specific formats vary for specific countries and federal governments.

FIGURE 13.4   REFERENCES PAGE

NED AVERS
45 Chester Street
Watertown, IA 62205
(530) 443-1565
na@gmail.com

REFERENCES

Leona Harden
Manager of Teller Services
Bank of Iowa
345 Main Street
Watertown, IA 65009
530-555-3209
lharden@bankofiowa.com
Relationship: Immediate supervisor, 2011 to 2013

Fred Murray, Instructor
Accounting Department
Watertown Community College
Postal Drop ACC 201
Watertown, IA 65009
530-855-8956
fmurray@wcc.edu
Relationship: Academic adviser and instructor for accounting courses

Linda Larsen, Manager
Watertown Boys and Girls Club
437 Oak Street
Watertown, IA 65009
530-855-3232
llarsen@wbgc.org

Relationship: Supervisor for volunteer activities

Includes professor and immediate supervisors as references, but excludes friends, relatives, or clergy to avoid potential bias.

Includes for each reference full contact information, including email address, if available, and relationship to job applicant.

Format Pointers
Prepares reference page at same time as résumé and makes available immediately after successful interview. Paper (color, texture, and size) and print type match résumé.

Balances references attractively.

silently at conferences, business meetings, and power lunches, similar to exchanging business cards.[9]

Electronic submissions are quick and easy but present new challenges and many opportunities to jeopardize your employment chances and compromise your privacy.

Just consider recent struggles you might have faced in dealing with viruses and unwelcomed emails, attempting to access nonworking links, and more. Before sending your résumé into cyberspace, follow these suggestions to ensure that your electronic submission is both professional and technically effective:

- **Choose postings for your résumé with purpose.** Online résumé postings are not confidential. Once your

résumé is online, anyone can read it, including your current employer. You might also begin to receive junk mail and cold calls from companies who see your résumé online; even more seriously, you could become a victim of identity theft. To protect your privacy online, limit personal information disclosed in the résumé and post only to sites with password protection allowing you to approve the release of your résumé to specific employers. Dating your electronic résumé will also prevent embarrassment should your employer find an old version of your résumé, which could occur as a result of the exchange of résumés between career sites, and delays in updating postings.

FIGURE 13.5 FUNCTIONAL RÉSUMÉ, PAGE 1

JERAD BARKER

134 Caswell Avenue.
Middleton, CT 03055
821-111-1212 (home)
821-222-3434 (cell)
JBarker@hotmail.com

Dedicated civil engineer with experience in structural and transportation design and proven leadership abilities.

CORE COMPETENCIES

- ☑ Structural Investigation & Design
- ☑ Computer Aided Design (CAD)
- ☑ Conceptual Design & Development
- ☑ Traffic Engineering
- ☑ Land Development
- ☑ Construction Drawings
- ☑ Project Management
- ☑ Hydraulics & Hydrology

- ☑ Soils & Earthwork
- ☑ Budgeting and Scheduling
- ☑ Impact Studies & Specifications
- ☑ Groundwater Monitoring
- ☑ Floodplain Management
- ☑ Construction Drawings
- ☑ Standard Specifications

EDUCATION

Bachelor of Science: Civil Engineering, emphasis in Structures   May 2013
Northern State University, Uptown, NY

Relevant Projects

Urban Lake and Park Development for City of Hartford, CT

Scope of design included storm water runoff, earthwork, structural analysis of retaining wall, and parking/sidewalk design.

- Designated Project Manager of four-member team.
- Retained quality control over project scope to preserve manageable size and avoid State violations.
- Initiated communication with city engineers and Fish & Game personnel on project-related issues and guidance.
- Maintained project schedule and completed on time. Received an 'A' grade on project.

Highway Design for State of Connecticut

The project scope included design of one-mile stretch of highway through private and public lands. Design challenges included steep terrain, storm water runoff, super-elevation for curves, and negotiating homes, businesses, and cemetery.

- Design included horizontal and vertical design based on minimal earthwork and minimal disturbance to local businesses and public land.
- Maintained project schedule and completed on time. Received an 'A' grade on project.

(continued on next page)

Includes clear objective and descriptive summary statements to grab attention and invite close reading.

Arranges qualifications into sections that emphasize applicant's relevant skills and accomplishments.

Uses employers' names to match skills with work history.

Limits education history to quick overview of basic qualifications and accommodates employers' preference for chronological format.

Format Pointers
Places name at top center, where it can be easily seen.

Uses bold font to distinguish identification section and headings from remaining text.

Creates visual appeal with easy-to-read columnar format and balanced page arrangement.

FIGURE 13.5 | FUNCTIONAL RÉSUMÉ, PAGE 2

SELECTED ACHIEVEMENTS

- Earned status of Engine Boss and Incident Commander Type 4 and oversaw wildfire control, including methods of attack, personnel and equipment requirements, and strategic planning; maintained personnel and public safety.
- Supervised up to 150 personnel and all equipment needs including air tankers, engines, helicopters, and water tenders.
- Used sound judgment and decision-making skills to preserve safety of crew and implement strategic plans of attack against wildfires.
- Developed strong leadership and communication skills as demonstrated by high-level of performance by crewmembers.
- Implemented training regimens for crew; many members promoted as a result.

EMPLOYMENT HISTORY

Delivery/Yard Crew: Big Tree Lumber Co., Hartford, CT	2015–Present
Forestry Technician: Danbury City Park, Danbury, CT	FT Seasonal, 2013–2015
Type 2, 3, and 6 Crewmember: Metro Fire Dept., Newport, CT	FT Seasonal, 2012–2013

TECHNICAL & RELATED

MS Word, Excel, PowerPoint, and Project/AutoCAD/HEC-HMS/Haestad Methods: WaterCAD, SewerCAD, and Flowmaster

Familiar Codes and Methods: NEPA, UBC, ASD, NDS, and LRFD

Connecticut Commercial Driver's License

Protect your references' privacy by omitting their names when posting online. Withholding this information will prevent unwelcomed calls by recruiters and other inappropriate contacts and threats to privacy. Because technology allows you to broadcast your résumé to all available positions on a career site, read postings carefully, and apply only to those that match your qualifications. This action improves the efficiency of the job selection process for the company and the applicant, and depicts fair, ethical behavior.

- **Don't hurry.** The speed, convenience, and informality of filling in online boxes or composing an email cover letter for an attached résumé can lead to sloppiness that reflects negatively on your abilities and attitude. Make sure every aspect of your electronic submission is top-notch just as you would for a print résumé. Provide all information exactly as requested; write concise, clear statements relevant to the job sought, and proofread carefully for grammatical and spelling errors. If you direct an employer to an electronic portfolio, devote necessary time to make it attractive, informative, and technically sound. Double-check your files to ensure they can be opened and retain an appealing format. Finally, read the posting carefully to learn how long your résumé will remain active, how to update it, and how to delete it from the site.

- **Include your résumé in the format requested by the employer or job bank.** You could be instructed to send the résumé as an attachment to the message or include it in the body of an email message, known as an **inline résumé**. The inline résumé is becoming the preferred choice as fear of computer viruses and daily email overload prevent employers from opening attachments. Unless instructed to send your attachment in a specific format such as Word, save your résumé and cover letter in one file, beginning with the cover letter as an ASCII or Rich Text Format file with line length limited to 65 characters and spacing. A plain text version, referred to as a **text résumé**,

inline résumé a résumé included in the body of an email message

text résumé a plain text (unformatted) version of a résumé removes formatting and lacks the appeal of your designed résumé; however, you can be confident that an employer can open the file and won't have to spend time "cleaning up" your résumé if it doesn't transmit correctly. For this reason, you'll also paste the text version of your résumé below your email message when sending an inline résumé.

As an added safeguard, send yourself and a couple of friends a copy of the résumé and see how it looks on different computers before sending it out to an employer. If you wish, follow-up with a print résumé and cover letter on high-quality paper.

- **Include a keyword summary after the identification section.** You'll want to grab the employer's attention by placing the keywords on the first screen (within the first 24 lines of text). Providing this relevant information will motivate the employer to keep scrolling down to see how the keywords are supported rather than click to the next résumé.

- **Email a cover message to accompany an online résumé.** Some companies consider this cover email message to be prescreening for a job interview. Write a formal, grammatically correct message just as you would if you were sending an application letter in the mail.

Some print résumés become electronic files when they are scanned by the employer into an electronic database where they can be read and sorted by a computer. Companies of all sizes are using **electronic applicant-tracking systems** to increase efficiency of processing the volume of résumés received in a competitive market. Such systems store scanned résumés in an electronic database where they can be sorted by keywords, with a resulting ranking of applicants. The system can also automatically prepare letters of rejection and interview offers and store the résumés of hired applicants for future promotion consideration. When seeking a job with a company that scans résumés into an electronic database, you will need to submit a **scannable résumé** as well as a print résumé that will be read by a person. If you are unsure whether a company scans résumés, call and ask. If still in doubt, take the safe route and submit your résumé in both formats.

FORMATTING A SCANNABLE RÉSUMÉ

To ensure that the scanner can read your résumé accurately and clearly, you must prepare a plain résumé with no special formatting. Follow these guidelines to prepare an electronic résumé that can be scanned accurately:

- **Use popular, nondecorative typefaces.** Typefaces such as Cambria and Times New Roman are clear and distinct and will not lose clarity in scanning.

- **Use 10- to 14-point font.** Computers cannot read small, tight print well. With a larger font, your résumé may extend to two pages, but page length is not an issue because a computer is reading the résumé.

- **Do not include italics, underlining, open bullets, or graphic lines and boxes.** Use boldface or all capitals for emphasis. Italicized letters that touch and underlining that runs into the text result in a garbled scanned image. Design elements such as graphic lines, shading, and shadowing effects can confuse equipment. Use solid bullets (•) because an open bullet (◦) could be read as an "o."

- **Use ample white space.** Use at least one-inch margins. Leave plenty of white space between the sections of a résumé so that the computer recognizes the partitions.

- **Print on one side of white, standard-size paper with sharp laser print.** Colored and textured paper scans poorly, and the scanner can pick up dirty specks on a photocopy.

- **Use a traditional résumé format.** Complex layouts that simulate catalogs or newspaper columns can confuse scanners.

- **Do not fold or staple your résumé.** If you must fold it, do not do so on a line of text.

MAKING A SCANNABLE RÉSUMÉ SEARCHABLE

You have two concerns in preparing a scannable résumé. You want to (1) be certain information is presented in a manner the computer can read, and (2) maximize the number of "hits" your résumé receives in a computerized résumé search. Follow these guidelines for making your print résumé searchable:

- **Position your name as the first readable item on the page.** Follow with your address, phone number, fax number, and email below your name on separate lines.

- **Add powerful keywords in a separate section called "Keywords" or "Keyword Summary" that follows the identification.** To identify keywords, ask yourself what words best describe your qualifications. Make maximum use of industry jargon and standard, easily recognizable abbreviations (e.g., B.A., M.S.) in the keyword summary and the body of the résumé, as these buzzwords will likely be matches with the computer's keywords.

electronic applicant-tracking systems systems that increase the efficiency of processing résumés by storing scanned résumés in an electronic database where they can be sorted by keywords, with a resulting ranking of applicants

scannable résumé a résumé formatted to ensure a scanner can accurately read and convert it into a digital format

THE POWER OF KEYWORDS

- **Format the keyword summary to maximize hits.** Capitalize the first letter of each word, and separate each keyword with a period. Position keywords describing your most important qualifications first, and then move to the least important ones. Order is important because some systems stop scanning after the first 80 keywords. The usual order is (a) job title, occupation, or career field; (b) education; and (c) essential skills for a specific position. Be certain to include keywords that describe interpersonal traits, such as *adaptable, flexible, sensitive, team player, willing to travel, ethical, industrious, innovative, open minded,* and *detail oriented.*

- **Support your keywords with specific facts in the body of the résumé.** Use synonyms of your keywords in the body in the event the computer does not recognize the keyword (e.g., use *M.B.A.* in the keyword summary and *Master of Business Administration* in the body; use *presentation graphics software* in the keyword summary and a specific program in the body). One unfortunate applicant reported using "computer-assisted design" consistently throughout his résumé when the computer

> Although portfolios were once thought of as only for writers, artists, or photographers, they are now seen as appropriate for other fields of work when the applicant wants to showcase abilities.

professional portfolio a portfolio presented in digital format and distributed to prospective employers via a website, CD/DVD, or other media; also called an *electronic portfolio* or *e-portfolio*

was searching for "CAD." Also, use a specific date of graduation in the education section. Some computer programs read two dates beside an institution to mean the applicant did not earn the degree (e.g., 2007–2011).

The scannable résumé Kerri Sears prepared when seeking a position in information management at a bank appears in Figure 13.6. The scannable résumé is formatted for scanning into an electronic database to be matched with employer requirements.

13-4 SUPPLEMENTING A RÉSUMÉ

Some candidates feel their career accomplishments are not appropriately captured in a standard résumé. Two additional tools for communicating your qualifications and abilities are the portfolio and the employment video.

13-4a Professional Portfolios

The **professional portfolio** (also called the *electronic portfolio* or *e-portfolio* when presented in a digital format) can be used to illustrate past activities, projects, and accomplishments. It is a collection of artifacts that demonstrate your communication, people, and technical skills. Although portfolios were once thought of as only for writers, artists, or photographers, they are now seen as appropriate for other fields of work when the applicant wants to showcase abilities.

Many portfolios are now presented in digital format, making the portfolio easier to organize and distribute to prospective employers via a website or burned to a CD or other media. With the availability of user-friendly software, college campuses are offering e-portfolio systems that aid students in reflecting on their experiences and producing e-portfolios. Just as students currently are not asked if they have an email account, predictions are that soon they will also be expected to have "a Web space that represents their learning and their assessment."[10]

FIGURE 13.6　SCANNABLE RÉSUMÉ, PAGE 1

KERRI SEARS

ksears@purdue.edu

Current Address

420 Jaker Ave., Apt. 22

West Lafayette, IN 47906

(765) 555-2424

Permanent Address

2800 N. Creekside St.

Fort Wayne, IN 46825

(260) 555-1234420

OBJECTIVE

A full-time position developing management information systems in the banking industry, which will allow me to apply my database development and financial analysis skills

EDUCATION

Purdue University, West Lafayette IN, expected May 2017 GPA: 3.6/4.0 (Major GPA: 3.8/4.0)

Bachelor of Science in Management

Minor: Management Information Systems

SIGNIFICANT COURSES

Database Management Systems, Applied Systems Analysis and Design, Decision Support and Expert

Systems, Computer Communications Systems

COMPUTER SKILLS

Proficient with IBM and MAC computers and with MS Office (Word, Excel, PowerPoint, and Access), Lotus,

Visual Basic, PowerBuilder, Oracle, SQL, and MS Publisher

WORK EXPERIENCE

Assistant Coordinator/Tutor

Purdue University Writing Lab, West Lafayette, IN January 2015 to Present

- Hire, train, and supervise tutors while creating a motivational climate
- Coordinate promotions through the production of marketing materials and promotional events
- Tutor students with business writing needs

Financial Analyst Intern

Merrill Lynch, Chicago, IL Summer 2016

- Prepared balance sheet and income statement analyses
- Evaluated various tax statements and other financial publications
- Joined a project team for establishing databases of pertinent information for use in analyzing future plans, forecasts, and acquisitions

Business Analyst Intern

State Farm, Bloomington, IL Summer 2015

- Assisted in developing and maintaining computer-based systems and procedures

(continued on next page)

Positions name as first readable item.

Includes position sought and reason to hire in separate section.

Omits references to use space for additional qualifications; references furnished when requested.

Edges out competition by expanding on related experience and work achievements.

Format Pointers

Keeps résumé simple and readable by computer: easy-to-read font of 10 to 14 points; solid bullets; and no italics, underlining, or graphic lines or borders.

Mails cover letter and print résumé unfolded and unstapled in large envelope.

FIGURE 13.6 SCANNABLE RÉSUMÉ, PAGE 2

- Analyzed financial systems and provided systems analysts with documentation of business requirements for proposed systems
- Developed written procedures for new system applications

ACTIVITIES/HONORS

AIESEC International Exchange Organization Vice President, fall 2016 to present

Alpha Sigma Phi Fraternity Treasurer, fall 2015 to 2016

Lions Club Fundraising Assistant, fall 2014 to spring 2015

National City Bank Scholarship Award, June 2013

Dean's list: fall 2014 to fall 2016

A clear understanding of your audience's needs and your qualifications will allow you to develop a logical organizational structure for your portfolio. Some possible items to include are

- sample speeches with digitized audio or video clips of the delivery;
- performance appraisals;
- awards;
- certificates of completion;
- reports, proposals, or written documents prepared for classes or on the job;
- brochures or programs describing workshops attended; and
- commendation messages, records, or surveys showing client or customer satisfaction with service.

Andrey_Popov/Shutterstock.com

After selecting the items for inclusion in your portfolio, select the appropriate software or binder you will use to showcase your accomplishments. Once you're organized, you can add items that demonstrate you have the characteristics the employer is seeking. Maintain your portfolio even after you are hired because it can demonstrate your eligibility for promotion, salary increase, or advanced training, or even justify why you should not be laid off.

For illustration purposes, take a look at Samuel Barkley's electronic portfolio shown in Figure 13.7 on the next page, which was created using a Microsoft Web template and posted to her personal website.

multimedia résumés a résumé created with presentation software, such as Camtasia Studio, and sent to prospective employers on CD/DVD or posted on an applicant's personal website

video résumé a résumé created as a video for posting on sites such as YouTube

13-4b Employment Videos

A video recording can be used to extend visually the impact of the printed résumé. A video can capture your stage presence and ability to speak effectively, and add a human dimension to the written process. Current technology enables applicants to embed video segments into **multimedia résumés** created with presentation software, such as Camtasia Studio, and sent to prospective employers on CD or DVD or posted on an applicant's personal website.

Video résumés, which job seekers post on sites such as YouTube, are the latest trend in developing creative job qualifications. You can learn some important lessons for your video project by taking a look at the abundance of good and bad examples already posted. If possible,

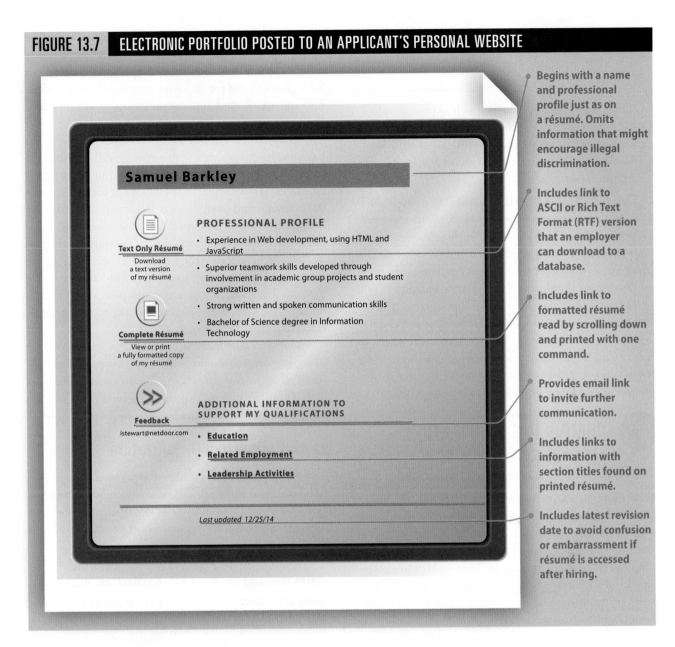

Samuel Barkley

Text Only Résumé
Download
a text version
of my résumé

Complete Résumé
View or print
a fully formatted copy
of my résumé

Feedback
istewart@netdoor.com

PROFESSIONAL PROFILE

- Experience in Web development, using HTML and JavaScript
- Superior teamwork skills developed through involvement in academic group projects and student organizations
- Strong written and spoken communication skills
- Bachelor of Science degree in Information Technology

ADDITIONAL INFORMATION TO SUPPORT MY QUALIFICATIONS

- Education
- Related Employment
- Leadership Activities

Last updated 12/25/14

Callouts:
- Begins with a name and professional profile just as on a résumé. Omits information that might encourage illegal discrimination.
- Includes link to ASCII or Rich Text Format (RTF) version that an employer can download to a database.
- Includes link to formatted résumé read by scrolling down and printed with one command.
- Provides email link to invite further communication.
- Includes links to information with section titles found on printed résumé.
- Includes latest revision date to avoid confusion or embarrassment if résumé is accessed after hiring.

---

solicit the help of someone with film experience and follow these simple suggestions for creating a visually enhanced résumé that is brief, showcases your key qualifications, and reflects your personality[11]:

- Keep your video simple with one stationary shot using a good camera and tripod. Avoid gimmicky effects and excessive panning that distract from the message.
- Use proper lighting, making sure that the employer can see your face. Avoid light behind you that casts shadows.
- Invest in a good-quality microphone, and speak clearly and at an appropriate pace for easy listening.
- Choose clothing appropriate for the job you are seeking. Video yourself wearing different clothing, and watch the video to select the ideal choice. Avoid clothing that gaps and bunches when you sit, as well as bright colors and clothing patterns that tend to vibrate when filmed.
- Edit your video to eliminate dead air and other imperfections that detract from a professional image.

Employment videos are more commonly used to obtain employment in career fields for which verbal delivery or visual performance is a key element. These fields include broadcasting and the visual and performing arts. The following guidelines apply when preparing an employment video:

- Be sure the video makes a professional appearance and is complimentary to you. A "home movie" quality recording will be a liability instead of an asset to your application.

- Avoid long "talking head" segments. Include segments that reflect you in a variety of activities; shots that include samples of your work are also desirable.
- Remember that visual media (such as photographs and videos) encourage the potential employer to focus on your physical characteristics and attributes, which might lead to undesired stereotyping and discrimination.

Be sure to advertise the availability of your portfolio and employment video to maximize its exposure. List your URL address in the identification section of your résumé. In your application letter, motivate the prospective employer to view your portfolio or video by describing the types of information included. Talk enthusiastically about the detailed supplementary information available during your job interview, and encourage the interviewer to view it when convenient. Note Karen Cunningham's promotion of her work in marketing when you read her application letter later in this chapter (see Figure 13.8).

13-5 COMPOSING APPLICATION MESSAGES

When employers invite you to send either a print or electronic résumé, they may expect you to include an **application message** (also known as a *cover message*). Because most applications are now made online, fewer employers ask for application letters. However, you should be knowledgeable about composing an application message for those situations in which they are expected.

As you have learned, a résumé summarizes information related to the job's requirements and the applicant's qualifications. An application message complements a résumé by speaking more directly to a specific job posting by (1) introducing the applicant, (2) attracting interest to the résumé, and (3) interpreting the résumé in terms of employer benefits.

Because it creates interest and points out employer benefits, the application message is persuasive and, thus, written inductively. It is designed to convince an employer that qualifications are adequate just as a sales message is designed to convince a buyer that a product will satisfy a need. Like sales messages, application messages can be either solicited or unsolicited. Job advertisements *solicit* applications. Unsolicited application messages have greater need for attention-getters; otherwise, solicited and unsolicited application messages are based on the same principles.

Unsolicited application messages are the same basic message (perhaps with slight modifications) sent to many prospective employers. By sending unsolicited messages, you increase your chances of locating potential openings and possibly alert employers to needs they had not previously identified for someone of your abilities. However, sending unsolicited messages has some disadvantages. Because the employer's specific needs are not known, the opening paragraph will likely be more general (less targeted to a specific position) than the opening paragraph in solicited messages. The process could also be time consuming.

Karen Cunningham wrote the letter in Figure 13.8 to accompany a chronological résumé she prepared after completing the company/job profile for a marketing assistant. The time Karen devoted to analyzing the job, the company, and her qualifications was well spent.

13-5a Persuasive Organization

A persuasive message is designed to convince the reader to take action, which, in this case is to read the résumé and invite you to an interview. Because an application message is persuasive, organize it as you would a sales message:

Sales Message	Application Message
Gets attention	Gets attention
Introduces product	Introduces qualifications
Presents evidence	Presents evidence
Encourages action	Encourages action
=	=
(sells a product, service, or idea)	(results in an interview)

Like a well-written sales message, a well-written application message uses a central selling feature as a theme. The central selling feature is introduced in the first or second paragraph and is stressed in the paragraphs that follow. Two to four paragraphs are normally sufficient for supporting evidence. Consider the order of importance as a basis for their sequence, with the most significant aspects of your preparation coming first.

application message a message placed on top of the résumé so it can be read first by the employer; also called a *cover message*

unsolicited application message an unrequested message sent to many prospective employers that contains the same basic message

FIGURE 13.8 **EXAMPLE OF AN APPLICATION LETTER**

Karen Cunningham
455 Ash Lane, Apt. 3
Birmingham, AL 67003
(504) 345-9876
kcunningham@gmail.com

Larry Canton, **Hiring Manager**
Dayton Ltd.
120 Main Street
Birmingham, AL 67012

March 12, 2017

Dear Mr. Canton:

I am interested in your position of Marketing Assistant, which was posted on your corporate website. The combination of my natural ability, technical expertise, and work experience all make me an ideal candidate for this role.

As a recent graduate of Alabama State University with an emphasis in Marketing, I am intimately familiar with developments in social media promotion and data mining applications. I would also bring value to a company like yours through my experience in the private sector in various internship positions and my positive "can do" attitude.

For the past six months, I have interned in the Marketing Department of Ajax Corp., where I participated in the development of a marketing program for a new computer-networking product. As part of that team, I also wrote promotional materials for the company website and sent a weekly email newsletter to current customers.

I consider myself to be a productive worker with a solid work ethic who exerts optimal effort to ensure that all tasks given to me are completed on time and to the highest standards. My personal strengths include, but are not limited to the following:

- Being a motivated self-starter who takes the initiative, and can work with minimal supervision.

- Being committed to providing a superior service to any company for which I work.

- Being computer literate with extensive software knowledge and proficiency covering a wide variety of applications.

Greater details of my accomplishments and achievements can be found in my attached resume. I am available for interview at any time and can start work at short notice. Thank you for the time you have taken to consider my application, and I eagerly look forward to hearing from you.

Yours sincerely,
Karen Cunningham

- Addresses letter to specific person, using correct name and job title.

- Identifies how applicant learned of the position, the specific position sought, and background.

- Discusses how education relates to job requirements.

- Introduces résumé for additional information.

- Encourages employer to take action without sounding pushy or apologetic.

Format Pointers

Formats as formal business letter because the message is accompanying a print résumé.

An abbreviated email message including an online résumé in ASCII or RTF format would be appropriate for electronic submission.

Uses the same high-quality, standard size and neutral colored paper as was used for the résumé.

Includes the writer's address and contact information.

GAIN THE RECEIVER'S ATTENTION

To gain attention, begin the message by identifying the job sought and describing how your qualifications fit the job requirements. This information will provide instant confirmation that you are a qualified applicant for an open position. An employer who reads hundreds of application letters and résumés will appreciate this direct, concise approach.

For an announced job, you should indicate in the first paragraph how you learned of the position—for example, employee referral, customer referral, executive referral, newspaper advertising, or job fair. Your disclosure will confirm that you are seeking an open job; and it will also facilitate an evaluation of the company's recruiting practices. Note that the opening of the letter in Figure 13.8 indicates that the applicant learned of the position through a posting on the company's corporate website.

An opening for an unsolicited message must be more persuasive: you must convince the interviewer to continue to read your qualifications even though a job might not exist. As in the opening of a solicited message, indicate the type of position sought and your qualifications, but be more creative in gaining attention. The following paragraph uses the applicant's knowledge of recent company developments and an intense interest in the company's future to gain receiver attention.

In the past three years, OfficeWorx has experienced phenomenal growth through various acquisitions, mergers, and market expansion. With this growth comes new opportunities, new customers, and the need for new team players to work in store management. While following the growth of OfficeWorx, I have become determined to join this exciting team and am eager to show you that my educational background, leadership abilities, and internship experience qualify me for the job.

PROVIDE EVIDENCE OF QUALIFICATIONS

For graduates entering the world of full-time work for the first time, educational backgrounds are usually more impressive than work histories. They can benefit from interpreting their educational experiences as meaningful, job-related experiences. An applicant for a human resources position should do more than merely report having taken courses in organizational behavior.

In my business communication class, I could see the specific application of principles encountered in my organizational behavior and marketing classes. Questions about leadership and motivation seemed to recur throughout the course: What really motivates people? Why do people fear change? How can those fears be overcome? What communication practices can be used to motivate people and help them accept change? The importance of communication was a focus of many courses and my research report, "How to Get the Most from Others."

Your application message will not necessarily refer to information learned in a class. Recognizing that managers must be tactful (a point on which the person reading the message will surely agree), the applicant included some details of a class. This technique is basic in persuasion: Do not just say a product or idea is good; say what makes it good. Do not just say that an educational or work experience was beneficial; say what made it so.

By making paragraphs long enough to include interpretation of experiences on a present or previous job, you show an employer that you are well prepared for your next job. For example, the following excerpt from an applicant whose only work experience was at a retail outlet is short and general:

I have been the assistant manager at Fashion Flash for the past year and have helped supervise a team of five associates. I received high performance evaluations for my work as a leader.

Tom Wang/Shutterstock.com

Added details and interpretation could make the value of the work experience more convincing:

As assistant manager at Fashion Flash, I have learned to listen to associates' concerns and make them feel valued by acting on their suggestions. I have trained associates in policies and procedures, and learned to reinforce those procedures for existing employees. I am able to preserve a good working relationship with my team even in sometimes difficult conversations.

The applicant has called attention to qualities that managers like to see in employees: willingness to listen, speed, accuracy, concern for clients or customers, a positive attitude, fairness, and tact. As a learning experience, the Fashion Flash job has taught or reinforced principles that the employer sees as transferrable to the job being sought.

In this section, you can discuss qualifications you have developed by participating in student organizations, student government, athletics, or community organizations. Be specific in describing gained skills that can be applied directly on the job—for example, organization, leadership, spoken and written communication skills, and budgeting and financial management. You can also use your involvement as a channel for discussing important personal traits vital to the success of a business, such as interpersonal skills, motivation, imagination, responsibility, and team orientation.

> Be specific in describing gained skills that can be applied directly on the job—for example, organization, leadership, spoken and written communication skills, and budgeting and financial management.

For the past year, I have served as treasurer for Alpha Chi Epsilon. In that duty, I have managed a $200,000 annual budget. By coordinating our yearly charitable fundraising event, I have exercised leadership and organizational and communication skills.

Finally, end this section with an indirect reference to the résumé. If you refer to it in the first or second paragraph, readers might turn from the message at that point and look at the résumé. Avoid the obvious statement "Enclosed please find my résumé" or "A résumé is enclosed." Instead, refer indirectly to the résumé while restating your qualifications. The following sentence emphasizes that references can confirm the applicant's qualifications:

References listed on the enclosed résumé would be glad to comment on my marketing education and experience.

ENCOURAGE ACTION

Once you have presented your qualifications and referred to your enclosed résumé, the next move is to encourage the receiver to extend an invitation for an interview. The goal is to introduce the idea of action without apologizing for doing so and without being demanding or "pushy." If the final paragraph (action closing) of your message is preceded by impressive paragraphs, you need not press hard for a response. Just mentioning the idea of a future discussion is probably sufficient. If you have significant related experience that you have developed as a central selling feature, mentioning this experience in the action closing adds unity and stresses your strongest qualification one last time. Forceful statements about *when* and *how* to respond are unnecessary and irritating. Avoid these frequently made errors:

- **Setting a date.** "May I have an appointment with you on January 15?" The date you name could be inconvenient; or even if it is convenient for the employer, your forwardness in setting it could be resented.

- **Expressing doubt.** "If you agree," "I hope you will," and "Should you decide" use subjunctive words that indicate a lack of confidence.

- **Sounding apologetic.** "May I take some of your time?" or "I know how busy you are" might seem considerate, but an apology is inappropriate when discussing ways you can contribute to a company.

- **Sounding overconfident.** "I will call you next week to set an appointment time that works for both of us." This statement is presumptuous and egotistical.

- **Giving permission to call.** "You may call me at 555-6543." By making the call sound like a privilege ("may call") you could alienate the reader. Implied meaning: You are very selective about the calls you take, but the employer does qualify.

FIGURE 13.9 | EXAMPLE OF APPLICATION MESSAGE SENT BY EMAIL

New Message

To: Tina Fredericks [tfredericks@atlas.com]

From: Laura Chu [lchu@hotmail.com]

Subject: Career Fair Follow-up: Resume for Laura Chu

Attachment: laura_chu_resume.docx

Dear Ms. Fredericks,

It was a pleasure meeting you at the career fair this morning and discussing your position of Assistant Communications Director. I believe my internship experiences make me an excellent fit for this position.

During my internship in the Communications Department of Luminous Inc., I wrote articles for the company website, managed contributing articles, and wrote and sent a weekly email newsletter to subscribers.

While interning for Assemblyperson Janet Brown, I researched, drafted and amended legislation, wrote press releases, and was responsible for office communications and correspondence.

My resume is attached, as requested. If I can provide you with any further information on my background and qualifications, please let me know.

I look forward to hearing from you.

Thank you for your consideration.

Laura Chu
Cell: 208-556-8899
Email: lchu@hotmail.com
LinkedIn Profile: linkedin.com/in/laurachu
Online Résumé: sites.google.com/site/laurachu
Résumé text included in email below and attached as MS Word attachment.

Annotations:

- Provides specific subject line that ensures the message will be opened.
- Email program automatically shows attached file containing résumé.
- Reveals how the applicant learned of the position and confirms knowledge of and interest in the company.
- Condenses persuasive application message to one screen. Avoids the tendency to send an impersonal message stating that the résumé is attached.
- Introduces résumé and reminds interviewer that submission was requested.
- Encourages employer to take action without sounding pushy or apologetic.
- Includes email address in .sig file to simplify access to all contact information without opening the attached résumé.
- Includes enclosure notation pointing out that résumé is sent as required by the company.

Format Pointers

Formats as formal business letter with complete address, exactly as done when job credentials are sent by mail. Complete letter and printed copy of résumé will be sent as a follow-up to the email.

you but cannot see your email address. Exclude quotes from your signature block that could be misunderstood or offensive. Add an enclosure notation drawing attention to your résumé attachment provided as requested by the employer, such as "Résumé attached as Word document."

To compete with the high volumes of junk mail, daily messages, and fear of computer viruses, you must provide a motive for an interviewer to open an unexpected message from an unknown person. Messages with missing or vague subject lines might be ignored or deleted immediately. To bring attention to your message, include the name of the person referring you to the position directly in the subject line or mention your email is a follow-up to a conversation, for example, "RE: Follow-up: Résumé for…." If the message is unsolicited, describe the specific value you can add to the company, for example, "Résumé for Forensics Accountant with Extensive ACL Skills." Stay away from tricks such as marking an email "urgent" or adding "re" to pass your message off as a reply to an earlier message.

Check any instructions provided by the prospective employer, and follow them precisely. Typically, however, you will want to send a complete letter and copy of your résumé by regular mail as a follow-up to the email submission. Figure 13.9 shows a sample application email an applicant sent after talking with a prospective employer at a career fair.

Include these steps in your finishing phase:

- Regardless of your delivery option, address your application letter or email message to the specific individual who is responsible for hiring for the position you are seeking, rather than sending the document to the "Human Resources Department" or "To Whom It May Concern." If necessary, consult the company's annual report or website, or call the company to locate this information.

- Verify the correct spelling, job title, and address, and send a personalized message to the appropriate individual.

- Keep the message short and easy to read. A one-page letter is sufficient for most applications from students and graduates entering the job market.

- Apply visual enhancements—learned previously—to enhance the appeal and readability of the message and to draw attention to your strengths.

- Definitely keep the paragraphs short, and consider listing your top four or five achievements or other important ideas in a bulleted list.

- In print documents, include "Enclosure" below the signature block to alert the employer that a résumé is enclosed. The proper letter format is shown in the example in Figure 13.8.

- Get opinions from qualified individuals, and make revisions where necessary.

STUDY TOOLS 13

LOCATED AT THE BACK OF THE TEXTBOOK
☐ Tear-Out Chapter Review Card

LOCATED AT WWW.CENGAGEBRAIN.COM
☐ Review Key Term flashcards and create your own cards

☐ Track your knowledge and understanding of key concepts in business communication

☐ Complete practice and graded quizzes to prepare for tests

☐ Complete interactive content within BCOM9 Online

☐ View the chapter highlight boxes for BCOM9 Online

14 | Interviewing for a Job and Preparing Employment Messages

PeopleImages.com/Getty Images

LEARNING OBJECTIVES

After studying this chapter, you will be able to ...

14-1 Explain the nature of structured, unstructured, stress, group, phone, and virtual interviews.

14-2 Explain the steps in the interview process.

14-3 Prepare effective answers to questions often asked in job interviews, including illegal interview questions.

14-4 Compose effective messages related to employment (including application, follow-up, thank-you, job-acceptance, job-refusal, resignation, and recommendation request messages).

After finishing this chapter, go to **PAGE 287** for **STUDY TOOLS.**

14-1 UNDERSTANDING TYPES OF EMPLOYMENT INTERVIEWS

Most companies conduct various types of interviews before hiring a new employee. Although the number and type of interviews vary among companies, applicants typically begin with a screening interview often completed by phone or videoconferencing, an in-depth interview, an on-site interview with multiple interviewers, and, sometimes, a stress interview. Depending on the goals of the interviewer, interviews follow a structured or an unstructured approach.

14-1a Structured Interviews

In a **structured interview**, the interviewer follows a predetermined agenda, including a checklist of questions and statements designed to elicit necessary information and reactions from the interviewee. Because each applicant answers the same questions, the interviewer has comparable data to evaluate. A particular type of structured interview is the behavior-based interview, in which you are asked to give specific examples of occasions in which you demonstrated particular behaviors or skills. The interviewer already knows what skills, knowledge, and qualities successful candidates must possess. The examples you provide will indicate whether you possess them.[1]

About Computer assisted

Many companies are finding computer-assisted interviews to be a reliable and effective way to conduct screening interviews. Applicants use a computer to provide answers to a list of carefully selected questions. A computer-generated report provides standard, reliable information about each applicant that enables an interviewer to decide whether to invite the applicant for a second interview. The report flags any contradictory responses (e.g., an applicant indicated he was terminated for absenteeism but later indicated that he thought his former employer would give him an outstanding recommendation), highlights any potential problem areas (e.g., an applicant responded that she would remain on the job less than a year), and generates a list of structured interview questions for the interviewer to ask (e.g., "Todd, you said you feel your former employer would rate you average. Why don't you feel it would be higher?").

Research has shown that applicants prefer computer-assisted interviews to human interviews and that they respond more honestly to a computer, feeling less need to give polite, socially acceptable responses. Because expert computer systems can overcome some of the inherent problems with traditional face-to-face interviews, the overall quality of the selection process improves. Typical interviewer errors include talking too much, forgetting to ask important questions, being reluctant to ask sensitive or tough questions, forming unjustified negative first impressions, obtaining unreliable and illegal information that makes an applicant feel judged, and using interview data ineffectively.[2] Regardless of whether the interview is face to face or computer assisted, you will need to provide objective, truthful evidence of your qualifications as they relate to specific job requirements.

> Many companies are finding computer-assisted interviews to be a reliable and effective way to conduct screening interviews.

14-1b Unstructured Interviews

An **unstructured interview** is a freewheeling exchange and can shift from one subject to another, depending on the interests of the participants. Some experienced interviewers are able to make a structured interview seem unstructured. The goal of many unstructured interviews is to explore unknown areas to determine the applicant's ability to speak comfortably about a wide range of topics.

14-1c Stress Interviews

A **stress interview** is designed to place the interviewee in an anxiety-producing situation so that an evaluation can be made of the interviewee's performance under stress. In all cases, interviewees should attempt to assess the nature of the interview quickly and adjust behavior accordingly. Understanding that interviewers sometimes deliberately create anxiety to assess your ability to perform under stress should help you handle such interviews more effectively. As the following discussion of different interviewer styles reveals, you can perform much better when you understand the interviewer's purpose.

structured interview an interview format generally used in the screening process, in which the interviewer follows a predetermined agenda, including a checklist of items or a series of questions and statements designed to elicit the necessary information or interviewee reaction

unstructured interview a freewheeling exchange that may shift from one subject to another, depending on the interests of the participants

stress interview an interview format designed to place the interviewee in an anxiety-producing situation so that an evaluation of the interviewee's performance under stress may be made

Monkey Business Images /shutterstock.com

14-1d Series Interviews

As organizations have increased emphasis on the team approach to management and problem solving, selecting employees who best fit their cultures and styles has become especially important. Involving key people in the organization in the candidate selection process has led to new interview styles. In a series interview, the candidate meets individually with a number of different interviewers. Each interviewer will likely ask questions from a differing perspective; for instance, a line manager might ask questions related to the applicant's knowledge of specific job tasks, while the vice president of operations might ask questions related to the applicant's career goals. Some questions will likely be asked more than once in the process. A popular trend in organizations that desire a broad range of input in the hiring decision but want to avoid the drawn-out nature of series interviews is to conduct group interviews.

14-1e Phone Interviews

Employers use telephone interviews as a way of identifying and recruiting candidates for employment. Phone interviews are often used to screen candidates in order to narrow the pool of applicants who will be invited for in-person interviews. They are also used as a way to minimize the expenses involved in interviewing out-of-town candidates.

While you're actively job searching, it's important to be prepared for a phone interview on a moment's notice. You never know when a recruiter or a networking contact might call and ask if you have a few minutes to talk.

Prepare for a phone interview just as you would

virtual interview
interview conducted using videoconferencing technology

for a regular interview. Compile a list of your strengths and weaknesses, as well as a list of answers to typical phone interview questions. In addition, plan on being prepared for a phone conversation about your background and skills. Other considerations to make when preparing for a phone interview include:

- keeping your résumé in clear view, on the top of your desk, or taping it to the wall near the phone, so it's at your fingertips when you need to answer questions;

- having a short list of your accomplishments available to review;

- having a pen and paper handy for note taking; and

- turning call-waiting off so your call isn't interrupted.

Unless you're sure your cellphone service is going to be perfect, you might consider using a landline rather than your cellphone to avoid a dropped call or static on the line.

14-1f Virtual Interviews

Technology is allowing much business activity, including job interviews, to be conducted virtually. Companies such as IBM, Microsoft, Nike, and Hallmark Cards save money and time by screening candidates through video interviews from remote locations. **Virtual interviews** help widen the applicant pool, decrease the cost of travel because they can be conducted regardless of geography, and fill the position more quickly. The consensus is that the video interview is excellent for screening applicants, but a face-to-face interview is appropriate whenever possible for the important final interview.

Various companies have direct hookups with the career services centers of colleges and universities to interview students. These virtual interviews allow students to meet large companies whose representatives typically would not visit colleges with small applicant pools, and to interview with companies whose representatives could not travel because of financial constraints or other reasons. Students simply sit in front of a camera, dial in, and interview with multiple interviewers; in some cases, several applicants are interviewed simultaneously. As you would imagine, some candidates who interview well in person can fail on camera or in a group conference call. Virtual interviewing is an excellent method for screening out candidates who are unable to communicate their competence, enthusiasm, and conviction in a technology-rich environment.

You should prepare for a virtual interview differently than you would for a traditional interview. First, suggest a preliminary telephone conversation with the interviewer to establish rapport. Arrive early and acquaint yourself with the equipment; know how to adjust the volume and other camera functions for optimal performance after the interview begins. Second, concentrate on projecting strong nonverbal skills: speak clearly, but do not slow down; be certain you are centered in the frame; sit straight; look up, not down; and use gestures and an enthusiastic voice to communicate energy and reinforce points while avoiding excessive motion that will appear blurry. Third, realize voices can be out of step with the pictures if there is a lag between the video and audio transmissions. You will need to adjust to the timing (e.g., slow down your voice) to avoid interrupting the interviewer.

14-2 PREPARING FOR AN INTERVIEW

College students frequently schedule on-campus interviews with representatives from various business organizations. Following the on-campus interviews, successful candidates often are invited for further interviews at the company location. The purpose of the second interview is to give executives and administrators, other than the human resources interviewer, an opportunity to appraise the candidate. Whether on campus or at the company location, interview methods and practices vary with the situation.

Pre-interview planning involves learning something about the company or organization, studying yourself, and making sure your appearance and mannerisms will not detract from the impression you hope to make.

Rawpixel.com/Shutterstock.com

14-2a Research the Company

Nothing can hurt a job candidate more than knowing little about the organization. Preparation will also arm candidates with information needed to develop pertinent qualifications and point their stories to solve an employer's specific problems.

> The interviewer does not want to waste precious interview time providing candidates with information they should have considered long before.

Companies that have publicly traded stock are required to publish annual reports that are available in school libraries or online. Be sure to read news items and blog posts, and sign up to receive news alerts from the prospective company for current company information up until the day of the interview. Use social networking utilities, such as LinkedIn and Hoovers.com, to find profiles of company leaders and gain insights into the types of managers this company employs.

Employees of the company or other applicants who have interviewed might be of help to the interviewee. Employee reviews of selected companies, salaries, and sample interview questions are available online, and some universities share taped interviews with various company recruiters. Information about the company and the job seen as pertinent in an interview includes the following:

COMPANY INFORMATION

Be sure to research the following on the companies with which you interview:

▸ **Name.** Know, for example, that the publishing company, Cengage Learning, was named to reflect the company's mission to be a "center of engagement" for its global customers.[3]

▸ **Status in the industry.** Know the company's share of the market, its *Fortune* 500 standing (if any), its sales, and its number of employees.

- ▸ **Latest stock market quote.** Be familiar with current market deviations and trends.

- ▸ **Recent news and developments.** Read current business periodicals, news, and blogs for special feature articles on the company, its new products, and its corporate leadership.

- ▸ **Scope of the company.** Is it local, national, or international?

- ▸ **Corporate officers.** Know the names of the chairperson, president, and chief executive officer.

- ▸ **Products and services.** Study the company's offerings, target markets, and innovative strategies.

JOB INFORMATION

Be sure to know the following about the job you are seeking:

- ▸ **Job title.** Know the job titles of typical entry-level positions.

- ▸ **Job qualifications.** Understand the specific knowledge and skills desired.

- ▸ **Probable salary range.** Study salaries in comparable firms, as well as regional averages.

- ▸ **Career path of the job.** What opportunities for advancement are available?

XiXinXing/Shutterstock.com

14-2b Study Yourself

When you know something about the company, you will also know something about the kinds of jobs or training programs the company has to offer. Next, compare your qualifications to the company/job profile. This systematic comparison of your qualifications and job requirements helps you identify pertinent information (strengths or special abilities) to be included in your résumé. If you cannot see a relationship between you and the job or company, you might have difficulty demonstrating the interest or sincerity needed to sell yourself.

14-2c Plan Your Appearance

An employment interviewer once said she would not hire a job applicant who did not meet her *extremities* test: fingernails, shoes, and hair must be clean and well kept. This interviewer felt that if the candidate did not take care of those details, the candidate could not really be serious about, or fit into, her organization. Other important

guidelines include avoiding heavy makeup and large, excessive jewelry. Select conservative clothes, and be certain clothing is clean, unwrinkled, and properly fitted. Additionally, avoid smoking, drinking, or wearing heavy fragrance.

You can locate a wealth of information on appropriate interview dress from numerous electronic and printed sources. Also, talk with professors in your field, professors of business etiquette and professional protocol, personnel at your career services center, and graduates who have recently acquired jobs in your field. Research the company dress code—real or implied—ahead of time. If you *look* and *dress* like the people who already work for the company, the interviewer will be able to visualize you working there.

14-2d Plan Your Time and Materials

One of the worst things you can do is be late for an interview. If something should happen to prevent your arriving on time, phone an apology. Another mistake is to miss the interview entirely. Plan your time so that you will arrive early and can unwind and mentally review the things you plan to accomplish. Be sure to bring a professional briefcase or notebook that contains everything you will need during the interview. These items might include copies of your résumé, a list of references and/or recommendations, a professional-looking pen, paper for taking notes, highlights of what you know about the company, a list of questions you plan to ask, and previous correspondence with the company.

14-2e Practice

The job interview could be the most important face-to-face interaction you ever have. You will be selling yourself in competition with others. How you listen and how you talk are characteristics the interviewer will be able to measure. Your actions, your mannerisms, and your appearance will combine to give the total picture of how you are perceived. Added to the marketable skills you have acquired from your education, experience, and activities, your interview performance can give a skilled interviewer an excellent picture of you. Practicing for an interview will prepare you to handle the nervousness that is natural when interviewing. However, do not memorize answers, as it will sound rehearsed and insincere. Instead, think carefully about how your accomplishments match the job requirements and practice communicating these ideas smoothly, confidently, and professionally.

Prepare for standard interview questions and other interview issues by following suggestions provided later in this chapter. Once you are satisfied you have identified your key selling points, have a friend ask you interview questions you have developed and surprise you with others. Participate in mock interviews with someone in your career services center or with a friend, alternating roles as interviewer and interviewee. Then, follow each practice interview with a constructive critique of your performance.

 14-3 ## CONDUCTING A SUCCESSFUL INTERVIEW

The way you handle an interview will vary somewhat depending on your stage in the hiring process. Regardless of whether you are being screened by a campus recruiter in person, by phone, or by videoconference, or have progressed to an on-site visit, an interview will have three parts: the opening formalities, an information exchange, and the closing.

14-3a The Opening Formalities

According to management consultant Dan Burns, most candidates don't realize that in the first 60 seconds, interviewers typically decide whether the candidate will be

pan_kung/Shutterstock.com

moved to the top of the list or dropped from consideration. Burns emphasizes that skills missing during the interview are important because he assumes these same deficiencies will carry over during employment.[4] Clearly, because the impression created during the first few seconds of an interview often determines the outcome, you cannot afford to take time to warm up in an interview. You must enter the door selling yourself!

Common courtesies and confident body language can contribute to a favorable first impression in the early moments when you have not yet had an opportunity to talk about your qualifications:

- **Use the interviewer's name, and pronounce it correctly.** Even if the interviewer calls you by your first name, always use the interviewer's surname unless specifically invited to do otherwise.

- **Apply a firm handshake.** Usually, the interviewer will initiate the handshake, although you may do so. In either case, apply a firm handshake. You do not want to leave the impression that you are weak or timid. At the same time, you do not want to overdo the firm grip and leave an impression of being overbearing.

- **Wait for the interviewer to ask you to be seated.** If you aren't invited to sit, choose a chair across from or beside the interviewer's desk.

- **Maintain appropriate eye contact, and use your body language to convey confidence.** Sit erect and lean forward slightly to express interest. For a professional image, avoid slouching, chewing gum, and fidgeting.

- **Be conscious of nonverbal messages.** If the interviewer's eyes are glazing over, end your answer, but expand it if eyes are bright and the head is nodding vigorously. If the interviewer is from a different culture, be conscious of subtle differences in nonverbal communication that could affect the interviewer's perception of you. For example, a North American interviewer who sees eye contact as a sign of trust

"Do you have a disability that would interfere with your ability to perform the job?" "Have you ever been injured on the job?" "Have you ever been treated by a psychiatrist?" "How much alcohol do you consume each week?" "What prescription drugs are you currently taking?"

○ *Marital status, spouse's employment, or dependents.* "Are you married?" "Who is going to care for your children if you work for us?" "Do you plan to have children?" "Is your spouse employed?" Additionally, employers may not ask the names or relationships of people with whom you live.

○ *Arrests or criminal convictions that are not related to the job.* "Have you ever been arrested other than for traffic violations? If so, explain." Keep in mind that the arrest/conviction record of a person applying for a job as a law enforcement officer or a teacher could be highly relevant to the job, but the same information could be illegal for a person applying for a job as an engineer.

As interviewers may ask illegal questions because of lack of training or an accidental slip, you must decide how to respond. You can refuse to answer and state that the question is improper, though you risk offending the interviewer. A second option is to answer the inappropriate question, knowing it is illegal and unrelated to job requirements. A third approach is to provide a low-key response such as "How does this question relate to how I will do my job?" or to answer the legitimate concern

that likely prompted the question. For example, an interviewer who asks, "Do you plan to have children?" is probably concerned about how long you might remain on the job. An answer to this concern would be, "I plan to pursue a career regardless of whether I decide to raise a family." If you can see no legitimate concern in a question, such as "Do you own your home, rent, or live with parents?" answer, "I'm not sure how that question relates to the job. Can you explain?"[12]

ASKING QUESTIONS OF THE INTERVIEWER

Both the interviewer and interviewee want to know as much as possible about each other before making a commitment to hire. A good way to determine whether the job is right for you is to ask pertinent questions.

Good questions show the interviewer that you have initiative and are interested in making a well-informed decision. Responses can provide insight to job requirements that you can then show you possess. Therefore, be sure not to say, "I don't have any questions." Focus on questions that help you gain information about the company and the job that you could not learn from published

sources or persons other than the interviewer. Respect the interviewer's time by avoiding questions that indicate you are unprepared (e.g., questions about the company's scope, products or services, job requirements, or new developments). Avoid questions about salary, required overtime, and benefits that imply you are interested more in money and the effort required than in the contribution you can make.

14-3c The Closing

The interviewer will provide cues indicating that the interview is completed by rising or making a comment about the next step to be taken. At that point, do not prolong the interview needlessly. Simply rise, accept the handshake, thank the interviewer for the opportunity to meet, and close by saying you look forward to hearing from the company. The tact with which you close the interview can be almost as important as the first impression you made. Be enthusiastic. If you really want the job, you must ask for it.

Your ability to speak confidently and intelligently about your abilities will help you secure a desirable job. Effective interviewing skills will be just as valuable once you begin work. You will be involved in interviews with your supervisor for various reasons: to seek advice or information about your work and working conditions, to receive informal feedback about your progress, to receive a deserved promotion, and to discuss other personnel matters. In addition, your supervisor will likely conduct a performance appraisal interview to evaluate your performance. This formal interview typically occurs annually on the anniversary of your start of employment.

14-3d Additional Considerations for Phone Interviews

Although many of the guidelines for interviewing also apply to phone interviews, some additional considerations are useful. For example, you will need to make sure that you are located in a quiet place, so that no distracting noises can be heard in the background. Other persons should be asked to leave, and pets should be put in another room or outside.

If you receive an unexpected call from an interviewer and the time isn't convenient, ask if you could talk at another time, and suggest some alternatives.

During the interview, you should

- avoid smoking, chewing gum, eating, or drinking;
- keep a glass of water handy, in case you need to wet your mouth;
- smile—smiling will add enthusiasm to your voice and help to project a positive image to the listener;
- speak slowly and enunciate clearly;
- use the person's title (Mr. or Ms. and their last name) and only use a first name if he or she asks you to;
- avoid interrupting the interviewer;
- pause if you need to collect your thoughts; and
- give short answers.

Remember, your goal is to set up a face-to-face interview. After you thank the interviewer, ask if it would be possible to meet in person.

14-4 PREPARING OTHER EMPLOYMENT MESSAGES

Preparing a winning résumé and application letter is an important first step in a job search. To expedite your job search, you will need to prepare other employment messages. For example, you might complete an application form, send a follow-up message to a company that does not respond to your résumé, send a thank-you message after an interview, accept a job offer, reject other job offers, and communicate with references. A career change will require a carefully written resignation letter.

> Increasing numbers of companies are designing employment forms as mechanisms for acquiring information about a candidate that often is not included in the résumé.

14-4a Application Forms

Before beginning a new job, you will almost certainly complete the employer's application and employment forms. Some application forms, especially for applicants who apply for jobs with a high level of responsibility, are very long. They can actually appear to be tests in which applicants give their answers to hypothetical questions and write defenses for their answers. Application forms also ensure consistency in the information received from each candidate and can prevent decisions based on illegal topics which might be presented in a résumé.

14-4b Follow-Up Messages

When an application message and résumé do not elicit a response, a follow-up message might bring results. Sent a few weeks after the original message, it includes a reminder that an application for a certain job is on file, presents additional education or experience accumulated and its relationship to the job, and closes with a reference

to a desired action. In addition to conveying new information, follow-up messages indicate persistence (a quality that impresses some employers). Figure 14.3 shows a good example of a follow-up message.

14-4c Thank-You Messages

What purposes are served in sending a thank-you message, even though you expressed thanks in person after the interview or after a discussion with a special employer at a career fair? After a job interview, a written message of appreciation is a professional courtesy and enhances your image within the organization. To be effective, it must be sent promptly. For maximum impact, send a thank-you message the day of the interview or the following day. Even if during the interview you decided you do not want the job, or you and the interviewer mutually agreed that the job is not for you, a thank-you message is appropriate. As a matter of fact, if you've made a positive impression, interviewers might forward your résumé to others who are seeking qualified applicants.

The medium you choose for sending this message depends on the intended audience. If the company you've interviewed with prefers a traditional style, send a letter in complete business format on high-quality paper that matches your résumé and application letter. If the company has communicated with you extensively by

---

FIGURE 14.3   EXAMPLE OF A FOLLOW-UP MESSAGE   Good.

Dear Ms. Nelson:

Recently I applied for an auditing position with Frederick Associates and now have additional qualifications to report.

The enclosed, updated résumé shows that I attended the annual Fraud Conference and Exhibition sponsored by the Association of Certified Fraud Examiners. I attended sessions in the technology track and learned about a variety of tools used to detect fraudulent financial transactions. In a post-conference session, I was introduced to interrogation techniques.

Ms. Nelson, I would welcome the opportunity to visit your office and talk more about the contributions I could make as an auditor with Frederick Associates. Please write or call me at (812) 455-9803.

States main idea and clearly identifies position being sought.

Refers to enclosed résumé; summarizes additional qualifications.

Assures employer that applicant is still interested in job.

Format Pointers

Format as formal business letter, but could be sent as an electronic message if previous communication with the employer had been by email.

Print letter and envelope with laser printer on paper that matches résumé and application letter.

---

email, follow the pattern and send a professional email that can be read in a timely manner. Choosing to send an email rather than using slower mail delivery can give you a competitive edge over other candidates whose mailed letters arrive several days later than yours.

After an interview has gone well and you think a job offer is a possibility, include these ideas in the message of appreciation: express gratitude, identify the specific job applied for, refer to some point discussed in the interview (the strength of the interview), and close by making some reference to the expected call or message that conveys the employer's decision. The tone of this business message should remain professional regardless of the personal relationship you might have developed with the interviewer and the informality encouraged by email. The message could be read by many others once it is placed in your personnel file as you complete annual appraisals and compete for promotions. Specific points to cover are illustrated in Figure 14.4.

FIGURE 14.4 EXAMPLE OF A THANK-YOU MESSAGE

Good

New Message

TO: Juan Ortiz [jortiz@insurancepros.com]
FROM: Kenneth Lowe [klowe@hotmail.com]
SUBJECT: Appreciation for job interview opportunity

Dear Mr. Ortiz:

Thank you for meeting with me this morning to discuss the executive assistant position. I enjoyed our conversation, and I am very excited about the possibility of joining your team.

I know what it takes to run a busy and successful insurance office. In my last position as an administrative assistant for Brooks Awnings, Inc., I helped manage all aspects of the operation, handling tasks such as bookkeeping, customer service, claims processing, report preparation, and ongoing communications with the district manager.

You mentioned that you need an assistant who has strong people skills, and this is an area in which I excel. At Brooks Awnings, I helped the manager build a loyal client base by consistently providing excellent service. My last supervisor said, "Ken is one of the hardest-working employees I have known. His friendly and professional customer-service skills helped the firm achieve a 20 percent revenue increase last year, and I couldn't have done it without him."

I will bring these same skills to Insurance Pros, helping you manage the day-to-day operations, volunteering for special projects, and ensuring the company is positioned for growth and increased profitability.

Again, thank you for considering me for this exciting opportunity. As you requested, I'm enclosing a list of professional references. Please feel free to call me if you need additional information, have any questions, or would like to offer me the job! Thank you for your time, and I look forward to hearing from you.

Sincerely,

Kenneth Lowe
Enclosure: List of References

- States main idea of appreciation for interview and information gained.

- Includes specific points discussed during interview, increasing sincerity and recall of applicant.

- Assures employer of applicant's continued interest in position.

- Politely reminds employer that applicant is awaiting reply.

Format Pointers
Prepare as email message because previous communication with the organization has been by email.

The résumé, application letter, and thank-you message should be stored in a computer file and adapted for submission to other firms when needed. Develop a database for keeping a record of the dates on which documents and résumés were sent to certain firms and answers were received, names of people talked with, facts conveyed, and so on. When an interviewer calls, you can retrieve and view that company's record while you are talking with the interviewer.

14-4d Job-Acceptance Messages

A job offer may be extended either by phone or in writing. If a job offer is extended over the phone, request that the company send a written confirmation of the job offer. The confirmation should include the job title, salary, benefits, starting date, and anything else negotiated.

Often, companies require a written acceptance of a job offer. Note the deductive sequence of the message shown in Figure 14.5: acceptance, details, and closing (confirms the report-for-work date).

14-4e Job-Refusal Messages

Like other messages that convey unpleasant news, job-refusal messages are written inductively—with a beginning that reveals the nature of the subject, explanations that lead to a refusal, the refusal, and a pleasant ending. Of course, certain reasons (even though valid in your mind) are better left unsaid, such as questionable company goals or methods of operation,

negative attitude of present employees, possible bankruptcy, unsatisfactory working conditions, and so on. The applicant who prefers not to be specific about the reason for turning down a job might write this explanation: *After thoughtfully considering job offers received this week, I have decided to accept a job in the finance department of a commercial bank.*

You might want to be more specific about your reasons for refusal when you have a positive attitude toward the company or believe you will want to reapply at some later date. The letter excerpt in Figure 14.6 includes the reasons for refusal.

14-4f Resignation Messages

Resigning from a job requires effective communication skills. You might be allowed to give your notice in person or be required to write a formal resignation. Your supervisor will inform you of the company's policy. Regardless of whether the resignation is given orally or in writing, show empathy for your employer by giving enough time to allow the employer to find a replacement. Because your employer has had confidence in you, has benefited from your services, and will have to seek a replacement, your impending departure is bad news. As such, the message may be written inductively or deductively, as shown in Figure 14.7. It calls attention to your job, gives your reasons for leaving it, conveys the resignation, and closes on a positive note.

A resignation is not an appropriate instrument for telling managers how a business should be operated.

FIGURE 14.5 **EXAMPLE OF A JOB-ACCEPTANCE MESSAGE** Good

I accept your employment offer as a management trainee. Thank you for responding so quickly after our discussion last week.

- States main idea of the job acceptance.

As you requested, I have signed the agreement outlining the specific details of my employment. Your copy is enclosed, and I have kept a copy for my records.

- Continues with any necessary details.

If you should need to communicate with me before I report to work on May 15, please call me at 777-2323.

- Confirms beginning employment date.

FIGURE 14.6 | EXAMPLE OF A JOB-REFUSAL MESSAGE

Good

Thank you very much for offering me the assistant manager position. After careful consideration, I regret that I must decline your offer.

Although you were most encouraging in outlining future advancement possibilities within Techline Inc., I have accepted another opportunity that is more in line with my skills and career goals.

I enjoyed meeting you and the rest of your team. You have been most kind and gracious throughout the interview process, and I only wish that circumstances allowed me to accept your offer.

Best wishes for your continued success.

- Begins with a neutral but related idea to buffer the bad news.

- Diplomatically presents the reasons that led to the refusal.

- Ends message on a positive note that anticipates future association with the company.

Lim Yong Hian/Shutterstock.com

Harshly worded statements could result in immediate termination or cause human relations problems during your remaining working days. If you can do so sincerely, recall positive experiences you had with the company. Doing so will leave a lasting record of your goodwill, making it likely that your supervisor will give you a good recommendation in the future.

14-4g Recommendation Requests

Companies seek information from references at various stages. Some prefer talking with references prior to an interview, and others, after a successful interview. Specific actions on your part will ensure that your references are treated with common courtesy and that references are prepared for the employer's call.

- **Remind the reference that he or she had previously agreed to supply information about you.** Identify the job for which you are applying, give a complete address to which the message is to be sent, and indicate a date by which the prospective employer needs the message. By sharing information about job requirements and reporting recent job-related experiences, you can assist the reference in writing an effective message. Indicate your gratitude, but do not apologize for making the request. The reference has already agreed to write on your behalf and will likely take pleasure in assisting a deserving person.

- **Alert the reference of imminent requests for information, especially if considerable time has elapsed since the applicant and reference have last seen each other.** Enclosing a recent résumé and providing any other pertinent information (e.g., name change) will enable the reference to write a message that is specific and convincing. To ensure on-target job references, politely explain the types of information you perceive relevant to the job sought: specific job skills, work ethic, attitude and demeanor

FIGURE 14.7   EXAMPLE OF A RESIGNATION MESSAGE

Good

New Message

To: Robert Johnson [rjohnson@Fredericks&Johnson.com]
From: Lynn Redbird [lredbird@Fredericks&Johnson.com]
Subject: Tendering my resignation

Dear Robert,

Please accept this letter as notice of my resignation from my position as staff accountant. My last day of employment will be July 22, 2017.

I received an offer to serve as a senior accountant of a Fortune 500 company, and after careful consideration, I realize that this opportunity is too exciting for me to decline.

It has been a pleasure working with you and your team over the last three years. One of the highlights of my career was collaborating with you to automate Frederick and Johnson's accounting, financial, and balance systems, and setting up your accounting infrastructure. Your company is poised for continued growth and I wish you much success with your upcoming acquisition of Rogers Tax Accounting.

I would like to help with the transition of my accounting duties so that systems continue to function smoothly after my departure. I am available to help recruit and train my replacement, and I will make certain that all reporting and records are updated before my last day of work.

Robert, thank you again for the opportunity to work for Fredericks and Johnson. I wish you and your staff all the best and I look forward to staying in touch with you. You can email me anytime at lredbird@gmail.com or call me at 501-667-5523.

Sincerely,

Lynn Redbird

Begins with statement of purpose.

Presents reasons that lead to the main idea: the resignation.

Provides contact information to ensure a smooth transition.

Conveys genuine appreciation for the experience gained and ends on a cordial note.

---

toward work, leadership style, and so on. If the job search becomes longer than anticipated, a follow-up message to references explaining the delay and expressing gratitude for their efforts is appropriate.

- **Send a sincere, original thank-you message after a position has been accepted.** This thoughtful gesture will build a positive relationship with a person who might continue to be important to your career. The message in Figure 14.8 is brief and avoids clichés and exaggerated expressions of praise, but instead gives specific examples of the importance of the reference's recommendation.

FIGURE 14.8 | **EXAMPLE OF A THANK-YOU MESSAGE TO A REFERENCE**

Good.

As you may be aware, I have been applying for various employment opportunities over the past few months. I just received a very attractive offer to fill a vacant position at a innovative and exciting company.

While my résumé, experience, and performance at the interview contributed a great deal to grasping this opportunity, I feel that your recommendation played a central role in the company's decision to offer me the job.

I wish to express my gratitude for your consideration and time in supporting my endeavors. Your encouragement and support mean a lot to me.

Implies main idea of appreciation for recommendation. Informs reference of success in locating a job.

Communicates sincere appreciation for assistance; uses specific examples and avoids exaggeration.

Restates main idea and anticipates continued relationship; is original and sincere.

STUDY TOOLS 14

LOCATED AT THE BACK OF THE TEXTBOOK
☐ Tear-Out Chapter Review Card

LOCATED AT WWW.CENGAGEBRAIN.COM
☐ Review Key Term flashcards and create your own cards

☐ Track your knowledge and understanding of key concepts in business communication

☐ Complete practice and graded quizzes to prepare for tests

☐ Complete interactive content within BCOM9 Online

☐ View the chapter highlight boxes for BCOM9 Online

GRAMMAR & USAGE APPENDIX

Polishing your language skills will aid you in preparing error-free documents that reflect positively on you and your company. This text appendix is an abbreviated review that focuses on common problems frequently encountered by business writers and offers a quick refresh of key skills.

GRAMMAR

Sentence Structure

1. Rely mainly on sentences that follow the normal subject-verb-complement sequence for clarity and easy reading.

   <u>Jennifer</u> and <u>I</u> <u>withdrew</u> for two <u>reasons</u>.
   (subject)   (verb)   (complement)

Original	Better
There are two <u>reasons</u> for our withdrawal.	Two <u>reasons</u> for our withdrawal are….
	<u>Jennifer and I</u> withdrew for two reasons.
<u>It</u> is necessary that we withdraw.	<u>We</u> must withdraw.
<u>Here</u> is a copy of my résumé.	The enclosed <u>résumé</u> outlines….

   There, *it*, and *here* are *expletives*—filler words that have no real meaning in the sentence.

2. Put pronouns, adverbs, phrases, and clauses near the words they modify.

Incorrect	Correct
Angie put a new type of gel in her hair, <u>which</u> she had just purchased.	Angie put a new type of <u>gel</u>, <u>which</u> she had just purchased, in her hair.
He works <u>only</u> in the call center during peak periods.	He works in the call center <u>only</u> during peak periods.
The clerk stood near the fax machine <u>wearing a denim skirt</u>.	The clerk <u>wearing a denim skirt</u> stood near the fax machine.

3. Do not separate subject and predicate unnecessarily.

Incorrect	Clear
<u>She</u>, hoping to receive a bonus, <u>worked</u> rapidly.	Hoping to receive a bonus, <u>she</u> <u>worked</u> rapidly.

4. Place an introductory phrase near the subject of the independent clause it modifies.
Otherwise, the phrase dangles. To correct the dangling phrase, change the subject of the independent clause, or make the phrase into a dependent clause by assigning it a subject.

Incorrect	Correct
<u>When</u> a young boy, <u>my mother</u> insisted I learn a second language.	<u>When I was a young boy</u>, my mother insisted I learn a second language.
[Implies that the mother was once a young boy]	
<u>Working</u> at full speed every morning, <u>fatigue</u> overtakes me in the afternoon.	<u>Working</u> at full speed every morning, <u>I</u> become tired in the afternoon.
[Implies that "fatigue" was working at full speed]	<u>Because I work</u> at full speed every morning, <u>fatigue</u> overtakes me in the afternoon.
<u>To function</u> properly, <u>you</u> must oil the machine every hour.	<u>If the equipment</u> is to function properly, <u>you</u> must oil it every hour.
[Implies that if "you" are "to function properly," the machine must be oiled hourly]	<u>To function properly</u>, the <u>equipment</u> must be oiled every hour.

5. Express related ideas in similar grammatical form (use parallel construction).

Incorrect	Correct
The machine operator made three resolutions: (1) <u>to be punctual,</u> (2) <u>following instructions carefully,</u> and third, <u>the reduction of waste</u>.	The machine operator made three resolutions: <u>to be punctual</u>, <u>to follow instructions carefully</u>, and <u>to reduce waste</u>.
The human resources manager is concerned with the <u>selection</u> of the right worker, <u>providing</u> appropriate orientation and the <u>worker's progress</u>.	The human resources manager is concerned with <u>selecting</u> the right worker, <u>providing</u> appropriate orientation, and <u>evaluating</u> the worker's progress.

6. Do not end a sentence with a needless preposition.

Where is the new sushi bar to be <u>located</u> (not *located at*)?

The applicant did not tell us where he was <u>going</u> (not *going to*).

End a sentence with a preposition if for some reason the preposition needs emphasis.

I am not concerned about what he is paying <u>for</u>. I am concerned about what he is paying <u>with</u>.

The prospect has everything—a goal to work <u>toward</u>, a house to live <u>in</u>, and an income to live <u>on</u>.

SOLUTIONS TO EXERCISES

Exercise 1—Sentence Structure

1. You must learn to design spreadsheets that make financial information meaningful to users.

2. Many online tools are available that build relationships with customers.

3. I am submitting an employee testimonial, which I first posted to a presentations blog, to the company website.

4. More companies are videoconferencing because of the need to reduce travel costs significantly.

5. You must perform periodic maintenance on your computer to keep it operating efficiently. [The introductory phrase dangles.]

6. Planned store improvements include widening the aisles, improving lighting, and lowering shelves for a sophisticated feel.

   Planned store improvements include widened aisles, improved lighting, and lowered shelves for a sophisticated feel.

Exercise 2—Pronoun Reference

1. affect
2. was
3. her
4. was
5. its
6. its
7. this oversight

Exercise 3—Pronoun Case

1. us
2. her
3. she; who
4. his
5. whom

Exercise 4—Verb Agreement, Tense, and Mood

1. has
2. are
3. were
4. were
5. is
6. has
7. is
8. doesn't
9. started
10. were

Exercise 5—Adjectives and Adverbs

1. infrequently
2. impatiently
3. quickly
4. best
5. any other

Exercise 6—Commas

1. Correct

2. Emoticons, which are created by keying combinations of symbols to produce "sideway faces," communicate emotion in electronic messages.

3. Sean Cohen, a new member of the board, remained silent during the long, bitter debate.

4. Top social networking sites include Facebook, MySpace, and Flickr.

5. The entire population was surveyed, but three responses were unusable.

6. If you tag websites in a social bookmarking site, you can locate them easily for later use.

7. To qualify for the position, applicants must have technology certification.

8. We should be spending less money, not more.

9. On May 9, 2013, the company's Twitter site was launched.

10. Yes, the president approved a team-building event to replace our annual golf outing.

Exercise 7—Semicolons and Colons

1. Some privacy concerns have become less important in recent years; however, most people feel extremely vulnerable to privacy invasion.

2. The following agents received bonuses: Barnes, $750; Shelley, $800; and Jackson, $950.

3. Employees were notified today of the plant closing; they received two weeks' severance pay.

4. This paint does have some disadvantages, for example, a lengthy drying time.

5. Soon after the applications are received, a team of judges will evaluate them; but the award recipients will not be announced until January 15.

6. Correct

7. The new bakery will offer frozen yogurt, candies, and baked goods.

8. We are enthusiastic about the plan because (1) it is least expensive, (2) its legality is unquestioned, and (3) it can be implemented quickly.

Exercise 8—Apostrophes

1. hire's; manager's
2. company's; its
3. week's
4. Vendors; weeks
5. employees'

Exercise 9—Hyphens

1. Web-based; denial-of-service attack
2. State-of-the-art; timely business
3. Correct
4. two-thirds; 5 percent
5. one half; highly educated

Exercise 10—Quotation Marks and Italics

1. Cynthia Cooper's *Extraordinary Circumstances* is required reading in some forensic accounting classes. [Italicizes a book title]
2. The article "How to Persuade People to Say Yes" appeared in the May 2009 issue of *Training Journal*. [Encloses the name of an article in quotation marks and italicizes the title of a journal]
3. The consultant's "accomplishments" are summarized on her opening blog page. [Uses quotation marks to introduce doubt about whether *accomplishments* is the right label; her undertakings may have been of little significance]
4. Connie said, "I want to participate in a volunteer program that serves such a worthy cause." [Uses quotations marks in a direct quotation]
5. The term *flame* is online jargon for "a heated, sarcastic, sometimes abusive message or posting to a discussion group." [Italicizes a defined term and encloses the definition in quotes]
6. Limit random "tweets," but focus on ideas and issues that are interesting and relevant. [Uses quotation marks to emphasize or clarify a word for the reader]

Exercise 11—Dashes, Parentheses, and Periods

1. Additional consultants—programmers and analysts—were hired to complete the computer conversion.
2. The dividend will be raised to 15 cents a share (approved by the Board of Directors on December 1, 2013).
3. Would you please link this YouTube video to my slide show. [Uses a period to follow a courteous request that requires no verbal response]

Exercise 12—Number Usage

1. The question was answered by 61 percent of the respondents.
2. The meeting is scheduled for 10 a.m. on February 3.
3. These three figures appeared on the expense account: $21.95, $30, and $35.14.
4. The purchasing manager ordered fifty, 4-GB Flash drives.
5. Twenty-one members voted in favor of the $2 million proposal.
6. Approximately 100 respondents requested a copy of the results. [Approximations above nine that can be expressed in one or two words may be written in either figures or words, but figures are more emphatic.]
7. Mix 2 quarts of white with 13 quarts of brown.
8. Examine the cost projections on page 8.

Exercise 13—Capitalization

1. The first question Professor Burney asked me during Interviewing 101 was "Why do you want to work for us?"
2. The remodeling will give the store a more sophisticated feel according to the public relations director.
3. As the summer season arrives, gas prices are expected to rise.
4. We recently purchased Digital Juice, an excellent source for copyright-free animated images.
5. Thomas Frieden, director of the Centers for Disease Control, is the agency's key communicator.

Exercise 14—Words Frequently Misused

1. effect
2. advise
3. number
4. site
5. compliment; complement
6. one another
7. farther
8. fewer
9. infer
10. losing; its; different from
11. led; lead
12. personal
13. principal
14. they're; their
15. two; to; too

REFERENCES

1

1. Koncz, A. (2007, March 15). Employers cite communication skills, honesty/integrity as key for job candidates. National Association of Colleges and Employers. Retrieved from www.naceweb.org/press/display .asp?year=2007&prid+254.

2. *Huffington Post* (2013). What big businesses can teach you about building company culture. Retrieved May 13, 2014 from http://www.huffingtonpost .com/2013/12/10/what-big-business-can-tea_n_4194514.html.

3. Tapscott, D. (2008, December 8). Supervising Net Gen. Business Week Online, 5. Retrieved from Business Source Complete Database.

4. Slayton, M. (1980). *Common sense and everyday ethics*. Washington, D.C.: Ethics Resource Center.

5. Brzezinski, N. (2014). Diversity and ethics, keys to corporate success: Interview with Global CEO Skanska. *Huffington Post*. Retrieved May 13, 2014 from http://www.huffingtonpost.com/ natalia-lopatniuk-brzezinski/diversity-ethics-keys-to-_b_4901755.html.

6. A gift or a bribe? (2002, September). *State Legislatures*, 2 (8), 9.

7. Mathison, D. L. (1988). Business ethics cases and decision models: A call for relevancy in the classroom. *Journal of Business Ethics*, 10, 781.

8. Wile, R. (2014). France didn't actually ban work email after 6 PM—But what did happen is still really funny. *Business Insider*. Retrieved May 13, 2014 from http://www.businessinsider. com/the-truth-about-frances-work-email-ban-2014-4#ixzz31dgeCZqP.

9. Carson, E. (2015). Top 5 worst social media brand blunders of 2015. *Tech Republic*. Retrieved June 1, 2016 from http://www.techrepublic .com/article/top-5-worst-social-media-brand-blunders-of-2015/.

10. Earley, P. C., & Ang, S. (2003). *Cultural Intelligence: Individual Interactions Across Cultures*. Stanford: Stanford Business Books.

11. Kaplan A. M. & Haenlein M. (2010). Users of the world, unite! The challenges and opportunities of social media. *Business Horizons*, 53 (1), 61.

12. Felts, C. (1995). Taking the mystery out of self-directed work teams. *Industrial Management*, 37 (2), 21–26.

13. Miller, B. K., & Butler, J. B. (1996, November/December). Teams in the workplace. *New Accountant*, 18–24.

14. Ray, D., & Bronstein, H. (1995). *Teaming Up*. New York: McGraw-Hill.

15. The trouble with teams. (1995, January 4). *Economist*, 61.

16. Frohman, M. A. (1995, April 3). Do teams … but do them right. *Industry Week*, 21–24.

17. Zuidema, K. R., & Kleiner, B. H. (1994). New developments in developing self-directed work groups. *Management Decision*, 32 (8), 57–63.

18. Barry, D. (1991). Managing the baseless team: Lessons in distributed leadership. *Organizational Dynamics*, 20 (1), 31–47.

19. Powell, A., Piccoli, G., & Ives. B. (2004). Virtual teams: A review of current literature and directions for future research. *The DATABASE for Advances in Information Systems*, 35 (1).

2

1. Interpersonal intelligence. (2009). My Personality. Retrieved from www.mypersonality.info/ multiple-intelligences/interpersonal/.

2. Luft, J., & Ingham, H. (1955). *The Johari window, a graphic model of interpersonal awareness*. Proceedings of the western training laboratory in group development. Los Angeles: University of California, Los Angeles.

3. Hershey, P., & Blanchard, K. H. (1982). *Management of Organizational Behavior: Utilizing Human Resources* (4th Ed.). Englewood Cliffs, NJ: Prentice-Hall.

4. Felts, C. (1995). Taking the mystery out of self-directed work teams. *Industrial Management*, 37 (2), 21–26.

5. Mehrabian, A. (1971). *Silent Messages*. Belmont, CA: Wadsworth.

6. Wolvin, A.D., & Coakley, C.G. (1996). Listening, 5th Ed. Madison, WI: Brown and Benchmark, p. 15.

7. Purdy, M. The listener wins, http:// featuredreports.monster.com/listen/ overview.

8. Senge, Peter M, Kleiner, Art, Roberts, Charlotte, Ross Richard B, & Smith, Bryan J. (1994). *The Fifth Discipline Fieldbook*. New York: Currency Doubleday.

9. Drucker, Peter. (1990). The Fifth Discipline. The art and practice of the learning organization. London: Random House.

10. Gratton, L. (2007, June 6). Working together … When apart. *Wall Street Journal*. Retrieved

from http://online.wsj.com/news/articles/SB118165895540732559.

11. Baldrige, L. (2003). *Letitia Baldrige's New Complete Guide to Executive Manners*. New York: Simon and Schuster.

12. Hunt, V. D. (1993). *Managing for quality: Integrating quality and business strategy* (121). Homewood, IL: Business One Irwin.

13. Munter, M. (1998, June). Meeting technology: From low-tech to high-tech. *Business Communication Quarterly*, 61 (2), 80–87.

3

1. Canavor, N., & Meirowitz, C. (2005). Good corporate writing: Why it matters, and what to do; Poor corporate writing—in press releases, ads, brochures, web sites and more—is costing companies credibility and reviews. Here's how to put the focus back on clear communication. *Communication World*, 22 (4), 30–34.

2. Schein, E. H. (1992). *Educational Culture and Leadership (p.12)*. New York: Jossey-Bass.

3. Stallard, M. L. (2011, January 21). Has SAS Institute's goodnight cracked the code on corporate culture? Insights on Leadership and Employee Engagement. Retrieved from http://www.michaelleestallard.com/has-sasinstitutes-goodnight-cracked-the-code-oncorporate-culture.

4. Cameron, K. S., & Quinn, R. E. (2011). *Diagnosing and Changing Organizational Culture: Based on the Competing Values Framework*. New York: John Wiley & Sons.

5. Bradford, J. (2013). 5-Hour Energy accused of false advertising over "no crash" claim. *The Huffington Post*. Retrieved May 15, 2014 from http://www.huffingtonpost.com/2013/01/03/5-hour-energy-no-crash-false-advertising_n_2403015.html.

6. Karoub, J. (2013). McDonald's to pay $700,000 to settle allegations franchise falsely claimed food complied with halal. *The Huffington Post*. Retrieved May 15, 2014 from http://www.huffingtonpost.com/2013/01/21/mcdonalds-halal_n_2522254.html.

7. Thomas, E. (2014). Vibram, "barefoot running shoe" company, settles multi-million dollar lawsuit. *The Huffington Post*. Retrieved May 15, 2014 from http://www.huffingtonpost.com/2014/05/10/_n_5302213.html.

8. Mackay, M. (2012). Ex-Yahoo CEO Scott Thompson and seven other cases of resume fraud. *The Huffington Post*. Retrieved May 15, 2014 from http://www.huffingtonpost.com/2012/05/15/yahoo-ceo-scott-thompsons-resume-fraud_n_1516061.html.

9. Telushkin, J. (1997). Avoid words that hurt. *USA Today*, 74.

4

1. Charlton, J. (Ed.). (1995). *The Writer's Quotation Book*. Stamford, CT: Ray Freeman.

2. Is email making bosses ruder? (2005). *European Business Forum*, 21, 72.

3. Rindegard, J. (1999). Use clear writing to show you mean business. *InfoWorld*, 21 (47), 78.

4. Dyrud, M. A. (1996). Teaching by example: Suggestions for assignment design. *Business Communication Quarterly*, 59 (3), 67–70.

5. Redish, J. C. (1993). Understanding readers. In C. M. Barnum & S. Carliner (Eds.), *Techniques for Technical Communicators*. New York: Prentice-Hall.

6. Ibid.

7. Good, C. (2009, March 20). Quote of the Day: Special Olympics Chairman Tim Shriver on Obama's Special Olympics Joke. Retrieved from http://www.theatlantic.com/politics/archive/2009/03/quote-of-the-day-special-olympics-chairman-tim-shriver-on-obamas-special-olympics-joke/1689/.

8. Neuwirth, R. (1998). Error message: To err is human, but darn expensive. *Editor & Publisher*, 131 (29), 4.

9. UCSD sends acceptance email to wrong list. (2009, April 2). *eSchool News*. Retrieved from http://www.eschoolnews.com/news/around-the-web/index.cfm?i=58045.

5

1. Collins, K. (2015, March 18). *A quick guide to the worst corporate hack attacks*. *Bloomberg News*. Retrieved June 3, 2016 from http://www.bloomberg.com/graphics/2014-data-breaches/

2. Garcia, A. (2015, December. 2). *Target settles for $39 million over data breach*. *CNN*. Retrieved June 14, 2016 from http://money.cnn.com/2015/12/02/news/companies/target-data-breach-settlement/

3. Hear no evil, see no evil: Business e-mail overtakes the telephone. (2007, August 20). *Network*. Retrieved from www.networkworld.com/community/node/18555.

4. Silverman, D. (2009, April 14). Words at work: How to revise an email so that people will read it. Retrieved from http://blogs.harvardbusiness.org/silverman/2009/04/how-to-revise-an-email-so-that.html.

5. Silverman, D. (2009, April 14). Words at work: Is your email businesslike—or brusque? Retrieved from http://blogs.harvardbusiness.org/silverman/2009/04/is-your-email-businesslike-or.html.

6. New technology makes work harder. (1999, June 1). *BBC News*. Retrieved from http://news.bbc.co.uk/2/hi/science/nature/357993.stm.

7. Lacy, S. (2006, January 6). IM security one tough sell. *Business Week Online*, 11.

8. Knapp, L. (2007, January 20). Switching to texting has pluses, minuses: Getting started. *Seattle Times*, E6. Retrieved from General Business File database.

9. McGrath, C. (2006, January 22). The pleasures of the text. *The New York Times*, 15.

10. Knapp, L. (2007, January 20). Switching to texting has pluses, minuses: Getting started. *Seattle Times*, E6. Retrieved from General Business File database.

11. Electronic Privacy Information Center. (2008, September 15). Public opinion on privacy. Retrieved from www.epic.org/privacy/survey.

12. 9th circuit court rules on text-messaging privacy. (2008, July 15). Law.com. Retrieved from www.law.com/jsp/legaltechnology/pubArticleLT-jsp?id=1202422970200.

13. Brown, P. B. (2005, December 31). Resolved: I will take good advice. *The New York Times*. Retrieved from http://www.nytimes.com/2005/12/31/business/31offline.html.

14. Mabrey, V., Scott, D. W., & Foster, M. (2008, March 24). Charges filed in Detroit mayor scandal. *ABC News*. Retrieved from http://abcnews.go.com/print?id=4355795.

15. Varchaver, N. (2003). The perils of e-mail. *Fortune*, 147 (3), 96+.

16. Ibid.

17. Downer, K. (2008). A great website in five steps. *Third Sector*, 9.

18. Tierney, J. (2007, April). Ignore universal web design at your own peril. *Multi-channel Merchant*, 8.

19. Fichter, D. (2001, November/December). Zooming in: Writing content for intranets. Online, 25(6), 80+.

20. McAlpine, R. (2001). *Web Word Wizardry: A Guide to Writing for the Web and Intranet*. Berkeley, CA: Ten Speed Press.

21. Seventy-nine percent of large international companies are using. (2010, February 23). *Bloomberg*. Retrieved from http://www.bloomberg.com/apps/news?pid=newsarchive&sid=a_M.jlgajlbw.

22. Weblog. (2005). Loosely coupled. Retrieved from www.looselycoupled.com/glossary/weblog.

23. Quible, Z. K. (2005). Blogs and written business communication courses: A perfect union. *Journal of Education for Business*, 80 (6), 327–332.

24. Jones, D. (2005, May 10). CEOs refuse to get tangled up in messy blogs. *USA Today*. Retrieved from Academic Search Premier database.

25. DeBare, I. (2005, May 5). Tips for effective use of blogs in business. *San Francisco Chronicle*, C6.

26. Hutchins, J. P. (2005, November 14). Beyond the water cooler. *ComputerWorld*, 39 (46), 45–46.

27. How to write for the web. (2008, March 26). *The Online Journalism Review*. Retrieved from www.ojr.org/ojr/wiki/writing.

28. Goodnoe, E. (2005, August 8). How to use wikis for business. *Information Week*. Retrieved from www.informationweek.com/news/management/showArticle.jhtml?articleID=16760331&pgno=3&queryText=&isPrev=.

29. Johnson, C. Y. (2008, July 7). Hurry up, the customer has a complaint: As blogs expand the reach of a single voice, firms monitor the Internet looking for the dissatisfied. *The Boston Globe*. Retrieved from www.Boston.com.

30. How to get the most out of voice mail. (2000, February). *The CPA Journal*, 70 (2), 11.

31. Leland, K., & Bailey, K. (1999). *Customer Service for Dummies* (2nd Ed.). New York: Wiley.

32. Berkley, S. (2003, July). Help stamp out bad voicemail! *The Voice Coach Newsletter*. Retrieved from www.greatvoice.com/archive_vc/archiveindex_vc.html.

33. McCarthy, M. L. (1999, October). Email, voicemail and the Internet: How employers can avoid getting cut by the double-edged sword of technology. *Business Credit*, 100 (9), 44+.

34. Norris, D. (2007). Sales communications in a mobile world: Using the latest technology and retaining the personal touch. *Business Communication Quarterly*, 70, 492–498.

35. Cell phone etiquette. (2001, March). Office Solutions, 18 (3), 13.

36. Krotz, J. L. (2008). Cell phone etiquette: 10 dos and don'ts. *Microsoft Business*. Retrieved from www.microsoft.com/smallbusiness/resources/technology/communications/cell-phone-etiquette-10-dos-and-donts.aspx#Cellphoneetiquettedosanddonts.

37. Cell phone etiquette. (2001, March). *Office Solutions*, 18 (3), 13.

38. Minton-Eversole, T. (2012, July 19). Virtual teams used by most global organizations, survey says. *Society for Human Resource Management*. Retrieved June 3, 2016 from https://www.shrm.org/hrdisciplines/orgempdev/articles/pages/virtualteamsusedmostbyglobalorganizations,surveysays.aspx.

39. Radley, N. (2014, July 17). How team members prefer to communicate on virtual teams. *Software Advice*. Retrieved June 3, 2016 from http://blog.softwareadvice.com/articles/project-management/survey-communication-virtual-projects-0714/.

40. Ibid.

6

1. Williamson, M. (2008, June 11). Twittering the Internet. *TechnologyStory.com*.

Retrieved from http://www.technologystory.com/2008/06/11/twittering-the-internet.

7

1. Swisher, K. (2007, October 15). AOL layoffs letter from CEO Randy Falco. *All Things Digital*. Retrieved from http://allthingsd.com/20071015/aol-layoffs-letter-from-randy-falco/.

2. Ethical workforce reflects honest management. (2008, June). *Internal Auditor*, 18–19.

3. Advice from the pros on the best way to deliver bad news. (2003, February). *IOMA's Report on Customer Relationship Management*, 5–6.

4. Purina on pet food recall 4-26-07. (2007). American Kennel Club. Retrieved from http://clubs.akc.org/brit/NEWS/07.PurinaPetFoodRecall.htm.

5. Workers get better at bearing bad news. (2005, October 11). *Personnel Today*, 46.

6. Expert offers advice about how to lay off employees. (2008, October 9). *Immediate Care Business*. Retrieved from http://www.immediatecarebusiness.com/hotnews/layingoff-employees.html.

7. Coombs, W. T. (2007). Protecting organization reputations during a crisis: The development and application of situational crisis communication theory. *Corporate Reputation Review 10* (3), 163–176; Coombs, W. T. (2004). Impact of past crisis on current crisis communications: Insights from situational crisis communication theory. *Journal of Business Communication 41* (3), 265–289; Coombs, W. T., & Holladay, S. J. (2002). Helping crisis managers protect reputational assets: Initial tests of the situational crisis communication theory. *Management Communication Quarterly 16* (2), 165–186.

8. Coombs, W. T. (2007). Protecting organization reputations during a crisis: The development and application of situational crisis communication theory. *Corporate Reputation Review 10* (3), 163–176; Coombs, W. T. (2004). Impact of past crisis on current crisis communications: Insights from situational crisis communication theory. *Journal of Business Communication 41* (3), 265–289; Coombs, W. T. & Holladay, S. J. (2002). Helping crisis managers protect reputational assets: Initial tests of the situational crisis communication theory. *Management Communication Quarterly 16* (2), 165–186.

8

1. Cody, S. (1906). *Success in letter writing: Business and social* (pp. 122–126). Chicago: A. C. McClurg.

2. Lotus Cars. Retrieved July 28, 2013 from www.lotuscars.com/gb/our-cars/current-range/elise-range.

3. Apple. Retrieved July 28, 2013 from www.apple.com/ipad/why-ipad-retina/.

4. http://home.mcafee.com/Store/PackageDetail.aspx?pkgid=275.

5. Sinclair, B. (2003, July 20). Handle client complaints. *The Web design business kit*. Retrieved from http://www.sitepoint.com/article/handle-client-complaints/.

9

1. Grimes, B. (2003, May 6). Fooling Google. *PC Magazine*, 22(8), 74.

2. McIntyre, Douglas A., Ashley C. Allen, Samuel Weigley, & Michael B. Sauter. (October 17, 2012). The worst business decisions of all time. 24/7 *Wall St*. Retrieved from http://247wallst.com/specialreport/2012/10/17/the-worst-businessdecisions-of-all-time/3/.

10

1. Gallo, C. (2008, December 10). Making YouTube work for your business. *Business Week Online*. Retrieved from www.businessweek.com/stories/2008-12-09/making-youtube-work-for-yourbusinessbusinessweek-business-news-stockmarket-and-financial-advice.

2. Martin, M. H. (1997, November 27). The man who makes sense of numbers. *Fortune*, 273–275.

3. Simons, T. (2004). The multimedia paradox. *Presentations*, 18(9), 24–25.

11

No endnotes.

12

1. Kalytiak, T. (2008, October). Overcoming speaking anxiety: Toastmasters sculpt shy speakers into outstanding orators. *Alaska Business Monthly*. Retrieved from http://www.akbizmag.com.

2. Axtell, R. E. (1992). *Do's and Taboos of Public Speaking: How to Get Those Butterflies Flying in Formation*. New York: John Wiley.

3. National Center for Biotechnology Information, U.S. National Library of Medicine, *The Associated Press*. (2014). Retrieved May 25, 2014 from http://statisticbrain.com/attention-span-statistics/.

4. Britz, J. D. (1999, October). You can't catch a marlin with a meatball. *Presentations*, 13 (10), A1–22.

5. Hughes, M. (1990). Tricks of the speechwriter's trade. *Management Review*, 9 (11), 56–58.

6. Somerville, J. (2003). Presentation tip: Stop the verbal spam. About.com:Entrepreneurs. Retrieved from http://entrepreneurs.about.com/cs/marketing/a/infodumping.htm.

7. Simmons, A. (2007). *Whoever Tells the Best Story Wins: How to Use Your Own Stories to Communicate with Power and Impact*. New York: Amacon.

8. Gallo, C. (2009, April 8). Making your presentations relevant. *Business Week Online*, 15.

9. Axtell, R. E. (1992). *Do's and Taboos of Public Speaking: How to Get Those Butterflies Flying in Formation*. New York: John Wiley.

10. Decker, B. (1992). *You've Got to Be Believed to Be Heard*. New York: St. Martin's Press.

11. Hillary Clinton's campaign sends "docu-points" to House Dems. (2008, May 10). *Presentation Zen*. Retrieved from http://www.presentationzen .com/presentationzen/2008/05/ hillary-campaig.html.

12. Earnest, W. (2007). *Save Our Slides: PowerPoint Design That Works*. Dubuque, IA: Kendall/Hunt.

13 CNN Staff (2008, April 5). Jonathan Knight exists New Kids on the Block show mid-concert. *CNN Entertainment*.

14. Decker, B. (1992). *You've Got to Be Believed to Be Heard*. New York: St. Martin's Press.

15. Boromisza-Habashia, D., Hughesa, J. M.F., & Malkowski, J. A. (2015, December.). Public speaking as cultural ideal: Internationalizing the public speaking curriculum. *Journal of International and Intercultural Communication*, 1–15.

16. Miller, A.N. (2002). An exploration of Kenyan public speaking patterns with implications for the American introductory public speaking course. *Communication Education*, 51, 168–182. doi:10.1080/03634520216505, p. 180.

17. Carbaugh, D. (2005). *Cultures in Conversation*. Mahwah, NJ: Lawrence Erlbaum Associates..

18. Liberman, K. (1990). Intercultural communication in Central Australia. In D. Carbaugh (Ed.), *Cultural Communication and Intercultural Contact* (pp. 177–183). Hillsdale, NJ: Lawrence Erlbaum Associates.

19. Ibid., p. 177.

20. Albert, E. (1964). "Rhetoric," "logic," and "poetics" in Burundi: Culture patterning of speech behavior. *American Anthropologist*, 66 (6), 35–54; Bauman, R. (1975). Verbal art as performance. *American Anthropologist*, 77 (2), 290–311; and Habashi et al.

21. Kulick, D., & Schieffelin, B.B. (2004). Language socialization. In A. Duranti (Ed.), *A Companion to Linguistic Anthropology* (pp. 349–368). Malden, MA: Blackwell.

22. Carbaugh; Liberman.

23. Hanke, J. (1998, January). Presenting as a team. *Presentations*, 12 (1), 74–82.

24. Ibid.

25. Ibid

26. Ibid

27. Davids, M. (1999). Smiling for the camera. *Journal of Business Strategy*, 20 (3), 20–24.

28. Turner, C. (1998, February). Become a web presenter? (Really it's not that hard). *Presentations*, 12 (2), 26–27.

29. Sturges, D. L. (1994). Communicating through crisis: A strategy for organizational survival. *Management Communication Quarterly*, 7, 297–316.

30. Mitroff, I.I., & Alpasian, M. C. (2004, Spring). A toolkit for managing crises and preparing for the unthinkable. *The Mitroff Report*, 1, 81–88.

13

1. Jackson, T. (2003). Find a job you love and success will follow. *Career Journal* (*The Wall Street Journal*). Retrieved from http:// www.careerjournal.com/jobhunting/ strategies/20030415-jackson.html.

2. Top 15 Most Popular Job Websites. (2014, May). Retrieved May 26, 2014 from http://www.ebizmba.com/articles/ job-websites.

3. Riley, M. F. (2009). The Riley guide: Employment opportunities and job resources on the Internet. Retrieved from http://www.rileyguide.com.

4. Ireland, S. (2002, July–August). A resume that works. *Searcher*, 10 (7), 98–110.

5. Harshbarger, C. (2003). You're out! *Strategic Finance*, 84 (11), 46–50.

6. Elefant, C. (2008, March 11). Do employers using Facebook for background checks face legal risks? Legal Blog Watch. Retrieved from http://legalblogwatch.typepad. com/legal_blog_watch/2008/03/ do-employers-us.html.

7. Garone, E. (2009, March 18). Do references really matter? WSJ. com: Careers Q&A. Retrieved from http://online.wsj.com/article/ SB123672074032087901.html.

8. Are you using the wrong resume? (2009). Careerbuilder. com. Retrieved from http:// www.careerbuilder.com/Article/ CB-998-Cover-Letters-and-Resumes-Are-You-Using-the-Wrong-R%C3%A9sum5C%A9/.

9. Resumes you don't see everyday. (2006). Retrieved from http:// www.dummies.com/WileyCDA/ DummiesArticle/id-1610.html.

10. Young, J. (2002). "E-portfolios" could give students a new sense of their accomplishments. *Chronicle of Higher Education*, 48 (26), 31–32.

11. Sipper, R. A. (2007, October 15). Tips for creating a YouTube video resume. Retrieved from http://www .associatedcontent.com/article/414702/ tips_for_creating_a_youtube_video_ resume.html?cat=3.

14

1. Vogt, P. (2006). Acing behavioral interviews. *Career Journal. com*. Retrieved from www .careerjournaleurope.com/jobhunting/ interviewing/19980129-vogt.html

2. Marion, L. C. (1997, January 11). Companies tap keyboards to interview applicants. *The News and Observer*, p. B5.

3. Thomson Learning announces name change to Cengage Learning. (2007, October). High Beam Research. Retrieved from www .highbeam.com/doc/1G1-168632242. html (pay to view).

4. Burns, D. (2009). *The first 60 seconds: Win the job interview before it begins*. Naperville, IL: Sourcebooks.

5. Lai, P., & Wong, I. (2000). The clash of cultures in the job interview. *Journal of Language for International Business*, 11 (1), 31–40.

6. Austin, N. K. (1996, March). The new job interview. *Working Woman*, 23–24.

7. Kennedy, J. L., & Morrow, T. J. (1994). *Electronic résumé revolution: Create a winning résumé for the new world of job seeking*. New York: John Wiley.

8. Kleiman, P. (2003, May). Armed for a multitude of tasks. *The Times Higher Education Supplement*, p. 4.

9. MIT Career Development Center (2008, September 16). *STAR method: Behavioral interviewing*. Retrieved from www.lpnet.org/site/programs/docs/ STAR%20MethodHandout.pdf.

10. Stern, L. (2005, January 17). The tough new job hunt. *Newsweek*, 73–74.

11. Gray. E. (2015, June 22). Do you understand why stars twinkle? Would you rather read than watch TV? Do you trust data more than your instincts? And other strange questions you need to get a job in the era of optimized hiring. *Time*, 40–47.

12. Interviews: Handling illegal interview questions. *JobWeb*. Retrieved from http://www.jobweb.org/interviews. aspx?id=1343.

BCOM
ONLINE

REVIEW FLASHCARDS
ANYTIME, ANYWHERE!

**Create Flashcards
from Your StudyBits**

**Review Key Term
Flashcards Already
Loaded on the
StudyBoard**

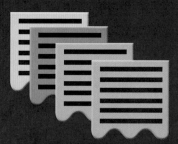

**4LTR
PRESS**

Access BCOM **ONLINE** at www.cengagebrain.com

INDEX

graphs, 66
group communication, 19, 29–31
grouped bar charts, 182
groups
 becoming teams, 34
 common goals, 31
 competitive behaviors, 30
 cooperation focus, 30–31
 effective characteristics, 31–32
 increasing focus on, 29–31
 leadership, 32
 negative group roles, 32
 norms, 32, 33
 positive group roles, 32
 presenting information and
  persuasive messages to, 3
 roles, 32–33
 size, 31–32
 status, 30, 32
Gunning, Robert, 67

H

Hallmark Cards, 272
Harvard University, 92
headings, 66
Hersey, Paul, 24
Hewlett-Packard, 18
hierarchy culture, 42
hierarchy of needs, 23, 139
hits, 163, 257, 258
hoaxes, 85
honors and activities, 247
Hoovers.com, 273
horizontal communication, 8
humane orientation, 48
Hunt-Wesson, 18
hypothesis, 159–160

I

IBM, 272
ideas, 53
 emphasizing and de-emphasizing, 62
 linking, 59
 positioning, 58
 sequencing to achieve goals, 52–54
 words that label, 62
IKEA, 30
illegal behavior, 10–11
images, 66
impromptu presentations, 223
index, 195
inductive, 53
inductive approach in persuasive
 messages, 140
inductive paragraphs, 58
informal communication network, 5–6
informal reports, 157
 vs. formal reports, 191

informational reports, 157–158
in-group collectivism, 48
inline résumés, 257
instant messaging (IM), 86
institutional collectivism, 48
Intel Corp., 92
intensive listening, 28
intentional accidents, 235
intercultural communication barriers,
 13–14
interferences, 4
internal messages, 8
internal proposals, 205
internal reports, 158
Internet
 career guidance information, 243
 identifying job listings, 243
 job search, 243
 netiquette, 83
Internet conferencing, 233
interpersonal communication, 8, 31
interpersonal skills, 276–277
interviews
 appearance, 274
 asking questions of interviewer,
  280–281
 behavioral questions, 277
 closing, 281
 comparing qualifications to company/
  job profile, 274
 computer-assisted interviews, 271
 conducting successful, 275–281
 discriminatory hiring practices, 279
 extracurricular activities, 276
 face-to-face interviews, 271
 first impressions, 275
 information exchange, 276, 280–281
 interpersonal skills, 276–277
 key points to emphasize, 276
 logical thinking and creativity, 278
 nonverbal messages, 275
 opening formalities, 275–276
 personality testing, 279
 phone interviews, 272
 practicing for, 275
 preparing for, 273–275
 professional attitude, 278–279
 researching company, 273–274
 salary and benefits, 279
 series interviews, 272
 standard questions, 277
 STAR method (Situation or Task/
  Action/Result), 278
 stress interviews, 271–272
 structured interviews, 271
 time and materials, 274–275
 unstructured interviews, 271
 virtual interviews, 272–273
in-text parenthetical citations, 171, 195
intranets, 16

intrapersonal communication, 8
introduction
 formal reports, 194
 presentations, 216–217
iPad, 144
iPhone, 91

J

jargon, 67
 email, 83
 presentations, 217
JetBlue, 279
job-acceptance messages, 284
job and/or career objective, 244–245
job-refusal messages, 284
job search
 career services centers, 241
 electronic employment resources,
  242–243
 employers' websites and office
  locations, 241
 employment agencies and
  contractors, 241
 gathering essential information, 239
 identifying job listings, 243
 identifying job listings, 228–229
 identifying potential career
  opportunities, 239–243
 internet, 242, 243
 locating career guidance
  information, 243
 networks, 240–241
 printed sources, 239–240
 professional organizations, 241–242
 social media, 240
 traditional sources, 239–240
Johari Window, 23–24
*Jones' Parliamentary Procedure at a
 Glance*, 36
justification reports, 159

K

Karlstrom, Johan, 10
Kennedy, Joyce, 276
Kilpatrick, Kwame, 88
Kimi Räikkönen, 144
kinesic messages, 25–26
kinesics, 14
Knight, Jonathan, 226
Kraft Foods, Inc., 18

L

laptops, 16
lateral communication, 8
lateral reports, 158
law and electronic messaging, 87–89

leadership
    groups, 32
    social constructionist view of, 25
legal behavior, 10
legal constraints, 9–12
letters, 99
    short reports, 200
    unified, 60
LexisNexis Academic Universe, 162, 163
Library of Congress classification
    system, 161
Likert scales, 168
Lincoln, Abraham, 69
Lincoln Business Data, Inc., 146
line charts, 182
lines, 60
LinkedIn, 91, 240, 273
listening, 27–28
Living Essentials, 50
Loeb, Daniel S., 51
LogicTech, 143
Lombardi, Vince, 142
longitudinal studies, 161
long reports, 157
Lotus Dynamic Performance
    Management (DPM), 144

M

management
    contrasting styles, 24–25
    explaining and clarifying procedures
        and work assignments, 3
    social constructionist view of
        leadership, 25
    Theory X style, 24
    Theory Y style, 24
    unethical tone set by, 10
managers
    communication, 3
    empowering employees, 25
    organizational development (OD), 24
manuscript presentations, 223
maps, 184
market culture, 42
Maslow, Abraham, 23, 139
McAfee Total Protection technology,
    145
McDonald's, 50
McGregor, Douglas, 24
measures of central tendency, 172
me attitude, 50
meetings, 35–38
    consensus, 37
    distributing agenda in advance, 36
    effective, 36–38
    electronic meetings, 36
    encouraging participation, 36
    face-to-face meetings, 35–36
    generic agenda, 37

identifying purpose of, 36
    maintaining order, 36–37
    managing conflict, 37
    minutes, 37–38
    negative attitudes of workers, 34–35
    purpose, 81
    satisfactory arrangements for, 36
    toward, 34
memorized presentations, 223
memos, 99, 113, 200
    unified, 60
messages
    adapting to audience needs and
        concerns, 49–52
    adjustment messages, 104
    central idea, 53
    chunking, 64, 65
    claim messages, 103–104
    clear and understandable ideas, 51
    clichés, 68–69
    communicating ethically and
        responsibly, 49–50
    concise communication, 69–71
    contextual forces, 41–43
    deductive sequence, 99
    direct sequence, 99
    effective sentences and coherent
        paragraphs, 57–63
    evaluating effectiveness, 65
    good-news messages, 99–102
    grabbing audience's attention, 63–67
    headings, 66
    honor, honesty, and credibility, 51
    informing and persuading others, 3
    misunderstanding, 3
    National Advertising Division, 50
    negative tone, 71–73
    neutral-news messages, 99
    organizational culture, 42–43
    organizing, 52, 53
    outdated expressions, 68
    passive voice, 71–73
    persuasive requests, 106
    planning and preparing, 41
    positive tone, 71–72
    procedural messages, 113–115
    profanity, 69
    proofreading, 65
    readability and appeal of text, 61
    receiver-centered statements, 50
    redundancies, 69–70
    routine messages, 109–113
    routine requests, 106–109
    sender-centered statements, 50
    style and tone, 67–76
    topics, 59
    viewpoint supported with objective
        facts, 51
    visual enhancements, 65–67
    white space, 65

metacommunication, 25
metaphors, 68
methodology, 161
MicroDenier Polyester Suede, 145
Microsoft, 91, 272
Microsoft job search log, 239
Microsoft Word, 67
Mindvalley, 42
Mobile Web Accessibility Guidelines, 90
Morrow, Thomas, 276
motivation, 14
Motorola, 18
multimedia résumés, 260
MySpace, 85
MyWebSearch, 163

N

National Advertising Division, 50
National Commission on Writing, 41
National Federation of the Blind, 90
natural disasters, 235
negative group roles, 32
negative organizational news messages
    breaking bad news, 131
    responding to crisis situations,
        131–135
netiquette, 83
networks, 240–241
neutral-news messages, 99
New Kids on the Block, 226
Nike, 272
nonverbal communication, 44, 45
    face-to-face communication, 3
    kinesic messages, 25–26
    metacommunication, 25
nonverbal messages, 25, 26
    interviews, 275
non-words, 224
normal accidents, 235
normative survey research, 164
norming, 34, 35
norms, 32, 33
notes pages, 223
null hypothesis, 160

O

Obama, Barack, 74
observational studies, 164
OfficeMax, 62
OfficeWorx, 264
100% bar charts, 182
online job banks, 242
oral briefings, 213
oral communication, 44
organizational charts, 4–5, 184
organizational communication, 4
organizational culture, 42–43
organizational development (OD), 24

R

racial/ethnic bias, 76
readability
  active voice, 70
  bias-free language, 75–76
  clichés, 68–69
  concise communication, 69–71
  condescending or demeaning
    expressions, 73–74
  connotative meaning, 74
  denotative meaning, 74
  euphemisms, 73
  improving readability, 67–68
  profanity, 69
  redundancies, 69–70
  sentences, 67
  simple, informal words, 69
  specific language, 74–75
  subjunctive sentences, 72
receiver-centered statements, 50
reciprocal sharing, 23
recommendation requests, 285–287
recommendations, 174, 194
redundancies, 69–70
references, 195, 248–249
  electronic résumé submissions, 254
refusing request message, 123–125
reports
  analytical reports, 158
  analyzing data, 172
  characteristics, 157–159
  conclusions, 172
  correlation analysis, 172
  defining terms clearly, 161
  divisions, 63
  documenting procedures, 161
  external reports, 158
  findings, 174
  formal reports, 157, 191–195
  functional reports, 158–159
  hypothesis, 159–160
  informal reports, 157
  informational reports, 157–158
  information-gathering methods,
    161–165
  internal reports, 158
  interpreting data, 172–174
  lateral reports, 158
  limited audience, 157
  limiting scope of problem, 160–161
  logically organized, 157
  longitudinal studies, 161
  long reports, 157
  measures of central tendency, 172
  objectivity, 157
  periodic reports, 158
  problem-solving process, 159–161
  problem statements, 159–160
  proposals, 159, 205–209
  recognizing and defining problem,
    159–161
  recommendations, 174
  secondary research, 161–163
  short reports, 157, 200–205
  statement of purpose, 159
  tabulation techniques, 172
  traveling upward in organization, 157
  vertical reports, 158
request for proposals (RFPs),
    159, 205
requests for information, 106–107,
    151–152
researching company, 273–274
resignation messages, 284–285
responding to crisis situations message,
    131–135
résumé padding, 51
résumés, 239
  action verbs, 247
  application messages, 262–269
  beamer, 252
  best length for, 252
  career services centers, 241
  career summary, 245
  chrono-functional résumés, 250
  chronological résumés, 249–250
  education, 245–246
  electronic employment resources,
    242–243
  electronic résumé submissions,
    252–257
  employers' websites and office
    locations, 241
  employment agencies and
    contractors, 241
  employment videos, 260–262
  functional résumés, 250
  gathering essential information, 239
  goals of, 243
  honors and activities, 247
  identifying job listings, 243
  identifying potential career
    opportunities, 239–243
  inline résumés, 257
  internet, 242
  job and/or career objective, 244–245
  locating career guidance
    information, 243
  multimedia résumés, 260
  networks, 240–241
  personal information, 248
  printed sources, 239–240
  print (designed) résumés, 251–252
  professional organizations, 241–242
  professional portfolios, 258–260
  qualifications, 245
  references, 248–249
  scannable résumés, 257
  standard parts of, 244–249
  supplementing, 258–262
  targeted résumés, 243–250
  text résumés, 256
  traditional sources, 239–240
  video résumés, 260–262
  work experience, 246–247
  your identification, 244
revising messages, 64
Robert's Rules of Order, 36
roles, 32–33
routine claims, 102–106
routine messages
  acknowledgment messages, 109
  credit information, 109–111
  extending credit messages, 111–112
routine requests
  favorable response to, 107
  form messages for routine
    responses, 108
  positive response to favor request,
    107–108
  requests for information, 106–107

S

sales messages
  action oriented, 143–144
  attention-getter, 142
  central selling point, 142, 143, 147
  comparison, 145
  creating desire with convincing
    evidence, 144–16
  incentive for quick action, 147
  introducing product, service, or idea,
    142–143
  motivating action, 147–148
  objectivity, 145–146
  preposterous statements, 146
  presenting and interpreting factual
    evidence, 144–145
  relationship between audience and
    product, service, or idea, 142
  restating reward for taking action, 147
  subordinating price, 146
  testimonials, guarantees, and
    enclosures, 146
sales promotional material, 104
sampling, 164
Save Our Slides (Earnest), 219
scannable résumés, 257
Schweitzer, Albert, 10
scripted presentations, 223
search engines, 163
segmented bar charts, 182
sender-centered statements, 50
Senge, Peter, 27

visual kinesic communication, 25
vocal kinesic communication, 26
vocal qualities, 224–226
voice mail, 92–93

W

Warby Parker, 6
Web 2.0, 90
webcasting, 233
Web Content Accessibility
    Guidelines, 90
webinars, 95
weblogs, 90–91
websites
    communication, 89–90
    hits, 163
    writing, 90

white space, 65
wikis, 91
win/lose philosophy, 30
win/win philosophy, 30
word processors
    addenda, 192
    improving sentence readability, 67–68
work experience, 246–247
workplace, 3
    diversity challenges, 12–13
    employees, 5
works cited, 195
works consulted, 195
work teams, 18–19, 34
World Wide Web Consortium (W3C), 90
writer's pride of ownership, 64
writing, 41
    application messages, 266–267
    bad-news messages, 120–121

blogs, 90–91
electronic communication, 64
email, 82–89
formal reports, 198–200
planning persuasive messages before,
    139–140
revising, 63–65
websites, 90
wikis, 91
"Writing: A Ticket to Work...or a Ticket
    Out" report, 41
written communication, 44

Y

Yahoo!, 51
you attitude, 50
YouTube, 92, 260
    presentations, 178

Preparing Spoken and Written Messages

Rough Draft of a Letter (excerpt)

April 1, 2017

Fax Transmission

Louisa Fox, Marketing Manager
Learner Consumer Products Group
2304 Pike Market Street
Seattle, Washington 90322   *(WA)*

Dear Ms. Fochs: *(Fox)*

Are you looking for help developing your organization's social media platform? . . . improve your retail marketing? . . . plan your external communication program? . . . enhance your mass advertising strategy? **Then you need the services of the full-service brand engagement firm Souther and Associates to develop an integrated media plan that ensures your company's continued success.**

With Souther and Associates full-service capabilities, you will receive support in all of the following areas:

- Social media. Leverage the millions of conversations taking place through the use of social media by taking advantage of our four-step approach®™ which tracks conversations and dialogue; extracts insights from consumer conversations; interacts with key influences, brand advocates, and detractors; and measures consumer sentiment, advocacy, and engagement.
- Retail marketing. Engage consumers away from the noise and competing advertising, and reach them on an intimate, meaningful, and locally relevant level that will help you to drive trial, traffic, and sales.
- Communication planning. Build preference for your brand by translating emotional insights into high-impact brand strategy and innovation. Our experts bypass consumers' rational thinking with tools and techniques that are reactive and observational. Then, we integrate these emotional insights with your brand's functional benefits to create the foundation for lasting behavior change.
- Influence marketing. Mass advertising still plays an important role in branding, but these days, credibility is especially important, and who is more credible than a trusted professional? We identify professionals to give your products that powerful endorsement.

~~Interested customers can~~ visit www.souther.com today and check out the list of consulting services we provide and read real-life stories from past clients about how we increased brand awareness for them. If you contact us before May 15, you will also receive a free assessment of your current marketing program from our proprietary MarketLab analysis tool. Our team is ready to assist you in improving the impact of your marketing programs today. Please call me at 509-788-1302 to make an appointment with a consultant.

Sincerely,

Frank Forester

Frank Forester
Engagement Director
Enclosure

- Adds mailing notation.
- Uses two-letter state abbreviation.
- Corrects spelling of name.
- Adds smooth transition to next paragraph.

- Bullet list for emphasis and conciseness.
- Divides into two sentences to enhance readability.

- Recasts from receiver's viewpoint.
- Includes specific action ending.

Errors Undetectable by Spell-Check

Verify spelling of names.

Correct proofreading grammatical error.

Check correctness of word substitutions, such as "to" for "too" and "your" for "you."

Step 1: Evaluate and respond to advice given for grammar and style errors detected.

Step 2: Use counts, averages, and readability indexes as guides for adjusting writing level appropriately.

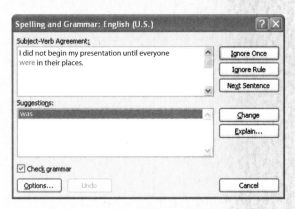

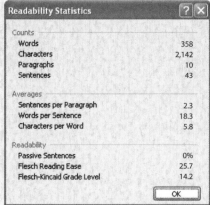

IMPROVING YOUR WRITING WITH THE COMPUTER

Hone your computer skills to spend more time writing and less time formatting.

☑ Draft in a font style and size that can be easily read on-screen; postpone formatting until the revision is done.

☑ Use the *Find* and *Go To* commands to search and make changes.

☑ Learn time-saving keyboard shortcuts for frequently used commands such as *Copy* and *Cut*. Customize software so that you can access these commands easily.

☑ Use automatic numbering to arrange numerical or alphabetical lists and to ensure accuracy.

☑ Save time by using built-in styles such as cover pages, headers/footers, list and table formats, text boxes, and graphical effects.

☑ Save frequently used text such as a letterhead or your signature line so you can insert it with a single click.

☑ Use the *Citations and Bibliography* command to format references and the *Document Styles* feature to automatically generate a content page and index.

Use formatting features to create an organized and polished appearance.

☑ Add spacing between lines and paragraphs, and use crisp, open fonts such as Calibri for a contemporary look that is easy to read on-screen.

☑ Apply color-infused document themes and built-in styles to reflect a consistent brand identity.

Use proofing features to locate errors.

☑ Use the spell-checker frequently as you draft and revise. Be aware that the spell-checker will not identify miskeyings (*than* for *then*), commonly misused words, homophones (*principle, principal*), omitted words, missing or out-of-order enumerations, and content errors.

☑ Use grammar check to provide feedback on usage, reading level, comprehension factors, and other errors and weaknesses that cannot be detected electronically.

☑ Use a thesaurus only when you can recognize the precise meaning needed.

Communicating Electronically

Email Format

New Message

To: Pablo Gonzales [pgonzales@computersolutions.com]
From: Jennifer Reagan [jreagan@lauder.com]
Subject: Laptop Repair or Replacement Needed ● Includes descriptive subject line.

Mr. Gonzales,

Please repair or send us a replacement for the laptop computer listed on the attached sales agreement. It has a faulty cooling fan. You should receive the computer tomorrow via overnight freight.

The computer was purchased six months ago under our agreement with your company to provide our salespeople with laptops. The computers are covered by a 12-month warranty for faulty parts replacement. I spoke with your sales manager, Tom Wilkins, this morning, and he instructed me to contact you for extradited service.

Our salesperson Maria Rodriguez eagerly awaits the return of her laptop. Our salespeople are highly dependent on their computers because they spend so much time on the road.

Thanks,

Jennifer Reagan

● **Includes signature file that identifies writer.**

Format Pointers

Includes single-spaced, unindented paragraphs and short lines for complete screen display.

Uses mixed case for easy reading.

Keeps format simple for quick download and compatibility.

• Email Format

While certain email formats are standard, some degree of flexibility exists in formatting email messages. Primarily, be certain your message is easy to read and represents the standards of formality that your company has set. The following guidelines and the model email illustrated above will assist you in formatting professional email messages:

- *Include an appropriate salutation and closing.* You might write "Dear" and the person's name or simply the person's first name when messaging someone for the first time. Casual expressions such as "Hi" and "Later" are appropriate for personal messages, but not serious business email. A closing of "Sincerely" or "Regards" is considered quite formal for email messages; instead, a simple closing such as "Best wishes" or "Thank you" provides a courteous end to your message.

- *Include a signature file at the end of the message.* The signature file (known as a .sig file) contains a few lines of text that include your full name and title, mailing address, telephone number, and any other information you want people to know about you. You might include a clever quote that you update frequently.

- *Format for easy readability.* Follow these suggestions:

  - Limit each message to one screen to minimize scrolling. If you need more space, consider a short email message with a lengthier message attached as a word-processing file. Be certain the recipient can receive and read the attachment.

- Limit the line length to 60 characters so that the entire line is displayed on the monitor without scrolling.

- Use short, unindented paragraphs. Separate paragraphs with an extra space.

- Use mixed case for easy reading. Typing in all capital letters is perceived as shouting in email and considered rude online behavior.

- Emphasize a word or phrase by surrounding it with quotation marks or keying in uppercase letters.

- ***Use emoticons or email abbreviations in moderation when you believe the receiver will understand and approve. Emoticons,*** created by keying combinations of symbols to produce "sideways" faces, are a shorthand way of lightening the mood, adding emotion to email messages, and attempting to compensate for nonverbal cues lost in one-way communication:

:-)	smiling, indicates humor or sarcasm	%-(	confused
:-(	frowning, indicates sadness or anger	:-0	surprised

Alternately, you might put a "g" (for grin) or "smile" in parentheses after something that is obviously meant as tongue-in-cheek to help carry the intended message to the receiver. Abbreviations for commonly used phrases save space and avoid unnecessary keying. Popular ones include BCNU (be seeing you), BTW (by the way), FYI (for your information), FWIW (for what it's worth), HTH (hope this helps), IMHO (in my humble opinion, AFAIK (as far as I know), F2F (face-to-face), IOW (in other words), and LOL (laugh out loud).

Some email users feel strongly that emoticons and abbreviations are childish or inappropriate for serious email and decrease productivity when the receiver must take time for deciphering. Before using them, be certain the receiver will understand them and that the formality of the message and your relationship with the receiver justify this type of informal exchange. Then use only in moderation to punctuate your message.

 Good Example of an Email Message

New Message	
To: Linda Roberts, Loan Officer	
From: Juan Alvarez, Director of Loan Compliance	
Subject: New Policies Affect Loans to Real-Estate Investors	

Linda,

Please be aware of the new policies regarding mortgages to real-estate investors.

Loans can no longer be made to mortgage applicants who already have four or more outstanding mortgages. Because of the problems caused by the sub-prime lending situation, we are required to limit our exposure to mortgage debt. Applicants who have four or more active mortgages are now considered too risky because of a potential lack of liquidity in their current asset portfolio.

You will find this latest policy change attached to this message. Please come by my office if you have additional questions after reading the attached policy statement.

Regards,

Juan

● **Provides subject line that is meaningful to the reader and the writer.**

● **Includes salutation and closing to personalize the message.**

Format Pointer

Composes short, concise message limited to one idea and one screen.

Delivering Good- and Neutral-News Messages

 Good Example of an Apology

New Message

To: Allen Melton [amelton@meltonpr.com]

cc:

Subject: Yesterday's Advertising Presentation

Allen:

Please accept my apology for the inconvenience you experienced yesterday because of the unavailability of computer equipment. Fortunately, you saved the day with your backup transparencies and gave an effective presentation on the new advertising campaign.

The next time you make a presentation at our company, I'll be sure to schedule the LGI room. This room has the latest technology to support multimedia presentations. Just call and let me know the date.

Later,

Thomas Lee Raferty
Administrative Assistant

• States the apology briefly without providing an overly specific description of the error.

• Reports measures taken to avoid repetition of such incidents, which strengthens the credibility of the apology.

• Closes with a positive statement.

Format Pointers

Limits the message to a single idea—the apology.

Composes a short, concise message that fits on one screen.

Includes a salutation and closing to personalize the message.

Good Example of an Appreciation Message

New Message

> **To:** Ellen Meyer [emeyer@techno.com]
> **cc:** Martha Riggins [mriggins@techno.com]
> **Subject:** Appreciation for Outstanding Contribution
>
> Ellen,
>
> Thank you for spearheading the initiative to improve interpersonal communication within the office and for arranging for the training sessions to achieve that goal. It was a big commitment on your part in addition to your regular duties.
>
> Your efforts are already paying off. I have observed the techniques we learned in the training sessions being used in the department on several occasions already. In times of uncertainty, anxiety can often spill over into people's professional lives, so the seminar was very timely in helping to ensure a collaborative and civil workplace where everyone is treated respectfully.
>
> You have proven yourself a dedicated and insightful employee, a true asset to the continued success of our organization.
>
> Best regards,
> Martha

- Extends appreciation for employee's efforts to improve departmental communication.

- Provides specific evidence of worth of experience without exaggerating or using overly strong language or mechanical statements.

- Assures writer of tangible benefits to be gained from the training session.

Format Pointer

Uses short lines, mixed case; omits special formatting such as emoticons and email abbreviations for improved readability.

Delivering Bad-News Messages

Developing the Components of a Bad-News Message

The current sub-prime mortgage situation and its subsequent effects on the economy have provided an opportunity to better educate loan seekers about the types of financial risk they might safely assume. For this reason, mortgage seekers may be restricted in the number of mortgage loans they might hold.

As part of the effort to help loan seekers reduce their financial risk, banks now limit the number of mortgages a person might judiciously hold to no more than four. Because of current sluggishness in the housing market, house sellers now have more difficulty selling homes in a timely manner, making such assets much less liquid. If a mortgage holder gets into trouble, he/she will have less ability to resell the property and recover the loan amount. This puts the mortgage holder and the lender at greater financial risk.

In order to secure an additional mortgage, you must first pay off one of your current mortgages. Alternately, our affiliated real-estate brokers are available to help you sell one of your properties so that you might secure another. Please call me at 213-555-3400 to discuss these services.

- Begins with a statement with which both can agree. Sets stage for reasons for bad news.
- Reveals subject of message and transitions into reasons.
- Provides rule and clearly applies rule to the situation.
- States refusal positively and clearly using complex sentence and positive language.
- Includes counterproposal as alternative.
- Closes with sales promotion for other services, inferring a continuing business relationship.

Note the closing paragraph is a positive, forward-looking statement that includes sales promotion of other services the mortgage firm and its affiliated real-estate brokers can offer.

Good Example of a Claim Denial

June 14, 2017

Meera Biswas
Snowcap Limited
1905 Southhaven Street
Santa Fe, NM 87501-7313

Dear Ms. Biswas:

Restocking of Returned Merchandise

The HighFly skis you stocked this past season are skillfully crafted and made
from the most innovative materials available. Maintaining a wide selection
of quality skiing products is an excellent strategy for developing customer
loyalty and maximizing your sales.

Our refund policies provide you the opportunity to keep a fully stocked
inventory at the lowest possible cost. You receive full refunds for
merchandise returned within 10 days of receipt. For unsold merchandise
returned after the primary selling season, a modest 15 percent restocking fee
is charged to cover our costs of holding this merchandise until next season.
The credit applied to your account for $2,069.75 covers merchandise you
returned at the end of February.

While relaxing from another great skiing season, take a look at our new
HighFly skis and other items available in the enclosed catalog for the 2018
season. You can save 10 percent by ordering premium ski products before
May 10.

Sincerely,

Galen Fondren

Galen Fondren
Credit Manager
Enclosure: Catalog

- Begins with a statement with which the reader can agree to get the message off to a good start.

- Presents a clear explanation for the additional charge.

- Shifts emphasis away from the refusal by presenting sales promotion on other services.

Format Pointer
Illustrates block format—all lines begin at the left margin.

Delivering Persuasive Messages

 Good Good Example of a Persuasive Claim

Palmdale Galleria
3109 Overlook Drive / Palmdale, CA 93550
P: (661) 555-2130 \ F: (661) 555-3129

October 27, 2017

Samantha Reynolds
Senior Architect
Primera Design
3400 Wilshire Boulevard
Los Angeles, CA 90052-3674

Dear Samantha:

When Palmdale Galleria selected your firm to redesign our retail space, we were impressed by the work that you had done in a number of hotels and mall properties in Las Vegas and other upscale developments throughout the country. We were most impressed with the fantasy world that you created for the Insight Hotel's shopping galleria, a space that attended to every aspect of the consumer's shopping experience, including sight, sound, smell, taste, and sensation, through the implementation of the latest technological and design advances.

• Seeks attention by giving sincere compliment that reveals the subject of the message.

In our meeting with your creative team, we asked for attention to the visual design, the entertainment elements, and the creation of an ambiance that addressed all aspects of the consumers' sensual experience. After reviewing the initial plan for our redesign, we find the degree of incorporation of entertainment and sensual experiences for consumers to be disappointing. The redesign incorporates the latest trends in architectural design but needs more attention to entertainment features, including spaces for "street" entertainers, mini-concerts, and amusement park rides, including bungee jumping, etc. We also expected a more complete integration of water features, such as fountains, waterfalls, and streams, with the associated opportunities for entertainment, such as a simulated river rafting experience. In the tropical forest region of the mall, we hoped to have a better integration of spaces for zoo animals and an apparatus to create the "smells" and "sounds" of the jungle. Consumers no longer go to malls to simply shop, but want to be transported to a world of leisure, pampering, and entertainment, one that appeals to all of their senses.

• Continues central appeal—commitment to creative redesign—while providing needed details.

• Presents reasoning that leads to request and subtle reminder of central appeal.

• Connects specific request with firm's commitment to develop a creative redesign.

With Primera Design's reputation for creative productions, we are confident the redesign plan for the Palmdale Galleria will be revised to incorporate these elements. Please let us know if you would like to meet to discuss and clarify any of the design issues raised here. Because of the importance of this project, I am at your disposal. Please call me at 444-1920 to schedule a meeting.

Legal and Ethical Consideration
Uses letter rather than less formal email format to emphasize importance of these differences regarding contractual agreement.

Sincerely,

Martinique Cole

Martinique Cole
General Manager
Palmdale Galleria

Good Good Example of a Persuasive Request

Down-Home Restaurants

83 South Pass Road • Chattanooga TN 37426-2723 • (423) 555-5320

March 15, 2017

Mrs. Joyce Smith
976 Thompson Road
Crossville, TN 38555-0976

Dear Mrs. Smith:

Meeting you and touring the building on your property last week was a pleasure. That little building provided me with a fascinating glimpse of the past. You must have found it convenient using the building as a big "attic," storing all your canned goods and old farm implements over the years.

As the manager of the Down-Home Barbeque in Mena, I am constantly looking for items to build and display in our restaurants. Our restaurants are constructed of weathered wood to create a genuine rustic atmosphere, which we think complements our "down-home" menu.

As I toured your building, I couldn't help but notice some of the unique items inside and the old weathered boards hanging outside. The wood from the building and its contents would enable us to build and furnish a new restaurant in Clarksville and refurbish our Jackson location. Marc Lane, owner of Down-Home Restaurants, has asked me to extend you the offer explained in the enclosed proposal.

Naturally, no amount of money can compensate you for a building that holds so many memories for you. However, we would be happy to purchase the entire contents of the building, excluding any special items of sentimental value that you may want to keep.

Although the thought of selling the building may sadden you, think of the "second life" that the old farm equipment, dishes, washboards, seed bags, and weathered boards would have in our restaurants. People who would otherwise never see such Americana will have the opportunity to learn a little about its rich past.

After you have reviewed the proposal, please call me at 555-3253 to discuss our offer to display your treasures in our restaurants.

Sincerely,

Karla Ash

Karla Ash, Manager
Chattanooga Store
Enclosure

Opens with a compliment that introduces an appeal to the owner's pride in the old property.

Introduces the writer's interest in acquiring property and continues the primary appeal (desire to preserve the past).

Offsets reluctance to sell by acknowledging the sentimental value and suggesting options.

Stresses benefits of selling property in terms of the primary appeal.

Connects the specific request for action with the reward for saying "Yes."

Format Pointers
Illustrates modified block format—the date and closing lines (complimentary close and signature block) begin at the horizontal center.

Uses mixed punctuation—a colon follows the salutation, and a comma follows the complimentary close.

Uses an enclosure notation to alert the reader that something is included.

Understanding the Report Process and Research Methods

Example of an Effective Questionnaire

- Uses variety of items to elicit different types of responses.

- Uses clear, concise language to minimize confusion.

- Provides clear instructions for answering each item.

- Provides additional lines to allow for individual opinions.

- Provides even number of rating choices to eliminate "fence" responses.

- Asks for easily recalled information.

- Provides non-overlapping categories of response and open-ended final category.

Format Pointers
Provides adequate space for answering open-ended item.

Keeps length as short as possible while meeting survey objectives.

Includes instructions for submitting completed questionnaire.

---

1. Rank the following new vehicle purchase factors in order of their importance to you.

		1	2	3	4	5	6
a.	Price						
b.	Overall performance						
c.	Reliability						
d.	Comfort						
e.	Driving enjoyment						
f.	Safety record						
g.	Fuel economy						
h.	Other (specify)						

2. Which of the following is the single most important purchase factor that you feel needs more attention by today's car makers? (Please select only one.)

- Price
- Overall performance
- Reliability
- Comfort
- Safety record
- Fuel economy
- Other (specify)

3. Would you purchase this vehicle again?

Definitely not 1	Probably not 2	I'm not sure 3	Only if improved 4	Probably would 5	Definitely yes 6

4. How would you rate your overall purchase satisfaction?

Very unsatisfied 1	Somewhat dissatisfied 2	Neutral 3	Somewhat satisfied 4	Satisfied 5	Very satisfied 6

5. Indicate your age group:

- 20–29
- 30–39
- 40–49
- 50–59
- 60–69
- 70 years and over

6. Indicate how many vehicles you have previously purchased.

- None
- 1–3
- 4–6
- 7–10
- More than 10

7. What could the car maker do to enhance your satisfaction with your new car purchase?

Thanks for your participation. Click to submit your questionnaire.

Submit

6

• Sample Report and References Pages in APA (6th Edition) Style

Culturally diverse virtual teams do have a greater potential for conflict than do teams that are homogeneous and are able to meet face to face ("Collaborative Teams," 2008). While variations in beliefs, behaviors, and expectations occur within all cultural groups, certain generalities about one based on his or her cultural group can be useful for others seeking better understanding. "Given little or no other information about an individual's values and behaviours, culture provides a good first impression of that person" (Maznevski & Peterson, 1997, p. 37).

Neyer and Harzing (2008) found that experiences in cross-cultural interactions do serve to improve one's abilities to adapt in such situations. One advantage gained through experience is the overcoming of cultural stereotypes which often stand in the way of effective communication (Williams & O'Reilly, 1998). Cross-cultural experience also leads to the establishment of norms that support interaction among individuals and to the development of mutual consideration for others (Neyer & Harzing, 2008). Studies have established that individuals who learn a foreign language also gain appropriate culturally determined behavior and are thus better able to adapt to specific characteristics of the other culture (Harzing & Feely, 2008).

In addition to possessing strong technical skills, qualities that are important to successful membership on cross-cultural virtual teams include the following (Adler, 1991; Hurn & Jenkins, 2000):

▶ Flexibility and adaptability
▶ Strong interpersonal skills
▶ Ability to think both globally and locally
▶ Linguistic skills

References

Adler, N. J. (1991). *International dimensions of organizational behavior.* Boston: PWS Kent.

Collaborative teams. (2008, June). *Bulletpoint 152,* 3–5.

Hurn, B. F., & Jenkins, M. (2000). International peer group development. *Industrial and Commercial Training, 32*(4), 128–131. doi: 10.1108/00197850010372205

Maznevski, M. L., & Peterson, M. F. (1997). Societal values, social interpretation, and multinational teams. In C. Granrose (Ed.), *Cross-Cultural Workgroups* (pp. 27–29). Thousand Oaks, CA: Sage.

Neyer, A., & Harzine, A. (2008). The impact of culture on interactions: Five lessons learned from the European Commission. *European Management Journal 26*(5), 325–334. doi: 10.1016/j.emj .2008.05.005

Williams, K. Y., & O'Reilly, C. A. (1998). Demography and diversity in organizations. In B. M. Staw & R. M. Sutton (Eds.), *Research in Organizational Behavior* (pp. 77–140). Stamford, CT: JAI.

Managing Data and Using Graphics

Choosing the Appropriate Graphic to Fit Your Objective

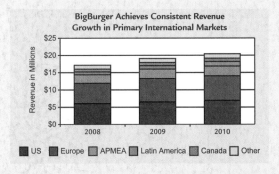

	October 2, 2013		October 2, 2014	
Quarter	High	Low	High	Low
Fourth	$23.94	$21.29	$26.35	$23.08
Third	22.09	18.62	28.13	22.78
Second	19.48	16.15	30.80	24.79
First	16.50	14.40	31.94	23.53

KoffeeKup Corporation — Market Price of Common Stock

Source: KoffeeKup Corporation, Annual Report, 2013

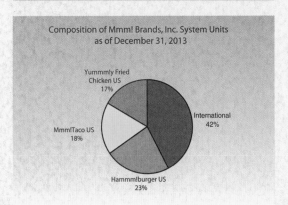

Graphic Type and Objective

Table—To show exact figures

Bar Chart—To compare one quantity with another

Line Chart—To illustrate changes in quantities over time

Pie Chart—To show how the parts of a whole are distributed

Graphic Type and Objective

Gantt Chart—To track progress toward completing a project

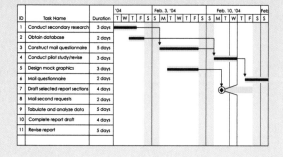

Map—To show geographic relationships

Flowchart—To illustrate a process or procedure

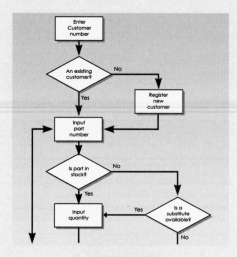

Photograph—To provide a realistic view of a specific item or place

Organizing and Preparing Reports and Proposals

Good

Short, Periodic Report in Memorandum Format

ETO Industries

233 State Boulevard
Kansas City, MO 64123-7600

TO: Candice Russell, Director, Human Resources
FROM: Tim Johnson, Manager, In-House Exercise Program
DATE: January 1, 2017
SUBJECT: Annual Report on In-House Exercise Program

The in-house exercise center has made significant gains in the past year. Data related to participation in our programs and current staffing follow:

Enrollment:	506 employees, up from 384 at end of 2015
Staff:	One full-time trainer/manager and two part-time trainers

Our goal for the coming year is to increase our enrollment in the in-house exercise programs another 10 percent. We also have plans to create a nutrition program that will be rolled out next month. If that program is successful initially, we may need to hire a certified nutritionist. This person might also be used part-time in the company cafeteria to improve the nutritional value of the lunches and snacks provided there.

Employees report overall satisfaction with the quality of the current program. At the end of 2016, we asked program participants to complete a questionnaire. Eighty-eight percent indicated that they were very satisfied or extremely satisfied with our program. The most frequently mentioned suggestion for improvement was the extension of hours until 7 p.m. This change would allow employees to work late and still take advantage of the exercise facility. A copy of the questionnaire is provided for your review.

Call me should you wish to discuss the nutritional program, extended service hours, or any other aspects of this report.

Attachment

- Includes header to serve formal report functions of transmittal and title page.

- Includes horizontal line to add interest and separate transmittal from body of memo.

- Uses deductive approach to present this periodic report requested by management on an annual basis.

- Uses headings to highlight standard information; allows for easy update when preparing subsequent report.

- Includes primary data from survey completed by program participants.

- Attaches material to memorandum, which would be an appendix item the in formal report.

Format Pointer
Uses memorandum format for brief periodic report prepared for personnel within the company.

CommPlus Consultants, Inc.
101 MAIN STREET, SUITE 203
ST. LOUIS, MO 54011
800-555-3000

January 10, 2017

John Simpson
Franklin Associates
345 Plum Street
St. Louis, MO 54002

Dear Mr. Simpson:

The communication audit of Franklin Associates' external communication program has been completed. You will find a brief summary of our findings and conclusions and recommendations below.

FINDINGS

Findings from our audit can be found below:

1. Franklin Associates is a consultant to the oil and gas industry. It is a well-established business with a 100-year history. Its branding is well recognized, but in recent years, it has been surpassed by several new entrants who have marketed themselves as innovative and using the latest technologies. This has created a challenge for Franklin Associates in terms of its external branding.
2. Franklin's major external stakeholders include its clients, the media, investors, government agencies, competitors, and the public. In terms of its clients, Franklin has focused its marketing efforts on the largest oil and gas producers. Because there are so few, this has created some competitive challenges for Franklin.
3. Franklin's most common methods for communicating its corporate message includes press releases; a company website; and personal communications with its clients through use of written, oral, and electronic media.

CONCLUSIONS AND RECOMMENDATIONS

The following recommendations are made:

1. Continue advertising and service promotion at current levels but with some changes that help you better reach mid-sized clients and increase your market share.
2. Update the design for your company logo, and roll out a campaign that introduces this new image to current and prospective customers.
3. Develop a plan for shaping public opinion on issues important to Franklin Associates. As a consultant for the oil industry, it is important to show that your organization is interested in addressing global climate issues.

Thank you for the opportunity to assist you in reviewing your external communication program. We are also available to help you in completing the final step in the audit process: Create, refine, and test new messages with the appropriate stakeholders. If you are interested in continuing our consulting relationship in order to develop an implementation plan, please call me at 415-640-9001.

Sincerely,

Louise Parker

Louise Parker
Chief Auditor

Letterhead and letter address function as title page and transmittal.

Introduces overall topic and leads into procedures and findings.

Uses side heading to denote the beginning of the body.

Closes with appreciation for business and offer to answer questions.

Format Pointers
Uses letter format for short report prepared by outside consultant.

Includes reference initials of typist, who did not write message.

Designing and Delivering Business Presentations

Selecting an Appropriate Presentation Visual

VISUAL	ADVANTAGES	LIMITATIONS
 HANDOUTS	• Provide detailed information that audience can examine closely • Extend a presentation by providing resources for later use • Reduce the need for note taking and aid in audience retention	• Can divert audience's attention from the speaker • Can be expensive
BOARDS AND FLIPCHARTS	• Facilitate interaction • Are easy to use • Are inexpensive if traditional units are used	• Require turning speaker's back to audience • Are cumbersome to transport, can be messy and not professional looking • Provide no hard copy and must be developed on-site if traditional units are used
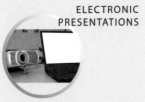 ELECTRONIC PRESENTATIONS	• Meet audience's expectations of visual standards • Enhance professionalism and credibility of the speaker • Provide special effects to enhance retention, appeal, flexibility, and reuse	• Can lead to poor delivery if misused • Can be time consuming to create • Pose technology failure and transportability challenges
 MODELS OR PHYSICAL OBJECTS	• Are useful to demonstrate an idea	• Can compete with the speaker for attention

Writing Effective Slide Content: Poor (left) and Good (right) Examples

Humor

- Important element in any presentation
- Easy connection with the audience
- Gets attention
- Alleviates boredom
- Reduces mental tension
- Discourages conflict
- Enhances comprehension
- Shouldn't embarrass people
  - Ethnic jokes are inappropriate
  - Profane language is definitely not recommended

Value of Humor in a Presentation

- Establishes a connection with the audience
- Increases audience's willingness to listen
- Makes message more understandable and memorable
- Alleviates negativity associated with sensitive subjects

The revised slide

- Includes a descriptive title that captures the major idea of a slide, in this case, the value of humor.
- Omits items unrelated to the value of humor. Specifically, "important element in any presentation" is a verbal transition and not needed on a slide; "shouldn't embarrass people" and related subpoints will appear on a separate slide focusing on tips for using humor.
- Collapses remaining content into a few memorable points that use parallel structure for clarity and grammatical accuracy (singular action verbs).
- Proofreads carefully to avoid misspellings that damage credibility, such as "conflect" in original slide.

Engaging Conceptual Slide Design: Poor (left) and Good (right) Examples

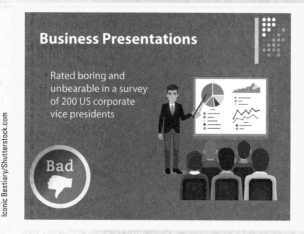

Iconic Bestiary/Shutterstock.com

Monkey Business Images/Used under license from Shutterstock.com

The revised slide

- Uses descriptive title that captures central idea of dissatisfaction with typical business presentation.
- Selects images that imply intended message—ineffectiveness of business presenters; enlarges images for slide appeal and balance.
- Trims text to emphasize central idea and eliminates bullet, as bulleted list should have at least two items.
- Moves source to less prominent slide position to add credibility to research data while keeping focus on central idea.

Preparing Résumés and Application Messages

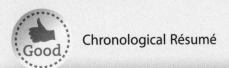 Chronological Résumé

JOSEPH PRIESTLEY
89 Lincoln Street
Santa Fe, NM 78285-9063
512 555-9823
jpriestley@hotmail.com

- Includes email address that reflects professional image.

Professional Profile
- Technical proficiency in ERP systems, ACL, database, and spreadsheet software.
- Hands-on experience in accounting gained through internship with well-regarded local firm.
- Excellent interpersonal communication and teamwork skills developed through course projects and active involvement in student organizations.
- Ability to manage time effectively, excellent work ethic, and dedication to high-quality work as demonstrated by 3.87 GPA and part-time work to finance my education.

- Highlights professional skills.

- Positions education as top qualification for recent graduate. Includes high GPA (B or better).

EDUCATION
B.B.A., Accounting,
University of New Mexico, May 2014, GPA 3.87
- Dean's List, 2010–2014
- Deanna D. Darling Academic Scholarship

- Edges out competition reflecting related experience and work achievements.

RELATED EXPERIENCE
Intern, Gerald and Associates, CPAs, Santa Fe, NM
June–August 2013
- Shadowed auditor and helped write numerous auditing reports for corporate clients.
- Created and maintained spreadsheets and databases, containing client audit information.
- Worked with audit teams to hone communication skills and developed phone skills necessary to effectively interact with professional clientele.

- Uses separate section to emphasize language proficiencies listed in job requirements.

OTHER EXPERIENCE
- Server, Bubba's BBQ, Santa Fe, NM 2011–2013
- Stockperson, University of New Mexico Bookstore, Santa Fe, NM 2010–2011

- Emphasizes activities that reflect service attitude, high level of responsibility, and people-oriented experiences.

LANGUAGES
- **Fluent in English**
- **Conversational Spanish**

Format Pointers

Places name at top center, where it can be easily seen when employers place it in file drawer (top right is also acceptable).

LEADERSHIP ACTIVITIES
Beta Alpha Psi, honorary accounting society, 2012–2014, Chapter president, 2012–2013
Chess Team, 2010–2014; president, 2013–2014

Creates visual appeal through custom format rather than commonly used template, short readable sections focusing on targeted qualifications, and streamlined bulleted lists.

Clarence Foster
715 Armadillo Circle
San Antonio, TX 78710-0715
(512) 555-1396
cfoster@hotmail.com

Position in retail clothing sales with advancement to sales   OBJECTIVE
management.

CUSTOMER SERVICE
- Processed customer financial transactions within assigned limits and established guidelines.
- Provided excellent customer service in completing transactions efficiently and in a friendly, professional manner.
- Met sales and referral goals by identifying and selling financial products and services beneficial to the customer needs.
- Identified fraudulent activity to prevent potential losses to the bank.

SALES
- Provided quality customer service to store patrons.
- Handled cash transactions and daily receipt balances.
- Usually surpassed weekly goal of opening new credit accounts.
- Employee of the month.

COMMUNICATION SKILLS AND WORK ETHIC
- Ability to communicate effectively over the phone and in person.
- Ability to work well unsupervised.
- Experience working on team projects both at work and in courses.
- Report consistently and promptly when scheduled for work.

COMPUTER SKILLS
Proficient in spreadsheet and word-processing software.

Sales Associate, Claremont Department Store, 2012–Present   EMPLOYMENT
                                                            HISTORY
Customer Service Associate, Union Bank, 2011–2012

B.S., Marketing, Claremont State College, Expected   EDUCATION
graduation, May 2013

Clare Randall, Sales Manager, Claremont Department Store,   REFERENCES
435 Main Street, Claremont, TX 78009, (818) 555-2345

Daniel Shore, Professor, Marketing Department, Claremont State College,
890 Alamo Street, San Antonio, TX 87003, (803) 555-8907

Lisa Cox, Senior Teller, Union Bank, 900 Main Street, Claremont, TX 87303,
(818) 555-1234

- Includes clear objective statement to grab attention and invite close reading.

- Uses headings that show applicant knows what skills are needed to succeed in sales.

- Arranges qualifications into sections that emphasize applicant's relevant skills and accomplishments.

- Uses employers' names and dates to match skills with work history.

- Lists references for employer convenience and to strengthen résumé.

Format Pointers
Creates visual appeal with easy-to-read columnar format and balanced page arrangement.

Places name at top center, where it can be easily seen.

Uses bold font to distinguish identification section and headings from the remaining text.

Lists education and work history as quick overview of basic qualifications and to accommodate employers' preference for chronological format.

Interviewing for a Job and Preparing Employment Messages

Example of a Follow-Up Letter

Dear Mr. Wagner:

Thank you for taking the time to meet with me today to discuss the position of Financial Planning Analyst with Carson Fine Foods.

During our discussion, you stated that you're looking for an organized and outgoing candidate to join your team. Through my previous work and life experience, I gained organizational and customer development skills and learned how to meet goals through teamwork. In my position with Biotech Inc., I communicated with internal and external customers and assisted in efficiency and customer relations for the Fraud Detection program. I am confident that my skills and background will make me an asset as a Financial Planning Analyst with Carson Fine Foods.

I am eager to discuss this opportunity with you further. Please let me know what additional information I can provide you and your colleagues in order to secure this position and begin working for your organization.

- States main idea and clearly identifies the position being sought.
- Assures employer that the applicant is still interested in job.

Format Pointers
Formats as formal business letter but could have sent message electronically if previous communication with employer had been by email.

Prints letter and envelope with laser printer on paper that matches résumé and application letter.

Example of a Thank-You Message to a Reference

Thank you so much for the letter of recommendation you prepared for my application to law school. I learned today that I have been accepted by Cleveland University for the fall semester.

Because of the rigor of that law program, I believe your comments about my work ethic, dedication to high-quality work, and willingness to seek out feedback for improvement carried a great deal of weight. The dean commented that she was impressed with the detailed evidence and examples you provided to support your statements, unlike the general recommendations she often receives.

Dr. Kenney, I appreciate your helping me secure a seat in a highly competitive academic discipline with such a well-regarded law program. Thanks for the recommendation and your outstanding instruction. I will keep you informed about my law school experience and hope to stop by your office next time I am in town to catch up.

- States main idea of appreciation for recommendation. Informs reference of success in acceptance to academic program.
- Communicates sincere appreciation for assistance; uses specific examples and avoids exaggeration.
- Restates main idea and anticipates continued relationship; is original and sincere.

MODEL DOCS

Example of a Thank-You Message

New Message

To: wrfann@viking.com
From: mperkins@hotmail.com
Subject: Appreciation for Plant Interview

Dear Mr. Fann:

Thank you for the opportunity to visit Viking Range for a plant interview yesterday. I enjoyed meeting you and appreciated the complete tour of the operation and the opportunity to learn about the exciting research efforts underway at Viking.

Viking's success in developing higher quality products than its competitors after such a short time in the refrigeration market is impressive. Additionally, I was impressed with the many friendly, enthusiastic employees who were willing to share with me their knowledge and commitment to Viking.

After visiting your plant on Thursday, I am confident that my interest and previous experience in research and development at the DIAL labs in Starkville would allow me to contribute to Viking's important research efforts in the refrigeration area. I would also gain valuable real-world experience needed to enhance the mechanical engineering degree I'm pursuing at Mississippi State.

Mr. Fann, I am eager to receive an offer from Viking for the co-op position. If you need additional information in the meantime, please contact me.

Thanks,

Matt Perkins

- States main idea of appreciation for interview and information gained.

- Includes specific points discussed during interview, increasing sincerity and recall of applicant.

- Assures employer of continued interest in position.

- Politely reminds employer that the applicant is awaiting reply.

Format Pointer
Prepared as email message because previous communication with the company has been by email.

Example of a Job-Refusal Message

I appreciate your spending time with me discussing the sales associate position.

Your feedback regarding my fit for your organization and the opportunities available to me were particularly valuable. Having received offers in both sales and marketing, I feel that a career in the latter field better suits my personality and long-term career goals. Today, I am accepting an entry-level marketing position with Fashion Trends, Inc.

Thank you for your confidence demonstrated by the job offer. When I hear about Marasol's continued success, I will think of the dedicated people who work for the company.

- Begins with neutral but related idea to buffer bad news.

- Presents reasons diplomatically that lead to refusal.

- Ends message on positive note that anticipates future association with the company.

1-1 **Define communication and describe the value of communication in business.** Communication is the process of exchanging information and meaning between or among individuals through a common system of symbols, signs, and behavior. Managers spend most of their time in communication activities.

1-2 **Explain the communication process model and the ultimate objective of the communication process.** People engaged in communication encode and decode messages while simultaneously serving as both senders and receivers. In the communication process, feedback helps people resolve possible misunderstandings and thus improves communication effectiveness. Feedback and the opportunity to observe nonverbal signs are always present in face-to-face communication, the most complete of the three communication levels.

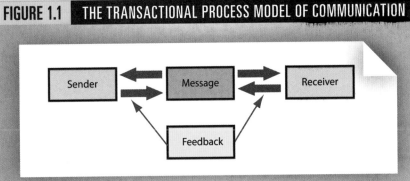

FIGURE 1.1 THE TRANSACTIONAL PROCESS MODEL OF COMMUNICATION

interferences also called *barriers*; numerous factors that hinder the communication process

1-3 **Discuss how information flows in an organization.** Both formal and informal communication systems exist in every organization; the formal system exists to accomplish tasks, and the informal system serves a personal maintenance purpose that results in people feeling better about themselves and others. Communication flows upward, downward, and horizontally or laterally. These flows often defy formal graphic description, yet each is a necessary part of the overall communication activity of the organization. Communication takes place at five levels: intrapersonal (communication within one person), interpersonal (communication between two people), group (communication among more than two people), organizational (communication among combinations of groups), and public (communication from one entity to the greater public).

organizational communication the movement of information within the company structure

formal communication network a network of communication flow typified by the formal organizational chart; dictated by the technical, political, and economic environment of the organization

informal communication network a network of communication flow that continuously develops as people interact within the formal system to accommodate their social and psychological needs

downward communication a type of communication that flows from supervisor to employee, from policy makers to operating personnel, or from top to bottom on the organizational chart

upward communication a type of communication that is generally a response to requests from supervisors

horizontal (or lateral) communication interactions between organizational units on the same hierarchical level

internal messages messages intended for recipients within the organization

external messages messages directed to recipients outside the organization

1-4 **Explain how legal and ethical constraints, diversity challenges, changing technology, and team environment act as contextual forces that influence the process of business communication.** Communication occurs within an environment constrained by legal and ethical requirements, diversity challenges, changing technology, and team environment requirements.

- International, federal, state, and local laws impose legal boundaries for business activity, and ethical boundaries are determined by personal analysis that can be assisted by application of various frameworks for decision making.
- Communication is critically impacted by diversity in nationality, culture, age, gender, and other factors that offer tremendous opportunities to maximize talent, ideas, and productivity but pose significant challenges in interpretation of time, personal space requirements, body language, and language translation.
- Significant strides have occurred in the development of tools for data collection and analysis, creation of messages that are clearer and more effective, and quick and easy communication with audiences in remote locations. The use of technology, however, poses legal and ethical concerns in regard to ownership, access, and privacy.
- Team environment challenges arise because communication in teams differs from communication in traditional organizational structures. The result of effective teams is better decisions, more creative solutions to problems, and higher worker morale.

context a situation or setting in which communication occurs

stakeholders people inside and outside the organization who are affected by decisions

ethics the principles of right and wrong that guide one in making decisions that consider the impact of one's actions on others as well as on the decision maker

diversity skills the ability to communicate effectively with both men and women of all ages, cultures, and minority groups

ethnocentrism the assumption that one's own cultural norms are the right way to do things

stereotypes mental pictures that one group forms of the main characteristics of another group, creating preformed ideas of what people in this group are like

chronemics the study of how a culture perceives time and its use

proxemics the study of cultural space requirements

kinesics the study of body language, which is not universal, but, instead, learned from one's culture

telecommuting also called *teleworking*; working at home or other remote locations and sending and receiving work from the company office electronically

social media a group of Internet-based applications that allow the creation and exchange of user-generated content

virtual team three or more people who collaborate from different physical locations, perform interdependent tasks, have shared responsibility for the outcome of the work, and rely on some form of technology to communicate with one another.

team a small number of people with complementary skills who work together for a common purpose

synergy a situation in which the whole is greater than the sum of the parts

GRAMMAR QUIZ Sentence Structure

Identify the weakness in each sentence and write an improved version.

1. It is essential that you learn to design spreadsheets that make financial information meaningful to users.

2. There are many online tools available that build relationships with customers.

3. I am submitting an employee testimonial to the company website, which I first posted to a presentation blog.

4. More companies are videoconferencing because of the need to significantly reduce travel costs.

5. To operate efficiently, you must perform periodic maintenance on your computer.

6. Planned store improvements include widening the aisles, improved lighting, and lower shelves for a sophisticated feel.

GRAMMAR QUIZ SOLUTIONS

1. You must learn to design spreadsheets that make financial information meaningful to users.

2. Many online tools are available that build relationships with customers.

3. I am submitting an employee testimonial, which I first posted to a presentations blog, to the company website.

4. More companies are videoconferencing because of the need to reduce travel costs significantly.

5. You must perform periodic maintenance on your computer to keep it operating efficiently.

6. Planned store improvements include widening the aisles, improving lighting, and lowering shelves for a sophisticated feel.

Planned store improvements include widened aisles, improved lighting, and lowered shelves for a sophisticated feel.

CHAPTER 2 LEARNING OBJECTIVES / KEY TERMS

2-1 **Explain how behavioral theories about human needs, trust and disclosure, and motivation relate to business communication.** Behavioral theories that address human needs, trust and disclosure, and motivation are essential aspects of interpersonal communication. The needs of all individuals to be heard, appreciated, wanted, and reinforced significantly affect their interpersonal communications.

interpersonal intelligence the ability to read, empathize, and understand others

stroke an emotional response one gets during a communication interaction that has either a positive or a negative effect on feelings about oneself and others

directive behavior characterized by leaders who give detailed rules and instructions and monitor closely that they are followed

supportive behavior characterized by leaders who listen, communicate, recognize, and encourage their followers

total quality management focuses on creating a more responsible role for the worker in an organization by distributing decision-making power to the people closest to the problem, empowering employees to initiate continuous improvements

FIGURE 2.1 **THE JOHARI WINDOW**

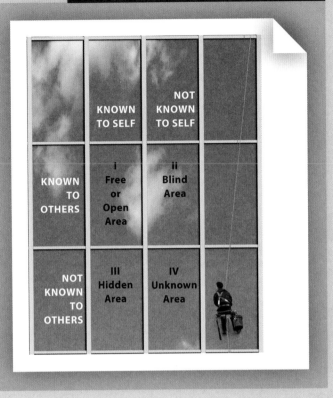

	KNOWN TO SELF	NOT KNOWN TO SELF
KNOWN TO OTHERS	i Free or Open Area	ii Blind Area
NOT KNOWN TO OTHERS	III Hidden Area	IV Unknown Area

2-2 **Describe the role of nonverbal messages in communication.** Nonverbal communication conveys a significant portion of meaning and includes metacommunications, which are wordless messages that accompany words, and kinesic communications, which are expressed through body language. The meanings of nonverbal messages are culturally derived.

metacommunication a nonverbal message that, although not expressed in words, accompanies a message that is expressed in words

visual kinesic communication gestures, winks, smiles, frowns, sighs, attire, grooming, and all kinds of body movements

vocal kinesic communication intonation, projection, and resonance of the voice

2-3 **Identify aspects of effective listening.** Effective listening, which requires effort and discipline, is crucial to effective interpersonal communication and leads to career success. Various types of listening require different strategies.

Casual listening listening for pleasure, recreation, amusement, and relaxation

listening for information listening that involves the search for data or material

intensive listening listening to obtain information, solve problems, or persuade or dissuade

active listening requires that the listener fully concentrates, understands, responds, and then remembers what is being said

empathetic listening listening to others in an attempt to share their feelings or emotions

2-4 **Identify factors affecting group and team communication.** Organizations are increasingly using group structures to achieve goals. Effective group communication results from shared purpose, constructive activity and behaviors, and positive role fulfillment among members. A team is a special type of group that is typified by strong commitment among members; this commitment results in behaviors that produce synergy.

role tasks employees assume that can involve power and authority that surpass their formal position in the organizational chart

status one's formal position in the organizational chart

norm a standard or average behavior

task force a team of workers that is generally given a single goal and a limited time to achieve it

quality assurance team a team that focuses on product or service quality; projects can be either short or long term *(continues)*

CHAPTER REVIEW

CHAPTER 2 LEARNING OBJECTIVES / KEY TERMS

(continued)

cross-functional team a team that brings together employees from various departments to solve a variety of problems

product development team usually cross-functional in nature; a group of employees who concentrate on innovation and the development cycle of new products

forming stage one of team development, in which team members become acquainted with each other and the assigned task

storming stage two of team development, in which team members deal with conflicting personalities, goals, and ideas

norming stage three of team development, in which team members develop strategies and activities that promote goal achievement

performing stage four of team development, in which team members reach the optimal performance level

---

2-5 **Discuss aspects of effective meeting management.** Face-to-face meetings and electronic meetings each offer certain advantages and disadvantages. Effective meeting management techniques and behaviors can enhance the success of meetings.

agenda a meeting outline that includes important information (e.g., date, beginning and ending times, place, topics to be discussed, and responsibilities of those involved)

brainstorming the generation of many ideas by team members

consensus represents the collective opinion of the group, or the informal rule that all team members can live with at least 70% of what is agreed upon

---

CHECK YOUR COMMUNICATION Nonverbal Communication

METACOMMUNICATION

Metacommunication is a message that, although not expressed in words, accompanies a message that is expressed in words.

KINESIC MESSAGES

Kinesic communication is an idea expressed through nonverbal behavior. In other words, receivers gain additional meaning from what they see and hear—the visual and the vocal:

- Visual—gestures, winks, smiles, frowns, sighs, attire, grooming, and all kinds of body movements.
- Vocal—intonation, projection, and resonance of the voice.

UNDERSTANDING NONVERBAL MESSAGES

Metacommunications and kinesic communication have characteristics that all communicators should take into account. Nonverbal messages

- cannot be avoided.
- may have different meanings for different people.
- vary between and within cultures.
- may be intentional or unintentional.
- can contradict the accompanying verbal message and affect whether your message is understood or believed.
- may receive more attention than verbal messages.
- provide clues about the sender's background and motives.
- are influenced by the circumstances surrounding the communication.
- may be beneficial or harmful.
- may vary depending upon the person's gender.

GRAMMAR QUIZ Sentence Structure

Correct the error in pronoun reference or verb form.

1. Conversation skills and good listening (affect, affects) a leader's effectiveness.

2. Each sales rep (was, were) trained to encourage customers to buy more than one size or color since shipping is free.

3. The production manager, not the controller, presented (her, their) strongly opposing views.

4. Neither Stephen nor Lydia (was, were) recognized for his or her contribution.

5. The company restructured (its, their) recreation event to avoid a frivolous perception.

6. The committee will present (its, their) recommendation at the next staff meeting.

7. Jenna forgot to retain her receipts; (this, this oversight) caused a delay in reimbursement.

GRAMMAR QUIZ SOLUTIONS

1. affect
2. was
3. her
4. was
5. its
6. its
7. this oversight

CHAPTER 3 LEARNING OBJECTIVES / KEY TERMS

3-1 **Consider contextual forces that may affect whether, how, to whom, and when a message is sent.** Chapter 1 discussed four contextual forces that may affect whether, how, to whom, and when a message is sent. These were legal and ethical constraints, diversity challenges, changing technology, and team environment. In addition to these four forces, communication patterns within an organization are a contextual force that should also be considered when planning a message. The organizational culture as well as the four dimensions of

context may influence how, whether, and when a message is sent. These two issues are discussed in the sections that follow.

organizational culture a pattern of shared basic assumptions that the group has learned as it solved its problems with external adaptation and internal integration, and which has worked well enough to be taught to new members as the correct way to perceive, think, and feel in relation to these problems

3-2 **Identify the purpose of the message and the appropriate channel and medium.** Writing is a systematic process that begins by determining the purpose of the message (central idea) and identifying how the central idea will affect the receiver. In view of its effect on the receiver, you can determine the appropriate channel and medium for sending a particular message (e.g., face-to-face, phone call, text, letter, memo, email, instant message, blog, voice mail, or fax).

3-3 **Develop clear perceptions of the audience to enhance the impact and persuasiveness of the message, improve goodwill, and establish and maintain the credibility of the communicator.** Before you compose the first draft, commit to overcoming perceptual barriers that will limit your ability to see an issue from multiple perspectives and thus plan an effective message. Then consider all you know about the receiver, including age, economic level, educational or occupational background, culture, existing relationship, expectations, and needs.

3-4 **Apply tactics for adapting messages to the audience, including those for communicating ethically and responsibly.** The insights you gain from seeking to understand your receiver will allow you to adapt the message to fit the receiver's needs. Developing concise, sensitive messages that focus on the receiver's point of view will build and protect goodwill and demand the attention of the receiver. Communicating ethically and responsibly involves stating information truthfully and tactfully, eliminating embellishments or exaggerations, supporting viewpoints with objective facts from credible sources, and designing honest graphics.

libel written defamatory remarks   **slander** spoken defamatory remarks

3-5 **Recognize the importance of organization when planning the first draft.** Outlining involves identifying the appropriate sequence of pertinent ideas. Outlining encourages brevity and accuracy, permits concentration on one phase at a time, saves writing time, increases confidence to complete the task, and facilitates appropriate emphasis of ideas. From a receiver's point of view, well-organized messages are easier to understand and promote a more positive attitude toward the sender.

outlining the process of identifying central ideas and details, and arranging them in the right sequence; this should be completed prior to writing

deductive a message in which the major idea precedes the details

inductive a message in which the major idea follows the details

CHECK YOUR COMMUNICATION Guidelines for Planning a Written Message

FOCUS ON THE RECEIVER'S POINT OF VIEW

- Present ideas from the receiver's point of view, conveying the tone that the message is specifically for the receiver.
- Give sincere compliments.

COMMUNICATE ETHICALLY AND RESPONSIBLY

- Present information truthfully, honestly, and fairly.
- Include all information relevant to the receiver.

- Avoid exaggerating or embellishing facts.
- Use objective facts to support ideas.
- Design graphics that avoid distorting facts and relationships.
- Express ideas clearly and understandably.
- State ideas tactfully and positively to build future relationships.

(continues)

WWW.CENGAGEBRAIN.COM **3**

CHECK YOUR COMMUNICATION Guidelines for Planning a Written Message *(continued)*

BUILD AND PROTECT GOODWILL

- Use euphemisms to present unpleasant thoughts politely and positively. Use dysphemisms only when they will be viewed humorously. Avoid using euphemisms as well as dysphemisms when they will be taken as excessive, sarcastic, or cruel.

- Avoid doublespeak or corporate speak that confuses or misleads the receiver.

- Avoid using condescending or demeaning expressions.

- Rely mainly on denotative words. Use connotative words that will elicit a favorable reaction, are easily understood, and are appropriate for the setting.

- Choose vivid words that add clarity and interest to your message.

- Use bias-free language:

  - Do not use the pronoun he when referring to a group of people that may include women or she when a group may include men.

  - Avoid referring to men and women in stereotyped roles and occupations, using gender-biased occupational titles, or differentiating genders in an occupation.

  - Avoid referring to groups (based on gender, race and ethnicity, age, religion, and disability) in stereotypical and insensitive ways.

  - Do not emphasize race and ethnicity, age, religion, or disability when these factors are not relevant.

CONVEY A POSITIVE, TACTFUL TONE

- Rely mainly on positive words that speak of what can be done instead of what cannot be done, and of the pleasant instead of the unpleasant. Use negative words when the purpose is to sharpen contrast or when positive words have not evoked the desired reaction.

- Use second person and active voice to emphasize pleasant ideas. Avoid using second person for presenting negative ideas; instead, use third person and passive voice to de-emphasize the unpleasant.

- Consider stating an unpleasant thought in the subjunctive mood.

USE SIMPLE, CONTEMPORARY LANGUAGE

- Avoid clichés and outdated expressions that make your language seem unnatural and unoriginal.

- Use simple words for informal business messages instead of using more complicated words that have the same meaning.

WRITE CONCISELY

- Avoid redundancy—unnecessary repetition of an idea.

- Use active voice to shorten sentences.

- Avoid unnecessary details; omit ideas that can be implied.

- Shorten wordy sentences by using suffixes or prefixes, making changes in word form, or substituting precise words for phrases.

GRAMMAR QUIZ Pronoun Case

Choose the correct pronoun case in the following sentences.

1. The professor agreed to award (we, us) partial credit for the confusing question.

2. Stacey requested that the tasks be divided equally between Addison and (her, she).

3. It was (her, she) (who, whom) recommended revising the company's technology policy to include social networking sites.

4. The manager seemed unaware of (him, his) inability to relate to younger employees.

5. Emma is a leader in (who, whom) we have great confidence.

GRAMMAR QUIZ SOLUTIONS

1. us
2. her
3. she, who
4. his
5. whom

CHAPTER 4 LEARNING OBJECTIVES / KEY TERMS

4-1 **Apply techniques for developing effective sentences and unified and coherent paragraphs.** Well-written sentences and unified and coherent paragraphs will help the receiver understand the message clearly and respond favorably. To craft powerful sentences, rely on active voice and emphasize important points. To write effective paragraphs, develop deductive or inductive paragraphs consistently; link ideas to achieve coherence; keep paragraphs unified; and vary sentence and paragraph length.

topic sentence a sentence that identifies the portion of the topic being discussed and presents the central idea of the paragraph

deductive paragraph a paragraph in which the topic sentence precedes the details

inductive paragraph a paragraph in which the topic sentence follows the details

coherence cohesion, so that each sentence is linked to the preceding sentences in some way

passive voice when the subject of a sentence is the receiver of an action

active voice when the subject of a sentence is the doer of an action

4-2 **Prepare visually appealing documents that grab the audience's attention and increase comprehension.** Visually appealing documents entice the reader to read the document and focus attention on important ideas, and they move the reader smoothly through the organization of the document without adding clutter. Techniques for preparing appealing, easy-to-read documents include enumerations, enumerated or bulleted lists, headings, tables and graphs, lines and borders, and drawing tools and clip art.

4-3 **Identify factors affecting readability, and revise sentences to improve readability.** The readability of a message is affected by the length of the sentences and the difficulty of the words. For quick, easy reading, use simple words and short sentences. A readability index (grade level at which the receiver must read in order to understand the material) in the eighth- to eleventh-grade range is appropriate for most business writing. Writing a message with a readability index appropriate for an audience does not guarantee understanding but does provide feedback on the average length of the sentences and the difficulty of the words.

clichés overused expressions that can cause their users to be perceived as unoriginal, unimaginative, lazy, and perhaps even disrespectful

jargon specialized terminology that professionals in some fields use when communicating with colleagues in the same field

redundancy a phrase in which one word unnecessarily repeats an idea contained in an accompanying word (e.g., "exactly identical")

tone the way a statement sounds; it conveys the writer's or speaker's attitude toward the message and the receiver

subjunctive sentences sentences that speak of a wish, necessity, doubt, or condition contrary to fact, and employ such conditional expressions as *I wish, as if, could, would,* and *might*

euphemism a kind word substituted for one that may offend or suggest something unpleasant

doublespeak also called doubletalk or corporate speak; euphemisms that deliberately mislead, hide, or evade the truth

goodwill an attitude of kindness or friendliness that results in a good relationship

denotative meaning the literal meaning of a word that most people assign to it

connotative meaning the literal meaning of a word plus an extra message that reveals the speaker's or writer's qualitative judgment

4-4 **Revise and proofread a message for content, organization, style, and tone; mechanics; and format and layout.** Be willing to revise a document as many times as necessary to be certain that it conveys the message effectively and is error free. Use spell-check to locate keying errors, and then follow systematic procedures for proofreading an onscreen and/or printed copy of the document. Proofread systematically for content, organization, and style; mechanics; and then for format and layout.

CHECK YOUR COMMUNICATION Preparing and Proofreading a Rough Draft

POWERFUL SENTENCES

- Use correct structure when writing simple, compound, complex, and compound-complex sentences. Avoid run-on sentences and comma splices.

- Use active voice to present important points or pleasant ideas. Use passive voice to present less significant points or unpleasant ideas.

- Emphasize important ideas:

  - Place an idea in a simple sentence.

  - Place an idea in an independent clause; for de-emphasis, place an idea in a dependent clause.

  - Use an important word more than once in a sentence.

  - Place an important idea first or last in a sentence, paragraph, or document.

  - Use words that label ideas as significant or insignificant.

  - Use headings, graphics, and additional space to emphasize important ideas.

COHERENT PARAGRAPHS

- Write deductively if the message will likely please or at least not displease. Write inductively if the message will likely displease or if understanding the major idea is dependent on prior explanations.

- Make sure the message forms a unit with an obvious beginning, middle, and ending and that the middle paragraphs are arranged in a systematic sequence, either deductively or inductively, as needed.

- Avoid abrupt changes in thought, and link each sentence to a preceding sentence. Place transition sentences before major headings.

- Vary sentence and paragraph length to emphasize important ideas.

- Limit paragraphs in letters, memos, email messages, and web pages to six lines and paragraphs in reports to 9 to 10 lines to maximize comprehension.

READABILITY

- Use simple words and short sentences for quick, easy reading (and listening).

- Strive for short paragraphs, but vary their lengths.

- Create appealing, easy-to-read documents by

  - using enumeration or bulleted or enumerated lists for stronger emphasis.

  - using headings, tables and graphs, lines and borders, and images to focus attention on important information.

SYSTEMATIC PROOFREADING

- Use spell-check to locate simple keying errors.

- Proofread once concentrating on content, organization, and style; a second time on mechanics; and a third time on format and layout.

GRAMMAR QUIZ Verb Agreement, Tense, and Mood

In each of the following sentences, select the correct word in parentheses.

1. Only one of the free smartphone applications (has, have) value to me.

2. Taxpayers, not the government, (are, is) held accountable for paying the national debt.

3. Neither the manager nor the employees (was, were) aware of the policy change.

4. Both Josh and Krystal (was, were) notified of the impending layoffs.

5. The news from the rescue mission (is, are) encouraging.

6. Good to Great (has, have) been placed in the company library.

7. The sales manager announced that Portsmouth, South Carolina, (is, was) the site for the annual sales meeting.

8. Taylor (don't, doesn't) expect preferential treatment.

9. The client studied the financial analysis for a minute and (starts, started) asking questions.

10. If the applicant (was, were) experienced with databases, she would have been hired.

GRAMMAR QUIZ SOLUTIONS

1. has
2. are
3. were
4. were
5. is
6. has
7. is
8. doesn't
9. started
10. were

5-1 **Discuss the effective use of email, instant messaging, and text messaging in business communication.** Email can be sent to receivers both inside and outside the organization. Email provides a fast, convenient way to communicate by reducing telephone tag and telephone interruptions, facilitating the transmission of a single message to multiple recipients, reducing telephone bills, eliminating time barriers, and fostering open communication among users in various locations. Although general writing principles apply, email formats are less formal than business letter formats. Real-time email, known as instant messaging, allows two or more people to converse online. Text messaging occurs primarily between users of portable devices. Abbreviations and online "shorthand" help speed these means of rapid communication.

5-2 **Explain principles for writing effectively for the Web.** Web pages facilitate an organization's continual communication with a wide audience. HTML and a Web browser turn ordinary text into a web page. Writing for web pages should be concise, jargon free, and chunked to allow for scanning of content. Weblogs serve important needs in capturing information for further use but should be considered public and not confidential.

netiquette the buzzword for proper behavior on the Internet

social networking sites websites that provide virtual communities in which people with shared interests can communicate

instant messaging (IM) a real-time email technology that blends email with conversation; sender and receiver who are online at the same time can type messages that both see immediately

text messaging messages that can be sent from one cellphone to another, a cellphone to a computer, or computer to computer; a refinement of computer instant messaging

5-3 **Discuss the effective use of voice and wireless technologies in business communication.** Voice recordings and messages should be clear and complete and considered as permanent records. Cellphones should be used with consideration for the receiver and the public. Cellphones communications should not be viewed as secure communications. Text messaging offers a limited avenue for exchanging quick, quiet messages. Applications and equipment to accommodate wireless communications continue to expand and offer flexibility for transmitting voice and data. Business decisions can be improved through the appropriate use of voice and wireless technologies.

weblog (or blog) a type of online journal, typically authored by an individual, that does not allow visitors to change the original material posted, but only to add comments

webinars seminars that are held using the Internet for transmission.

5-4 **Consider legal and ethical implications associated with the use of communication technology.** The following legal and ethical considerations should be taken into account when communicating through technology: (a) Be certain that information technology does not violate basic rights of individuals and that you abide by all laws related to the use of technology; (b) understand that email is not private and can be monitored by a company; (c) develop and use procedures that protect the security of information; and (d) develop a clear and fair privacy policy.

CHECK YOUR COMMUNICATION Electronic Communication

EMAIL MESSAGES

Organization, Content, Style, and Mechanics

- Provide a subject line that is meaningful to the recipient.
- Include only one main message idea related to the receiver's needs.
- Show empathy and logic to determine the idea sequence.
- Use jargon, technical words, and shortened terms carefully.
- Use bulleted lists, tables, graphs, or images as needed.
- Avoid flaming and use of overly emotional language.

Format

- Include an appropriate salutation, ending, and signature line (your name, address, phone, etc.)
- When possible, limit message width and length to one screen. Use attachments for longer messages.
- Single-space lines with a blank space between unindented paragraphs.
- Use mixed-case letters unless emphasis is needed with capital letters or quotation marks.
- Use emoticons and abbreviations in moderation only if the receiver understands them and content is informal.

(continues)

CHECK YOUR COMMUNICATION Electronic Communication *(continued)*

INSTANT MESSAGES

Organization, Content, Style, and Mechanics
- Consider previously listed email guidelines.
- Choose your message participants appropriately.
- Be aware of unwanted eavesdropping.

Format
- Use understandable shorthand and abbreviations for frequent words and phrases.
- Focus more on efficiency and less on spelling and grammar.

Text Messages
- Choose for exchanging quick, quiet messages.
- Avoid using text messaging as a substitute for richer communication mediums.

WEB COMMUNICATION AND SOCIAL MEDIA

Writing for Websites
- Create brief, simple documents for easy reading. Break longer documents into smaller chunks.
- Use eye-catching headlines and techniques.
- Use jargon and technical terms cautiously.
- Avoid placing critical information only in graphic form that may be skipped by users of slow systems.

SOCIAL MEDIA

Writing for Weblogs
- Consider previously listed email guidelines.
- Communicate responsibly and ethically when writing anonymously.
- Develop a clear goal that leads to relevant content for the target audience. Revise and update regularly, and promote actively to attract and retain readers.

Writing for Wikis
- Avoid first-person language, and conform to tone and flow of existing article.
- Present factual information in clear, concise, and neutral language.

VOICE AND WIRELESS COMMUNICATIONS

Voice Recordings
- Leave your email address, fax number, or mailing address on your greeting if helpful to callers.
- Encourage callers to leave detailed messages.
- Instruct callers in how to review their messages or be transferred to an operator.
- Check voice mail regularly, and reply within 24 hours.

Voice Messages
- Speak slowly and clearly.
- Repeat your name and phone number at the beginning and end, spelling your name if helpful.
- Leave a detailed, specific message.
- Keep your message brief, typically 60 seconds or less.
- Ensure your message is understood; avoid calling from noisy environments and weak-signal areas.

Voice and Wireless Etiquette
- Use judgment about silencing or turning off your phone.
- Respect others around you by speaking in low conversational tones and monitoring your content.
- Practice safety when using wireless communication devices while driving.

GRAMMAR QUIZ Adjectives and Adverbs

In each of the following sentences, select the correct word in parentheses.

1. Despite the dangers, employees change their computer passwords (infrequent, infrequently).
2. Daniel looked (impatient, impatiently) at the new production assistant.
3. The server moved (quick, quickly) from table to table.
4. Of the several people I met during the speed networking event, Olivia made the (better, best) impression.
5. The Chicago plant has a higher safety record than (any, any other) plant.

GRAMMAR QUIZ SOLUTIONS

1. infrequently
2. impatiently
3. quickly
4. best
5. any other

CHAPTER REVIEW

6-1 Describe the deductive outline for good and neutral news and its adaptations for specific situations and for international audiences. When the receiver can be expected to be pleased by the message, the main idea is presented first and details follow. Likewise, when the message is routine and not likely to arouse a feeling of pleasure or displeasure, the main idea is presented first. The deductive approach is appropriate for positive news and thank-you and appreciation messages, routine claims, routine requests, responses to routine requests, routine messages, and responses about credit and orders. Cultural differences of international audiences may necessitate adjustments in writing style and to the typical deductive pattern for good- and neutral-news messages.

good-news messages messages that convey pleasant information

neutral-news messages messages that are of interest to the reader but are not likely to generate an emotional reaction

deductive (or direct) sequence when the message begins with the main idea followed by supporting details

6-2 Prepare messages that convey good news, including thank-you and appreciation messages. The deductive approach for letters, memos, and email messages that contain positive news as the central idea. Thank-you messages express appreciation for a kindness or special assistance and should reflect sincere feelings of gratitude. Appreciation messages highlight exceptional performance and should avoid exaggerations and strong, unsupported statements that the receiver may not believe.

6-3 Write messages presenting routine claims and requests and favorable responses to them. A routine claim requests the adjustment in the first sentence because you assume the company will make the adjustment without persuasion. It continues with an explanation of the problem to support the request and an expression of appreciation for taking the action. An adjustment extends the adjustment in the first sentence and explains the circumstances related to correcting the problem. The closing may include sales promotional material or other future-oriented comments indicating your confidence that the customer will continue doing business with a company that has a reputation for fairness. A routine request begins with the major request, includes details that will clarify the request, and alludes to the receiver's response. A response to a routine request provides the information requested, provides necessary details, and closes with a personal, courteous ending.

claim a request for an adjustment

routine claims messages that assume that a claim will be granted quickly and willingly, without persuasion

persuasive claims messages that assume that a claim will be granted only after explanations and persuasive arguments have been presented

adjustment messages messages that are fair responses by businesses to legitimate requests in claim messages by customers

resale a discussion of goods or services already bought

sales promotional material statements made about related merchandise or service

6-4 Write messages acknowledging customer orders, providing credit information, and extending credit. Form or computer-generated acknowledgment messages or email messages ensure customers that orders will be filled quickly. With individualized acknowledgments that confirm shipment and include product resale, the company generates goodwill and future business. When providing credit information, provide only verifiable facts to avoid possible litigation. A message extending credit begins with an approval of credit, indicates the basis for the decision, and explains credit terms. The closing may include sales promotional material or future-oriented comments. Credit extension messages must adhere to legal guidelines.

routine requests messages that assume that a request will be granted quickly and willingly, without persuasion

persuasive requests messages that assume that a requested action will be taken after persuasive arguments are presented

6-5 Prepare procedural messages that ensure clear and consistent application. When preparing instructions, highlight the steps in a bulleted or numbered list or a flow chart, and begin each step with an action statement. Check the accuracy and completeness of the document, and incorporate changes identified by following the instructions to complete the task and asking another person to do likewise.

acknowledgment message a document that indicates that an order has been received and is being processed

CHECK YOUR COMMUNICATION Good- and Neutral-News Messages

Content

- Clearly identify the principal idea (pleasant or routine idea).
- Present sufficient supporting details in logical sequence.
- Ensure the accuracy of facts or figures.
- Structure the message to meet legal requirements and ethical dimensions.

Organization

- Place the major idea in the first sentence.
- Present supporting details in logical sequence.
- Include a final idea that is courteous and indicates a continuing relationship with the receiver; it may include sales promotional material.

Style

- Ensure that the message is clear and concise (e.g., words will be readily understood).
- Use active voice predominantly and first person sparingly.
- Make ideas cohere by avoiding abrupt changes in thought.
- Use contemporary language; avoid doublespeak and clichés.
- Use relatively short sentences that vary in length and structure.
- Emphasize significant thoughts (e.g., position and sentence structure).
- Keep paragraphs relatively short.
- Adjust formality and writing style to the particular medium of delivery (letter, memo, email, text message, etc.).

Mechanics

- Ensure that keyboarding, spelling, grammar, and punctuation are perfect.

Format

- Use a correct message format.
- Ensure that the message is appropriately positioned.
- Include standard message parts in appropriate position and special parts as needed (subject line, enclosure, copy, etc.).

Cultural Adaptations

- Avoid abbreviations, slang, acronyms, technical jargon, sports and military analogies, and other devices particular to your own culture.
- Avoid words that trigger emotional responses.
- Use simple terms but attempt to be specific.
- Consider the communication style of the culture when selecting an organizational pattern.
- Use graphics, visual aids, and forms, when possible, to simplify the message.
- Use figures for expressing numbers to avoid confusion.
- Be aware of differences in the way numbers and dates are written, and write out the name of the month to avoid confusion.
- Adapt the document format for expectations of the recipient's country.

GRAMMAR QUIZ Commas

Insert needed commas. Write "correct" if you find no errors.

1. The employee who is featured in our latest television commercial is active in the community theater.
2. Emoticons which are created by keying combinations of symbols to produce "sideways faces" communicate emotion in electronic messages.
3. Sean Cohen a new member of the board remained silent during the long bitter debate.
4. Top social networking sites include Facebook, MySpace, and Flickr.
5. The entire population was surveyed but three responses were unusable.
6. If you tag websites in a social bookmarking site you can locate them easily for later use.
7. To qualify for the position applicants must have technology certification.
8. We should be spending less money not more.
9. On May 9, 2011 the company's Twitter site was launched.
10. Yes the president approved a team-building event to replace our annual golf outing.

GRAMMAR QUIZ SOLUTIONS

1. Correct.
2. Emoticons, which are created by keying combinations of symbols to produce "sideways faces," communicate emotion in electronic messages.
3. Sean Cohen, a new member of the board, remained silent during the long, bitter debate.
4. Correct.
5. The entire population was surveyed, but three responses were unusable.
6. If you tag sites in a social bookmarking site, you can locate them easily for later use.
7. To qualify for the position, applicants must have technology certification.
8. We should be spending less money, not more.
9. On May 9, 2011, the company's Twitter site was launched.
10. Yes, the president approved a team-building event to replace our annual golf outing.

CHAPTER 7 LEARNING OBJECTIVES / KEY TERMS

7-1 **Explain the steps in the inductive outline, and understand its use for specific situations.** Because the receiver can be expected to be displeased by the message, the inductive approach is appropriate for messages denying an adjustment, refusing an order for merchandise, refusing credit, sending constructive criticism, or conveying negative organizational messages. The steps in the inductive outline include (1) introducing the topic with a neutral idea that sets the stage for the explanation; (2) presenting a concise, logical explanation for the refusal; (3) implying or stating the refusal using positive language; (4) offering a counterproposal or "silver lining" statement that shifts focus toward the positive; and (5) closing with a positive, courteous ending that shifts the focus away from the bad news. Although bad-news messages are typically expressed using paper documents or face-to-face means, electronic channels may be appropriate under certain circumstances. The deductive approach can be used to communicate bad news when (a) the message is the second response to a repeated request; (b) a very small, insignificant matter is involved; (c) a request is obviously ridiculous, immoral, unethical, illegal, or dangerous; (d) a writer's intent is to "shake" the receiver; or (e) a writer–reader relationship is so close and long-standing that satisfactory human relations can be taken for granted.

7-2 **Discuss strategies for developing the five components of a bad-news message.** The introductory paragraph should buffer the bad news and tactfully identify the subject. Following the introduction should be a logical discussion of the reasons for the refusal or bad news. The bad-news statement itself should be positioned strategically and (a) use the inductive approach, (b) not be set in a paragraph by itself, and (c) should sit in a dependent clause of a complex sentence. A counterproposal or silver lining should follow the bad-news statement, and the concluding paragraph of the message should demonstrate empathy.

counterproposal in a bad-news message, an alternative to the action requested that follows the negative news and can assist in preserving future relationships with the audience

7-3 **Prepare messages refusing requests and claims.** A message refusing a request begins with a neutral idea and presents the reasons before the refusal. The close may offer a counterproposal—an alternative to the action requested. A message denying a claim begins with a neutral or factual sentence that leads to the reason for the refusal. In the opening sentence, you might include resale to reaffirm the reader's confidence in the merchandise or services. Next, present the explanation for the refusal and then the refusal in a positive, nonemphatic manner. Close with a positive thought such as sales promotion that indicates you expect to do business with the customer again.

7-4 **Prepare messages handling problems with customers' orders and denying credit.** A message refusing an order implies receipt of the order and uses resale to reaffirm the customer's confidence in the merchandise or service. Continue with reasons for your procedures or actions and benefits to the customer. Close with information needed for the customer to reorder or anticipate later delivery. Credit refusal messages must comply with laws related to fair credit practices and should be reviewed carefully by legal counsel. Begin the message by implying receipt of an order and using resale that could convince the applicant to buy your merchandise on a cash basis when he or she learns later that credit has been denied. You must provide an explanation for the refusal (in writing or verbally) and may encourage the customer to apply for credit later or offer a discount on cash purchases. Your legal counsel may advise that you omit the explanation and invite the applicant to call or come in to discuss the reasons or to obtain more information from the credit reporting agency whose name, address, and telephone number you provide in the message.

7-5 **Prepare messages providing constructive criticism.** Because of the importance of maintaining goodwill with employees and outside parties, convey constructive criticism organizational news in a sensitive, honest, and timely manner; use the inductive approach. The motive for delivering constructive criticism should be to help, not to get even. The message includes verifiable facts and omits evaluative words, allowing the recipient to make logical judgments based on facts.

Fair Credit Reporting Act a federal law that provides consumers the right to know the nature of the information in their credit file and gives them other protections when they apply for and are denied credit

7-6 **Prepare messages communicating negative organizational news.** Negative information about an organization should be timely, honest, empathetic, and helpful. If handled well, bad-news messages can build unity and trust among employees, customers, and the general public.

7-7 **Prepare messages responding to crises.** Crisis communication should be well planned and organized and should demonstrate concern, compassion, and control. A command center, chain of command, and a means of disseminating critical information should be determined before a crisis occurs. Potential crises should be anticipated in areas of vulnerability.

CHECK YOUR COMMUNICATION Bad-News Messages

Content

- Be sure the principal idea (the unpleasant idea or the refusal) is sufficiently clear.
- Use sufficient supporting details, and present them in a logical sequence.
- Verify accuracy of facts or figures.
- Structure the message to meet ethical and legal requirements.
- Make appropriate cultural adaptations (e.g., organizational pattern, format, and language usage).

Organization

- Structure the first sentence to introduce the general subject
  - without stating the bad news.
  - without leading a receiver to expect good news.
  - without including obvious statements (e.g., "I am replying to your letter").
- Precede the main idea (bad news) with meaningful discussion.
- Follow up the bad news with a counterproposal or silver lining statement that moves discussion in a positive direction.
- Use a closing sentence that is positive (an alternative, resale, or sales promotion).

Style

- Write clearly and concisely (e.g., use words that are easily understood).

- Use techniques of subordination to keep the bad news from emerging with unnecessary vividness. For example, bad news may
  - appear in a dependent clause.
  - be stated in passive voice.
  - be revealed through indirect statement.
  - be revealed through the use of subjunctive mood.
- Use first person sparingly or not at all.
- Make ideas cohere by avoiding abrupt changes in thought.
- Keep sentences and paragraphs relatively short, and vary length and structure.
- Use original expression (sentences are not copied directly from the definition of the problem or from sample documents in the text); omit clichés.

Mechanics

- Ensure that keyboarding, spelling, grammar, and punctuation are perfect.

Format

- Use a correct document format.
- Include standard document parts in appropriate position.
- Include special parts if necessary (subject line, enclosure, copy, etc.).

GRAMMAR QUIZ Semicolons and Colons

In each of the following sentences, insert or delete semicolons and colons where necessary. Write "correct" if you find no errors.

1. Some privacy concerns have become less important in recent years, however, most people feel extremely vulnerable to privacy invasion.
2. The following agents received bonuses Barnes, $750, Shelley, $800, and Jackson, $950.
3. Employees were notified today of the plant closing they received two weeks' severance pay.
4. This paint does have some disadvantages for example a lengthy drying time.
5. Soon after the applications are received, a team of judges will evaluate them, but the award recipients will not be announced until January 15.
6. The program has one shortcoming: flexibility.
7. The new bakery will offer: frozen yogurt, candies, and baked goods.
8. We are enthusiastic about the plan because: (1) it is least expensive, (2) its legality is unquestioned, and (3) it can be implemented quickly.

GRAMMAR QUIZ SOLUTIONS

8. We are enthusiastic about the plan because (1) it is least expensive; (2) its legality is unquestioned; and (3) it can be implemented quickly.
7. The new bakery will offer frozen yogurt, candies, and baked goods.
6. Correct.
5. Soon after the applications are received, a team of judges will evaluate them; but the award recipients will not be announced until January 15.
4. This paint does have some disadvantages; for example, a lengthy drying time.
3. Employees were notified today of the plant closing; they received two weeks' severance pay.
2. The following agents received bonuses: Barnes, $750; Shelley, $800; and Jackson, $950.
1. Some privacy concerns have become less important in recent years; however, most people feel extremely vulnerable to privacy invasion.

CHAPTER 8 LEARNING OBJECTIVES / KEY TERMS

8-1 **Develop effective outlines and appeals for messages that persuade.** The purpose of a persuasive message is to influence others to take a particular action or to accept your point of view. Effective persuasion involves understanding the product, service, or idea you are promoting; knowing your audience; presenting convincing evidence; and having a rational response to anticipated resistance to your arguments. Effective persuasive communications build on a central selling point interwoven throughout the message. The receivers, rather than the product, serve as the subject of many of the sentences. Therefore, receivers can envision themselves using the product, contracting for the service, or complying with a request. Persuasive messages are written inductively.

persuasion the ability of a sender to influence others to accept his or her point of view

AIDA the four basic steps of the persuasive process, including gaining attention, generating interest, creating desire, and motivating action

central selling point the primary appeal on which a persuasive message focuses

8-2 **Write effective sales messages.** A sales message is written inductively following the four AIDA steps for selling:

- **Gain attention.** Use an original approach that addresses one primary receiver's benefit (the central selling point) in the first paragraph.

- **Introduce the product, service, or idea.** Provide a logical transition to move the receiver from the attention-getter to information about the product, service, or idea. Hold the receiver's attention by using action-oriented sentences to stress the central selling point.

- **Create desire by providing convincing evidence.** Provide specific facts and interpretations that clarify features and quality. Include nonexaggerated, believable evidence and research and testimonials that provide independent support. De-emphasize price by presenting convincing evidence before the final paragraph, showing how money can be saved, stating price in small units, illustrating that the price is reasonable, or placing the price in a sentence that summarizes the benefits.

- **Motivate action.** State confidently the specific action to be taken and the benefits for complying. Present the action as easy to take, and provide a stimulus for acting quickly.

8-3 **Write effective persuasive requests (making a claim or asking for a favor or information) and persuasion within an organization.** A persuasive request is written inductively, is organized around a primary appeal, and is longer than a typical routine message because you must provide convincing evidence of receiver benefit.

- **Persuasive claim**—To convince an adjuster, gain the receiver's attention, develop a central appeal that emphasizes an incentive for making the adjustment, and end with the request for an adjustment you consider fair.

- **Request for a favor or information**—Gain the receiver's attention, build interest by emphasizing the reward for taking action, and encourage the receiver to grant the favor or send the information.

- **Persuasion within an organization**—When persuading an employee or supervisor to take specific actions, gain the receiver's attention, introduce and build interest and support for the proposed idea, address any major resistance, and encourage the receiver to take a specific action.

CHECK YOUR COMMUNICATION Persuasive Messages

SALES MESSAGES

Content

- Convince the reader that the product or service is worthy of consideration.
- Include sufficient evidence of usefulness to the purchaser.
- Reveal price (in the message or an enclosure).
- Make the central selling point apparent.
- Identify the desired specific action.
- Ensure that the message is ethical and abides by legal requirements.

Organization

- Use an inductive sequence of ideas.
- Ensure that the first sentence is a good attention-getter.
- Introduce the central selling point in the first few sentences, and reinforce it throughout the message.
- Introduce price only after presenting receiver benefits.
- Associate price (what the receiver gives) directly with reward (what the receiver gets).
- End with a final paragraph that makes action easy and includes (a) the specific action desired, (b) the receiver's reward for taking action, and (c) incentive for quick action.

(continues)

WWW.CENGAGEBRAIN.COM

CHECK YOUR COMMUNICATION Persuasive Messages *(continued)*

Style

- Use objective language.
- Ensure that active verbs and concrete nouns predominate.
- Keep sentences relatively short but varied in length and structure.
- Place significant words in emphatic positions.
- Make ideas cohere by avoiding abrupt changes in thought.
- Frequently call the central selling point to receiver's attention through repeated reference.
- Use original expression (sentences that are not copied directly from templates or sample documents). Omit clichés.
- Achieve unity by including in the final paragraph a key word or idea (central selling point) that was introduced in the first paragraph.

Mechanics

- Ensure that keyboarding, spelling, grammar, and punctuation are perfect.

Format

- Use correct document format.
- Include standard document parts in their appropriate positions.
- Include special parts if necessary (subject line, enclosure, copy, etc.).

PERSUASIVE REQUESTS

Content

- Convince the receiver that the idea is valid and that the proposal has merit.
- Point out ways in which the receiver will benefit.
- Incorporate the primary appeal (central selling feature).

- Identify the specific action desired.

Organization

- Use an inductive sequence of ideas.
- Use a first sentence that gets attention and reveals the message's subject.
- Introduce the major appeal in first few sentences and reinforce it throughout the message.
- Point out receiver benefits.
- Associate desired action with the receiver's reward for taking action.
- Include a final paragraph that makes reference to the specific action desired and the primary appeal. Emphasize easy, quick action.

Style

- Use objective and positive language.
- Ensure that active verbs and concrete nouns predominate.
- Keep sentences relatively short, but vary them in length and structure.
- Place significant words in emphatic positions.
- Make ideas cohere by ensuring that changes in thought are not abrupt.
- Call the primary appeal to the receiver's attention frequently through repeated reference.
- Use original expression (sentences that are not copied directly from templates or model documents). Omit clichés.
- Achieve unity by including the primary appeal in the final paragraph.

Mechanics

- Ensure that keyboarding, spelling, grammar, and punctuation are perfect.

GRAMMAR QUIZ Apostrophes

Correct the possessives.

1. The new hires confidence was crushed by the managers harsh tone.
2. This companies mission statement has been revised since it's recent merger.
3. Employees who are retained may be asked to accept a reduction of one weeks pay.
4. Vendors' have submitted sealed bids for the construction contract that will be opened in two week's.
5. Younger workers must appreciate older employees extensive company knowledge.

GRAMMAR QUIZ SOLUTIONS

1. hire's; manager's
2. company's; its
3. week's
4. Vendors; weeks
5. employees'

9-1 Identify the characteristics of a report and the various classifications of business reports.
The basis of a report is a problem that must be solved through data collection and analysis. Reports are usually requested by a higher authority, are logically organized and highly objective, and are prepared for a limited audience. Reports can be classified as formal or informal, short or long, informational or analytical, vertical or lateral, internal or external, or a proposal.

formal report a carefully structured report that is logically organized and objective, contains a lot of detail, and is written in a style that tends to eliminate such elements as personal pronouns

informal report usually a short message written in natural or personal language

informational report a report that carries objective information from one area of an organization to another

analytical report a report that presents suggested solutions to problems

vertical report a report that can be upward- or downward-directed

lateral report a report that travels between units on the same organizational level

internal report a report that travels within an organization, such as a production or sales report

external report a report prepared for distribution outside an organization

periodic report a report that is issued on regularly scheduled dates

functional report a report that serves a specified purpose within a company

proposal a written description of how one organization can meet the needs of another

9-2 Apply steps in the problem-solving process and methods for solving a problem.
The four steps in the problem-solving process must be followed to arrive at a sound conclusion. The four steps are as follows: (1) Recognize and define the problem; (2) select an appropriate secondary and/or primary method for solving the problem; (3) collect and organize data, using appropriate methods; and (4) interpret the data to arrive at an answer. Research methods in report preparation involve locating information from appropriate secondary sources to identify research that has already been done on the topic and then collecting the primary data needed to solve the problem. Primary data collection may include observational, experimental, or survey research processes.

problem statement the particular problem that is to be solved by the research

statement of purpose the goal of the study; includes the aims or objectives the researcher hopes to accomplish

hypothesis a statement to be proved or disproved through research

procedures (or methodology) the steps a writer takes in preparing a report; often recorded as a part of the written report

longitudinal studies reports that study the same factors in different time frames

9-3 Use appropriate printed, electronic, and primary sources of information.
Location of secondary sources of information involves appropriate use of printed indexes and application of electronic search techniques that can lead the researcher to books, periodicals, and other documents needed for topic exploration. Methods for collecting survey data include mailed questionnaires, email polling, telephone surveys, personal interviews, and participant observation. Collecting data through a survey involves selecting a sample that is representative of the entire population. Effective survey design and unbiased data collection are essential to ensuring the validity and reliability of the data reported.

secondary research provides information that has already been reported by others

primary research data collected for the first time, usually for a specific purpose

observational studies studies in which the researcher observes and statistically analyzes certain phenomena in order to assist in establishing new principles or discoveries

experimental research the study of two samples that have exactly the same components before a variable is added to one of the samples

normative survey research research to determine the status of something at a specific time

sampling a survey technique that eliminates the need for questioning 100% of the population

validity the degree to which the data measure what the researcher intends to measure

reliability the level of consistency or stability over time or over independent samples

9-4 Demonstrate appropriate methods of collecting, organizing, and referencing information.
Information from published sources should be carefully read and interpreted. To avoid plagiarism, both direct quotes and paraphrases must be referenced using an acceptable method. Surveys are a common method for collecting data. Instruments should be carefully designed to solicit needed information, avoid ambiguity and confusion, and reflect accurate information. The researcher must work to avoid various data-gathering pitfalls including using small or unrepresentative samples, using biased sources or irrelevant information, and excluding relevant information.

plagiarism the presentation of someone else's ideas or words as your own

CHAPTER REVIEW

CHAPTER 9 LEARNING OBJECTIVES / KEY TERMS

9-5 **Explain techniques for the logical analysis and interpretation of data.** Arriving at an answer in the research process involves proper analysis using appropriate statistical techniques. To maintain the integrity of the research, the interpretation of data should be objective and unbiased. Carefully presented findings give way to sound conclusions that lead to logical recommendations.

CHECK YOUR COMMUNICATION Report Process and Research Methods

Problem Formation

- Decide what type of report is required.

- Formulate the problem statement.

- Determine boundaries for the research.

- Define specialized terms used in the report.

Research Methodology

- Select appropriate methods of solution, including relevant secondary and primary resources.

- Gather appropriate published and electronic sources.

- Plan appropriate primary research, using observational, experimental, or normative techniques.

Data Collection and Organization

- Document all quoted and paraphrased information using the appropriate referencing method.

- Develop effective data collection instruments; pilot test and refine prior to conducting research.

- Avoid data-collection errors that can minimize your research effort.

Data Interpretation

- Analyze data accurately and ethically.

- Interpret data to reach logical conclusions.

- Make recommendations that are well supported by the data presented.

- Avoid overgeneralizing results of research conducted in one setting to another group or setting.

GRAMMAR QUIZ Hyphens

In each of the sentences below, add necessary hyphens and delete unnecessary hyphens. Write "correct" if you find no errors.

1. The Web based application was unavailable because of a denial of service attack.

2. State of the art computers provide quick access to timely business information.

3. A large portion of holiday orders are time sensitive.

4. A two thirds majority is needed to pass the 5% increase in employee wages.

5. Nearly one-half of the respondents were highly-educated professionals.

GRAMMAR QUIZ SOLUTIONS

1. Web-based; denial-of-service
2. State-of-the-art
3. Correct
4. two-thirds
5. one half; highly educated

10-1 Communicate quantitative information effectively. Graphics complement text by clarifying complex figures and helping readers visualize major points. Tabulating data and analyzing data using measures of central tendency aid in summarizing or classifying large volumes of data into manageable information you can interpret. You can then communicate this meaningful data using common language—fractions, ratios, and percentages—that the reader can easily understand.

common language reduces difficult figures to the common denominators of language and ideas

10-2 Apply principles of effectiveness and ethical responsibilities in the construction of graphic aids. A graphic aid should clarify, reinforce, or emphasize a particular idea and should contribute to the overall understanding of the idea under discussion. It should be uncluttered and easily understood and depict information honestly. Graphic aids used in spoken presentations should be large enough to be seen by the entire audience.

graphics all types of illustrations used in written and spoken reports

10-3 Select and design appropriate and meaningful graphics. The type of graphic used in a presentation should be chosen based on its ability to communicate the information most effectively. Tables present data in systematic rows and columns. Bar charts (simple, grouped, and stacked) compare quantities for a specific period. Line charts depict changes in quantities over time and illustrate trends. Pie charts, pictograms, and segmented and area charts show the proportion of components to a whole. Gantt charts track progress toward completing a series of events over time. Maps help readers visualize geographic relationships. Flowcharts visually depict step-by-step procedures for completing a task; organization charts show the organizational structure of a company. Floor plans, photographs, cartoons, blueprints, and lists also enhance reports.

table a graphic that presents data in columns and rows, which aid in clarifying large quantities of data in a small space

bar chart a graphic used to compare quantities

grouped bar chart a graphic used for comparing more than one quantity (set of data) at each point along the y-axis (vertical) or x-axis (horizontal); also called a *clustered bar chart*

segmented bar chart a graphic used to show how different facts (components) contribute to a total; also called a *subdivided*, *stacked bar*, or *100% bar chart*

pictogram a graphic that uses pictures or symbols to illustrate objects, concepts, or numerical relationships

Gantt chart a specific type of bar chart that is useful for tracking progress toward completing a series of events over time

line chart a graphic that depicts changes in quantitative data over time and illustrates trends

area chart a graphic that shows how different factors contribute to a total; also referred to as a *cumulative line chart* or *surface chart*

pie chart a graphic that shows how the parts of a whole are distributed

map a graphic that shows geographic relationships

flowchart a step-by-step diagram of a procedure, or a graphic depiction of a system or organization

10-4 Integrate graphics within documents. A graphic should always be introduced in text before it is presented. The graphic will then reinforce your conclusions and discourage readers from drawing their own conclusions before encountering your ideas. An effective introduction for a graphic tells something meaningful about what is depicted in the graphic and refers the reader to a specific figure number. The graphic should be placed immediately after its introduction if possible or positioned at the top of the next page after filling the previous page with text that ideally would have followed the graphic. Analysis or interpretation follows the graphic, avoiding a mere repetition of what the graphic clearly shows.

CHECK YOUR COMMUNICATION Types of Graphic Aids

Tables
- Number tables and all other graphics consecutively throughout the report.
- Give each table a title that is complete enough to clarify what is included without forcing the reader to review the table.
- Label columns of data clearly enough to identify the items.
- Indent the second line of a label for the rows (horizontal items) two or three spaces.
- Place a superscript symbol beside an entry that requires additional explanation, and include the explanatory note beneath the visual.
- Document the source of the data presented in a visual by adding a source note beneath the visual.

(continues)

CHECK YOUR COMMUNICATION Types of Graphic Aids *(continued)*

Bar Charts

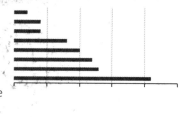

- Begin the quantitative axis at zero, divide the bars into equal increments, and use bars of equal width.
- Position chronologically or in some other logical order.
- Use variations in color to distinguish among the bars when the bars represent different data.
- Avoid using 3D-type formatting that makes values more difficult to distinguish.
- Include enough information in the scale labels and bar labels for clear understanding.

Line Charts

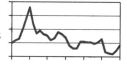

- Use the vertical axis for amount and the horizontal axis for time.
- Begin the vertical axis at zero.
- Divide the vertical and horizontal scales into equal increments.

Pie Charts

- Position the largest slice or the slice to be emphasized at the 12 o'clock position.
- Label each slice and include information about the quantitative size (percentage, dollars, acres, square feet, etc.) of each slice.
- Draw attention to one or more slices for desired emphasis.
- Avoid using 3D-type formatting that makes values more difficult to distinguish.

Maps

- Use to show geographic information visually.

Flowcharts

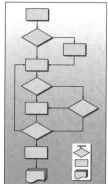

- Use to show step-by-step procedures or graphic depiction of a system or organization.

GRAMMAR QUIZ Quotation Marks and Italics

Add necessary quotation marks and italics.

1. Cynthia Cooper's Extraordinary Circumstances is required reading in some forensic accounting classes.

2. The article How to Persuade People to Say Yes appeared in the May 2014 issue of Training Journal.

3. The consultant's accomplishments are summarized on her opening blog page. [Indicate that a word other than accomplishments may be a more appropriate word.]

4. Connie said I want to participate in a volunteer program that serves such a worthy cause. [direct quotation]

5. The term flame is online jargon for a heated, sarcastic, sometimes abusive message or posting to a discussion group.

GRAMMAR QUIZ SOLUTIONS

1. Cynthia Cooper's *Extraordinary Circumstances* is required reading in some forensic accounting classes. [Italicizes a book title.]

2. The article "How to Persuade People to Say Yes" appeared in the May 2014 issue of *Training Journal*. [Encloses the name of an article in quotation marks and italicizes the title of a journal.]

3. The consultant's "accomplishments" are summarized on her opening blog page. [Uses quotation marks to introduce doubt about whether "accomplishments" is the right label. His undertakings may have been of little significance.]

4. Connie said, "I want to participate in a volunteer program that serves such a worthy cause." [Uses quotation marks in a direct quotation.]

5. The *term flame* is online jargon for "a heated, sarcastic, sometimes abusive message or posting to a discussion group." [Italicizes a word used as a term and encloses its definition in quotation marks.]

CHAPTER 11 LEARNING OBJECTIVES / KEY TERMS

11-1 **Identify the parts of a formal report and the contribution each part makes to the report's overall effectiveness.** As reports increase in length from one page to several pages, they also grow in formality with the addition of introductory and addenda items. As a result, reports at the formal end of the continuum tend to be repetitious. These report parts and their purposes are summarized in Figure 11-1.

preliminary parts report sections included to add formality to a report, emphasize report content, and aid the reader in locating information in the report quickly and understanding the report more easily

executive summary short summary of the essential elements in an entire report; also called an *abstract*, *overview*, or *précis*

analytical report a type of report designed to solve a specific problem or answer research questions

addenda may include all materials used in the research but not appropriate to be included in the report itself

11-2 **Organize report findings.** Organizing the content of a report involves seeing the report problem in its entirety and then breaking it into its parts. After the research or field work has been completed, the writer may begin with any of the report parts and then complete the rough draft by putting the parts in logical order. Writers determine the format and style best able to communicate the intended message.

justification report a report that outlines comparative information clearly to the reader; used commonly when comparing items for purchase

11-3 **Prepare effective formal reports using an acceptable format and writing style.** In preparing effective long reports, outlining assists the writer with logical sequencing. Appropriate headings lead the reader from one division to another. The writing style should present the findings and data interpretation clearly and fairly, convincing the reader to accept the writer's point of view, but in an unemotional manner. Opinions should be clearly identified as such.

11-4 **Prepare effective short reports in memorandum, email, and letter formats.** Short reports are typically written in a personal writing style and in memorandum, email, or letter format. Form reports provide accuracy, save time, and simplify tabulation of data when a need exists for numerous, repetitive reports.

short reports reports that include only the minimum supporting materials to achieve effective communication

form reports reports that meet the demand for numerous, repetitive reports; include college registration forms, applications for credit, airline tickets, and bank checks

11-5 **Prepare effective proposals for a variety of purposes.** Proposals can be written for both internal and external audiences. Proposals call for thorough organization and require writing methods that will be not only informative but convincing. Because they have discrete parts that can be prepared in any order and then assembled into whole reports, they are conducive to preparation by teams.

internal proposals proposals used by managers to justify or recommend purchases or changes in the company

external proposal a proposal written to generate business; one organization describes how it can meet the needs of another by, for example, providing a product or service

solicited proposals proposals generated when a potential buyer submits exact specifications or needs in a bid request

unsolicited proposal a proposal prepared by an individual or firm who sees a problem to be solved and proposes a solution

CHECK YOUR COMMUNICATION Formal Reports

Transmittal Letter or Memorandum

Use a letter-style transmittal in reports going outside the organization. For internal reports, use a memorandum transmittal.

- Transmit a warm greeting to the reader.
- Open with a "Here is the report you requested" tone.
- Establish the subject in the first sentence.

- Follow the opening with a brief summary of the study. Expand the discussion if a separate summary is not included in the report.
- Acknowledge the assistance of those who helped with the study.
- Close the message with a thank-you and a forward look.

(continues)

CHECK YOUR COMMUNICATION Formal Reports *(continued)*

Title Page
- Include the title of the report, succinctly worded.
- Provide full identification of the authority for the report (the person or organization for whom the report was prepared and the preparer(s) of the report).
- Provide the date of the completion of the report.
- Use an attractive layout.

Table of Contents
- Use *Table of Contents* or *Contents* as the title.
- Use indentation to indicate the heading degrees used in the report.
- List numerous figures separately as a preliminary item called *Table of Figures or Figures*. (Otherwise, figures should not be listed, because they are not separate sections of the outline but only supporting data within a section.)

Executive Summary
- Use a descriptive title, such as *Executive Summary, Synopsis*, or *Abstract*.
- Condense the major report sections.
- Use effective, generalized statements that avoid detail available in the report itself.

Report Text
- Avoid the personal *I* and *we* pronouns in formal writing. Minimize the use of the *writer, the investigator*, and *the author*.
- Use active construction to give emphasis to the *doer* of the action; use passive voice to give emphasis to the *results* of the action.
- Use proper tense.
- Avoid ambiguous pronoun references (they hinder clarity).
- Avoid expletive beginnings such as *There is* and *There are*.
- Use bulleted or enumerated lists for three or more items if listing will make reading easier.
- Incorporate transition sentences to ensure coherence.
- Use parallel construction in headings of equal degree in the same report section.

- Number consecutively figures (tables, graphics, and other illustrations) used in the report.
- Give each graph or table a descriptive title.
- Question each statement for its contribution to the solution of the problem.
- Use units of production, percentages, or ratios to express large numbers.
- Use objective reporting style that avoids emotional terms, assumptions and opinions, and unwarranted judgments and inferences.
- State the conclusions carefully and clearly, and be sure they grow out of the findings.

Citations
- Include a citation (in-text reference, footnote, or endnote) for material quoted or paraphrased from another source.
- Adhere to an acceptable, authoritative style or company policy.
- Present consistent citations, including adequate information for readers to locate the source in the reference list.

References
- Include an entry for every reference cited in the report.
- Adhere to an acceptable, authoritative style or company policy.
- When in doubt, include more information than might be necessary.
- Include separate sections (e.g., books, articles, and nonprint sources) if the references section is lengthy and your referencing style allows it.

Appendix
- Include cover messages and all other items that provide information but are not important enough to be included in the report body.
- Subdivide categories of information beginning with Appendix A, Appendix B, and so on.
- Identify each item with a title.

GRAMMAR QUIZ Dashes, Parentheses, and Periods

In each of the following sentences, add necessary dashes, parentheses, or periods.

1. Additional consultants, programmers and analysts, were hired to complete the computer conversion. [Emphasize the appositive.]
2. The dividend will be raised to 15 cents a share approved by the Board of Directors on December 1, 2015. [Deemphasize the approval.]
3. Would you link this YouTube video to my slide show?

GRAMMAR QUIZ SOLUTIONS

1. Additional consultants—programmers and analysts—were hired to complete the computer conversion.
2. The dividend will be raised to 15 cents a share (approved by the Board of Directors on December 1, 2015).
3. Would you link this YouTube video to my slide show. [Uses a period to follow courteous request that requires no verbal response.]

12-1 **Plan a business presentation that accomplishes the speaker's goals and meets the audience's needs.** Determine what you want to accomplish in your presentation, and direct your presentation to the specific needs and interests of the audience. Identify the general characteristics (age, gender, experience, etc.), size, and receptiveness of the audience.

oral briefings informal presentations prepared and presented with little time for planning and developing

12-2 **Organize and develop the three parts of an effective presentation.** An effective presentation has an introduction, body, and closing. The introduction should capture the audience's attention, involve the audience and the speaker, present the purpose statement, and preview major points. The body is limited to a few major points that are supported and clarified with relevant statistics, anecdotes, quotes from prominent people, appropriate humor, presentation visuals, and so forth. The closing should be a memorable idea that supports and strengthens the purpose statement.

12-3 **Select, design, and use presentation visuals effectively.** Using visual aids reduces the time required to present a concept and increases audience retention. Available aids include handouts, models and physical objects, whiteboards, flip charts, overhead transparencies, electronic presentations, videotapes, and audiotapes. Each type provides specific advantages and should be selected carefully. An effective visual presents major ideas in a simple design large enough for the audience to read. Permissions should be obtained for the use of copyrighted multimedia content.

12-4 **Deliver speeches with increasing confidence.** Business speakers use the impromptu and extemporaneous speech methods more frequently than the memorized or scripted methods. Professional vocal qualities include a medium or low voice pitch, adequate volume, varied tone and rate, and the absence of distracting verbal fillers. Articulate speakers enunciate words precisely and ensure proper pronunciation. Preparation, professional demeanor, and staying in tune with the audience are keys to a successful speech.

memorized presentation a presentation in which a speaker writes out a speech, commits it to memory, and recites it verbatim

manuscript presentation a presentation in which a speaker writes out the entire speech and reads it to the audience; also called a *scripted presentation*

impromptu presentation a presentation in which a speaker is called on without prior notice

extemporaneous presentation a presentation in which a speaker plans, prepares, and rehearses but does not write everything down; brief notes prompt the speaker, but the exact words are chosen spontaneously as the speaker interacts with the audience and identifies its specific needs

phonation the production and variation of a speaker's vocal tone

articulation smooth, fluent, and pleasant speech

pronunciation using principles of phonetics to create accurate sounds, rhythm, stress, and intonation

12-5 **Discuss strategies for presenting in alternate delivery situations such as culturally diverse audiences, teams, and distance presentations.** When communicating with other cultures, use simple, clear speech. Consider differences in presentation approach, nonverbal communication, and social protocol that may require flexibility and adjustments to your presentation style. Effective team presentations result from the selection of an appropriate leader and team members with complementary strengths and styles who plan ahead and rehearse thoroughly. When delivering a videoconference or live Web presentation, determine whether a distance delivery method is appropriate for the presentation, attempt to establish rapport with the participants prior to the distance presentation, become proficient in delivering and using distance technology, and develop high-quality graphics appropriate for the distance format.

Internet conferencing a method of real-time conferencing that allows a company to conduct a presentation in real time over the Internet simultaneously with a conference telephone call; also called *webcasting*

CHECK YOUR COMMUNICATION Presentation Skills

Planning and Organizing a Presentation

- **Identify your purpose.** Know what you hope to accomplish and choose supporting content.
- **Analyze your audience.** Identify common characteristics, number in audience, seating arrangements, and time of day.
- **Develop an effective opening.** Ensure that the opening captures attention, initiates rapport with the audience, presents the purpose, and previews the main points.

- **Develop the body.** Select a few major and supporting points: statistics, anecdotes, quotes, and appropriate humor. Use simple, nontechnical language and understandable sentences.
- **Develop an effective closing.** Call for the audience to accept your idea or provide a strong conclusion with recommendations.

Selecting an Appropriate Presentation Visual

- Select a presentation visual appropriate for the audience and topic.

(continues)

CHECK YOUR COMMUNICATION Presentation Skills (continued)

- Use whiteboards and flip charts for small audiences in an informal setting and when no special equipment is available. Prepare flip charts in advance when possible.
- Use overhead transparencies for small, informal audiences.
- Use slides for presentations requiring photography. Sequence the slides appropriately and show them in a darkened room.
- Use electronic presentations for large audiences and to enliven the topic with multimedia.
- Use models and physical objects to convey the idea presented.

Designing and Using Presentation Visuals

- Limit the number of visual aids to avoid overload.
- Clear all copyrights for multimedia content.
- Write descriptive titles and parallel bulleted lists.
- Create a standard design for each visual following these slide design principles:
  - Include only the major idea to be remembered.
  - Make the design concise, simple, and readable.
  - Avoid graphics that distort facts.
  - Proofread the visual carefully to eliminate errors.
- Paraphrase rather than read, and step to one side for audience viewing.

DELIVERING A PRESENTATION

Before the Presentation

- Prepare thoroughly to minimize natural nervousness.
- Prepare easy-to-read note cards or pages to prompt recall.
- Rehearse to identify organizational flaws or verbal potholes.
- Use a lectern for steadiness, but not to hide behind.
- Request a proper, impressive introduction.
- Dress appropriately to convey a professional image.
- Arrive early to check out the room and last-minute details.

During the Presentation

- Use clear, articulate speech and proper pronunciation.
- Use vocal variety, and adjust volume and rate to emphasize ideas.
- Avoid verbal fillers and annoying speech habits.
- Maintain steady eye contact with various audience members.
- Smile genuinely and use gestures naturally to communicate confidence and warmth.
- Watch your audience for important feedback, and adjust your presentation accordingly.
- Handle questions from the audience politely.
- Keep within the time limit.

After the Presentation

- Be prepared for a question-and-answer period.
- Distribute handouts at the appropriate time.

Adapting to a Culturally Diverse Audience

- Use simple English and short sentences.
- Use a straightforward, direct approach.
- Adjust to differences in nonverbal communication and social protocol.

Delivering a Team Presentation

- Select a leader to lead in developing a cohesive presentation strategy and team members with complementary strengths and styles.
- Plan the presentation as a team.
- Rehearse thoroughly for cohesion and uniformity.

Delivering a Distance Presentation

- Determine whether a distance delivery method is appropriate for the presentation.
- Establish rapport with participants prior to the presentation.
- Become proficient in using distance technology.
- Develop high-quality, appropriate graphics.

GRAMMAR QUIZ Number Usage

Correct the number usage in the following sentences taken from a letter or a report.

1. The question was answered by sixty-one percent of the respondents.
2. The meeting is scheduled for 10:00 a.m. on February 3rd.
3. These 3 figures appeared on the expense account: $21.95, $30.00, and $35.14.
4. The purchasing manager ordered 50 4-GB flash drives.
5. 21 members voted in favor of the $2,000,000 proposal.
6. Approximately 100 respondents requested a copy of the results.
7. Mix two quarts of white with 13 quarts of brown.
8. Examine the cost projections on page eight.

GRAMMAR QUIZ SOLUTIONS

1. The question was answered by 61% of the respondents.
2. The meeting is scheduled for 10 a.m. on February 3.
3. These three figures appeared on the expense account: $21.95, $30, and $35.14.
4. The purchasing manager ordered fifty 4-GB flash drives.
5. Twenty-one members voted in favor of the $2 million proposal.
6. Approximately 100 respondents requested a copy of the results. [Approximations above nine that can be expressed in one or two words may be written in either figures or words, but figures are more emphatic.]
7. Mix 2 quarts of white with 13 quarts of brown.
8. Examine the cost projections on page 8.

13-1 **Prepare for employment by considering relevant information about yourself as it relates to job requirements.** As a job candidate, you should complete systematic self-, career-, and job analyses. Gather information to make wise career decisions, asking questions about yourself, about a possible career, and about a specific job in your chosen field. Interview people already working. Recording and analyzing this information will aid in selecting a satisfying career and preparing an effective résumé and application message.

résumé a vital communication tool that provides a basis for judgment about a person's capabilities on the job

13-2 **Identify career opportunities using traditional and electronic methods.** A job candidate can use traditional and electronic methods for the employment search. Names and addresses of possible employers may be obtained from networks, career services centers at schools, employers' offices, employment agencies and contractors, online databases and printed sources, professional organizations, electronic job fairs, news groups, and chat sessions.

targeted résumé a résumé that reflects the requirements of a specific job listing

chronological résumé the traditional organizational format for résumés, with headings that spotlight an applicant's education and experience

functional résumé the organizational format for résumés that highlights an applicant's transferable skills

chrono-functional résumé a résumé that combines features of chronological and functional résumés

13-3 **Prepare an organized, persuasive résumé that is adapted for print and electronic postings.** A résumé typically includes identification, an objective, a career summary, qualifications, personal information, and references. The most effective résumé for a particular candidate could be a chronological, functional, or chrono-functional résumé.

- Chronological résumés have headings such as "Education" and "Experience" and list experiences in reverse chronological order; they are appropriate for applicants who have the apparent qualifications for the job.
- Functional résumés show applicant qualifications as headings; this format is especially effective for applicants who lack the appropriate education and experience.

- The chrono-functional résumé lists education and experience as headings and uses functional headings that emphasize qualifications.

Effective print (designed) résumés concisely highlight key qualifications and are formatted for quick, easy reading. Electronic résumé posting varies considerably, with popular options including a job bank posting, a website entry, a link to a personal web page, an email attachment, and an inline résumé within the body of an email message. Scannable résumés are designed so that information can be scanned and processed by an applicant-tracking system. An effective keyword section summarizes qualifications and helps ensure that the résumé is identified during a search for matching requirements.

beamer a quick version of a résumé designed in a format suitable for broadcasting on smartphones; also called a *beamable résumé*

inline résumé a résumé included in the body of an email message

text résumé a plain text (unformatted) version of a résumé

electronic applicant-tracking systems systems that increase the efficiency of processing résumés by storing scanned résumés in an electronic database where they can be sorted by keywords, with a resulting ranking of applicants

scannable résumé a résumé formatted to ensure a scanner can accurately read and convert it into a digital format

13-4 **Use employment tools other than the résumé that can enhance employability.** The résumé may be supplemented with other employment tools that include a professional portfolio and a video recording of the applicant. Content for a portfolio or video should be carefully chosen to reflect the skills necessary for effective job performance and should complement information in the résumé.

professional portfolio a portfolio presented in digital format and distributed to prospective employers via a website, CD/DVD, or other media; also called an *electronic portfolio* or *e-portfolio*

multimedia résumé a résumé created with presentation software, such as Camtasia Studio, and sent to prospective employers on CD/DVD or posted on an applicant's personal website

video résumé a résumé created as a video for posting on sites such as YouTube

13-5 **Write an application message that effectively introduces an accompanying print (designed) or electronic résumé.** The purposes of the application message are to introduce the applicant and the résumé, create interest in the information given on the résumé, and assist an employer in seeing ways in which the applicant's services would be desirable. As such, it is a persuasive message—beginning with an attention-getter, including a central appeal and convincing evidence, and closing with an indirect reference to the enclosed résumé and desired action (invitation to an interview).

application message a message placed on top of the résumé so it can be read first by the employer; also called a *cover message*

unsolicited application message an unrequested message sent to many prospective employers that contains the same basic message

CHECK YOUR COMMUNICATION Résumés and Application Messages

PRINT (DESIGNED) RÉSUMÉ

Content

- Include relevant qualifications compatible with the job requirements generated from analyses of self, career, and the job.
- Present qualifications truthfully and honestly.

Organization

- Choose an organizational pattern that highlights key qualifications: chronological, functional, or chrono-functional.
- Arrange headings in the appropriate sequence.
- Place significant ideas in an emphatic position.
- List experiences consistently, either in time sequence or in order of importance.

Style

- Omit personal pronouns.
- Use action verbs.
- Use past tense for previous jobs and present tense for present job.
- Place significant words in emphatic positions.

Mechanics

- Ensure there are no keying, grammar, spelling, or punctuation errors.
- Balance elements on the page.
- Use ample margins even if a second page is required.
- Include a page number on all pages except the first, and place "continued" at the bottom of the first page to indicate a multiple-page document.
- Position and format headings consistently throughout.
- Use an outline format or a bulleted list to emphasize multiple points.

ELECTRONIC RÉSUMÉS

Content

- Adapt general guidelines for résumé preparation to fit the particular requirements of the submission.
- Place "Keyword Summary" on the first screen (first 24 lines of text), listing qualifications that match.
- Include a link or reference to your electronic portfolio.
- For scannable résumés, position your name as the first readable item on each page.

PROFESSIONAL PORTFOLIO

Content

- Include items that showcase abilities and accomplishments.

Mechanics

- Choose an appropriate traditional or electronic format.
- For electronic formats, include links to your print résumé, plain text version of résumé, email address, and appropriate supplementary documents.

APPLICATION MESSAGE

Content

- Identify the message as an application for a certain job.
- Emphasize significant qualifications and exclude non-essential ideas.
- Make reference to the enclosed or attached résumé.
- End with an action closing that is neither apologetic nor pushy.

Mechanics

- Ensure that there are no keying, grammar, spelling, or punctuation errors.
- Include your address above the date or format as a letterhead because the letter is presented on plain paper that matches the résumé.
- Keep the first and last paragraphs relatively short; hold others to six or seven lines.

GRAMMAR QUIZ Capitalization

Copy each of the following sentences, making essential changes in capitalization.

1. The first question Professor Burney asked me during Interviewing 101 was "Why do you want to work for us?"
2. The remodeling will give the store a more sophisticated feel, according to the public relations director.
3. As the summer season arrives, gas prices are expected to rise.
4. We recently purchased Digital Juice, an excellent source of copyright-free animated images.
5. Thomas Frieden, director of the Centers for Disease Control, is the agency's key communicator.

GRAMMAR QUIZ SOLUTIONS

1. The first question Professor Burney asked me during Interviewing 101 was "Why do you want to work for us?"
2. The remodeling will give the store a more sophisticated feel, according to the public relations director.
3. As the summer season arrives, gas prices are expected to rise.
4. We recently purchased Digital Juice, an excellent source of copyright-free animated images.
5. Thomas Frieden, director of the Centers for Disease Control, is the agency's key communicator.

CHAPTER 14 LEARNING OBJECTIVES / KEY TERMS

14-1 **Explain the nature of structured, unstructured, stress, group, and virtual interviews.** Interviewers and interviewees can be considered as buyers and sellers: Interviewers want to know whether job candidates can meet the needs of their firms before making a "purchase"; interviewees want to sell themselves based on sound knowledge, good work skills, and desirable personal traits. Structured interviews follow a preset, specific format; unstructured interviews follow no standard format but explore for information. Computer-assisted interviews provide standard, reliable information on applicants during the preliminary interview stages. Stress interviews are designed to reveal how the candidate behaves in high-anxiety situations. Group interviews involve various personnel within the organization in the candidate interview process.

structured interview an interview format generally used in the screening process, in which the interviewer follows a predetermined agenda, including a checklist of items or a series of questions and statements designed to elicit the necessary information or interviewee reaction

unstructured interview a freewheeling exchange that may shift from one subject to another, depending on the interests of the participants

stress interview an interview format designed to place the interviewee in an anxiety-producing situation so that an evaluation of the interviewee's performance under stress may be made

virtual interview interview conducted using videoconferencing technology

14-2 **Explain the steps in the interview process.** Successful job candidates plan appropriately for the interview so that they will know basic information about the company, arrive on time dressed appropriately for the interview, and present a polished first impression following appropriate protocol. During the interview, the candidate presents his or her qualifications favorably and obtains information about the company to aid in deciding whether to accept a possible job offer.

14-3 **Prepare effective answers to questions often asked in job interviews, including illegal interview questions.** The successful job candidate effectively discusses key qualifications and skillfully asks questions that show initiative and genuine interest in the company. The candidate recognizes issues that fall outside the bounds of legal questioning. Refusing to answer an illegal question could be detrimental to your chances to secure a job, but answering the question may compromise your ethical values. An effective technique is to answer the legitimate concern behind the illegal question rather than to give a direct answer.

14-4 **Compose effective messages related to employment (including application, follow-up, thank-you, job-acceptance, job-refusal, resignation, and recommendation request messages).** The job applicant should complete application forms accurately, neatly, and completely, and should only send a follow-up message after a few weeks of no response to an application. An applicant should send a prompt thank-you message following an interview as a professional courtesy. If a job offer is extended, an applicant should write a deductive job-acceptance message that includes the acceptance, details, and a closing that confirms the date the employee will begin work. If the applicant does not accept the job, he or she should write an inductive job-refusal message that includes a buffer beginning, reasons that lead to the refusal, a tactful decline to the offer, and a goodwill closing. Resignation notices should confirm that termination plans are definite and emphasizes positive aspects of the job. Requests for recommendations should include specific information about the job requirements and the applicant's qualifications.

CHECK YOUR COMMUNICATION Interviewing for a Job and Preparing Employment Messages

INTERVIEWS
Planning Stage
- Learn as much as you can about the job requirements, range of salary and benefits, and the interviewer.
- Research the company with whom you are interviewing (e.g., its products/services, financial condition, and growth potential).
- Identify the specific qualifications for the job and other pertinent information about the company.
- Plan your appearance: arrive clean, well groomed, and appropriately dressed.
- Arrive early with appropriate materials to communicate promptness and organization.
- Try to identify the type of interview you will have (structured, unstructured, virtual, stress, or group).

Opening Formalities
- Greet the interviewer by name with a smile, direct eye contact, and a firm handshake.
- Wait for the interviewer to ask you to be seated.
- Sit erect and lean forward slightly to convey interest.
- Avoid distractions such as looking at your cellphone.

Body of the Interview
- Adapt your responses to the type of interview situation.
- Explain how your qualifications relate to the job requirements using multiple specific examples.
- Identify illegal interview questions; address the concern behind an illegal question or tactfully avoid answering the question.
- Ask pertinent questions that communicate intelligence and genuine interest in the company. Introduce questions throughout the interview where appropriate.
- Allow the interviewer to initiate a discussion of salary and benefits. Be prepared to provide a general salary range for applicants with your qualifications.

(continues)

CHECK YOUR COMMUNICATION Interviewing for a Job and Preparing Employment Messages *(continued)*

Closing the Interview

- Watch for cues the interview is ending; rise, accept the interviewer's handshake, and communicate enthusiasm.
- Express appreciation for the interview and say you are eager to hear from the company.

EMPLOYMENT MESSAGES

Application Forms

- Read the entire form before completing it and follow instructions precisely.
- Complete the form neatly and accurately.
- Respond to all questions; insert "N/A" for questions that do not apply.
- Retain a copy for your records.

Follow-Up Messages

- Remind the receiver that your application is on file and you are interested in the job.
- Present additional education or experience gained since previous correspondence; do not repeat information presented earlier.
- Close with a courteous request for an interview.

Thank-You Messages

- Express appreciation for the interview, and mention the specific job for which you have applied.
- Refer to a specific point discussed in the interview.
- Close with a reference to an expected call or document conveying the interviewer's decision.

Job-Acceptance Messages

- Begin by accepting the job offer; specify position.
- Provide necessary details.
- Close with a courteous ending that confirms the date employment begins.

Job-Refusal Messages

- Begin with a neutral, related idea that leads to the explanation for the refusal.
- Present the reasons that lead to a diplomatic statement of the refusal.
- Close positively, anticipating future association with the company.

Resignation Messages

- Begin with a positive statement about the job to cushion the bad news.
- Present the explanation, state the resignation, and provide any details.
- Close with an appreciative statement about experience with the company.

Recommendation Requests

- Begin with the request for the recommendation.
- Provide necessary details including reference to an enclosed résumé to ensure a targeted message.
- End with an appreciative statement for the reference's willingness to aid in the job search.
- Send a follow-up letter explaining delays and extended job searches and expressing appreciation for continued help.

Thank-You for a Recommendation

- Begin with expression of thanks for the recommendation.
- Convey sincere tone by avoiding exaggerated comments and providing specific examples of the value of the recommendation.
- End courteously, indicating future association with the reference.

GRAMMAR QUIZ

In each of the following sentences, select the correct word or phrase in parentheses.

1. What (affect, effect) will the change have on us?
2. The consultant plans to (advice, advise) the company to eliminate the fourth shift for at least three months.
3. The (amount, number) of complaints from customers declined with the addition of online chat.
4. The (cite, sight, site) of the new 24/7 fitness center is being debated.
5. I consider your remark a (compliment, complement); I agree that the granite countertops (compliment, complement) the deep, earthy tones in the room.
6. The three panelists were constantly interrupting (each other, one another).
7. Generally staple merchandise is placed (farther, further) from the cashier than impulse items.
8. Limit your discussion to five or (fewer, less) points.
9. The hurricane seems to be (losing, loosing) (its, it's) force, which is (different from, different than) predictions.
10. Customer perception is the (principal, principle) reason for the change.
11. (Their, There, They're) planning to complete (their, there, they're) strategic plan this week.
12. The (to, too, two) external auditors expect us (to, too, two) complete (to, too, two) many unnecessary reports.

GRAMMAR QUIZ SOLUTIONS

1. effect
2. advise
3. number
4. site
5. compliment, complement
6. one another
7. farther
8. fewer
9. losing, its, different from
10. principal
11. They're, their
12. two, to, too

Letter and Punctuation Styles

Decisions about page format impact the effectiveness of the message. Many companies have policies that dictate the page layout, letter and punctuation style, and other formatting issues. In the absence of company policy, make your format choices from among standard acceptable options illustrated on this style card.

• Page Layout, Punctuation, and Letter Style

The default margins set by word-processing software typically reflect the standard line length to increase the efficiency of producing business correspondence. Letters are balanced on the page with approximately equal margins on all sides of the letter, a placement often referred to as fitting the letter into a picture frame. Short letters (one or two paragraphs) are centered on the page; all other letters begin 1 inch from the top of the page. Side margins may be adjusted to improve the appearance of extremely short letters.

Current word-processing software has increased the default line spacing and space between paragraphs for easier on-screen reading. If you prefer the tighter, traditional spacing, simply adjust the line spacing to 1.0. Also, to conserve space but keep the fresh, open look, try reducing the line spacing in the letter address but retaining the wider line and paragraph spacing in the body of the letter. Another new default is a crisp, open font such as Calibri (replacing the common Times New Roman) designed for easy reading on monitors.

NEW DOCUMENT LOOK

July 24, 2017   **Tap Enter 2 times**

Mr. Abbie S. Jackson

1938 South Welch Avenue

Northwood, NE 65432-1938   **Tap Enter 1 time**

Dear Mr. Jackson,   **Tap Enter 1 time**

Your recent article, "Are Appraisers Talking to Themselves?" has drawn many favorable comments from local real estate appraisers.
          Tap Enter 1 time

The Southeast Chapter of the Society of Real Estate Appraisers …

TRADITIONAL SPACING

July 24, 2017   **Tap Enter 4 times (QS)**

Mr. Abbie S. Jackson

1938 South Welch Avenue

Northwood, NE 65432-1938   **Tap Enter 2 times (DS)**

Dear Mr. Jackson,   **Tap Enter 2 times (DS)**

Your recent article, "Are Appraisers Talking to Themselves?" has drawn many favorable comments from local real estate appraisers.
          Tap Enter 2 times (DS)

The Southeast Chapter of the Society of Real Estate Appraisers …

PUNCTUATION STYLES. Two punctuation styles are customarily used in business letters: mixed and open. Letters using mixed punctuation style have a colon after the salutation and a comma after the complimentary close. Letters using open punctuation style omit a colon after the salutation and a comma after the complimentary close. Mixed punctuation is the traditional style; however, efficiency-conscious companies are increasingly adopting the open style (and other similar format changes), which is easier to remember.

LETTER STYLES. Business letters are typically formatted in either block or modified block letter styles. The Sample Letters card has examples of these two styles:

- **Block.** Companies striving to reduce the cost of producing business documents adopt the easy-to-learn, efficient block format. All lines (including paragraphs) begin at the left margin.
- **Modified Block.** Modified block is the traditional letter format still used in many companies. The dateline, complimentary close, and signature block begin at the horizontal center of the page. Paragraphs may be indented ½ inch if the writer prefers or the company policy requires it. However, the indention creates unnecessary keystrokes that increase the production cost. All other lines begin at the left margin.

• Standard Letter Parts

Professional business letters include seven standard parts. Other parts are optional and may be included when necessary.

1

DATELINE. When the letterhead shows the company name, address, telephone and/or fax number, and logo, the letter begins with the **dateline.** Use the month-day-year format (September 2, 2016) for most documents prepared for US audiences. When preparing government documents or writing to an international audience, use the day-month-year format (2 September 2016). Company policy may require another format.

2

LETTER ADDRESS. The **letter address** includes a personal or professional title (e.g., Mr., Ms., or Dr.), the name of the person and company receiving the letter, and the complete address.

3

SALUTATION. The **salutation** is the greeting that opens a letter. To show courtesy for the receiver, include a personal or professional title (e.g. Mr., Ms., Dr., or Senator). Refer to the first line of the letter address to determine an appropriate salutation. "Dear Ms. Henson" is an appropriate salutation for a letter addressed to Ms. Donna Henson (first line of letter address). "Ladies and Gentlemen" is an appropriate salutation for a letter addressed to "Wyatt Enterprises," where the company name is keyed as the first line of the letter address.

4

BODY. The **body** contains the message of the letter. Because extra space separates the paragraphs, paragraph indention, which requires extra setup time, is not necessary. However, for organizations that require paragraph indention as company policy, the modified block format with indented paragraphs is the appropriate choice.

5

COMPLIMENTARY CLOSE. The **complimentary close** is a phrase used to close a letter in the same way that you say good-bye at the end of a conversation. To create goodwill, choose a complimentary close that reflects the formality of your relationship with the receiver. Typical examples are "Sincerely," "Regards," "Cordially," and "Respectfully." Using "yours" in the close has fallen out of popularity (as in "Sincerely yours" and "Very truly yours"). "Sincerely" is considered neutral and is thus appropriate in a majority of business situations. "Cordially" can be used for friendly messages, and "Respectfully" is appropriate when you are submitting information for the approval of another.

Letter and Punctuation Styles (continued)

6

SIGNATURE BLOCK. The *signature block* consists of the writer's name keyed below the complimentary close, allowing space for the writer to sign legibly. A woman may include a courtesy title to indicate her preference (e.g., Miss, Ms., or Mrs.), and a woman or man may use a title to distinguish a name used by both men and women (e.g., Shane, Leslie, or Stacy) or initials (E. M. Goodman). A business or professional title may be placed on the same line with the writer's name or directly below it as appropriate to achieve balance.

Title on the Same Line	Title on the Next Line
Ms. Leslie Tatum, President	Ms. E. M. Goodman
Perry Watson, Manager	Assistant Manager
Quality Control Division Head	Richard S. Templeton
	Human Resources Director

7

REFERENCE INITIALS. The *reference initials* consist of the keyboard operator's initials keyed in lowercase below the signature block. The reference initials and the signature block identify the persons involved in preparing a letter in the event of later questions. Reference initials are frequently omitted when a letter is keyed by the writer. However, company policy may require that the initials of all people involved in preparing a letter be placed in the reference initials line to identify accountability in the case of litigation. For example, the following reference initials show the indicated level of responsibility. The reference line might also include department identification or other information as required by the organization.

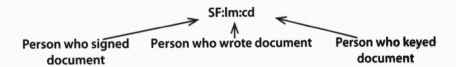

SF:lm:cd

Person who signed document   Person who wrote document   Person who keyed document

• Optional Letter Parts

DELIVERY AND ADDRESSEE NOTATIONS. A *delivery notation* provides a record of how a letter was sent. Examples include air mail, certified mail, Federal Express, registered mail, and fax transmission. Addressee notations such as "Confidential" or "Personal" give instructions on how a letter should be handled.

ATTENTION LINE. An *attention line* is used for directing correspondence to an individual or department within an organization while still officially addressing the letter to the organization. The attention line directs a letter to a specific person (Attention Ms. Laura Ritter), position within a company (Attention Human Resources Director), or department (Attention Purchasing Department). Current practice is to place the attention line in the letter address on the line directly below the company name and use the same format for the envelope address. The appropriate salutation in a letter with an attention line is "Ladies and Gentlemen."

REFERENCE LINE. A *reference line* (Re: Contract No. 983–9873) directs the receiver to source documents or to files.

SUBJECT LINE. A *subject line* tells the receiver what a letter is about and sets the stage for the receiver to understand the message. For added emphasis, use initial capitals or all capitals, or center the subject line if modified block style is used. Omit the word *subject* because its position above the body clearly identifies its function.

SECOND-PAGE HEADING. The second and succeeding pages of multiple-page letters and memorandums are keyed on plain paper of the same quality as the letterhead. Identify the second and succeeding pages with a ***second-page heading*** including the name of the addressee, page number, and the date. Place the heading 1 inch from the top edge of the paper, using either a vertical or horizontal format as illustrated. The horizontal format is more time consuming to format but looks attractive with the modified block format and may prevent the document from requiring additional pages.

Vertical Format

Communication Systems, Inc.

Page 2

January 19, 2017

Horizontal Format

Communication Systems, Inc.   2   January 19, 2017

COMPANY NAME IN SIGNATURE BLOCK. Some companies prefer to include the ***company name*** in the signature block, but often it is excluded because it appears in the letterhead. The company name is beneficial when the letter is prepared on plain paper or is more than one page (the second page of the letter is printed on plain paper). Including the company name also may be useful to the writer wishing to emphasize that the document is written on behalf of the company (e.g., a letter establishing an initial customer contact).

ENCLOSURE NOTATION. An ***enclosure notation*** indicates that additional items (brochure, price list, and résumé) are included in the same envelope. Key the plural form (Enclosures) if more than one item is enclosed. You may identify the number of enclosures (Enclosures: 3) or the specific item enclosed (Enclosure: Bid Proposal). Avoid abbreviations (Enc.) that may give the impression that your work is hurried and careless and may show disrespect for the recipient. Some companies use the word *Attachment* on memorandums when the accompanying items may be stapled or clipped and not placed in an envelope.

COPY NOTATION. A ***copy notation*** indicates that a courtesy copy of the document was sent to the person(s) listed. Include the person's personal or professional title and full name after keying "c" for *copy* or "cc" for *courtesy copy*. Key the copy notation below the enclosure notation, reference initials, or signature block (depending on the optional letter parts used).

POSTSCRIPT. A ***postscript***, appearing as the last item in a letter, is commonly used to emphasize information. A postscript in a sales letter, for example, is often used to restate the central selling point; for added emphasis, it may be handwritten or printed in a different color. Often handwritten postscripts of a personal nature are added to personalize the printed document. Postscripts should not be used to add information inadvertently omitted from the letter. Because its position clearly labels this paragraph as a postscript, do not begin with "PS."

COMPUTER FILE NOTATION. A ***computer file notation*** provides the path and file name of the letter. Some companies require this documentation on the file copy to facilitate revision. Place the computer file notation a single space below the last keyed line of the letter.

Sample Letters

Block Letter Style with Open Punctuation

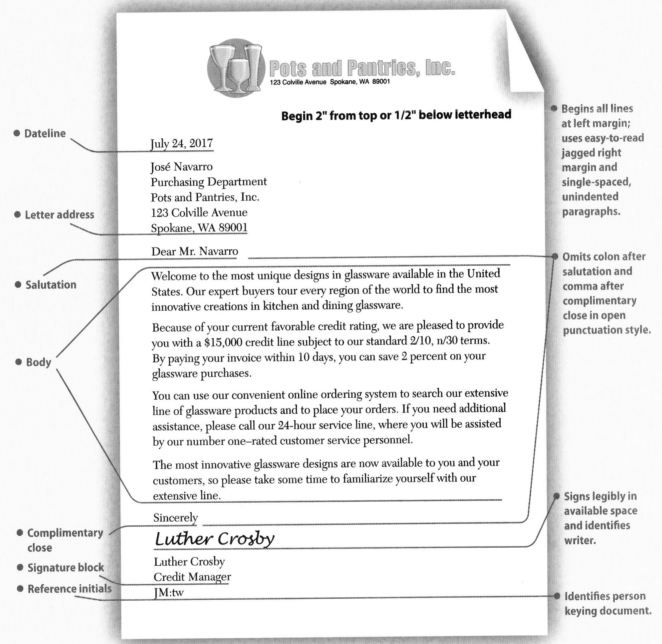

Pots and Pantries, Inc.
123 Colville Avenue Spokane, WA 89001

Begin 2" from top or 1/2" below letterhead

- **Dateline**

July 24, 2017

- **Letter address**

José Navarro
Purchasing Department
Pots and Pantries, Inc.
123 Colville Avenue
Spokane, WA 89001

- **Salutation**

Dear Mr. Navarro

- **Body**

Welcome to the most unique designs in glassware available in the United States. Our expert buyers tour every region of the world to find the most innovative creations in kitchen and dining glassware.

Because of your current favorable credit rating, we are pleased to provide you with a $15,000 credit line subject to our standard 2/10, n/30 terms. By paying your invoice within 10 days, you can save 2 percent on your glassware purchases.

You can use our convenient online ordering system to search our extensive line of glassware products and to place your orders. If you need additional assistance, please call our 24-hour service line, where you will be assisted by our number one–rated customer service personnel.

The most innovative glassware designs are now available to you and your customers, so please take some time to familiarize yourself with our extensive line.

Sincerely

Luther Crosby

- **Complimentary close**
- **Signature block**
- **Reference initials**

Luther Crosby
Credit Manager
JM:tw

- Begins all lines at left margin; uses easy-to-read jagged right margin and single-spaced, unindented paragraphs.

- Omits colon after salutation and comma after complimentary close in open punctuation style.

- Signs legibly in available space and identifies writer.

- Identifies person keying document.

The document illustrates contemporary spacing with 1.15 spaces between lines. If using traditional single spacing (1.0), tap Enter 2 times to double-space between paragraphs and 4 times to quadruple space after the dateline and the complimentary close.

Modified Block Letter Style with Mixed Punctuation

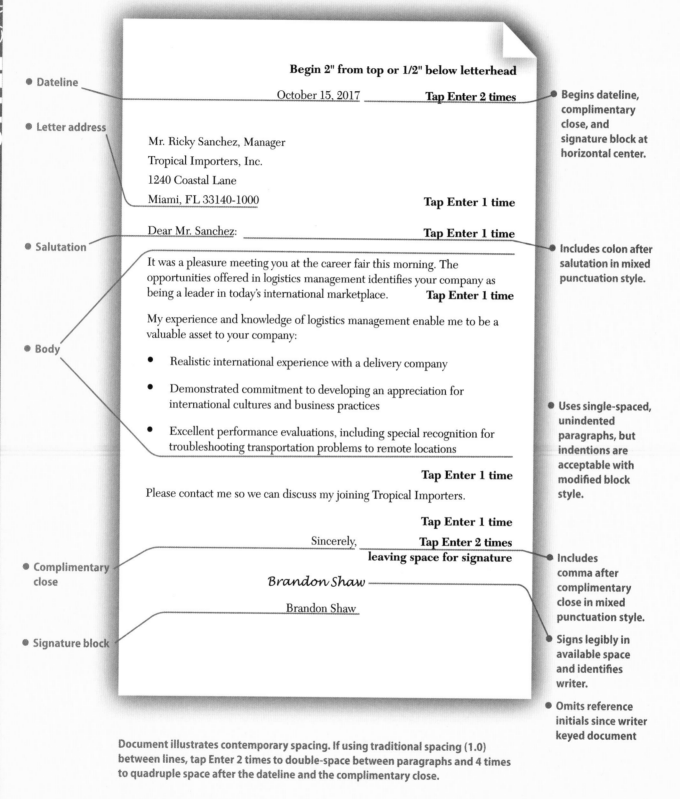

- Dateline

- Letter address

- Salutation

- Body

- Complimentary close

- Signature block

Begin 2" from top or 1/2" below letterhead

October 15, 2017   **Tap Enter 2 times**

Mr. Ricky Sanchez, Manager

Tropical Importers, Inc.

1240 Coastal Lane

Miami, FL 33140-1000   **Tap Enter 1 time**

Dear Mr. Sanchez: **Tap Enter 1 time**

It was a pleasure meeting you at the career fair this morning. The opportunities offered in logistics management identifies your company as being a leader in today's international marketplace.   **Tap Enter 1 time**

My experience and knowledge of logistics management enable me to be a valuable asset to your company:

- Realistic international experience with a delivery company

- Demonstrated commitment to developing an appreciation for international cultures and business practices

- Excellent performance evaluations, including special recognition for troubleshooting transportation problems to remote locations

    Tap Enter 1 time

Please contact me so we can discuss my joining Tropical Importers.

    Tap Enter 1 time

Sincerely,   **Tap Enter 2 times**
leaving space for signature

Brandon Shaw

Brandon Shaw

Begins dateline, complimentary close, and signature block at horizontal center.

Includes colon after salutation in mixed punctuation style.

Uses single-spaced, unindented paragraphs, but indentions are acceptable with modified block style.

Includes comma after complimentary close in mixed punctuation style.

Signs legibly in available space and identifies writer.

Omits reference initials since writer keyed document

Document illustrates contemporary spacing. If using traditional spacing (1.0) between lines, tap Enter 2 times to double-space between paragraphs and 4 times to quadruple space after the dateline and the complimentary close.

Envelope and Memo Styles

• Envelopes

An envelope should be printed on the same quality and color of paper as the letter and generated using the convenient envelope feature of your word-processing program. Adjust defaults as needed to adhere to the recommendations of the United States Postal Service (USPS). To increase the efficiency of mail handling, use the two-letter abbreviations for states, territories, and Canadian provinces. USPS official state abbreviations are available at **www.USPS.gov**.

Most companies today do not follow the traditional USPS recommendation to key the letter address in all capital letters with no punctuation. The mixed case format matches the format used in the letter address, looks more professional, and allows the writer to generate the envelope automatically without rekeying text. No mail-handling efficiency is lost as today's optical character readers that sort mail can read both uppercase- and lowercase letters easily. Proper placement of the address on a large envelope and a small envelope generated using an envelope template available with word-processing software is shown here:

No. 10 Envelope, Mixed Case Format

Match letter address exactly with all lines in block form

No. 6¾ Envelope, USPS Uppercase, No Punctuation Format

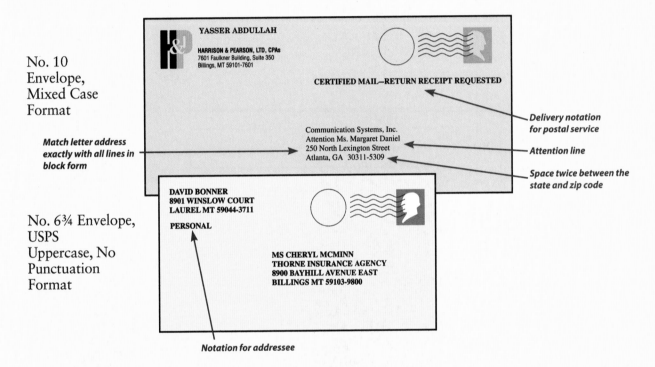

Notation for addressee

Additionally, to create a highly professional image, business communicators should fold letters to produce the fewest number of creases. Here are the proper procedures for folding letters for large (No. 10) and small (No. 6¾) envelopes:

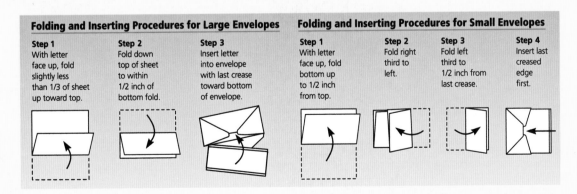

• Memorandum Formats

To increase productivity of memorandums (memos), which are internal messages, companies use formats that are easy to input and that save time. Most companies use customized or standard memo templates found in most word-processing software that include the basic headings (TO, FROM, DATE, and SUBJECT) to guide the writer in providing the needed transmittal information. Memos may be printed on memo forms, plain paper, or letterhead, depending on the preference of the company. Follow the guidelines for formatting a memo illustrated here.

Begin 2" from top of page or 1/2" below letterhead

TO: Sandra Linkletter, President

FROM: Donald Worthy, Sales Manager

DATE: April 1, 2017

SUBJECT: Monthly Sales Report, Appliance Department

Sales for the month remained at about the same level as previous months this year, at $23,819. Sales figures for the month by item are as follows:

Item	Quantity Sold	Total Revenue from Sales ($)
Washers	12	5,102
Dryers	11	6,543
Stoves	8	4,276
Refrigerators	10	5,899
Dish Washers	6	1,989

Marketing

This month, we continued to publish a circular, which was distributed each Thursday in the *News Tribune*. The cost of that circular is $2,400 per month. That was our only cost of advertising and marketing. Please see the attached file for a complete breakdown of the departments' costs and sales for the month.

Staffing

We continue to employ two full-time salespeople on the floor and two part-time salespersons to cover the weekend shift. Current staffing levels are sufficient for the current sales volume, but if the home construction sector improves, we expect appliance sales to increase along with that improvement. If this occurs, we will need to hire an additional full- and part-time salesperson to return to our 2008 employment numbers.

Future Plans

We are continuing to look at ways that we might increase our marketing presence in the local community. One suggestion offered by Dale, one of our full-time salespersons, is to have a weekly promotion that runs as a banner on our web page. We could institute this opportunity storewide and have banners for the other departments running randomly with ours throughout the week. The cost of such a promotional program storewide needs to be calculated; perhaps this is something that we might put on our agenda for next week's managers' meetings.

Attachment

Formal Report

• Formal Report Format

Page arrangement for reports varies somewhat, depending on the documentation style guide followed or individual company preferences. Take advantage of your software's automatic formatting features for efficient formatting and generating report parts. Portions of a sample report are shown below.

MARGINS. For formal reports, use 1-inch side margins. If the report is to be bound, increase the left margin by ½ inch. Use a 2-inch top margin for the first page of each report part (table of contents and executive summary) and a 1-inch top margin for all other pages. Leave at least a 1-inch bottom margin on all pages.

SPACING. Although documentation style guides typically specify double-spacing of text, company practice is often to single-space reports. Double-spacing accommodates editorial comments and changes but results in a higher page count. Even if you choose to double-space the body of a report, you may opt to single-space some elements, such as the entries in your references page and information in tables or other graphic components.

HEADINGS. Several levels of headings can be used throughout the report and are typed in different ways to indicate the level of importance. Suggested formatting guidelines for a report divided into three levels are illustrated in the document on the next page. Develop fourth- and fifth-level headings simply by using boldface, underline, and varying fonts.

Formal Report Parts

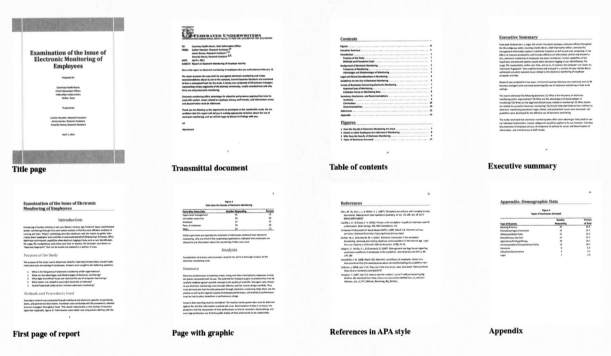

Title page

Transmittal document

Table of contents

Executive summary

First page of report

Page with graphic

References in APA style

Appendix

STYLE CARD

Report Format Using Preset Styles

- Capitalizes all letters in report title.

- Places first- and second-level headings at left margin and capitalizes initial letters. Larger font size makes the first level stand out.

- Includes intervening text between first- and second-level headings.

- Uses default indentation and decreased spacing between enumerated and bulleted items.

- Places third-level subheadings at left margin and capitalizes the first letter.

Format Pointers
This report document illustrates Word 2013 Style Set with style formats applied for the report title, the three heading levels, and the enumerated list. Creating a custom style set allows businesses to create a report style that is consistent with their company image and brand.

The increased spacing after each paragraph eliminates the need for indented paragraphs.

1" top margin

REPORT TITLE Title style (26-point Cambria font)

Tap Enter 1 time

xxx xxxxxx xxxxxxx xxxxx xxxxxxxxx xxxx xx xxxxx xxxxx xxxxxxx xxxxx xx xxxxxx xxxx x xxxxx xxxxx xxxxxxxxx xxx xxxx xxxxx xxxxx.

Tap Enter 1 time

First-Level Heading Heading 1 (14-point Cambria font)

Tap Enter 1 time

xxx xxxxxx xxxxxxx xxxxx xxxxxxxxx xxxx xxxxx xxxxx xxxxxxx xxxxx xx xxxxxx xxxx x xxxxx xxxxx xxxxxxxxx xxx xxxx xxxxx xxxxx.

Tap Enter 1 time

Second-Level Subheading Heading 2 (13-point Cambria font)

Tap Enter 1 time

xxx xxxxxx xxxxxxx xxxxx xxxxxxxxx xxxx xxxxx xxxxx xxxxxxx xxxxx xx xxxxxx xxxx x xxxxx xxxxx xxxxxxxxx xxx xxxx xxxxx xxxxx.

Tap Enter 1 time

1. xxxx x xxxxxx xx xxxxxx xxxx xxx xxxxxxxxx xx xxxxx xxxxx xx. xx xxxx xxx.

Space automatically reduced between enumerated items.

2. xxxx x xxxxxx xx xxxxxx xxxx xxx xxxxxxxxx xx xxxxx xxxxx xx. xx xxxx xxx xxxxx xxxx xx x xxxxxxxxxx.

Tap Enter 1 time

Second-Level Subheading

Tap Enter 1 time

xxx xxxxxx xxxxxxx xxxxx xxxxxxxxx xxxx xxxxx xxxxx xxxxxxx xxxxx xx xxxxxx xxxx x xxxxx xxxxx xxxxxxxxx xxx xxxx xxxxx xxxxx.

Tap Enter 1 time

Heading 3 (11-point Cambria font)

Third-Level Subheading. xxx xxxxxx xxxxxxx xxxxx xxxxxxxxx xxxx xxxxxx xxxxxx xxxxxxx xxxxx xx xxxxxx xxxx x xxxxx xxxxx xxxxxxxxx xxx xxxx xxxxx xxxxx.

Tap Enter 1 time

Third-Level Subheading. xxx xxxxxx xxxxxxx xxxxx xxxxxxxxx xxxx xxxxxx xxxxxx xxxxxxx xxxxx xx xxxxxx xxxx x xxxxx xxxxx xxxxxxxxx xxx xxxx xxxxx xxxxx.

MLA Referencing

A number of widely used reference styles are available for documenting the sources of information used in report writing. Two of the more popular style manuals for business writing are as follows:

Publication Manual of the American Psychological Association, 6th ed., Washington, DC: American Psychological Association, 2001.

Joseph Gibaldi, *MLA Handbook for Writers of Research Papers*, 7th ed., New York: Modern Languages Association of America, 2003. The *MLA Handbook* is designed for high school and undergraduate college students; the *MLA Style Manual and Guide to Scholarly Publishing*, 3rd ed. (2008) is designed for graduate students, scholars, and professional writers.

These sources, commonly referred to as the APA and MLA styles, provide general rules for referencing and give examples of the citation formats for various types of source materials. This style card reflects the rules along with examples for the MLA style. Whenever you are not required to use a particular documentation style, choose a recognized one and follow it consistently. Occasionally, you may need to reference something for which no general example applies. Choose the example that is most like your source, and follow that format. When in doubt, provide more information, not less. Remember that a major purpose for listing references is to enable readers to retrieve and use the sources. This style card illustrates citation formats for some common types of information sources and refers you to various electronic sites that provide further detailed guidelines for preparing electronic citations.

• In-Text Parenthetical Citations

The *MLA Handbook* supports the use of **in-text citations**. Abbreviated information within parentheses in the text directs the reader to a list of sources at the end of a report. The list of sources at the end contains all bibliographic information on each source cited in a report. This list is arranged alphabetically by the author's last name or, if no author is provided, by the first word of the title.

The in-text citations contain minimal information needed to locate the source in the complete list. The *MLA* style includes the author's last name and the page number for both quotes and paraphrases, but not the date of publication. Note the format of the in-text parenthetical citations shown below.

One author not named in the text, direct quotation

"A recent survey … shows that more and more companies plan to publish their annual reports on the Internet" (Prinn 13).

Direct quotation, no page number on source

According to James, "traditional college students have a perspective that is quite different from adult consumers" (par. 2).

Use par. 2 in place of missing page number only if paragraphs are numbered in original text.

Multiple authors for sources not named in the text wording

Globalization is becoming a continuous challenge for managers … (Tang and Crofford 29).

"For all its difficulty, teamwork is still essential … " (Nunamaker et al. 163).

For sources by more than three authors, use et al. *after the last name of the first author or include all last names. Do not underline or italicize* et al.

More than one source documenting the same idea

… companies are turning to micromarketing (Heath 48; Roach 54).

More than one source by the same author documenting the same idea

Past research (Taylor, "Performance Appraisal" 6, "Frequent Absenteeism" 89) shows …

Reference to author(s) or date in the text wording

Kent Spalding and Brian Price documented the results …

In 2006, West concluded … (E2).

Omit a page number when citing a one-page article or nonprint source.

No author provided

… virtues of teamwork look obvious ("Teams Triumph in Creative Solutions" 61).

Include full title or shortened version of it.

6

• Works Cited

The **works cited** page located at the end of your document contains an alphabetized list of the sources used in preparing a report, with each entry containing publication information necessary for locating the source. A researcher often uses sources that provide information but do not result in citations. If you want to acknowledge that you have consulted these works and provide the reader with a comprehensive reading list, include these sources in the list of works cited and refer to list as Works Consulted. Your company guidelines may specify whether to list works cited only or works consulted. If you receive no definitive guidelines, use your own judgment. If in doubt, include all literature cited and read, and label the page with the appropriate title so that the reader clearly understands the nature of the list.

To aid the reader in locating sources in lengthy bibliographies, you may include several subheadings denoting the types of publications documented, for example, books, articles, unpublished documents and papers, government publications, and nonprint media. Check your reference manual to determine if subheadings are allowed.

• Formats for Print and Recorded References

Reference styles for a variety of print and recorded sources prepared using the MLA style are shown in Figure 3. Note that the following rules apply for MLA works cited.

Indention and spacing	Begin first line of each entry at left margin and indent subsequent lines ½ inch. Although the MLA style manual specifies double-spacing within and between entries, common practice in preparing reports is to single-space each entry and double-space between entries.
Author names	List last name first for first author only. Use "and" before final author's name.
Date	Place date at the end of citation for books and after periodical title and volume for articles. Months are abbreviated.
Capitalization	In titles of books, periodicals, and article titles, capitalize all main words.
Italicizing and quotation marks	Italicize titles of books, journals, and periodicals (or underline if directed). Place titles of articles within quotation marks.
Page notations	Omit the use of *p.* or *pp.* on all citations.

MLA (7th Edition Style)

Writer's Last Name   5

Works Cited

Centento, Antonio. "The Appropriate Men's Attire for Every Occasion." *businessinsider.com*. Business Insider, 12 September 2014. Web. 23 October 2014.

Freeburg, Beth Winfrey, & Arnett, Sally E. "The Impact of Appearance Management Training, Work Status, and Plans After High School on Opinions Regarding Appearance at Work and School." *Journal of Career and Technical Education* 25.2 (2010).

"Proper Business Attire and Etiquette." *tcbsolutions.net*. The Country's Best Solutions, n.d. Web. 23 October 2014.

"Dress Speak for Men." *ECG*. Executive Communications Group, n.d. Web. 23 October 2014.

"Dress Speak for Women." *ECG*. Executive Communications Group, n.d. Web. 23 October 2014.

Goman, Carol Kinsey. "What It Really Means to Dress for Success." *Forbes.com*. Forbes, 20 March 2012. Web. 23 October 2014.

Smith, Jacquelyn. "Here's What 'Business Casual' Really Means." *businessinsider.com*. Business Insider, 19 August 2014. Web. 23 October 2014.

Heathfield, Susan M. "Dress for Work Success: A Business Casual Dress Code." *About.com*. About, n.d. Web. 23 October 2014.

Jensen, Andrew . "How Does Workplace Attire Affect Productivity?" *Andrew Jensen*. Andrew Jensen, 27 June 2014. Web. 23 October 2014.

LeTrent, Sarah. "Decoding the workplace dress code." *CNN.com*. Cable News Network, 15 August 2012. Web. 23 October 2014.

APA Referencing

Crediting Sources

According to the APA Style, references in the article follow the author-date citation system and are placed at the end of the article in the alphabetical order. This helps the reader determine the source from the text with the reference list. All references that are cited throughout the text must be listed in the reference section at the end of the article. Likewise, all the sources mentioned in the reference section need to be present in the text. Care needs to be taken while citing the two sources as they need to be indistinguishable. The authors' name and the year should be spelled correctly.

One Work by One Author

To cite one work by one author, the author-date method is used wherein the last name of the author (without any suffixes such as Jr.) and the year of publication should be added in the content.

Brown's (2006) recent report on the use of experiments shows a correlation between results and participants.

The most recent report on the use of experiments shows a correlation between results and participants (Brown, 2006).

In the first example, the name of the author is present as a part of the sentence. In such cases, only the year of publication should be cited in parentheses. In other cases (as in the second example), the name and the year can be placed at the end in parentheses and separated by a comma. The month of publication need not be included. In rare cases where the name and the year come along with discussion in the article, they need not be in parentheses.

In 2006, Brown's report on the use of experiments shows ….

One Work by Multiple Authors

If the source consists of only two authors, use both the names throughout the text when they are cited. If the source consists of more than two authors, mention all of them if it is the first time they are cited. In succeeding references, cite only the last name of the author followed by "et al." along with the year if it is the first cited reference in a paragraph. The "et al." should be followed by a period and should not be italicized.

Kernis, Cornell, Sun, Berry, Harlow, & Bach (1993) found (First citation)

Kernis et al. (1993) found (Succeeding first citation for each paragraph)

Groups as Authors

Authors in the name of groups such as universities, medical institutes, agencies, or study groups are usually spelled out every time they are referenced. In most cases, they are spelled out in the first instance and then abbreviated in the following instances. If the name of the group is better spelled out, for example the University of Arizona, then it doesn't need be abbreviated. If the name is lengthy and the abbreviation can be easily recalled, then it can be used as an abbreviation thereafter.

Authors with the Same Surname

If the source contains two (or more) authors with the same surname, include the initials of the authors to avoid confusion.

J. Dawson (1986) and T. Dawson (1986) accept the ….

Works with No Identified Author or with an Anonymous Author

If the source has an author that cannot be identified, cite the title and the year of the work. The title should be in double quotation marks and italicized if it is a report, a book, a brochure, or a periodical.

("Relativity," 2005)

College Bound Seniors (2008)

STYLE CARD

Two or More Works within the Same Parentheses

Cite references of two or more works within parentheses in the alphabetical order (as they would appear in the reference list). Also, for two or more works by the same author, arrange them in the same manner but by year of publication.

Training materials are available (Department of Veterans Affairs, 2001, 2003)

Secondary Sources

Secondary sources need to be used in moderation, for instance, when the original source cannot be availed. The secondary source is listed in the reference section, but while citing it in the text it should have the name of the original source followed by the citation of the secondary one.

Allport's diary (as cited in Nicholson, 2003)

Personal Communications

Interviews, lectures, email, phone conversations, messages, and the like that cannot be recovered are classified under personal communications. They should only be cited in the text/article and not in the reference list. Provide the initials and surname of the communicator and also the date if possible.

A. M. Raulson (personal communication, January 28, 2007) says …

Reference List

The sources cited at the end of the article classified under the reference list guides readers to recover and pinpoint each of them. Only sources that have been used for the exploration and basis for the article should be included. Journals using the APA Style broadly make use of reference lists and not bibliographies. The reference section should begin on a fresh page apart from the article, and the sources should be in a double-spaced format.

Reference List Format

The reference list is formatted using the following APA Style guidelines.

- The lines succeeding the first line of each source must be indented to ½ inch from the left margin.
- The authors' last name should be used first. Provide the last name and the initials for all authors of the same work. If there are more than seven authors cited, use ellipses after the sixth author's name, and then provide the last author's name.
- The list should be in alphabetical order by the surname of the first author of each source.
- If there are several works by one author, cite the sources in a sequential order starting from the oldest to the most recent.
- Sustain the capitalization and punctuation that is used in the original source.
- All major words in the titles of journals should be capitalized.
- Only the first letter of the first word in a title, subtitle, proper nouns, and the first word after a colon or a dash should be capitalized. This is done when you are referring to chapters, books, web pages, or articles. The second word in a hyphenated compound word should not be capitalized.
- Book and journal titles with longer works need to be italicized.
- Journal articles or essay titles with shorter works need not be italicized, underlined, or in quotes.